Chinese

3rd Edition

by Dr. Wendy Abraham

for
dummies®
A Wiley Brand

Chinese For Dummies®, 3rd Edition

Published by: **John Wiley & Sons, Inc.**, 111 River Street, Hoboken, NJ 07030-5774, www.wiley.com

For general information on our other products and services, please contact our Customer Care Department within the U.S. at 877-762-2974, outside the U.S. at 317-572-3993, or fax 317-572-4002. For technical support, please visit https://hub.wiley.com/community/support/dummies.

Wiley publishes in a variety of print and electronic formats and by print-on-demand. Some material included with standard print versions of this book may not be included in e-books or in print-on-demand. If this book refers to media such as a CD or DVD that is not included in the version you purchased, you may download this material at http://booksupport.wiley.com. For more information about Wiley products, visit www.wiley.com.

Library of Congress Control Number: 2018947818

ISBN 978-1-119-47544-6 (pbk); ISBN 978-1-119-47551-4 (ebk); ISBN 978-1-119-47550-7 (ebk)

Manufactured in the United States of America

C10003258_080918

Contents at a Glance

Table of Contents

Introduction

Globalization has made familiarity with other people, cultures, and languages not only preferable but also essential in the 21st century. With the help of the Internet and a bevy of social media growing at a dizzying rate, reaching out and touching someone on the other side of the earth has become as easy as clicking a mouse, using a smartphone, or clicking on to RenRen (the Chinese equivalent of Facebook) or Weibo (the Twitter of China). And yet nothing quite beats the excitement of a face-to-face encounter with someone who hails from the other side of the globe in his or her own language. Communication in cyberspace doesn't even come close.

Whether you're an inveterate traveler, going overseas for business, studying abroad, adopting a child, interested in frequenting Chinatown, befriending a Chinese-speaking classmate or co-worker, or just plain curious about China, *Chinese For Dummies,* 3rd Edition, can help you get acquainted with enough Chinese to carry on a decent conversation on any number of topics. You won't become fluent instantly, of course, but this book helps you greet a stranger, buy a plane ticket, talk to Chinese students, converse with business colleagues, and order some food. It also gives you some invaluable cultural tips so that you not only rattle off those newly acquired words and phrases but also back them up with the right behavior at the right time.

I designed this book to help guide you toward the successful use of one of the most difficult languages on earth. Chinese should also just be plain fun to learn.

About This Book

The good news is that you can use *Chinese For Dummies,* 3rd Edition, anytime, anywhere. No mandatory class sessions, no exams, and no homework assignments to dread. Need to get to a new city for a business meeting? Just turn to the chapters on travel or business to find out how to buy a plane ticket, get through customs, get to the airport on time, or do some negotiating. Have to make a sudden trip to the doctor? Turn to the chapter on your health and figure out in advance how to tell your caregivers exactly what ails you.

Pay attention to a few conventions that can help you navigate this book's contents:

>> Chinese terms are set in **boldface** to make them stand out.

>> Pronunciations and meanings appear in parentheses immediately after the Chinese terms. The English translations are in *italics*.

>> This book uses the **pīnyīn** 拼音 (pin-yin) (Literally: *spelling the way it sounds*) Romanization system of Chinese words. What does that mean? Well, if you go to China, you see signs in Chinese characters all around, but if you look for something in English, you may be hard-pressed to find it. Whatever signs you see in Roman letters will be of **pīnyīn,** the Romanization system developed by the Communists in the 1950s, so seeing **pīnyīn** in this book is good practice for you.

>> In this edition of *Chinese For Dummies,* Chinese characters have been added in many places and appear after the initial transliteration from the **pīnyīn.** Chinese characters are fun to try to decipher. The Chinese have been working at precisely that for thousands of years, especially for the more complicated characters that took as many as 20 separate strokes of the writing brush to create traditional Chinese characters.

Lucky for you, many of the more complicated Chinese characters were simplified in the early 20th century to make them easier to read and write, and these are used in mainland China today. (You can read more about Chinese characters in Chapter 2.) The original (or *traditional*) characters are still used in Taiwan. In this book, simplified characters appear first, followed in parentheses by the traditional characters. Characters that were never simplified don't have any separate notation in parentheses.

>> Another thing you should keep in mind as you begin to understand Chinese is that many of the English translations you see in this book aren't exactly literal. Knowing the gist of what you hear or see is more important than knowing what individual words in any given phrase mean. For example, the Chinese phrase meaning *so-so* literally translates as *horse horse tiger tiger* even though you're not actually talking about animals. Whenever I give a literal translation, I preface it with "Literally."

The following elements in this book help reinforce the new terms and phrases you're studying:

>> **Talkin' the Talk dialogues:** Nothing beats seeing and hearing an actual conversation to learn Chinese, so I intersperse dialogues throughout the book under the heading "Talkin' the Talk." They show you the Chinese words, the pronunciations, and the English translations, and I often put cultural do's and

don'ts into context, which should come in handy. Many of these dialogues appear in the accompanying online audio tracks so you can practice the sentences after you hear how they should sound. With the tonal nature of the Chinese language, this feature is indispensable as you learn Chinese.

>> **Words to Know:** These boxes come after the Talkin' the Talk dialogues and highlight useful additional words beyond the dialogue.

>> **Fun & Games activities:** Working through word games, cracking crossword puzzles, or recalling some phrases to fill in the blanks can be a fun way to review the words and phrases you encounter in each chapter. This element is a great way to gauge your progress and tease your brain at the same time. Look for these activities at the end of each chapter.

The beauty of this book is that it can be all things to all people. You don't have to memorize Chapter 5 before moving on to Chapter 6 if what Chapter 6 deals with is what you really need. Each chapter provides you with different bits of information about the Chinese language and highlights different parts of Chinese grammar. Read as much or as little as you want, as quickly or as slowly as you like. Whatever interests you is what you should focus on. And remember: You're discovering a language that simultaneously represents one of the world's oldest civilizations and one of its fastest-growing economies in the 21st century.

Foolish Assumptions

Some of the foolish assumptions I made about you while writing *Chinese For Dummies*, 3rd Edition, are that

>> You don't know any Chinese, except for maybe a couple of words you picked up from a good kung-fu movie or the word *tofu*, which you picked up while grocery shopping.

>> Your goal in life isn't to become an interpreter of Chinese at the U.N.; you just want to pick up some useful words, phrases, and sentence constructions to make yourself understood in a Chinese-speaking environment.

>> You have no intention of spending hours and hours memorizing Chinese vocabulary and grammar patterns.

>> You basically want to have fun while speaking a little Chinese.

Icons Used in This Book

Cute little icons occasionally appear in the left-hand margins, next to sidebars, and with the Talkin' the Talk dialogues throughout this book. These beacons shed light on what kind of information you're looking at and can help you locate certain types of information in a hurry. The five icons used in this book are as follows:

TIP

The bull's-eye appears wherever I've highlighted a great idea to help make your study of Chinese easier.

REMEMBER

This icon, appropriately showing a string around a finger, should serve as a reminder about particularly important information concerning Chinese.

WARNING

This icon should act as a stop sign in your mind. It warns you about things to avoid saying or doing so that you don't make a fool of yourself overseas or with a new Chinese friend.

CULTURAL WISDOM

This icon clues you in on fascinating bits of information about China and Chinese culture. Knowledge of a culture goes hand in hand with knowledge of a foreign language, so these icons help light the way as you embark on your journey.

GRAMMAR CHAT

This icon highlights various rules of grammar that may be out of the norm. Even though this book doesn't focus primarily on grammar, your successful execution of the language can only be enhanced by paying attention to little grammatical rules as they pop up.

Beyond the Book

This book is full of useful information, but you can find even more online! Check out this book's Cheat Sheet, which contains useful questions, common expressions, phrases used in emergencies, the Chinese calendar, and Chinese numbers all in a handy portable format. Just go to www.dummies.com and search for "Chinese For Dummies Cheat Sheet."

You can also hear all the Talkin' the Talk dialogues provided in the book to get a better handle on correct pronunciation. Just go to www.dummies.com/go/chinese.

Where to Go from Here

Chinese is often considered one of the toughest languages in the world to master. Don't worry. The good news is that you're not trying to master it. All you want to do is be understandable when you open your mouth so that you don't ask for the men's room when you really want the ladies' room. All you have to do now is keep listening to and repeating the words and phrases you find in this book. Turn to whichever chapter piques your curiosity, listen to the accompanying online audio tracks at home or in your car, and keep practicing your favorite Chinese phrases when you're with your family and friends in Chinatown.

1
Getting Started with Chinese

Chapter **1**

Chinese in a Nutshell: The Spoken Word

Time to get your feet wet with the basics of Chinese. This chapter gives you guidelines that help you pronounce words in standard Mandarin (the official language of both the People's Republic of China and Taiwan) like a native speaker and helps you get a handle on the four tones that distinguish Mandarin Chinese. You also find out about the kind of Chinese characters used to write in Taiwan (traditional) versus the kind of characters written in the People's Republic of China (simplified). (Spoiler alert: To get a jump-start on China's thousand-year-old writing system, check out Chapter 2.) After you have the basics down, I show you how to construct basic Chinese phrases.

But before you dive in, here's a bit of advice: Don't be intimidated by all the tones! The best thing you can do when learning a foreign language is to not worry about making mistakes the minute you open your mouth. Practice speaking Chinese first to your dog or cat, and then work your way up to a couple of goldfish or a niece or nephew under the age of 10. When you finally get the nerve to rattle off a few phrases to your local Chinatown grocer, you'll know you've made it. And when you visit China for the first time, you discover how incredibly appreciative the Chinese are of anyone who even remotely attempts to speak their language. All the hours you spent yakking away with the family pet start to pay off, and you'll be rewarded greatly. Still have doubts? You'll be amazed at how much you can say after snooping through *Chinese For Dummies*, 3rd Edition.

Encountering the Chinese culture is just as important as exploring the Chinese language. In fact, you can't quite master the language without absorbing a little of the culture by osmosis. Just making the effort to speak Chinese is an act of positive diplomacy. Don't worry about how you sound when you open your mouth — you're contributing to international friendship no matter what comes out.

Grasping Chinese Dialects

Give yourself a big pat on the back right now. Yup, right now — before you even begin to utter one iota of Chinese. If you don't do it now, you may be too shocked later on when it sinks in that you've taken on a language that has hundreds (yes, hundreds) of dialects — each one mutually incomprehensible to speakers of the other ones. Practically every major town, and certainly every province, in China has its own regional dialect that folks grow up learning. Of the seven major dialects (outlined in Table 1-1), Shanghainese, Taiwanese, and Cantonese are the ones you may have heard of before.

And then you have Mandarin, dialect of the masses. Mandarin Chinese is spoken by more people on earth than any other language today. Pretty much a quarter of humanity uses it, given China's immense population. So just why was this particular dialect chosen to become the official dialect taught in all schools throughout China, regardless of whatever additional dialects people speak at home or in their communities?

With only four tones, **Guānhuà** 官话 (官話) (Gwan-hwah) (*Mandarin* [Literally: *the language of the officials,* who were also known as Mandarins]) has served as the hybrid language of China since the 15th century because this dialect was based on the educated speech of the region around Beijing. Instead of referring to it as **Guānhuà,** mainlanders in China now call it **Pǔtōnghuà** 普通话 (普通話) (Poo-toong-hwah) (Literally: *the common language*). People in Taiwan, in Hong Kong, and in overseas Chinese communities call it **Guóyǔ** 国语 (國語) (Gwaw-yew) (Literally: *the national language*). You may also hear it referred to as **Zhōngwén** 中文 (Joong-wun) (*the language of the Chinese people*) and **Hànyǔ** 汉语 (漢語) (Hahn-yew) (*the language of the Han people*), because the Chinese have often referred to themselves as descendants of the Han dynasty (206 BCE–220 CE), one of the golden eras of Chinese history. Because Chinese is the language of ethnic Chinese and China's minority groups, the more all-encompassing term **Zhōngwén** is preferred.

The term **Pǔtōnghuà** is used to refer to Mandarin in the People's Republic of China, and the term **Guóyǔ** is the term used for Mandarin in Taiwan. You can simply say **Hànyǔ** anywhere.

TABLE 1-1

Major Chinese Dialects

Dialect	Pronunciation	Region Where Spoken
Pǔtōnghuà/Guóyǔ (Mandarin) 普通话 (普通話)/ 国语(國語)	Poo-toong-hwah/ Gwaw-yew	North of the Yangzi River, but is taught in schools everywhere; official language of the People's Republic of China and is spoken all over Taiwan
Wú 吴 (吳)	Woo	Shanghai, southeastern Anhui, and much of Zhejiang
Xiāng 湘	Shyahng	Hunan
Gàn 赣 (贛)	Gahn	Jiangxi, southern Anhui, and southeastern Hubei
Kèjiā (Hakka) 客家	Kuh–jyah	Scattered parts of eastern and southwestern Guangxi and in northern Guangdong (Canton)
Yuè (Cantonese) 粤 (粵)	Yweh	Southeastern Guangxi, Guangdong (Canton), and Hong Kong
Mǐn (Taiwanese) 闽 (閩)	Meen	Fujian, southern Zhejiang, northeastern Guangdong, Hainan, and Taiwan

Pīnyīn Spelling: Beijing, Not Peking

To spell the way it sounds . . . that's the literal meaning of **pīnyīn** 拼音. For decades, Chinese had been *transliterated* (written/spelled with the characters of other languages' alphabets) in any number of ways. Finally, in 1979, the People's Republic of China (PRC) officially adopted **pīnyīn** as its official Romanization system. After the adoption, U.S. libraries and government agencies diligently changed all their prior records from other Romanization systems into **pīnyīn**.

You should keep in mind the following quick facts about some of the initial sounds in Mandarin when you see them written in the relatively new **pīnyīn** system:

» **J:** Sounds like the **g** in *gee whiz*. An **i** often follows a **j. Jǐ kuài qián?** 几块钱? (幾塊錢?) (Jee kwye chyan?) means *How much money?*

» **Q:** Sounds like the **ch** in *cheek*. In Chinese, you never see it followed by a **u** like it is in English, but an **i** always follows it, possibly before another vowel or a consonant. **Qīngdǎo** 青岛 (青島) (Cheeng-daow) beer used to be spelled **Ch'ing tao** or **Tsingtao**.

» **X:** Sounds like the **sh** in *she*. It's the third letter that's often followed by an **i**. One famous Chinese leader, **Dèng Xiǎopíng** 邓小平 (鄧小平) (Dung Shyaow-peeng), boasted this letter in his name.

>> **Zh:** Unlike **j**, which often precedes a vowel to make it sound like you're opening your mouth, **zh** is followed by vowels that make it sound like your mouth is a bit more closed like you're about to play the flute — it sounds like the *ger* in *German.* Take **Zhōu Ēnlái** 周恩来 (周恩來) (Joe Un-lye), the great statesman of 20th-century China, for example. When you say his name, it should sound like Joe Un-lye.

>> **Z:** Sounds like a **dz.** You see it in the name of the PRC's first leader, **Máo Zédōng** 毛泽东 (毛澤東) (Maow Dzuh-doong), which used to be spelled **Mao Tse-tung.**

>> **C:** Pronounced like ts in such words as **cài** 菜 (tsye) (*food*) or **cèsuǒ** 厕所 (廁所) (tsuh-swaw) (*bathroom*).

Sounding Off: Basic Chinese Sounds

Don't worry about sounding like a native speaker the first time you utter a Chinese syllable — after all, who can? But the longer you procrastinate about becoming familiar with the basic elements of Chinese words, the greater your fear of this unique language may become. After you begin to practice the sounds (and eventually the tones) out loud, you may wonder if you'll ever come close to sounding like Bruce Lee in a **gōngfū** 功夫 (goong-foo) (*kung-fu*) movie or even like your local Chinatown grocer. Hearing Chinese spoken at a normal speed is definitely intimidating at the beginning, so you should enjoy taking plenty of baby steps and reveling in the praise from waiters who appreciate all your effort the next time you frequent a Chinese restaurant.

GRAMMAR CHAT

The main thing to remember about the Chinese language is that each *morpheme* (the smallest unit of meaning in a language) is represented by one syllable, which in turn consists of an initial sound and a final sound, topped off by a tone. This rule applies to each and every syllable. Without any one of these three components, your words may be incomprehensible to the average Chinese person. For example, the syllable **mā** 妈 (媽) is comprised of the initial **m** and the final **a,** and you pronounce it with what's called a first tone. Together, the parts mean *mother.* If you substitute the first tone for a third tone, which is written as **mǎ,** 马 (馬) you say the word *horse.* So be careful not to call your mother a horse when you practice the initials, finals, and tones. The following sections break up the three parts and give each their due.

REMEMBER

Before you can participate in sports or play games, you must become familiar with all the rules. The same goes for practicing a new language. Do your best to understand the basic rules of pronunciation, and keep practicing over and over to begin feeling comfortable speaking Chinese.

Starting off with initials

In Chinese, initials always consist of consonants. Table 1-2 lists the initials you encounter in the Chinese language. (*Note:* You can also hear these sounds by going online to www.dummies.com/go/chinese.)

TABLE 1-2

Chinese Initials

Chinese Letter	Sound	English Example
b	b	*but*
p	p	*paw*
m	m	*more*
f	f	*four*
d	d	*done*
t	t	*ton*
n	n	*null*
l	l	*lull*
g	g	*gull*
k	k	*come*
h	h	*hunt*
j	g	*gee*
q	ch	*cheat*
x	sh	*she*
z	dz	ds in *suds*
c	ts	ts in *huts*
s	s	*sun*
zh	jir	*germ*
ch	chir	*churn*
sh	sh	*shirt*
r	ir	er in *bigger*
w	w	*won*
y	y	*yup*

REMEMBER

The initials **-n** and **-r** in Table 1-2 can also appear as part of finals, so don't be surprised if you see them in Table 1-3, where I list finals.

Ending with finals

Chinese boasts many more consonants than vowels. In fact, the language has only six vowels all together: **a, o, e, i, u,** and **ü.** If you pronounce the vowels in sequence, your mouth starts off very wide and your tongue starts off very low. Eventually, when you get to **ü,** your mouth becomes much more closed and your tongue ends pretty high. You can also combine the vowels in various ways to form compound vowels. Table 1-3 lists the vowels and some possible combinations, which comprise all the finals in Chinese.

TABLE 1-3

Chinese Finals

Chinese Vowel	Sound	English Example
a	ah	*hot*
ai	i	*eye*
ao	ow	*chow*
an	ahn	*on*
ang	ahng	*thong*
o	aw	*straw*
ong	oong	*too + ng*
ou	oh	*oh*
e	uh	*bush*
ei	ay	*way*
en	un	*fun*
eng	ung	*tongue*
er	ar	*are*
i	ee	*tea*
ia	ya	*yack*
iao	yaow	*meow*
ie	yeh	*yet*
iu	yo	*Leo*

Chinese Vowel	Sound	English Example
ian	yan	*Cheyenne*
iang	yahng	*yang (as in yin–yang)*
in	een	*seen*
ing	eeng	*going*
iong	yoong	*you + ng*
u	oo	*too*
ua	wa	*suave*
uo	waw	*war*
ui	way	*way*
uai	why	*why*
uan	wan	*want*
un	one	*one*
uang	wahng	*wan + ng*
ueng	wung	*one + ng*
ü	yew	*ewe*
üe	yweh	*you + eh*
üan	ywan	*you + wan*
ün	yewn	*you + n*

Perfect pitch: Presenting . . . the four tones!

Mee meeeee (cough cough)! Pardon me. I'm getting carried away with warming up before I get into the four tones. Just think of the tones this way: They can be your best friends when it comes to being understood in Chinese, and they're the hip part of this ancient language.

If you combine all the possible initial sounds of Chinese with all the possible permutations of the final sounds, you come up with only about 400 sound combinations — not nearly enough to express all the ideas in your head. If you add the four basic tones of Mandarin to the mix, the number of possible permutations increases fourfold. Tones are also a great way to reduce the number of homophones in Chinese. Even so, any given syllable with a specific tone can often have more than one meaning. Sometimes, the only way to decipher the intended meaning is to see the written word.

Mandarin has only four tones. The best way to imagine what each of the four tones sounds like is to visualize these short descriptions:

>> **First tone:** High level. The first tone is supposed to be as high as your individual pitch range can be without wavering. It appears like this above the letter *a:* **ā.** (Imagine saying "Ta Da-a-a-ah!" and you've got the first tone.)

>> **Second tone:** Rising. The second tone sounds like you're asking a question. (Think: "Huh?") It goes from the middle level of your voice to the top. It doesn't automatically indicate that you're asking a question, however — it just sounds like you are. It appears like this above the letter *a:* **á.**

>> **Third tone:** Falling and then rising. The third tone starts in the middle level of your voice range and then falls deeply before slightly rising at the end. It looks like this above the letter *a:* **ǎ.** (Imagine someone being incredulous at something, saying "Say *whaaat?*")

>> **Fourth tone:** Falling. The fourth tone sounds like you're giving someone an order (unlike the more plaintive-sounding second tone). It falls from the high pitch level it starts at. Here's how it looks above the letter *a:* **à.** (This sounds more like the rather blasé, "Oh," once you've understood something — like the tone.)

I know this tone business (especially the nuances in the following sections) all sounds very complicated, but when you get the hang of tones, pronunciation becomes second nature. Just keep listening to the online audio files that accompany this book. These concepts will sink in quicker than you expect.

One third tone after another

Here's something interesting about tones: When you have to say one third tone followed by another third tone out loud in consecutive fashion, the first one actually becomes a second tone. If you hear someone say **Tā hěn hǎo.** 她很好. (Tah hun how.) (*She's very well.*), you may not realize that both **hěn** 很 and **hǎo** 好 individually are third-tone syllables. It sounds like **hén** is a second tone and **hǎo** is a full third tone.

Half-third tones

Whenever a third tone is followed by any of the other tones — first, second, fourth, or even a neutral tone — it becomes a half-third tone. You pronounce only the first half of the tone — the falling half — before you pronounce the other syllables with the other tones. In fact, a half-third tone barely falls at all. It sounds more like a level, low tone (kind of the opposite of the high-level first tone). Get it?

Neutral tones

A fifth tone exists that you can't exactly count among the four basic tones because it's actually toneless, or *neutral.* You never see a tone mark over a fifth tone, and you say it only when you attach it to grammatical particles or the second character of repetitive syllables, such as **bàba** 爸爸 (bah-bah) (*father*) or **māma** 妈妈 (媽媽) (mah-mah) (*mother*).

Tonal changes in yī and bù

Just when you think you're getting a handle on all the possible tones and tone changes in Chinese, I have one more aspect to report: The words **yī** 一 (ee) (*one*) and **bù** 不 (boo) (*not* or *no*) are truly unusual in Chinese, in that their tones may change automatically depending on what comes after them. You pronounce **yī** by itself with the first tone. However, when a first, second, or third tone follows it, **yī** instantly turns into a fourth tone, such as in **yì zhāng zhǐ** 一张纸 (一張紙) (ee jahng jir) (*a piece of paper*). If a fourth tone follows **yī**, however, it automatically becomes a second tone, such as in the word **yíyàng** 一样 (一樣) (ee-yahng) (*the same*).

Adding Idioms and Popular Expressions to Your Repertoire

The Chinese language has thousands of idiomatic expressions known as **chéngyǔ** 成语 (成語) (chung-yew). Most of these **chéngyǔ** originated in anecdotes, fables, fairy tales, or ancient literary works, and some of the expressions are thousands of years old. The vast majority consist of four characters, succinctly expressing morals behind very long, ancient stories. Others are more than four characters. Either way, the Chinese pepper these pithy expressions throughout any given conversation.

Here are a few **chéngyǔ** you frequently hear in Chinese:

>> **àn bù jiù bān** 按部就班 (ahn boo jyoe bahn) (*to take one step at a time*)

>> **hú shuō bā dào** 胡说八道 (胡說八道) (hoo shwaw bah daow) (*to talk nonsense* [Literally: *to talk nonsense in eight directions*])

>> **huǒ shàng jiā yóu** 火上加油 (hwaw shahng jyah yo) (*to add fuel to the fire/to aggravate the problem*)

» **mò míng qí miào.** 莫名其妙. (Maw meeng chee meow.) (Literally: *No one can explain the wonder and mystery of it all.*) This saying describes anything that's tough to figure out, including unusual behavior.

» **quán xīn quán yì** 全心全意 (chwan sheen chwan ee) (*wholeheartedly* [Literally: *entire heart, entire mind*])

» **rù xiāng suí sú.** 入乡随俗. (入鄉隨俗.) (Roo shyahng sway soo.) (*When in Rome, do as the Romans do.*)

» **yì jǔ liǎng dé** 一举两得 (一舉兩得) (ee jyew lyahng duh) (*to kill two birds with one stone*)

» **yì mó yí yàng** 一模一样 (一模一樣) (ee maw ee yahng) (*exactly alike*)

» **yǐ shēn zuò zé** 以身作则 (以身作則) (ee shun dzwaw dzuh) (*to set a good example*)

» **yì zhēn jiàn xiě** 一针见血 (一針見血) (ee jun jyan shyeh) (*to hit the nail on the head*)

Another fact you quickly become aware of when you start speaking with **chéngyǔ** is that the expressions are sometimes full of references to animals. Here are some of those:

» **chē shuǐ mǎ lóng** 车水马龙 (車水馬龍) (chuh shway mah loong) (*heavy traffic* [Literally: *cars flowing like water and horses, creating a solid line looking like a dragon*])

» **dǎ cǎo jīng shé** 打草惊蛇 (打草驚蛇) (dah tsaow jeeng shuh) (*to give a warning* [Literally: *to beat the grass to frighten the snake*])

» **duì niú tán qín** 对牛弹琴 (對牛彈琴) (dway nyo tahn cheen) (*to cast pearls before swine* [Literally: *to play music to a cow*])

» **gǒu zhàng rén shì.** 狗仗人势. (狗仗人勢.) (go jahng run shir.) (*to take advantage of one's connections with powerful people* [Literally: *The dog acts fierce when his master is present.*])

» **guà yáng tóu mài gǒu ròu** 挂羊头卖狗肉 (掛羊頭賣狗肉) (gwah yahng toe my go roe) (*to cheat others with false claims* [Literally: *to display a lamb's head but sell dog meat*])

» **huà shé tiān zú** 画蛇添足 (畫蛇添足) (hwah shuh tyan dzoo) (*to gild the lily/to do something superfluous* [Literally: *to paint a snake and add legs*])

» **hǔ tóu shé wěi** 虎头蛇尾 (虎頭蛇尾) (hoo toe shuh way) (*to start strong but end poorly* [Literally: *with the head of a tiger but the tail of a snake*])

» **xuán yá lè mǎ** 悬崖勒马 (懸崖勒馬) (shywan yah luh mah) (*to halt* [Literally: *to rein in the horse before it goes over the edge*])

FUN & GAMES

Listen to the online audio file to see whether you can imitate the following words, which are distinguished only by their tones. (Be on the lookout: Any given sound with the same accompanying tone may have several other meanings, distinguishable only by context or by seeing the appropriate written character.) Good luck!

» **mā** 妈 (媽) (*mother*)

» **má** 麻 (*hemp*)

» **mǎ** 马 (馬) (*horse*)

» **mà** 骂 (罵) (*to scold*)

» **fēi** 飞 (飛) (*to fly*)

» **féi** 肥 (*fat*)

» **fěi** 匪 (*bandit*)

» **fèi** 肺 (*lungs*)

Connect the tone on the left with the word in English on the right that is said with virtually the same tone.

ā	*Oh.*
á	*Ta–dah!*
ǎ	*Huh?*
à	*Say* what?

Chapter **2**

The Written Word: Checking Out Chinese Characters

Make no bones about it. (Oracle bones, that is.) China has literally hundreds of spoken dialects but only one written language. That's right: When a headline hits the news, people in Shanghai, Chongqing, and Henan are all yakking about it to their neighbors in their own regional dialects, but they're pointing to the exact same characters in the newspaper headlines. The written word is what's kept the Chinese people unified for over 4,000 years.

This chapter gives you the lowdown on how Chinese **wénzì** 文字 (wuhn-dzuh) (*writing*) actually began, how characters are constructed, and which direction they're going in when you read them. I describe how you may be able to identify the basic meaning of a character by looking at a key portion of it (called the radical) and how characters used by people living in Taiwan are different from characters used by people in mainland China. And because Chinese has no **zìmǔ** 字母 (dzuh-moo) (*alphabet*), I show you all sorts of ways you can look words up in a Chinese dictionary.

REMEMBER

Chinese has the multiple distinction of being the mother tongue of the oldest continuous civilization on earth as well as the language spoken by the greatest number of people. It arguably is one of the most intricate written languages in existence, with about 50,000 characters in a comprehensive Chinese dictionary. To read a newspaper with relative ease, though, you only need to know about 3,000 to 4,000 characters.

Perusing Pictographs, Ideographs, and the Six Scripts

You already know that Chinese words are written in beautiful, sometimes symbolic configurations called *characters*. But did you know that you can classify the characters in a variety of ways?

During the Hàn 汉 (漢) dynasty (206 BCE–220 CE), a lexicographer named Xǔ Shèn 许慎 (許慎) (Shyew Shuhn) identified six ways in which Chinese characters reflect meanings and sounds. These designations are known as the **Liù Shū** 六书 (六書) (Lyoe Shoo) (*the Six Scripts*). Of the six, four are the most common:

» **Xiàngxíng** 象形 (shyahng-sheeng) (*pictographs*): These characters resemble the shape of the objects they represent, such as **shān** 山 (shahn) (*mountain*) or **guī** 龜 (gway) (the traditional character for *turtle*; the simplified character for turtle — 龟 — doesn't really look as much like a turtle). Pictographs show the meaning of the character rather than the sound.

» **Biǎoyì** or **zhǐshì** 表意 or 指事 (byaow-ee or jir-shir) (*ideographs*): These characters represent more abstract concepts. The characters for **shàng** 上 (shahng) (*above*) and **xià** 下 (shyah) (*below*), for example, each have a horizontal line representing the horizon and another stroke leading out above or below the horizon.

» **Huìyì** 会意 (會意) (hway-ee) (*compound ideographs*): These characters are combinations of simpler characters that together represent more things. For example, by combining the characters for sun (日) and moon (月), you get the character 明**míng** (meeng), meaning *bright*.

>> **Xíngshēng** 形声 (形聲) (sheeng-shuhng) (*phonetic compounds*): These characters are formed by two graphic elements — one hinting at the meaning of the word (called the radical; see the following section), and the other providing a clue to the sound. More than 90 percent of all Chinese characters are phonetic compounds.

An example of a phonetic compound is the character **gū** 蛄 (goo). It's a combination of the radical **chóng** 虫 (choong) (*insect*) and the sound element of the character **gū** 古 (goo) (*ancient*). Put them together, and you have the character 蛄, meaning *cricket* (the insect, not the sport). It's pronounced with a first tone (**gū**) rather than a third tone (**gǔ**). So the sound of the word is similar to the term for ancient, even though that term has nothing to do with the meaning of the word. The actual meaning is connected to the radical referring to insects. Table 2-1 summarizes the Six Scripts.

TABLE 2-1   ## The Six Scripts

Type of Character	Chinese Character	Romanization and Pronunciation	Description
Pictographs	象形	**xiàngxíng** (shyahng-sheeng)	Simplified line drawings of concrete objects
Ideographs	表意 *or* 指事	**biǎoyì** *or* **zhǐshì** (byaow-ee *or* jir-shir)	Graphic representations of abstract ideas
Compound ideographs	会意 (會意)	**huìyì** (hway-ee)	Literally *joined meaning;* combination of two or more characters into a new compound character
Phonetic compounds	形声 (形聲)	**xíngshēng** (sheeng-shuhng)	Literally *form and sound;* combination of a visual meaning element with a phonetic element
Derivative cognates	轉注	**zhuǎnzhù** (jwahn joo)	Literally *reciprocal meaning;* characters given a new written form to better reflect a changed pronunciation over time
Phonetic loan characters	假借	**jiǎjiè** (jyah-jyeh)	Characters used to represent a homophone unrelated in meaning to the new word they represent

The Chinese Radical: A Few Clues to a Character's Meaning

What a radical idea! Two hundred and fourteen radical ideas, in fact.

GRAMMAR CHAT

The Chinese written language contains a total of 214 *radicals* — parts of the character that can help identify what it may signify. For example, if you see two or three short, staccato lines on the left-hand side of the character, you know the word is something connected to water. Here are some characters with the water radical appearing on the left-hand side:

冰 **bīng** (beeng) (*ice*)

冲 **chōng** (choong) (*to pour boiling water on something/to rinse or flush*)

汗 **hàn** (hahn) (*sweat*)

河 **hé** (huh) (*river*)

湖 **hú** (hoo) (*lake*)

Another example: The radical meaning *wood* — 木**mù** (moo) — originally represented the shape of a tree with branches and roots. Here are some characters with the wood radical in them (also on the left-hand side):

板 **bǎn** (bahn) (*board/plank*)

林 **lín** (leen) (*forest*)

树 (樹) **shù** (shoo) (*tree*)

Sometimes you find the radical at the top of the character rather than on the left-hand side. The radical meaning *rain* — 雨 **yǔ** (yew) — is one such character. Look for the rain radical at the top of these characters. (*Hint:* It looks slightly squished compared to the actual character for rain by itself.)

雹 **báo** (baow) (*hail*)

雷 **léi** (lay) (*thunder*)

露 **lù** (loo) (*dew*)

One of the most complicated radicals (number 214, to be precise) is the one that means *nose*: 鼻 **bí** (bee). It's so complicated to write, in fact, that only one other character in the whole Chinese language uses it: 鼾 **hān** (hahn) (*to snore*).

Following the Rules of Stroke Order

If you want to study **shūfǎ** 书法 (書法) (shoo-fah) (*calligraphy*) with a traditional Chinese **máobǐ** 毛笔 (毛筆) (maow-bee) (*writing brush*), or even just learn how to write Chinese characters with a plain old ballpoint pen, you need to know which stroke goes before the next. This progression is known as **bǐshùn** 笔顺 (筆順) (bee shwun) (*stroke order*).

All those complicated-looking Chinese characters are actually created by several individual strokes of the Chinese writing brush. **Bǐshùn** follows nine (count 'em) rules, which I lay out in the following sections.

TIP

Nowadays you don't have to master the art of Chinese calligraphy to write beautiful characters. All you have to do is press a key on a computer, and the character magically appears.

Rule 1

The first rule of thumb is that you write the character by starting with the topmost stroke.

For example, among the first characters students usually learn is the number one, which is written with a single horizontal line: 一. Because this character is pretty easy and has only one stroke, it's written from left to right.

The character for *two* has two strokes: 二. Both strokes are written from left to right; the top stroke is written first, following the top-to-bottom rule. The character for *three* has three strokes (三) and follows the same stroke-making pattern.

In the case of more complicated characters (for example, those with radicals that appear on the left-hand side), the radical on the left is written first, followed by the rest of the character. For example, to write the character meaning *tree* — 树 (樹) **shù** (shoo) — you first write the radical on the left (木) before adding the rest of the character to the right of the radical. To write the character meaning *thunder* — 雷 **léi** (lay) — you have to write the radical that appears on top (雨) first before writing the rest of the character underneath it.

Rules 2 through 9

Don't worry; the remaining rules require a lot less explanation than Rule 1 does:

>> **Rule 2:** Write horizontal strokes before vertical strokes. For example, the character meaning *ten* (十) is composed of two strokes, but the first one you

write is the one appearing horizontally: 一. The vertical stroke downward is written after that.

>> **Rule 3:** Write strokes that have to pass through the rest of the character last. Vertical strokes that pass through many other strokes are written after the strokes they pass through (like in the second character for the city of **Tiānjīn:** 天津 (tyan-jeen), and horizontal strokes that pass through all sorts of other strokes are written last (like in the character meaning *boat:* 舟**zhōu** [joe]).

>> **Rule 4:** Create diagonal strokes that go from right to left before writing the diagonal strokes that go from left to right. You write the character meaning *culture* — 文 **wén** (wuhn) — with four separate strokes: First comes the dot on top, then the horizontal line underneath it, then the diagonal stroke that goes from right to left, and finally the diagonal stroke that goes from left to right.

>> **Rule 5:** In characters that are vertically symmetrical, create the center components before those on the left or the right. Then write the portion of the character appearing on the left before the one appearing on the right. An example of such a character is the one meaning *to take charge of:* 承 **chéng** (chuhng).

>> **Rule 6:** Write the portion of the character that's an outside enclosure before the inside portion, such as in the word for *sun:* 日**rì** (ir). Some characters with such enclosures don't have bottom portions, such as with the character for *moon:* 月**yuè** (yweh).

>> **Rule 7:** Make the left vertical stroke of an enclosure first. For example, in the word meaning *mouth* — 口 **kǒu** (ko) — you write the vertical stroke on the left first, followed by the horizontal line on top and the vertical stroke on the right (those two are written as one stroke) and finally the horizontal line on the bottom.

>> **Rule 8:** Bottom enclosing components usually come last, such as with the character meaning *the way:* 道 **dào** (daow).

>> **Rule 9:** Dots come last. For example, in the character meaning *jade* — 玉 **yù** (yew) — the little dot you see between the bottom and middle horizontal lines is written last.

Up, Down, or Sideways? Deciphering the Direction of Characters

Because each Chinese character can be a word in and of itself or part of a compound word, you can read and understand them in any order — right to left, left to right, or top to bottom. If you see a Chinese movie, you can often see two different subtitles: one in English, going from left to right on one line, and Chinese characters, which may be going from right to left or left to right. You may go cross-eyed for a while trying to follow them both, but you'll get the hang of it soon enough.

Right to left and left to right are common enough, but why top to bottom, you may ask? Because before the invention of paper around the eighth century BCE, Chinese was originally written on strips of bamboo, which required the vertical writing direction.

CULTURAL WISDOM

You can see the role of bamboo strips in the character for *volume* (as in a volume of a book): 册 (冊) **cè** (tsuh). The simplified character consists of two bamboo strips connected by a piece of string. The traditional character (in parentheses) looks like even more bamboo strips are tied together by the string. I tell you more about simplified and traditional characters in the following section.

See whether you can tell what the following saying means, regardless of which way these characters are going. First, I tell you what the four characters each mean individually; then you can string them together and take a stab at the whole saying.

>> 知 **zhī** (jir) (*to know*)

>> 者 **zhě** (juh) (possessive article, such as *the one who*)

>> 不 **bù** (boo) (negative prefix, such as *no, not, doesn't*)

>> 言 **yán** (yeahn) (classical Chinese for *to speak*)

Okay, here's the saying in three different directions. See whether you can figure it out by the time it's written top to bottom.

Left to right: 知者不言, 言者不知

Right to left: 知不者言, 言不者知

Top to bottom:

知

者

不

言,

言

者

不

知

Give up? It means *Those who know do not speak, and those who speak do not know.* How's that for wisdom?

CULTURAL WISDOM

The saying "Those who know do not speak, and those who speak do not know" has been attributed to the sage **Lǎozǐ** 老子 (Laow-dzuh) in the sixth century BCE. It comes from the **Dàodé Jīng** 道德经 (道德經) (Daow-duh jeeng) (more commonly spelled **Tao Te Ching**), which contains many inspirational sayings; portions of the **Dàodé Jīng** appear in many Chinese paintings, poems, and works of calligraphy.

Traditional versus Simplified Characters: When to Use Which

Whether you're planning on visiting Taiwan or doing business in the People's Republic of China, you need to know the difference between **fántǐ zì** 繁体字 (繁體字) (fahn-tee dzuh) (*traditional characters*) and **jiántǐ zì** 简体字 (簡體字) (jyan-tee dzuh) (*simplified characters*) — especially if you plan on exchanging business cards at some point.

Fántǐ zì haven't changed much since **kǎishū** 楷书 (楷書) (kye-shoo) (*standard script*) was first created around 200 CE. These traditional characters are still used in Taiwan, Hong Kong, Macao, and many overseas Chinese communities today, where the proud but arduous process of learning complicated characters begins at a very early age and the art of deftly wielding a Chinese writing brush comes with the territory.

Jiántǐ zì are used solely in the People's Republic of China, Singapore, and Malaysia. When the People's Republic of China was established in 1949, the illiteracy rate among the general populace was about 85 percent — in large part because learning to write Chinese was so difficult and time consuming, especially when most of the population consisted of farmers who had to work on the land from dawn to dusk.

The new Communist government decided to simplify the writing process by reducing the number of strokes in many characters. Table 2-2 shows you some examples of the before (traditional characters) and after (simplified characters).

TIP

Simplification of the Chinese writing system has political overtones, so if you're planning on doing business in Taiwan, for example, make sure your business cards and other company materials are printed with *traditional* Chinese characters.

TABLE 2-2   **Traditional and Simplified Chinese Characters**

Traditional Character (# of Strokes)	Simplified Character (# of Strokes)	Romanization and Pronunciation	Meaning
見 (7 strokes)	见 (4 strokes)	**jiàn** (jyan)	*to see*
車 (6 strokes)	车 (4 strokes)	**chē** (chuh)	*vehicle*
聲 (17 strokes)	声 (7 strokes)	**shēng** (shuhng)	*sound*
國 (11 strokes)	国 (8 strokes)	**guó** (gwaw)	*country*
較 (13 strokes)	较 (10 strokes)	**jiào** (jyaow)	*relatively*

Using a Chinese Dictionary . . . without an Alphabet!

Whether you're looking at simplified or traditional characters (see the preceding section), you don't find any letters stringing them together like you see in English. So how in the world do Chinese people consult a Chinese dictionary? (Bet you didn't know I could read your mind.) Several different ways:

>> **Count the number of strokes in the overall character.** Because Chinese characters are composed of several strokes of the writing brush, one way to look up a character is by counting the number of strokes and then looking up the character under the portion of the dictionary that notes characters by strokes. But to do so, you have to know which radical to check under first.

>> **Determine the radical.** Each radical is itself composed of a certain number of strokes, so you have to first look up the radical by the number of strokes it contains. After you locate that radical, you start looking under the number of strokes left in the character after that radical to locate the character you wanted to look up in the first place.

>> **Check under the pronunciation of the character.** You can always just check under the pronunciation of the character (assuming you already know how to pronounce it), but you have to sift through every single *homonym* (characters with the same pronunciation) to locate just the right one. You also have to look under the various tones to see which pronunciation comes with the first, second, third, or fourth tone you want to locate. And because Chinese has so many homonyms, this task isn't as easy as it may sound (no pun intended). (You can read more about tones in Chapter 1.)

I bet now you feel really relieved that you're only focusing on spoken Chinese and not the written language.

FUN & GAMES

Fill in the blanks below to test your knowledge of the Chinese writing system. Refer to Appendix C for the correct answers.

1. The Chinese written language contains ____ radicals.

   a) 862   b) 194   c) 214   d) 2,140

2. The origins of the Chinese writing system can be found on ____.

   a) oracle bones   c) chopped liver

   b) bronze inscriptions   d) rice cakes

3. The direction of Chinese writing is ____.

   a) right to left   b) left to right   c) top to bottom   d) all of the above

4. The most complicated radical to write (鼻) means ____.

   a) eye   b) ear   c) nose   d) throat

5. Chinese characters that are simple line drawings representing an object are ____.

   a) ideographs   c) pictographs

   b) compound ideographs   d) phonetic compounds

Chapter 3

Warming Up with the Basics: Chinese Grammar

Maybe you're one of those people who cringe at the mere mention of the word *grammar*. Just the thought of all those rules on how to construct sentences can put you into a cold sweat.

Hey, don't sweat it! This chapter can just as easily be called "Chinese without Tears." It gives you some quick and easy shortcuts on how to combine the basic building blocks of Chinese (which, by the way, are the same components that make up English) — nouns to name things; adjectives to qualify the nouns; verbs to show action or passive states of being; and adverbs to describe the verbs, adjectives, or other adverbs. After you know how to combine these parts of any given sentence, you can express your ideas and interests spanning the past, present, and future.

When you speak English, I bet you don't sit and analyze the word order before opening your mouth to say something. Well, the same can hold true when you begin speaking Chinese. You probably didn't even know the word for grammar before someone taught you that it was the framework for analyzing the structure of a language. Instead of overwhelming you, this chapter makes understanding Chinese grammar as easy as punch.

If you're patient with yourself, have fun following the dialogues illustrating basic sentences, and listen to them on the accompanying online audio tracks, you'll do just fine.

REMEMBER

You can listen to all the Talkin' the Talk dialogues featured in this chapter. Go to www.dummies.com/go/chinese and click on the dialogue you want to hear.

The Basics of Chinese Nouns, Articles, and Adjectives

Admit it. Most of us took the better part of our first two years of life to master the basics when it came to forming English sentences. With this book, you can whittle this same skill in Chinese down to just a few minutes. Just keep reading this chapter. I promise it'll save you a lot of time in the long run.

The basic word order of Chinese is exactly the same as in English. Hard to imagine? Just think of it this way: When you say *I love spinach*, you're using the subject (I), verb (love), object (spinach) sentence order. It's the same in Chinese. Only in Beijing, the sentence sounds more like **Wǒ xǐhuān bōcài.** 我喜欢菠菜. (我喜歡菠菜.) (Waw she-hwahn baw-tsye). (*I like spinach.*)

And if that isn't enough to endear you to Chinese, maybe these tidbits of information will:

>> You don't need to distinguish between singular and plural nouns.

>> You don't have to deal with gender-specific nouns.

>> You can use the same word as both the subject and the object.

>> You don't need to conjugate verbs.

>> You don't need to master verb tenses. (Don't you just love it already?)

How could such news not warm the hearts of all those who've had grammar phobia since grade school? I get to the verb-related issues later in the chapter; in this section, I pull you up to speed on nouns and their descriptors.

The way you can tell how one part of a Chinese sentence relates to another is generally by the use of particles and what form the word order takes. (*Particles*, for those of you presently scratching your heads, can be found at the beginning or end of sentences and serve mainly to distinguish different types of emphatic statements but can't be translated in and of themselves.)

Nouns

Common nouns represent tangible things, such as **háizi** 孩子 (hi-dzuh) (*child*) or **yè** 叶 (葉) (yeh) (*leaf*). Like all languages, Chinese is just chock-full of nouns:

>> Proper nouns for such things as names of countries or people, like **Fǎguó** 法国 (法國) (Fah-gwaw) (*France*) and **Zhāng Xiānshēng** 张先生 (張先生) (Jahng Shyan-shung) (*Mr. Zhang*)

>> Material nouns for such non-discrete things as **kāfēi** 咖啡 (kah-fay) (*coffee*) or **jīn** 金 (jin) (*gold*)

>> Abstract nouns for such things as **zhèngzhì** 政治 (juhng-jir) (*politics*) or **wénhuà** 文化 (one-hwah) (*culture*)

Pronouns

Pronouns are easy to make plural in Chinese. Just add the plural suffix **-men** to the three basic pronouns:

>> **Wǒ** 我 (waw) (*I/me*) becomes **wǒmen** 我们 (我們) (waw-mun) (*we/us*).

>> **Nǐ** 你 (nee) (*you*) becomes **nǐmen** 你们 (你們) (nee-mun) (*you [plural]*).

>> **Tā** 他/她/它 (tah) (*he/him, she/her, it*) becomes **tāmen** 他们/她们/它们 (他們/她們/它們) (tah-mun) (*they/them*).

Sometimes you hear the term **zánmen** 咱们 (咱們) (dzah-mun) for *us* rather than the term **wǒmen**. **Zánmen** is used in very familiar settings when the speaker wants to include the listener in an action, like when you say **Zánmen zǒu ba**. 咱们走吧. (咱們走吧.) (Dzah-mun dzoe bah.) (*Let's go.*).

When you're speaking to an elder or someone you don't know too well and the person is someone to whom you should show respect, you need to use the pronoun **nín** 您 (neen) rather than the more informal **nǐ** 你 (nee). On the other hand, if you're speaking to several people who fit that description, the plural remains **nǐmen** 你们 (你們) (nee-men).

Classifiers

Classifiers are sometimes called *measure words*, even though they don't really measure anything. They actually help classify particular nouns. For example, the classifier **běn** 本 (bun) can refer to books, magazines, dictionaries, and just about anything else that's printed and bound like a book. You may hear **Wǒ yào yì běn shū.** 我要一本书. (我要一本書.) (Waw yaow ee bun shoo.) (*I want a book.*) just as easily as you hear **Wǒ yào kàn yì běn zázhì.** 我要看一本杂志. (我要看一本雜志.) (Waw yaow kahn ee bun dzah-jir.) (*I want to read a magazine.*).

Classifiers are found between a number (or a demonstrative pronoun such as *this* or *that*) and a noun. They're similar to English words such as *herd* (of elephants) or *school* (of fish). Although English doesn't use classifiers too often, in Chinese you find them wherever a number is followed by a noun, or at least an implied noun (such as *I'll have another one,* referring to a cup of coffee).

TIP

Because you have so many potential classifiers to choose from in Chinese, here's the general rule of thumb: When in doubt, use **ge** 个 (個) (guh). It's the all-purpose classifier and the one used the most in the Chinese language. You usually can't go wrong by using **ge.** If you're tempted to leave a classifier out altogether because you're not sure which one is the right one, don't give in! You may not be understood at all.

Chinese has lots of different classifiers because they're each used to refer to different types of things. For example, Table 3-1 lists classifiers for natural objects. Here are some other examples:

>> **gēn** 根 (gun): Used for anything that looks like a stick, such as a string or even a blade of grass

>> **zhāng** 张 (張) (jahng): Used for anything with a flat surface, such as a newspaper, table, or bed

>> **kē** 颗 (顆) (kuh): Used for anything round and tiny, such as a pearl

TABLE 3-1

Typical Classifiers for Natural Objects

Classifier	Pronunciation	Use
duǒ 朵	dwaw	flowers
kē 棵	kuh	trees
lì 粒	lee	grain (of rice, sand, and so on)
zhī 只(隻)	jir	animals, insects, birds
zuò 座	dzwaw	hills, mountains

Whenever you have a pair of anything, you can use the classifier **shuāng** 双(雙) (shwahng). That goes for **yì shuāng kuàizi** 一双筷子 (一雙筷子) (ee shwahng kwye-dzuh) (*a pair of chopsticks*) as well as for **yì shuāng shǒu** 一双手 (一雙手) (ee shwahng show) (*a pair of hands*). Sometimes a pair is indicated by the classifier **duì** 对 (對) (dway), as in **yí duì ěrhuán** 一对耳环 (一對耳環) (ee dway are-hwahn) (*a pair of earrings*).

Singular and plural: It's a non-issue

Chinese makes no distinction between singular and plural. If you say the word **shū** 书 (書) (shoo), it can mean *book* just as easily as *books*. The only way you know whether it's singular or plural is if a number followed by a classifier precedes the word **shū**, as in **Wǒ yǒu sān běn shū.** 我有三本书. (我有三本書.) (Waw yo sahn bun shoo.) (*I have three books.*).

One way to indicate plurality after personal pronouns **wǒ** 我 (waw) (*I*), **nǐ** 你 (nee) (*you*), and **tā** 他/她/它 (tah) (*he/she/it*) and human nouns such as **háizi** 孩子 (hi-dzuh) (*child*) and **xuéshēng** 学生 (學生) (shweh-shuhng) (*student*) is by adding the suffix **-men** 们 (們) (men). It acts as the equivalent of adding an *s* to nouns in English.

So many Chinese words are pronounced largely the same way (although each with different tones) that the only way to truly know the meaning of the word is by looking at the character. For example, the third person singular is pronounced "tah" regardless of whether it means *he, she,* or *it,* but each one is written with a different Chinese character.

GRAMMAR CHAT

TIP

Talkin' the Talk

Susan and Michael are looking at a beautiful field.

Susan: **Zhèr de fēngjǐng zhēn piàoliàng!**
           Jar duh fung-jeeng juhn pyaow-lyahng.
           This scenery is really beautiful!

Michael: **Nǐ kàn! Nà zuò shān yǒu nàmme duō shù, nàmme duō huā.**
           Nee kahn! Nah dzwaw shahn yo nummuh dwaw shoo, nummuh dwaw hwah.
           Look! That mountain has so many trees and flowers.

Susan:	**Duì le. Nèi kē shù tèbié piàoliàng. Zhè duǒ huā yě hěn yǒu tèsè.**	
	Dway luh. Nay kuh shoo tuh-byeh pyaow-lyahng. Jay dwaw hwah yeah hun yo tuh-suh.	
	You're right. That tree is particularly beautiful. And this flower is also really unique.	
Michael:	**Nà kē shù shàng yě yǒu sān zhī niǎo.**	
	Nah kuh shoo shahng yeah yo sahn jir nyaow.	
	That tree also has three birds in it.	

WORDS TO KNOW

guān niǎo 观鸟 (觀鳥)	gwan nyaow	bird-watching
wàngyuǎnjìn 望远镜 (望遠鏡)	wahng-ywan-jeeng	binoculars
hú 湖	hoo	lake
hé 河	huh	river
fēi yíng diào 飞蝇钓 (飛蠅釣)	fay yeeng dyaow	fly fishing

TIP

If a number and a measure word already appear in front of a pronoun or human noun, such as **sān ge háizi** 三个孩子 (三個孩子) (sahn guh hi–dzuh) (*three children*), don't add the suffix -men after **háizi** because plurality is already understood.

REMEMBER

Never attach the suffix **-men** to anything not human. People will think you're nuts if you start referring to your two pet cats as **wǒ de xiǎo māomen** 我的小猫们 (我的小貓們) (waw duh shyaow maow-mun). Just say **Wǒ de xiǎo māo hěn hǎo, xièxiè.** 我的小猫很好, 谢谢. (我的小貓很好, 謝謝.) (Waw duh shyaow maow hun how, shyeh-shyeh.) (*My cats are fine, thank you.*), and that should do the trick.

Definite versus indefinite articles

If you're looking for those little words in Chinese you can't seem to do without in English, such as *a, an,* and *the* — articles, as grammarians call them — you'll find they simply don't exist in Chinese. The only way you can tell if something is being referred to specifically (hence, considered definite) or just generally (and therefore indefinite) is by the word order. Nouns that refer specifically to something are usually found at the beginning of the sentence, before the verb:

Háizimen xǐhuān tā. 孩子们喜欢她. (孩子們喜歡她.) (Hi-dzuh-mun she-hwahn tah.) (*The children like her.*)

Pánzi zài zhuōzishàng. 盘子在桌子上. (盤子在桌子上.) (Pahn-dzuh dzye jwaw-dzuh-shahng.) (*There's a plate on the table.*)

Shū zài nàr. 书在那儿. (書在那兒.) (Shoo dzye nar.) (*The book[s] are there.*)

Nouns that refer to something more general (and are therefore indefinite) can more often be found at the end of the sentence, after the verb:

Nǎr yǒu huā? 哪儿有花? (哪兒有花?) (Nar yo hwah?) (*Where are some flowers?/Where is there a flower?*)

Nàr yǒu huā. 那儿有花. (那兒有花.) (Nar yo hwah.) (*There are some flowers over there./There's a flower over there.*)

Zhèige yǒu wèntí. 这个有问题. (這個有問題.) (Jay-guh yo one-tee.) (*There's a problem with this./There are some problems with this.*)

WARNING

These rules have some exceptions: If you find a noun at the beginning of a sentence, it may actually refer to something indefinite if the sentence makes a general comment (instead of telling a whole story), like when you see the verb **shì** 是 (shir) (*to be*) as part of the comment:

Xióngmāo shì dòngwù. 熊猫是动物. (熊貓是動物.) (Shyoong-maow shir doong-woo.) (*Pandas are animals.*)

Same thing goes if an adjective comes after the noun, such as

Pútáo hěn tián. 葡萄很甜. (Poo-taow hun tyan.) (*Grapes are very sweet.*)

Or if there's an auxiliary verb, such as

Xiǎo māo huì zhuā lǎoshǔ. 小猫会抓老鼠. (小貓會抓老鼠.) (Shyaow maow hway jwah laow-shoo.) (*Kittens can catch mice.*)

Or a verb indicating that the action occurs habitually, such as

Niú chī cǎo. 牛吃草. (Nyo chir tsaow.) (*Cows eat grass.*)

Nouns that are preceded by a numeral and a classifier, especially when the word **dōu** 都 (doe) (*all*) exists in the same breath, are also considered definite:

> **Sìge xuéshēng dōu hěn cōngmíng.** 四个学生都很聪明. (四個學生都很聰明.) (Suh-guh shweh-shung doe hun tsoong-meeng.) (*The four students are all very smart.*)

If the word **yǒu** 有 (yo) (*to exist*) comes before the noun and is then followed by a verb, it can also mean the reference is indefinite:

> **Yǒu shū zài zhuōzishàng.** 有书在桌子上. (有書在桌子上.) (Yo shoo dzye jwaw-dzuh-shahng.) (*There are books on top of the table.*)

If you see the word **zhè** 这 (這) (juh) (*this*) or **nà** 那 (nah) (*that*), plus a classifier used when a noun comes after the verb, it indicates a definite reference:

> **Wǒ yào mǎi nà zhāng huà.** 我要买那张画. (我要買那張畫.) (Waw yaow my nah jahng hwah.) (*I want to buy that painting.*)

Adjectives

As you learned in grade school (you were paying close attention, weren't you?), adjectives describe nouns. The question is where to put them. The general rule of thumb in Chinese is that if the adjective is pronounced with only one syllable, it appears immediately in front of the noun it qualifies:

> **cháng zhītiáo** 长枝条 (長枝條) (chahng jir-tyaow) (*long stick*)
>
> **lǜ chá** 绿茶 (綠茶) (lyew chah) (*green tea*)

If the adjective has two syllables, though, the possessive particle **de** 的 (duh) comes between it and whatever it qualifies:

> **cāozá de wǎnhuì** 嘈杂的晚会 (嘈雜的晚會) (tsaow-dzah duh wahn-hway) (*noisy party*)
>
> **gānjìng de yīfu** 干净的衣服 (乾淨的衣服) (gahn-jeeng duh ee-foo) (*clean clothes*)

And if a numeral is followed by a classifier, those should both go in front of the adjective and what it qualifies:

> **sān běn yǒuyìsī de shū** 三本有意思的书 (三本有意思的書) (sahn bun yo-ee-suh duh shoo) (*three interesting books*)
>
> **yí jiàn xīn yīfu** 一件新衣服 (一件新服裝) (ee jyan shin ee-foo) (*a [piece of] new clothing*)

One unique thing about Chinese is that when an adjective is also the predicate, appearing at the end of a sentence, it follows the subject or the topic without needing the verb shì:

Nà jiàn yīfu tài jiù. 那件衣服太旧. (那件衣服太舊.) (Nah jyan ee-foo tye jyo.) (*That piece of clothing [is] too old.*)

Tā de fángzi hěn gānjìng. 他的房子很干净. (他的房子很乾淨.) (Tah duh fahng-dzuh hun gahn-jeeng.) (*His house [is] very clean.*)

Getting into Verbs, Adverbs, Negation, and Possession

Some interesting characteristics of the Chinese language include the fact that there's no such thing as first, second, or third person (for example, *I eat* versus *he eats*); no such thing as active or passive voices (for example, *hear* versus *be heard*); and no such thing as past or present (*I like him* versus *I liked him*). In addition, the Chinese language has only two aspects — complete and continuous — whereas English has all sorts of different aspects: indefinite, continuous, perfect, perfect continuous, and so on. (Examples include ways of distinguishing among *I eat*, *I ate*, *I will eat*, *I said I would eat*, *I am eating*, and so on.) *Aspects* are what characterize the Chinese language in place of tenses. They refer to how a speaker views an event or state of being.

The following sections give you the lowdown on verbs, their friends the adverbs, and ways you can negate statements and express possession.

Verbs

Good news! You never have to worry about conjugating a Chinese verb in your entire life! If you hear someone say **Tāmen chī Yìdàlì fàn.** 他们吃意大利饭. (他們吃意大利飯.) (Tah-men chir Ye-dah-lee fahn.), it may mean *They eat Italian food.* just as easily as it may mean *They're eating Italian food.* Table 3-2 presents some common verbs; check out Appendix B for a more extensive list.

TABLE 3-2

Common Chinese Verbs

Chinese	Pronunciation	English
chī 吃	chir	*to eat*
kàn 看	kahn	*to see*
mǎi 买 (買)	my	*to buy*
mài 卖 (賣)	my	*to sell*
rènshi 认识 (認識)	run-shir	*to know (a person)*
shì 是	shir	*to be*
yào 要	yaow	*to want/to need*
yǒu 有	yo	*to have*
zhīdào 知道	jir-daow	*to know (a fact)*
zǒulù 走路	dzoe-loo	*to walk*
zuò fàn 做饭 (做飯)	dzwaw fahn	*to cook*

To be or not to be: The verb shì

Does the Chinese verb **shì** 是 (shir) really mean *to be?* Or is it not to be? **Shì** is indeed similar to English in usage because it's often followed by a noun that defines the topic, such as **Tā shì wǒ de lǎobǎn.** 他是我的老板. (他是我的老闆.) (Tah shir waw duh laow–bahn.) (*He's my boss.*) or **Nà shì yī ge huài huà.** 那是一个坏话. (那是一個壞話.) (Nah shir ee guh hwye hwah.) (*That's a bad word.*).

WARNING

Be careful not to put the verb **shì** in front of an adjective unless you really mean to make an emphatic statement. In the course of normal conversation, you may say **Nà zhī bǐ tài guì.** 那支笔太贵. (那支筆太貴.) (Nah jir bee tye gway.) (*That pen [is] too expensive.*). You wouldn't say **Nà zhī bǐ shì tài guì.** 那支笔是太贵. (那支筆是太貴.) (Nah jir bee shir tye gway.) unless you really want to say *That pen IS too expensive!*, in which case you'd emphasize the word **shì** when saying it.

GRAMMAR CHAT

To negate the verb **shì**, put the negative prefix **bù** 不 (boo) in front of it:

> **Shì búshì?** 是不是? (Shir boo-shir?) (*Is it or isn't it?*)

> **Zhè búshì táng cù yú.** 这不是糖醋鱼. (這不是糖醋魚.) (Jay boo-shir tahng tsoo yew.) (*This isn't sweet and sour fish.*).

Flip to the later section "**Bù** and **méiyǒu**: Total negation" for more on negation prefixes.

Feeling tense? Le, guò, and other aspect markers

Okay, you can relax now. No need to get tense about Chinese, because verbs don't indicate tenses all by themselves. That's the job of aspect markers, which are little syllables that indicate whether an action has been completed, is continuing, has just begun, and just about everything in between.

Take the syllable **le** 了 (luh), for example. If you use it as a suffix to a verb, it can indicate that an action has been completed:

> **Nǐ mǎile hěn duō shū.** 你买了很多书. (你買了很多書.) (Nee my-luh hun dwaw shoo.) (*You bought many books.*)

> **Tā dàile tā de yǔsǎn.** 他带了他的雨伞. (他帶了他的雨傘.) (Tah dye-luh tah duh yew-sahn.) (*He brought his umbrella.*)

And if you want to turn the sentence into a question, just add **méiyǒu** 没有 (mayo) at the end. It automatically negates the action completed by **le**:

> **Nǐ mǎile hěn duō shū méiyǒu?** 你买了很多书没有? (你買了很多書没有?) (Nee my-luh hun dwaw shoo may-yo?) (*Have you bought many books?/Did you buy many books?*)

> **Tā dàile tā de yǔsǎn méiyǒu?** 他带了他的雨伞没有? (他帶了他的雨傘没有?) (Tah dye-luh tah duh yew-sahn may-yo?) (*Did he bring his umbrella?*)

Another aspect marker is **guò** 过 (過) (gwaw). It basically means that something has been done at one point or another even though it's not happening right now:

> **Tā qùguò Měiguó.** 他去过美国. (他去過美國.) (Ta chyew-gwaw May-gwaw.) (*He has been to America.*)

> **Wǒmen chīguò Fǎguó cài.** 我们吃过法国菜. (我們吃過法國菜.) (Waw-mun chir-gwaw Fah-gwaw tsye.) (*We have eaten French food before.*)

If an action is happening just as you speak, you use the aspect marker **zài** 在 (dzye):

> **Nǐ māma zài zuòfàn.** 你妈妈在做饭. (你媽媽在做飯.) (Nee mah-mah dzye dzwaw-fahn.) (*Your mother is cooking.*)

> **Wǒmen zài chīfàn.** 我们在吃饭. (我們在吃飯.) (Waw-mun dzye chir-fahn.) (*We are eating.*)

TIP

When using the aspect marker **zài**, you can also add the word **zhèng** 正 (juhng) in front of it to add emphasis. It can be translated as *to be right in the middle of [doing something]*.

If something is or was happening continually and resulted from something else you did, just add the syllable **zhe** 着 (juh) to the end of the verb to say things like the following:

Nǐ chuānzhe yí jiàn piàoliàng de chènshān. 你穿着一件漂亮的衬衫. (你穿著一件漂亮的襯衫.) (Nee chwan-juh ee jyan pyaow-lyahng duh chuhn-shahn.) (*You're wearing a pretty shirt.*)

Tā dàizhe yí ge huáng màozi. 他戴着一个黄帽子. (他戴著一個黃帽子.) (Tah dye-juh ee guh hwahng maow-dzuh.) (*He's wearing a yellow hat.*)

Another way you can use **zhe** is when you want to indicate two actions occurring at the same time:

Tā zuòzhe chīfàn. 她坐着吃饭. (她坐著吃飯.) (Tah dzwaw-juh chir-fahn.) (*She is/was sitting there eating.*)

.... **Talkin' the Talk** ....

Carol and Joe have fun people-watching on the streets of Shanghai.

Carol:	**Nǐ kàn! Nà ge xiǎo háizi dàizhe yí ge hěn qíguài de màozi, shì búshì?** Nee kahn! Nah guh shyaow hi-dzuh dye-juh ee guh hun chee-gwye duh maow-dzuh, shir boo-shir? *Look! That little kid is wearing a really strange hat, isn't she?*
Joe:	**Duìle. Tā hái yìbiān zǒu, yìbiān chànggē.** Dway luh. Tah hi ee-byan dzoe, ee-byan chahng-guh. *Yeah. She's also singing while she walks.*
Carol:	**Wǒ méiyǒu kànguò nàmme kě'ài de xiǎo háizi.** Waw mayo kahn-gwaw nummuh kuh-eye duh shyaow hi-dzuh. *I've never seen such a cute child.*
Joe:	**Zài Zhōngguó nǐ yǐjīng kànle tài duō kě'ài de xiǎo háizi.** Dzye Joong-gwaw nee ee-jeeng kahn-luh tye dwaw kuh-eye duh shyaow hi-dzuh. *You've already seen too many adorable little kids in China.*

WORDS TO KNOW

xiūxí 休息	shyo-shee	relax
zài kāfēi ting zuò yīxià 在咖啡厅坐一下 (在咖啡廳坐一下)	dzye kah-fay teeng dzwaw ee-shyah	sit at a cafe
qù sànbù 去散步	chyew sahn-boo	go for a walk
qù hǎitān 去海滩 (去海灘)	chyew hye-tan	go to the beach

The special verb: Yǒu (to have)

Do you **yǒu** 有 (yo) a computer? No?! Too bad. Everyone else seems to have one these days. How about a sports car? Do you **yǒu** one of those? If not, welcome to the club. People who have lots of things use the word **yǒu** pretty often, translated as *to have* like in the following examples:

> **Wǒ yǒu sān ge fángzi: yí ge zài Ōuzhōu, yí ge zài Yàzhōu, yí ge zài Měiguó.** 我有三个房子: 一个在欧洲, 一个在亚洲, 一个在美国. (我有三個房子: 一個在歐洲, 一個在亞洲, 一個在美國.) (Waw yo sahn guh fahng-dzuh: ee guh dzye Oh-joe, ee guh dzye Yah-joe, ee guh dzye May-gwaw.) (*I have three homes: one in Europe, one in Asia, and one in America.*)

> **Wǒ yǒu yí wàn kuài qián.** 我有一万块钱. (我有一萬塊錢.) (Waw yo ee wahn kwye chyan.) (*I have $10,000.*)

Another way **yǒu** can be translated is as *there is* or *there are*:

> **Yǒu hěn duō háizi.** 有很多孩子. (Yo hun dwaw hi-dzuh.) (*There are many children.*), as opposed to **Wǒ yǒu hěn duō háizi.** 我有很多孩子. (Waw yo hun dwaw hi-dzuh.) (*I have many children.*)

> **Shūzhuō shàng yǒu wǔ zhāng zhǐ.** 书桌上有五张纸 (書桌上有五張紙.) (Shoo-jwaw shahng yo woo jahng jir.) (*There are five pieces of paper on the desk.*)

WARNING

To negate the verb **yǒu**, you can't use the usual negative prefix **bù**. Instead, you must use another term indicating negation, **méi** 没 (may):

> **Méiyǒu hěn duō háizi.** 没有很多孩子. (May-yo hun dwaw hi-dzuh.) (*There aren't many children.*)

> **Shūzhuō shàng méiyǒu wǔ zhāng zhǐ.** 书桌上没有五张纸. (書桌上沒有五張紙.) (Shoo-jwaw shahng may-yo woo jahng jir.) (*There aren't five pieces of paper on the desk.*)

You can read more about negation prefixes in "**Bù** and **méiyǒu**: Total negation" later in the chapter.

Asking for what you want: The verb yào

After Yao Ming, the 7-foot-6-inch basketball superstar from China, came on the scene, the verb **yào** 要 (yaow) (*to want*) got some great publicity in the United States. The character for his name isn't written quite the same as the verb **yào,** but at least everyone knows how to pronounce it already: yow!

Yào is one of the coolest verbs in Chinese. When you say it, you usually get what you want. In fact, the mere mention of the word **yào** means you want something:

> **Wǒ yào gēn nǐ yìqǐ qù kàn diànyǐng.** 我要跟你一起去看电影. (我要跟你一起去看電影.) (Waw yaow gun nee ee-chee chyew kahn dyan-yeeng.) (*I want to go to the movies with you.*)

> **Wǒ yào yì bēi kāfēi.** 我要一杯咖啡. (Waw yaow ee bay kah-fay.) (*I want a cup of coffee.*)

GRAMMAR CHAT

You can also give someone an order with the verb **yào,** but only if it's used with a second-person pronoun:

> **Nǐ yào xiǎoxīn!** 你要小心! (Nee yaow shyaow-sheen!) (*You should be careful!*)

> **Nǐ yào xǐshǒu.** 你要洗手. (Nee yaow she-show.) (*You need to wash your hands.*)

Adverbs

Adverbs serve to modify verbs or adjectives and always appear in front of them in Chinese. The most common adverbs you find in Chinese are **hěn** 很 (hun) (*very*) and **yě** 也 (yeah) (*also*).

GRAMMAR CHAT

If you want to say that something isn't just **hǎo** 好 (how) (*good*) but rather that it's very good, you say it's **hěn hǎo** 很好 (hun how) (*very good*). If your friend wants to put his two cents in and say that something else is also really good, he says **Zhèi ge yě hěn hǎo.** 这个也很好. (這個也很好.) (Jay guh yeah hun how.) (*This is also very good.*) because **yě** always comes before **hěn** (as well as before the negative prefix **bù**; refer to the following section.)

Bù and méiyǒu: Total negation

Boo! Scare you? Don't worry. I'm just being negative in Chinese. That's right: The word **bù** is pronounced the same way a ghost would say it (boo) and is often spoken with the same intensity.

Bù can negate something you've done in the past or the present (or at least indicate you don't generally do it these days), and it can also help negate something in the future:

> **Diànyǐngyuàn xīngqīliù bù kāimén.** 电影院星期六不开门. (電影院星期六不開門.) (Dyan-yeeng-ywan sheeng-chee-lyo boo kye-mun.) (*The movie theatre won't be open on Saturday.*)

> **Tā xiǎo de shíhòu bù xǐhuān chī shūcài.** 他小的时候不喜欢吃蔬菜. (他小的時候不喜歡吃蔬菜.) (Tah shyaow duh shir-ho boo she-hwahn chir shoo-tsye.) (*When he was young, he didn't like to eat vegetables.*)

> **Wǒ bú huà huàr.** 我不画画儿. (我不畫畫兒.) (Waw boo hwah hwar.) (*I don't paint.*)

> **Wǒ búyào chàng gē.** 我不要唱歌. (Waw boo-yaow chahng guh.) (*I don't want to sing.*)

TIP

The negative prefix **bù** is usually spoken with a fourth (falling) tone. However, when it precedes a syllable with another fourth tone, **bù** becomes a second (rising) tone instead, as in such words as **búqù** 不去 (boo–chew) (*won't/didn't/doesn't go*) and **búyào** 不要 (boo–yaow) (*don't/didn't/won't want*). For more about tones, head to Chapter 1.

In addition to being part of the question **yǒu méiyǒu** (*do you have/does it have*), **méiyǒu** is another negative prefix that also goes before a verb. It refers only to the past, though, and means either something didn't happen, or at least didn't happen on a particular occasion:

> **Wǒ méiyǒu kàn nèi bù diànyǐng.** 我没有看那部电影. (我沒有看那部電影.) (Waw may-yo kahn nay boo dyan-yeeng.) (*I didn't see that movie.*)

> **Zuótiān méiyǒu xiàyǔ.** 昨天没有下雨. (昨天沒有下雨.) (Dzwaw-tyan mayo shyah-yew.) (*It didn't rain yesterday.*)

If the aspect marker **guò** is at the end of the verb **méiyǒu**, it means the action never happened (up until now) in the past. By the way, you'll sometimes find that **méiyǒu** is shortened just to **méi**:

> **Wǒ méi qù guò Fǎguó.** 我没去过法国. (我沒去過法國.) (Waw may chyew gwaw Fah-gwaw.) (*I've never been to France.*)

> **Wǒ méi chī guò Yìndù cài.** 我没吃过印度菜. (我沒吃過印度菜.) (Wo may chir gwaw Een-doo tsye.) (*I've never eaten Indian food.*)

Talkin' the Talk

Peter, Stewie, and Lois discuss where to go for dinner.

Peter: **Nǐmen jīntiān wǎnshàng yào búyào qù fànguǎn chīfàn?**
Nee-mun jin-tyan wahn-shahng yaow boo-yaow chyew fahn-gwahn chir-fahn?
Do you both want to go to a restaurant tonight?

Stewie: **Nà tài hǎole. Dāngrán yào.**
Nah tye how-luh. Dahng-rahn yaow.
That's a great idea. Of course I'd like to go.

Lois: **Wǒ búyào. Wǒ méiyǒu qián.**
Waw boo-yaow. Waw may-yo chyan.
I don't want to. I have no money.

Peter: **Wǒ yě méiyǒu qián, dànshì méiyǒu guānxi. Wǒ zhīdào yí ge hěn hǎo, hěn piányì de Zhōngguó fànguǎn.**
Waw yeah may-yo chyan, dahn-shir may-yo gwahn-she. Waw jir-daow ee guh hun how, hun pyan-yee duh Joong-gwaw fahn-gwan.
I don't have any money either, but it doesn't matter. I know a great but very inexpensive Chinese restaurant.

Lois: **Hǎo ba. Zánmen zǒu ba.**
How bah. Dzah-men dzoe bah.
Okay. Let's go.

WORDS TO KNOW

Wǒ èle. 我饿了. (我餓了.)	Waw uh-luh.	I'm hungry.
Wǒ kǒu kě. 我口渴.	Waw ko kuh.	I'm thirsty.
Wǒ è sǐle. 我饿死了. (我餓死了.)	Waw uh suh- luh.	I'm starving.
Wǒ è dé kěyǐ chī yītóu dà xiàng. 我饿得可以吃一头大象. (我餓得可以吃一頭大象.)	Waw uh duh kuh-yee chir ee-toe dah shyahng.	I could eat a horse.

Getting possessive with the particle de

The particle **de** 的 is ubiquitous in Chinese. Wherever you turn, there it is. **Wǒ de tiān!** 我的天! (Waw duh tyan!) (*My goodness!*) Oops . . . there it is again. It's easy to use. All you have to do is attach it to the end of the pronoun, such as **nǐ de chē** 你的车 (你的車) (nee duh chuh) (*your car*), or other modifier, such as **tā gōngsī de jīnglǐ** 他公司的经理 (他公司的經理) (tah goong-suh duh jeeng-lee) (*his company's manager*), and — voilà — it indicates possession.

The particle **de** acts as the *'s* in English when it's not attached to a pronoun. It also makes the process of modification exactly the opposite of the French possessive **de** or the English *of*, with which you may be tempted to compare it.

Asking Questions

You have a few easy ways to ask questions in Chinese at your disposal. Hopefully you're so curious about the world around you these days that you're itching to ask lots of questions when you know how. I break them down in the following sections.

The question particle ma

By far the easiest way to ask a question is simply to end any given statement with a **ma.** That automatically makes it into a question. For example, **Tā chīfàn.** 他吃饭 (他吃飯) (Tah chir-fahn.) (*He's eating./He eats.*) becomes **Tā chīfàn ma?** 他吃饭吗? (他吃飯嗎?) (Tah chir-fahn mah?) (*Is he eating?/Does he eat?*). **Nǐ shuō Zhōngwén.** 你说中文. (你說中文.) (Nee shwaw Joong-one.) (*You speak Chinese.*) becomes **Nǐ shuō Zhōngwén ma?** 你说中文吗? (你說中文嗎?) (Nee shwaw Joong-one mah?) (*Do you speak Chinese?*).

Yes/no choice questions using bù between repeating verbs

Another way you can ask a Chinese question is to repeat the verb in its negative form. The English equivalent is to say something like: *Do you eat, not eat? Remember:* This format can be used for only yes-or-no questions, though. Here are some examples:

> **Nǐ shì búshì Zhōngguórén?** 你是不是中国人? (你是不是中國人?) (Nee shir boo-shir Joong-gwaw-run?) (*Are you Chinese?*)

Tāmen xǐhuān bùxǐhuān chī Zhōngguó cài? 他们喜欢不喜欢吃中国菜? (他們喜歡不喜歡吃中國菜?) (Tah-men she-hwahn boo-she-hwahn chir Joong-gwaw tsye?) (*Do they like to eat Chinese food?*)

Tā yào búyào háizi? 他要不要孩子? (Tah yaow boo-yaow hi-dzuh?) (*Does he want children?*)

To answer this type of question, all you have to do is omit either the positive verb or the negative prefix and the verb following it:

Nǐ hǎo bù hǎo? 你好不好? (Nee how boo how?) (*How are you?* [Literally: *Are you good or not good?*])

Wǒ hǎo. 我好. (Waw how.) (*I'm okay.*) or **Wǒ bùhǎo.** 我不好. (Waw boo-how.) (*I'm not okay.*)

GRAMMAR CHAT

Some Chinese verbs, such as **xǐhuān** 喜欢 (喜歡) (she-hwan) (*to like/to want*), have two syllables. When Chinese people speak quickly, they may leave out the second syllable in a few bi-syllabic verbs and even a few auxiliary verbs the first time they come up in the verb-**bù**-verb pattern. So instead of saying **Tā xǐhuān bùxǐhuān hē jiǔ?** 她喜欢不喜欢喝酒? (她喜歡不喜歡喝酒?) (Tah she-hwan boo-she-hwan huh jyo?) to mean *Does she like to drink wine?*, someone may say **Tā xǐ bùxǐhuān hē jiǔ?** 她喜不喜欢喝酒? (她喜不喜歡喝酒?) (Tah she boo-she-hwan huh jyoe?).

Interrogative pronouns

A third way to ask questions in Chinese is to use interrogative pronouns. The following are pronouns that act as questions in Chinese:

- ❯❯ **nǎ** 哪 (nah) + classifier (*which*)
- ❯❯ **nǎr** 哪儿 (哪兒) (nar) (*where*)
- ❯❯ **shéi** 谁 (誰) (shay) (*who/whom*)
- ❯❯ **shéi de** 谁的 (誰的) (shay duh) (*whose*)
- ❯❯ **shénme** 什么 (甚麼) (shummuh) (*what*)
- ❯❯ **shénme dìfāng** 什么地方 (甚麼地方) (shummah dee-fahng) (*where*)

WARNING

Don't confuse **nǎ** with **nǎr.** That one extra letter makes the difference between saying which (**nǎ**) and where (**nǎr**).

Figuring out where such interrogative pronouns should go in any given sentence is easy. Just put them wherever the answer would be found. For example:

Question: **Nǐ shì shéi?** 你是谁? (你是誰?) (Nee shir shay?) (*Who are you?*)

Answer: **Nǐ shì wǒ péngyǒu.** 你是我朋友. (Nee shir waw puhng-yo.) (*You're my friend.*)

Question: **Tā de nǚpéngyǒu zài nǎr?** 他的女朋友在哪儿? (他的女朋友在哪兒?) (Tah duh nyew-puhng-yo dzye nar?) (*Where is his girlfriend?*)

Answer: **Tā de nǚpéngyǒu zài jiālǐ.** 他的女朋友在家里. (他的女朋友在家裡.) (Tah duh nyew-puhng-yo dzye jyah-lee.) (*His girlfriend is at home.*)

TIP

A way to ask who or which person without sounding rude or too familiar is to use the term **něi wèi** 哪位 (nye way) (Literally: *which person*). For example, **Nǐ yéye shì něi wèi?** 你爷爷是哪位? (你爺爺是哪位?) (Nee yeh–yeh shir nay way?) (*Which one is your grandfather?*).

GRAMMAR
CHAT

You often find interrogative pronouns at the beginning of sentences if they're followed by the verb **yǒu** 有 (yo) (*to exist*), such as **Shéi yǒu wǒ de bǐ?** 谁有我的笔? (誰有我的筆?) (Shay yo waw duh bee?) (*Who has my pen?*).

FUN & GAMES

Match the Chinese questions with the English translations. (See Appendix C for the correct answers.)

1. **Shì búshì?** 是不是?

2. **Nǐ shuō Zhōngwén ma?** 你说中文吗? (你說中文嗎?)

3. **Nǐ shì shéi?** 你是谁? (你是誰?)

4. **Nà yǒu shénme guānxi?** 那有什么关系? (那有甚麼關係?)

5. **Nǐ yǒu méiyǒu yíge bǐjìběn diànnǎo?** 你有没有一个笔记本电脑? (你有沒有一個筆記本電腦?)

a. Who are you?

b. Isn't that so?

c. Do you have a laptop?

d. Who cares?

e. Do you speak Chinese?

Chapter **4**

Getting Started with Basic Expressions: Nǐ Hǎo!

Nǐ hǎo! 你好! (Nee how!) (*Hello!/How are you?*) Those are probably the two most important words you need to know to start a conversation with your Chinese neighbors, with your Chinese in-laws coming into town, with a Chinese classmate, or with airport personnel upon your arrival in China. When you say them, you take the first step in making new friends and establishing contact with just about anybody.

In this chapter, I show you how to start your new connection off with just the right words. The only other thing you have to do is smile. That's something all people understand, no matter what country they're from.

REMEMBER

You can listen to all the Talkin' the Talk dialogues featured in this chapter. Go to www.dummies.com/go/chinese and click on the dialogue you want to hear.

Making Introductions

Nothing beats making new friends at a **wǎnhuì** 晚会 (晚會) (wahn-hway) (*party*), a **xīn gōngzuò** 新工作 (sheen goong-dzwaw) (*new job*), on the **dìtiě** 地铁 (地鐵) (dee-tyeh) (*subway*), or just **zài lù shàng** 在路上 (dzye loo shahng) (*on the street*). You may meet someone right after reading this chapter who becomes a good friend for life. This section gives you a head start in making a good first impression. Go ahead and practice these greetings to get ready for anything.

Acquainting yourself

When you make Chinese acquaintances or travel abroad, you soon discover that a little knowledge of even a few key expressions in their native language goes a long way in creating good will between your two cultures. Chinese people in particular are very appreciative of anyone who takes the time to learn their intricate and difficult language, so your efforts will be rewarded many times over.

You have options other than **nǐ hǎo** when you first meet someone, such as **Hěn gāoxìng jiàndào nǐ.** 很高兴见到你. (很高興見到你.) (Hun gaow-sheeng jyan-daow nee.) (*Glad to meet you.*) or **Wǒ hěn róngxìng.** 我很荣幸. (我很榮幸.) (Waw hun roong-sheeng.) (*I'm honored to meet you.*). Go ahead and tell the person your **míngzi** 名字 (meeng-dzuh) (*name*) and take the conversation from there.

Don't know what to say after the first **Nǐ hǎo?** Here are a few common opening lines to get you started:

>> **Nǐ jiào shénme míngzi?** 你叫什么名字? (你叫甚麼名字?) (Nee jyaow shummuh meeng-dzuh?) (*What's your name?*)

>> **Qǐng ràng wǒ jièshào wǒ zìjǐ.** 请让我介绍我自己. (請讓我介紹我自己.) (Cheeng rahng waw jyeh-shaow waw dzuh-jee.) (*Please let me introduce myself.*)

>> **Wǒ jiào ____. Nǐ ne?** 我叫 ____. 你呢? (Waw jyaow ____. Nee nuh?) (*My name is ____. What's yours?*)

>> **Wǒ shì Měiguórén.** 我是美国人. (我是美國人.) (Waw shir May-gwaw-run.) (*I'm an American.*)

Introducing your friends and family

You can help your friends make even more friends if you start introducing them to each other. All you have to do is say **Qǐng ràng wǒ jièshào wǒ de péngyǒu, Carl.** 请让我介绍我的朋友, Carl. (請讓我介紹我的朋友, Carl.) (Cheeng rahng waw jyeh-shaow waw duh puhng-yo, Carl.) (*Let me introduce my friend, Carl.*). In addition to introducing your **péngyǒu** 朋友 (puhng-yo) (*friend*), you can introduce these important people:

>> **bàba** 爸爸 (bah-bah) (*father*)

>> **lǎobǎn** 老板 (老闆) (laow-bahn) (*boss*)

>> **lǎoshī** 老师 (老師) (laow-shir) (*teacher*)

>> **māma** 妈妈 (媽媽) (mah-mah) (*mother*)

>> **nán péngyǒu** 男朋友 (nahn puhng-yo) (*boyfriend*)

>> **nǚ péngyǒu** 女朋友 (nyew pung-yo) (*girlfriend*)

>> **tàitai** 太太 (tye-tye) (*wife*)

>> **tóngshì** 同事 (toong-shir) (*colleague*)

>> **tóngwū** 同屋 (toong-woo) (*roommate*)

>> **tóngxué** 同学 (同學) (toong-shweh) (*classmate*)

>> **wǒ de péngyǒu** 我的朋友 (waw duh puhng-yo) (*my friend*)

>> **zhàngfu** 丈夫 (jahng-foo) (*husband*)

TIP

When introducing two people to each other, always introduce the one with the lower social status and/or age to the person with the higher social status. The Chinese consider this progression polite.

Asking people for their names

Many situations call for informal greetings like **Wǒ jiào Sarah. Nǐ ne?** 我叫Sarah. 你呢? (Waw jyaow Sarah. Nee nuh?) (*My name is Sarah. And yours?*) or **Nǐ jiào shénme míngzi?** 你叫什么名字? (你叫甚麼名字?) (Nee jyaow shummuh meeng-dzuh?) (*What's your name?*), but you can show a greater level of politeness and respect by asking **Nín guì xìng?** 您贵姓? (您貴姓?) (Neen gway sheeng?) (Literally: *What's your honorable surname?*). But if you're asking this question of someone who's younger than you or lower in social status, you can easily just say **Nǐ jiào shénme míngzi?** 你叫什么名字? (你叫甚麼名字?) (Nee jyaow shummah meeng-dzuh?) (*What's your name?*). Even though **míngzi** usually means *given name*, asking this question may elicit an answer of first and last name. Keep practicing these different opening lines to ask who people are, and you're bound to make friends quickly (or you're at least bound to get to know a lot of Chinese names).

If someone asks you **Nín guì xìng?**, don't refer to yourself with the honorific **guì** when you answer. Your new acquaintance would consider you too boastful. Such a response is like saying "My esteemed family name is Smith." The best way to answer is to say **Wǒ xìng Smith.** 我姓 Smith. (Waw sheeng Smith.) (*My family name is Smith.*).

If a guy tells you his name in Chinese, you can be sure the first syllable he utters will be his surname, not his given name. So if he says his name is **Lǐ Shìmín,** for example, his family name is **Lǐ** and his given name is **Shìmín.** You should keep referring to him as **Lǐ Shìmín** (rather than just **Shìmín**) until you become really good friends. If you want to address him as **Xiānshēng** 先生 (shyan–shuhng) (*Mr.*), or if you're addressing a female as **Xiǎojiě** 小姐 (shyaow–jyeh) (*Miss*) or **Tàitài** 太太 (tye–tye) (*Mrs.*), you put that title after his or her last name and say **Lǐ Xiānshēng** or **Lǐ Xiǎojiě.** Even though the Chinese language has words for *Mr., Miss,* and *Mrs.,* it has no equivalent term for *Ms.* At least not yet.

Talkin' the Talk

Eva introduces her friends Oscar and David to each other.

Eva: **Oscar, qǐng ràng wǒ jièshào wǒ de péngyǒu David.**
Oscar, cheeng rahng waw jyeh-shaow waw duh puhng-yo David.
Oscar, allow me to introduce my friend David.

Oscar: **Nǐ hǎo. Hěn gāoxìng jiàndào nǐ.**
Nee how. Hun gaow-sheeng jyan-daow nee.
Hi. Nice to meet you.

David: **Hěn gāoxìng jiàndào nǐ. Wǒ shì Eva de tóngxué.**
Hun gaow-sheeng jyan-daow nee. Waw shir Eva duh toong-shweh.
Good to meet you. I'm Eva's classmate.

Oscar: **Hěn gāoxìng jiàndào nǐ.**
Hun gaow-sheeng jyan-daow nee.
Nice to meet you.

David: **Nǐmen zénme rènshì?**
Nee-mun dzummuh run-shir?
How do you happen to know each other?

Eva: **Wǒmen shì tóngshì.**
Waw-mun shir toong-shir.
We're co-workers.

WORDS TO KNOW

zǔfù 祖父	dzoo-foo	paternal grandfather (formal)
zǔmǔ 祖母	dzoo-moo	paternal grandmother (formal)
wàizǔfù 外祖父	wye-dzoo-foo	maternal grandfather (formal)
wàizǔmǔ 外祖母	wye-dzoo-moo	maternal grandmother (formal)
bǎomǔ 保姆	baow-moo	nanny
lǐfà shī 理发师 (理 髮師)	lee-fah shir	hairdresser
yīshēng 医生 (醫 生)	ee-shung	doctor
lǜshī 律师 (律師)	lyew-shir	lawyer
wǎngqiú dādàng 网球 搭档 (網球搭檔)	wahng-chyo dah-dahng	tennis partner

Greeting and Chatting

When you **dǎ zhāohu** 打招呼 (dah jaow-who) (*extend greetings*), you're sure to maintain and possibly even improve your connections with others. This goes for starting the day right with your **àirén** 爱人 (愛人) (eye-run) (*spouse*), showing respect for your **lǎoshī** 老师 (老師) (laow-shir) (*teacher*), keeping on the good side of your **lǎobǎn** 老板 (老闆) (laow-bahn) (*boss*), or paving the way for that deal with your new **shēngyì huǒbàn** 生意伙伴 (生意夥伴) (shuhng-ee hwaw-bahn) (*business partner*).

After the opening greeting, stick around to chat for a bit so you can get to know each other better. You can make new friends and find out more about each other through small conversations. This section gives you the important phrases to know.

Addressing new friends and strangers

In your hometown or home country, you may have plenty of **lǎo péngyǒu** 老朋友 (laow puhng-yo) (*old friends*), but in any other city or country, you need to get off on the right foot by addressing people the way they're used to being addressed. You can get chummier as time goes by, but try to avoid sounding too friendly or presumptuous too soon.

You can always safely greet people in professional settings by announcing their last name followed by their title, such as **Wáng Xiàozhǎng** 王校长 (王校長) (Wahng Shyaow-jahng) (*President [of an educational institution] Wang*) or **Jīn Zhǔrèn** 金主任 (Jeen Joo-run) (*Director Jin*). Here are some other examples of occupational titles:

>> **bùzhǎng** 部长 (部長) (boo-jahng) (*department head or minister*)

>> **fùzhǔrèn** 副主任 (foo-joo-run) (*assistant director*)

>> **jiàoshòu** 教授 (jyaow-show) (*professor*)

>> **jīnglǐ** 经理 (經理) (jeeng-lee) (*manager*)

>> **lǎoshī** 老师 (老師) (laow-shir) (*teacher*)

If you don't know someone's title, you can safely address the person by saying his or her family name and then either **Xiānshēng** 先生 (Shyan-shuhng) (*Mr.*) or **Xiǎojiě** 小姐 (Shyaow-jyeh) (*Miss*).

CULTURAL WISDOM

Chinese folks often instruct their young children to address older people as **shúshu** 叔叔 (shoo-shoo) (*uncle*) or **āyí** 阿姨 (ah-yee) (*aunt*). Getting to know a Chinese family makes you feel like you're actually part of the family in a new country.

TIP

Sometimes people add the terms **lǎo** 老 (laow) (*old*) or **xiǎo** 小 (shyaow) (*young*) in front of the last name and omit the first name completely. It indicates a comfortable degree of familiarity and friendliness that can only develop over time. But make sure you know which one to use — **lǎo** is for someone who's older than you, and **xiǎo** is for someone who's younger than you. Also keep in mind that these names can sometimes sound kind of funny to non-Chinese. If someone's surname is pronounced **Yáng** (Yahng), which sounds like the word for *goat*, you may end up sounding like you're calling the person an old goat when you become good friends.

Conversing around the clock

You can always say **Nǐ hǎo** when you meet someone, but at certain times of the day, you can use specific ways to express your greetings.

When you meet family, friends, co-workers, or fellow students in the morning, you can say **Zǎo.** 早. (Dzaow.) (*Good morning.*) or **Zǎo ān.** 早安 (Dzaow ahn.) (*Good morning.* [Literally: *early peace*]).

A WORD ABOUT CULTURALLY ACCEPTABLE BEHAVIOR

CULTURAL WISDOM

The Chinese are very friendly people and sometimes don't hesitate to come up to a foreigner on the street in order to practice their English. Such a situation can be a great chance to practice your Chinese as well. You have all sorts of cultural differences to get used to, however, so don't be surprised if a person you meet for the first time starts asking you about your salary or the cost of that cute sweater you're wearing. Subjects that are taboo as conversation pieces in the United States aren't off-limits in China. (Try not to inquire about a person's political views or love life unless you know the person really well, though, or you may hit a brick wall.)

In general, Chinese people are loath to show negative emotions in public. Anger and disappointment or disapproval are major no-nos. Try to do the same when you're in a Chinese setting, because you may run the risk of insulting someone unintentionally. To do so means that you make them lose face — a cardinal sin if you want to get along in China. The last thing you want to do is insult, yell at, or otherwise embarrass anyone publicly, so keep a lid on any negative reactions you may have. You earn respect by controlling your emotions.

You may be surprised that many Chinese have no compunction about performing certain bodily functions in public. The Chinese don't consider it rude, for example, to belch, spit, or even pass gas in front of others. And because there's no such thing as a nonsmoking area, most smokers don't even think to ask whether you mind their lighting up near you. In addition, you may find people pointing or even staring at you — especially in smaller towns and villages, which rarely get foreign visitors. These behaviors are considered perfectly acceptable, so don't let them get your dander up. Just go with the flow and offer a polite smile in return.

The Chinese have a different idea about keeping a certain polite physical distance when speaking to someone. You'll commonly find someone standing or sitting pretty close to you, no matter how much you keep trying to inch away. And if you find two friends of the same sex walking arm in arm or holding hands, don't jump to any conclusions. It just means that they're friends.

Note: Despite the more relaxed view of personal space, however, avoid slaps on the back to Chinese people you don't know well, no matter how excited you are to meet them. And when dealing with members of the opposite sex, any physical contact with folks you don't know too well will be misinterpreted, so try to avoid it.

In the evening or before you go to sleep, you can say **Wǎn ān.** 晚安. (Wahn ahn.) (*Good night.*). Just as **zǎo** means early, **wǎn** means late. So if someone says **Nǐ lái de tài wǎn.** 你来得太晚. (你來得太晚.) (Nee lye duh tye wahn.) or **Nǐ lái de tài zǎo.** 你来得太早. (你來得太早.) (Nee lye duh tye dzaow.), he means *You came too late.* or *You came too early.*

Talkin' the Talk

Julia and Christopher are good friends who meet in front of school one morning. Julia introduces Christopher to a new student named Lǐ.

Julia: **Zǎo. Nǐ zěnme yàng?**
Dzaow. Nee dzummuh yahng?
Good morning. How's it going?

Christopher: **Hěn hǎo, xièxiè. Nǐ ne?**
Hun how, shyeh-shyeh. Nee nuh?
Very well, thanks. And you?

Julia: **Wǒ yě hěn hǎo. Zhè wèi shì wǒmen de xīn tóngxué.**
Waw yeah hun how. Jay way shir waw-mun duh sheen toong-shweh.
I'm good, too. This is our new classmate.

Christopher: **Nǐ hǎo. Qǐng wèn, nǐ xìng shénme?**
Nee how. Cheeng one, nee sheeng shummuh?
Hi. What's your (sur)name?

Lǐ: **Wǒ xìng Lǐ. Nǐ jiào shénme míngzi?**
Waw sheeng Lǐ. Nee jyaow shummuh meeng-dzuh?
My last name is Lǐ. What's your (first) name?

Christopher: **Wǒ jiào Christopher. Nǐ xué shénme?**
Waw jyaow Christopher. Nee shweh shummuh?
My name is Christopher. What do you study?

Lǐ: **Wǒ xué lìshǐ. Nǐ ne?**
Waw shweh lee-shir. Nee nuh?
I study history. How about you?

Christopher: **Wǒ xué kuàijì.**
Waw shweh kwye-jee.
I study accounting.

WORDS TO KNOW

kāiyèchē 开夜车 (開夜車)	kye-yeh-chuh	to pull an all-nighter
dàxué zhuānyè 大学专业 (大學 專 業)	dah-shyweh jwan-yeh	college major
lǎoshī 老师 (老師)	laow-shir	teacher
dàxué xiān xiū wùlǐ kè 大学先修物理课 (大學先修物理課)	dah-shyweh shyan shyo woo-lee kuh	AP courses
gōnglì xuéxiào 公立学校 (公立學校)	goong-lee shyweh-shyaow	public school
sīlì xuéxiào 私立学校 (私立學校)	suh-lee shyweh-shyaow	private school

Talking about the weather

Talking about the **tiānqì** 天气 (天氣) (tyan-chee) (*weather*) is always a safe topic in any conversation. In fact, it's kind of the universal ice breaker. If the skies are blue and all seems right with the world, you can start by saying **Jīntiān de tiānqì zhēn hǎo, duì búduì?** 今天的天气真好, 对不对? (今天的天氣真好, 對不對?) (Jin-tyan duh tyan-chee juhn how, dway boo-dway?) (*The weather today sure is nice, isn't it?*). Here are some adjectives to describe temperature and humidity:

>> **lěng** 冷 (lung) (*cold*)

>> **liángkuài** 凉快 (涼快) (lyahng-kwye) (*cool*)

>> **mēnrè** 闷热 (悶熱) (mun-ruh) (*muggy*)

>> **nuǎnhuó** 暖和 (nwan-hwaw) (*warm*)

>> **rè** 热 (熱) (ruh) (*hot*)

REMEMBER

Only use the word **rè** to describe hot weather. For food that's hot temperature-wise, you say **tàng** 烫 (燙) (tahng). And if your food is spicy hot, you have to say it's **là** 辣 (lah) instead.

The **sìjì** (suh-jee) (*four seasons*) — **dōngtiān** 冬天 (doong-tyan) (*winter*), **chūntiān** 春天 (chwun-tyan) (*spring*), **xiàtiān** 夏天 (shyah-tyan) (*summer*), and **qiūtiān** 秋天 (chyo-tyan) (*fall*) — all have their charms. They also all have their distinctive characteristics when it comes to the weather, which you can express with the following words in any conversation:

» **bàofēngxuě** 暴风雪 (暴風雪) (baow-fuhng-shweh) (*blizzard*)

» **dàfēng** 大风 (大風) (dah-fuhng) (*gusty winds*)

» **duōyún** 多云 (多雲) (dwaw-yewn) (*cloudy*)

» **fēng hěn dà** 风很大 (風很大) (fuhng hun dah) (*windy*)

» **léiyǔ** 雷雨 (lay-yew) (*thunderstorm*)

» **qínglǎng** 晴朗 (cheeng-lahng) (*sunny*)

» **qíngtiān** 晴天 (cheeng-tyan) (*clear*)

» **xià máomáoyǔ** 下毛毛雨 (shyah maow-maow-yew) (*drizzle*)

» **xiàwù** 下雾 (下霧) (shyah-woo) (*fog*)

» **xiàxuě** 下雪 (shyah-shweh) (*snow*)

» **xiàyǔ** 下雨 (shyah-yew) (*rainy*)

» **yīntiān** 阴天 (陰天) (yeen-tyan) (*overcast*)

Talkin' the Talk

Gerry and Jean discuss the weather in Harbin, one of the coldest places in northern China.

Jean: **Hā'ěrbīn dōngtiān hěn lěng. Chángcháng xiàxuě.**
          Hah-are-been doong-tyan hun lung. Chahng-chahng shyah-shweh.
          Harbin is very cold in the winter. It snows often.

Gerry: **Zhēn de ma?**
          Jun duh mah?
          Really?

Jean: **Zhēn de. Yě yǒu bàofēngxuě. Xiàtiān hái hǎo. Bǐjiào nuǎnhuó.**
          Jun-duh. Yeh yo baow-fuhng-shweh. Shyah-tyan hi how. Bee-jyaow nwan-hwaw.
          Really. There are also blizzards. Summertime is okay, though. It's relatively warm.

Gerry: **Lěng tiān kéyǐ qù huáxuě, hái kéyǐ qù liūbīng. Nèmme Hā'ěrbīn dōngtiān de shíhòu dàgài hěn hǎo wán.**
Lung tyan kuh-yee chyew hwah-shweh, hi kuh-yee chyew lyo-beeng. Nummah Hah-are-been doong-tyan duh shir-ho dah-gye hun how wahn.
In cold weather, you can go skiing or ice skating. So Harbin during the winter is probably a lot of fun.

WORDS TO KNOW

diàoyú 钓鱼 (釣魚)	dyaow-yew	fishing
páshān 爬山	pah-shahn	mountain climbing
fú qiǎn 浮潜 (浮潛)	foo chyan	snorkeling
shēn qián 深潜 (深潛)	shun chyan	scuba diving

Finding out where people are from

Wondering where people are from when you first meet them is natural. Maybe they hail from your hometown. Maybe your new friend's mother and your father went to the same high school way back when. Whatever motivates you to pose the question, you ask it by saying **Nǐ shì nǎr de rén?** 你是哪儿的人? (你是哪兒的人?) (Nee shir nar duh run?) (*Where are you from?*). To answer this question, you replace the word **nǐ** 你 (nee) (*you*) with **wǒ** 我 (waw) (*I*) and put the name of wherever you're from where the word **nǎr** is.

REMEMBER

People in Taiwan say **nálǐ** 哪里 (哪理) (nah–lee) rather than **nǎr** 哪儿 (哪兒) (nar) for the word *where*. **Nǎr** indicates a northern accent and is used primarily by people from mainland China.

Here's a list of countries that may come up in conversation:

>> **Fǎguó** 法国 (法國) (Fah-gwaw) (*France*)

>> **Měiguó** 美国 (美國) (May-gwaw) (*America*)

>> **Rìběn** 日本 (Ir-bun) (*Japan*)

>> **Ruìdiǎn** 瑞典 (Rway-dyan) (*Sweden*)

>> **Ruìshì** 瑞士 (Rway-shir) (*Switzerland*)

» **Yìdàlì** 意大利 (Ee-dah-lee) (*Italy*)

» **Yuènán** 越南 (越南) (Yweh-nahn) (*Vietnam*)

» **Zhōngguó** 中国 (中國) (Joong-gwaw) (*China*)

Talkin' the Talk

Cynthia has just introduced herself to Adrienne at their mutual friend's house. Cynthia asks Adrienne where she is from.

Cynthia:	**Adrienne, nǐ shì nǎr de rén?**
	Adrienne, nee shir nar duh run?
	Adrienne, where are you from?

Adrienne:	**Wǒ shì Jiāzhōu rén. Nǐ ne?**
	Waw shir Jyah-joe run. Nee nuh?
	I'm from California. How about you?

Cynthia:	**Wǒ búshì Měiguórén. Wǒ shì Yīngguó Lúndūn lái de.**
	Waw boo-shir may-gwaw-run. Waw shir Eeng-gwaw Lwun-dun lye duh.
	I'm not American. I'm from London, England.

Adrienne:	**Nà tài hǎole.**
	Nah tye how-luh.
	That's great.

WORDS TO KNOW

Niǔyuē 纽约 (紐約)	Nyo yweh	New York
Bālí 巴黎	Bah-lee	Paris
Běijīng 北京	Bay-jeeng	Beijing
Lúndūn 伦敦 (倫敦)	Lwun-duhn	London

Taking (that is, rejecting) compliments

Chinese people are always impressed whenever they meet a foreigner who has taken the time to learn their language. So when you speak **Zhōngwén** 中文 (Joong-one) (*Chinese*) to a **Zhōngguórén** 中国人 (中國人) (Joong-gwaw-run) (*Chinese person*), he may very well say **Nǐ de Zhōngwén tài hǎole.** 你的中文太好了. (Nee duh joong-one tye how-luh.) (*Your Chinese is fantastic.*). Instead of patting yourself on the back, however, you should be slightly self-deprecating in your response. Don't give in to the temptation to accept the compliment easily and say **Xièxiè.** 谢谢 (謝謝). (Shyeh-shyeh.) (*Thanks.*), because doing so implies that you agree whole-heartedly with the complimentary assessment. Instead, try one of the following replies. Each of them can be roughly translated as *It's nothing*, or the equivalent of *No, no, I don't deserve any praise.*

>> **Guò jiǎng guò jiǎng.** 过讲过讲. (過講過講.) (Gwaw jyahng gwaw jyahng.)

>> **Nálǐ nálǐ.** 哪里哪里. (哪裡哪裡.) (Nah-lee nah-lee.)

>> **Nǎr de huà.** 哪儿的话. (哪兒的話.) (Nar duh hwah.)

Saying goodbye

When it comes time to say goodbye, you can always say **Zài jiàn.** 再见. (再見.) (Dzye jyan.) (*Goodbye.*). If you're just leaving for a little while and plan to be back soon, you can say **Yīhuǐr jiàn.** 一会儿见. (一會兒見.) (Ee-hwahr jyan.) (*See you in a bit.*). And if you won't see someone until the next day, you can say **Míngtiān jiàn.** 明天见. (明天見.) (Meeng-tyan jyan.) (*See you tomorrow.*). For a quick *See you later*, you can say **Huítóu jiàn.** 回头见. (回頭見.) (Hway-toe jyan.). Here are some other phrases you can use to say goodbye:

>> **Míngnián jiàn.** 明年见. (明年見.) (Meeng-nyan jyan.) (*See you next year.*)

>> **Xiàge lǐbài jiàn.** 下个礼拜见. (下個禮拜見.) (Shyah-guh lee-bye jyan.) (*See you next week.*)

>> **Xīngqī'èr jiàn.** 星期二见. (星期二見.) (Sheeng-chee-are jyan.) (*See you on Tuesday.*)

>> **Yílù píng'ān.** 一路平安. (Ee-loo peeng ahn.) (*Have a good trip.*)

For more days-of-the-week options to use in the next to last item in the list, head to Chapter 5.

FUN & GAMES

Match the situation with the appropriate expression. You can find the answers in Appendix C.

1. You see someone again after a long time.

2. You see your friend in the evening.

3. You see your teacher in the morning.

4. Someone compliments you on your new hairstyle.

5. Someone introduces you to his brother.

6. Your best friend is about to board a plane for France.

(A) Hěn gāoxìng jiàndào nǐ. 很高兴见到你. (很高興見到你.)

(B) Yílù píng'ān. 一路平安.

(C) Hǎo jiǔ méi jiàn. 好久没见. (好久沒見.)

(D) Wǎn ān. 晚安.

(E) Zǎo. 早.

(F) Nǎr de huà. 哪儿的话. (哪兒的話.)

Chapter **5**

Getting Your Numbers, Times, and Measurements Straight

Know how they figured out that China has more than a billion people? They counted, silly. Okay, they probably conducted an official census, but if you can learn your ABCs in English, you can at least learn to count to a hundred in Chinese. The words for Chinese numbers are really quite logical — easier than you think — and they're the cornerstone of this chapter.

After you know how to count, you can also say the days of the week and the months of the year. The chapter also covers cardinal and ordinal numbers, so you can tell which came first (the chicken or the egg). If you've got a train to catch, you can look to this chapter to figure out how to tell time so you won't be late. You can even tell your Chinese date what the date is in Chinese. Finally, I give you the lowdown on key Chinese holidays so you can plan your work and travel schedule accordingly, including showing you how to extend New Year's greetings and providing a whole list of which animals are coming up in the Chinese zodiac. What more could you ask for?

REMEMBER

You can listen to all the Talkin' the Talk dialogues featured in this chapter. Go to www.dummies.com/go/chinese and click on the dialogue you want to hear.

Counting in Chinese

Figuring out things like how to specify the number of pounds of meat you want to buy at the market, how much money you want to change at the airport, or how much that cab ride from your hotel is really going to cost can be quite an ordeal if you don't know the basic words for numbers. The following sections break down the Chinese counting rules and terms.

Numbers from 1 to 10

Learning to count from 1 to 10 in Chinese is as easy as **yī** 一 (ee) (*one*), **èr** 二 (are) (*two*), **sān** 三 (sahn) (*three*). Table 5-1 lists numbers from 1 to 10. People in China use Arabic numerals as well, though, so you can just as easily write *1*, *2*, *3*, and everyone will know what you mean.

TABLE 5-1

Numbers from 1 to 10

Chinese	Pronunciation	English
líng 零	leeng	*0*
yī 一	ee	*1*
èr 二	are	*2*
sān 三	sahn	*3*
sì 四	suh	*4*
wǔ 五	woo	*5*
liù 六	lyo	*6*
qī 七	chee	*7*
bā 八	bah	*8*
jiǔ 九	jyoe	*9*
shí 十	shir	*10*

If the number 2 comes before a classifier, use the word **liǎng** rather than **èr**. (As I discuss in Chapter 3, *classifiers* are the equivalent of English words such as *herd* [of elephants] or *school* [of fish]. They help classify particular nouns.) So to say that you have *two books,* you say that you have **liǎng běn shū** 两本书 (兩本書) (lyahng bun shoo) rather than **èr běn shū** 二本书 (二本書) (are bun shoo).

Numbers from 11 to 99

After the number *10,* you create numbers by saying the word *10* followed by the single digit that, when added to it, will combine to create numbers 11 through 19. It's really easy. For example, *11* is **shíyī** 十一 (shir-ee) — literally, *10 plus 1.* Same thing goes for 12, and so on through 19. Table 5-2 lists numbers from 11 to 19.

TABLE 5-2

Numbers from 11 to 19

Chinese	Pronunciation	English
shíyī 十一	shir-ee	11 (Literally: *10 + 1*)
shí'èr 十二	shir-are	12 (Literally: *10 + 2*)
shísān 十三	shir-sahn	13
shísì 十四	shir-suh	14
shíwǔ 十五	shir-woo	15
shíliù 十六	shir-lyo	16
shíqī 十七	shir-chee	17
shíbā 十八	shir-bah	18
shíjiǔ 十九	shir-jyoe	19

When you get to 20, you have to literally think *two 10s* — plus whatever single digit you want to add to that for 21 through 29, as shown in Table 5-3.

The same basic idea goes for **sānshí** 三十 (sahn-shir) (30 [Literally: *three 10s*]), **sìshí** 四十 (suh-shir) (40), **wǔshí** 五十 (woo-shir) (50), **liùshí** 六十 (lyo-shir) (60), **qīshí** 七十 (chee-shir) (70), **bāshí** 八十 (bah-shir) (80), and **jiǔshí** 九十 (jyoe-shir) (90). What could be easier?

TABLE 5-3

Numbers from 20 to 29

Chinese	Pronunciation	English
èrshí 二十	are-shir	20 (Literally: *two 10s*)
èrshíyi 二十一	are-shir-ee	21 (Literally: *two 10s + 1*)
èrshí'èr 二十二	are-shir-are	22
èrshísān 二十三	are-shir-sahn	23
èrshísì 二十四	are-shir-suh	24
èrshíwǔ 二十五	are-shir-woo	25
èrshíliù 二十六	are-shir-lyo	26
èrshíqī 二十七	are-shir-chee	27
èrshíbā 二十八	are-shir-bah	28
èrshí jiǔ 二十九	are-shir-jyoe	29

Numbers from 100 to 9,999

After the number 99, you can no longer count by tens. Here's how you say *100* and *1,000*:

>> *100* is **yìbǎi** 一百 (ee-bye).

>> *1,000* is **yìqiān** 一千 (ee-chyan).

Chinese people count all the way up to **wàn** 万 (萬) (wahn) (*10,000*) and then repeat in those larger amounts up to **yì** 亿 (億) (ee) (*100 million*).

TIP

In Chinese, numbers are represented with the higher units of value first. So the number *387* is **sānbǎi bāshíqī** 三百八十七 (sahn-bye bah-shir-chee). The number *15,492* is **yí wàn wǔqiān sìbǎi jiǔshí'èr** 一万五千四百九十二 (一萬五千四百九十二) (ee-wahn woo-chyan suh-bye jyoe-shir-are).

GRAMMAR CHAT

The number *1* **yī** 一 (ee) changes its tone from the first (high) to the fourth (falling) tone when followed by a first tone, as in **yìqiān** 一千 (ee-chyan) (*1,000*); by a second (rising) tone, as in **yì nián** 一年 (ee nyan) (*one year*); and by a third (low dipping) tone, as in **yìbǎi** 一百 (ee-bye) (*100*). And it changes to the second tone when followed by a fourth tone, as in **yí wàn** 一万 (一萬) (ee wahn) (*10,000*). It retains its original first tone mark only when people count numbers: one, two, three, and so on.

Numbers from 10,000 to 100,000 and beyond

Here are the big numbers:

>> *10,000* is **yí wàn** 一万 (一萬) (ee wahn) (Literally: *one unit of 10,000*).

>> *100,000* is **shí wàn** 十万 (十萬) (shir wahn) (Literally: *ten units of 10,000*).

>> *1 million* is **yìbǎi wàn** 一百万 (一百萬) (ee-bye wahn) (Literally: *100 units of 10,000*).

>> *100 million* is **yí yì** 一亿 (一億) (ee ee).

CULTURAL WISDOM

Numbers play an interesting role in everyday speech in China. Sometimes you'll hear someone say emphatically **Nǐ qiānwàn búyào xìn tā de huà!** 你千万不要信他的话! (你千萬不要信他的話!) (Nee chyan-wahn boo-yaow sheen tah duh hwah!) (*No matter what, you're not to believe what he says!*). **Qiān** means *1,000*, and **wàn** means *10,000*, but when you put those two words together in front of the negative prefix **bù**, you emphasize a point even more. Another phrase that has been heard often in the Chinese past is the partial phrase **wàn suì** 万岁 (萬歲) (wahn sway) (*long live*). After that phrase, the person may add the name of someone in power, so you hear something like **Máo Zhǔxí wàn suì!** 毛主席万岁! (毛主席萬歲!) (Maow Joo-she wahn sway!) (*Long live Chairman Mao!*). If you use this expression these days, you're kind of parodying a phrase taken extremely seriously just a few short decades ago.

How 'bout those halves?

So what happens if you want to add a half to anything? Well, the word for *half* is **bàn** 半 (bahn), and it can either come at the beginning, such as in **bàn bēi kělè**

(半杯可乐) (半杯可樂) (bahn bay kuh-luh) (*a half a glass of cola*), or after a number and classifier but before the object to mean *and a half*, such as in **yí ge bàn xīngqī** 一个半星期 (一個半星期) (ee guh bahn sheeng-chee) (*a week and a half*).

Ordinal numbers

If you want to indicate the order of something, add the word **dì** 第 (dee) before the numeral:

Chinese	Pronunciation	English
dì yī 第一	dee ee	*first*
dì èr 第二	dee are	*second*
dì sān 第三	dee sahn	*third*
dì sì 第四	dee suh	*fourth*
dì wǔ 第五	dee woo	*fifth*
dì liù 第六	dee lyo	sixth
dì qī 第七	dee chee	*seventh*
dì bā 第八	dee bah	*eighth*
dì jiǔ 第九	dee jyoe	*ninth*
dì shí 第十	dee shir	*tenth*

If a noun follows the ordinal number, a classifier needs to go between them, such as in **dì bā ge xuéshēng** 第八个学生 (第八個學生) (dee bah guh shweh-shuhng) (*the eighth student*) or **dì yī ge háizi** 第一个孩子 (第一個孩子) (dee ee guy hi-dzuh) (*the first child*).

Asking how many or how much

You have two ways to ask how much something is or how many of something there are. The first is the question word **duōshǎo** 多少 (dwaw-shaow), which you use when referring to something for which the answer is probably more than ten. The second is **jǐ** 几 (幾) (jee) or **jǐge** 几个 (幾個) (jee-guh), which you use when referring to something for which the answer is probably going to be less than ten:

Nàge qìchē duōshǎo qián? 那个汽车多少钱? (那個汽車多少錢?) (Nah-guh chee-chuh dwaw-shaow chyan?) (*How much is that car?*)

Nǐ xiǎo nǚ'ér jīnnián jǐ suì? 你小女儿今年几岁? (你小女兒今年幾歲?) (Nee shyaow nyew-are jin-nyan jee sway?) (*How old is your little girl this year?*)

Telling Time

All you have to do to find out the **shíjiān** 时间 (時間) (shir-jyan) (*time*) is take a peek at your **shǒubiǎo** 手表 (show-byaow) (*watch*) or look at the **zhōng** 钟 (鐘) (joong) (*clock*) on the wall. These days, even your computer or cellphone shows the time. And you can always revert to that beloved **luòdìshì dà bǎizhōng** 落地式大摆钟 (落地式大擺鐘) (lwaw-dee-shir dah bye-joong) (*grandfather clock*) in your parents' living room. You no longer have any excuse to **chídào** 迟到 (遲到) (chir-daow) (*be late*), especially if you own a **nào zhōng** 闹钟 (鬧鐘) (now joong) (*alarm clock*)!

Asking and stating the time

Want to know what time it is? Just walk up to someone and say **Xiànzài jǐdiǎn zhōng?** 现在几点钟? (現在幾點鐘?) (Shyan-dzye jee-dyan joong?). It almost literally translates into *Now how many hours are on the clock?* In fact, you can even leave off the word *clock* and still ask for the time: **Xiànzài jǐdiǎn?** 现在几点? (現在幾點?) (Shyan-dzye jee-dyan?). Isn't that easy?

To understand the answers to those questions, though, you need to understand how to tell time in Chinese. You can express time in Chinese by using the words **diǎn** 点 (點) (dyan) (*hour*) and **fēn** 分 (fun) (*minute*). Isn't using **fēn** fun? You can even talk about time in **miǎo** 秒 (meow) (*seconds*) if you like and sound like a cat. Table 5-4 shows you how to pronounce all the hours on the clock.

GRAMMAR CHAT

You can indicate the hour by saying **sān diǎn** or **sān diǎn zhōng**. **Diǎn** 点 (點) (dyan) means *hour*, but it's also a classifier, and **zhōng** 钟 (鐘) (joong) means *clock*. Feel free to use either to say what time it is.

REMEMBER

When mentioning 12:00, be careful! The way to say *noon* is simply **zhōngwǔ** 中午 (joong-woo), and the way to say *midnight* is **bànyè** 半夜 (bahn-yeh).

Specifying the time of the day

The Chinese are very precise when they tell time. You can't just say **sān diǎn zhōng** 三点钟 (三點鐘) (sahn dyan joong) when you want to say *3:00*. Do you mean to say **qīngzǎo sān diǎn zhōng** 清早三点钟 (清早三點鐘) (cheeng-dzaow sahn dyan joong) (*3:00 a.m.*) or **xiàwǔ sāndiǎn zhōng** 下午三点钟 (下午三點鐘) (shyah-woo sahn-dyan joong) (*3:00 p.m.*)? Another wrinkle: Noon and midnight aren't the only dividers the Chinese use to split up the day.

TABLE 5-4

Telling Time in Chinese

Chinese	Pronunciation	English
yī diǎn zhōng 一点钟 (一點鐘)	ee dyan joong	1:00
liǎng diǎn zhian 两点钟 (兩點鐘)	lyahng dyan joong	2:00
sān diǎn zhōng 三点钟 (三點鐘)	sahn dyan joong	3:00
sì diǎn zhōng 四点钟 (四點鐘)	suh dyan joong	4:00
wǔ diǎn zhōng 五点钟 (五點鐘)	woo dyan joong	5:00
liù diǎn zhōng 六点钟 (六點鐘)	lyo dyan joong	6:00
qī diǎn zhōng 七点钟 (七點鐘)	chee dyan joong	7:00
bā diǎn zhōng 八点钟 (八點鐘)	bah dyan joong	8:00
jiǔ diàn zhōng 九点钟 (九點鐘)	jyo dyan joong	9:00
shí diàn zhōng 十点钟 (十點鐘)	shir dyan joong	10:00
shíyī diǎn zhōng 十一 点钟 (十一點鐘)	shir-ee dyan joong	11:00
zhōngwǔ 中午	joong-woo	noon
bàn ye 半夜	bahn-yeh	midnight

Here's a list of the major segments of the day:

>> **qīngzǎo** 清早 (cheeng-dzaow): The period from midnight to 6:00 a.m.

>> **zǎoshàng** 早上 (dzaow-shahng): The period from 6:00 a.m. to noon

>> **xiàwǔ** 下午 (shyah-woo): The period from noon to 6:00 p.m.

>> **wǎnshàng** 晚上 (wahn-shahng): The period from 6:00 p.m. to midnight

The segment of the day that you refer to needs to come before the actual time itself in Chinese. Here are some samples of combining the segment of the day with the time of day:

> **qīngzǎo yì diǎn yí kè** 清早一点一刻 (清早一點一刻) (cheeng-dzaow ee dyan ee kuh) (*1:15 a.m.*)

> **wǎnshàng qī diǎn zhōng** 晚上七点钟 (晚上七點鐘) (wahn-shahng chee dyan joong) (*7:00 p.m.*)

> **xiàwǔ sān diǎn bàn** 下午三点半 (下午三點半) (shyah-woo sahn dyan bahn) (*3:30 p.m.*)

> **zǎoshàng bā diǎn èrshíwǔ fēn** 早上八点二十五分 (dzaow-shahng bah dyan are-shir-woo fun) (*8:25 a.m.*)

If you want to indicate half an hour, just add **bàn** (bahn) (*half*) after the hour:

> **sān diǎn bàn** 三点半 (三點半) (sahn dyan bahn) (*3:30*)

> **shíyī diǎn bàn** 十一点半 (十一點半) (shir-ee dyan bahn) (*11:30*)

> **sì diǎn bàn** 四点半 (四點半) (suh dyan bahn) (*4:30*)

Do you want to indicate a quarter of an hour or three quarters of an hour? Just use the phrases **yí kè** 一刻 (ee kuh) and **sān kè** 三刻 (sahn kuh), respectively, after the hour:

> **liǎng diǎn yí kè** 两点一刻 (兩點一刻) (lyahng dyan ee kuh) (*2:15*)

> **qī diǎn sān kè** 七点三刻 (七點三刻) (chee dyan sahn kuh) (*7:45*)

> **sì diǎn yí kè** 四点一刻 (四點一刻) (suh dyan ee kuh) (*4:15*)

> **wǔ diǎn sān kè** 五点三刻 (五點三刻) (woo dyan sahn kuh) (*5:45*)

When talking about time, you may prefer to indicate a certain number of minutes before or after a particular hour. To do so, you use either **yǐqián** 以前 (ee-chyan) (*before*) or **yǐhòu** 以后 (以後) (ee-ho) (*after*) along with the time (though you can also use it with days and months, concepts that I cover later in the chapter). Here are a couple of examples:

> **qīngzǎo sì diǎn bàn yǐhòu** 清早四点半以后 (清早四點半以後) (cheeng-dzaow suh dyan bahn ee-ho) (*after 4:30 a.m.*)

> **xiàwǔ sān diǎn zhōng yǐqián** 下午三点钟以前 (下午三點鐘以前) (shyah-woo sahn dyan joong ee-chyan) (*before 3 p.m.*)

GRAMMAR
CHAT

Of course, you have other ways to indicate time in Chinese. On the hour, half hour, and quarter of an hour aren't the only parts of time that exist, after all. For example, instead of saying **qī diǎn wǔshí fēn** 七点五十分 (七點五十分) (chee dyan woo–shir fun) (7:50), you can say **bā diǎn chà shí fēn** 八点差十分 (八點差十分) (bah dyan chah shir fun) (10 minutes to 8 [Literally: 8:00 minus 10 minutes]). **Chà** 差 (chah) means to lack. Unlike **fēn** 分 (fun) (minute), **kè** 刻 (kuh) (quarter of an hour), and **bàn** 半 (bahn) (half), you can use **chà** either before or after **diǎn** 点 (點) (dyan) (hour).

Here are some other examples of alternative ways to indicate the time:

chà shí fēn wǔ diǎn 差十分五点 (差十分五點) (chah shir fun woo dyan) (10 minutes to 5:00)

wǔ diǎn chà shí fēn 五点差十分 (五點差十分) (woo dyan chah shir fun) (10 minutes to 5:00)

sì diǎn wǔshí fēn 四点五十分 (四點五十分) (suh dyan woo-shir fun) (4:50)

chà yí kè qī diǎn 差一刻七点 (差一刻七點) (chah ee kuh chee dyan) (a quarter to 7:00)

qī diǎn chà yí kè 七点差一刻 (七點差一刻) (chee dyan chah ee kuh) (a quarter to 7:00)

liù diǎn sān kè 六点三刻 (六點三刻) (lyo dyan sahn kuh) (6:45)

liù diǎn sìshíwǔ fēn 六点四十五分 (六點四時五分) (lyo dyan suh-shir-woo fun) (6:45)

Talkin' the Talk

Wendy and Marilyn discuss their plans to see a movie.

Wendy: **Wǒmen jīntiān wǎnshàng qù kàn diànyǐng, hǎo bùhǎo?**
Waw-men jin-tyan wahn-shahng chyew kahn dyan-yeeng, how boo-how?
Let's go see a movie tonight, okay?

Marilyn: **Bùxíng. Wǒ de fùmǔ jīntiān wǎnshàng yídìng yào wǒ gēn tāmen yìqǐ chī wǎnfàn.**
Boo-sheeng. Waw duh foo-moo jin-tyan wahn-shahng ee-deeng yaow waw gun tah-men ee-chee chir wahn-fahn.
No can do. My parents are adamant that I have dinner with them tonight.

Wendy:	**Nǐmen jǐdiǎn zhōng chīfàn?**
	Nee-men jee-dyan joong chir-fahn?
	What time do you eat?

Marilyn:	**Píngcháng wǒmen liùdiǎn zhōng zuǒyòu chīfàn.**
	Peeng-chahng waw-men lyo-dyan joong dzwaw-yo chir-fahn.
	We usually eat around 6:00.

Wendy:	**Hǎo ba. Nǐ chīfàn yǐhòu wǒmen qù kàn yíbù jiǔdiǎn zhōng yǐqián de piānzi, hǎo bùhǎo?**
	How-bah. Nee chir-fahn ee-ho waw-men chyew kahn ee-boo jyo-dyan joong ee-chyan duh pyan-dzuh, how boo-how?
	Okay. How about we see a movie that starts before 9:00 after you're finished eating?

Marilyn:	**Hěn hǎo. Yìhuǐr jiàn.**
	Hun how. Ee-hwar jyan.
	Okay. See you later.

● ●

WORDS TO KNOW

zǒng shì 总是 (總是)	dzoong shir	always
yǒu de shíhòu 有的时候 (有的時候)	yo duh shir-ho	sometimes
yǒngyuǎn 永远 (永遠)	yoong-ywan	forever
jué bù 决不	jyweh boo	never

Save the Date: Using the Calendar and Stating Dates

So what day is **jīntiān** 今天 (jin-tyan) (*today*)? Could it be **Xīngqī liù** 星期六 (Sheeng-chee lyo) (*Saturday*), when you can sleep late and go see a movie in the evening with friends? Or is it **Xīngqī yī** 星期一 (Sheeng-chee ee) (*Monday*), when you have to be at work by 9:00 a.m. to prepare for a 10:00 a.m. meeting? Or maybe it's **Xīngqī wǔ** 星期五 (Sheeng-chee woo) (*Friday*), and you already have two tickets for the symphony that begins at 8:00 p.m. In the following sections, I give you the words you need to talk about days and months and put them together into specific dates. I also give you the lowdown on some major Chinese holidays.

Dealing with days of the week

You may not be a big fan of going to work Monday to Friday, but when the **zhōumò** 周末 (週末) (joe-maw) (*weekend*) comes, you have two days of freedom and fun. Before you know it, though, Monday comes again. Chinese people recognize seven days in the week just as Americans do, and the Chinese week begins on Monday and ends on **Xīngqī tiān** 星期天 (Sheeng-chee tyan) (*Sunday*). Table 5-5 spells out the days of the week.

TABLE 5-5

Days of the Week

Chinese	Pronunciation	English
Xīngqí yī 星期一	Sheeng-chee ee	*Monday*
Xīngqí'èr 星期二	Sheeng-chee are	*Tuesday*
Xīngqí sān 星期三	Sheeng-chee sahn	*Wednesday*
Xīngqí sì 星期四	Sheeng-chee suh	*Thursday*
Xīngqí wǔ 星期五	Sheeng-chee woo	*Friday*
Xīngqí liù 星期六	Sheeng-chee lyo	*Saturday*
Xīngqí tiān 星期天	Sheeng-chee tyan	*Sunday*

If you're talking about **zhèige xīngqí** 这个星期 (這個星期) (jay-guh sheeng-chee) (*this week*) in Chinese, you're talking about any time between this past Monday through this coming Sunday. Anything earlier is considered **shàngge xīngqí** 上个星期 (上個星期) (shahng-guh sheeng-chee) (*last week*). Any day after this coming Sunday is automatically part of **xiàge xīngqí** 下个星期 (下個星期) (shyah-guh sheeng-chee) (*next week*) at the earliest. Here are a few more week-related terms:

» **hòutiān** 后天 (後天) (ho-tyan) (*the day after tomorrow*)

» **míngtiān** 明天 (meeng-tyan) (*tomorrow*)

» **qiántiān** 前天 (chyan-tyan) (*the day before yesterday*)

» **zuótiān** 昨天 (dzwaw-tyan) (*yesterday*)

So **jīntiān Xīngqí jǐ?** 今天星期几? (今天星期幾?) (Jin-tyan Sheeng-chee jee?) (*What day is it today?*) Where does today fit in your weekly routine?

>> **Jīntiān Xīngqí'èr.** 今天星期二. (Jin-tyan Sheeng-chee are.) (*Today is Tuesday.*)

>> **Wǒmen měige Xīngqí yī kāihuì.** 我们每个星期一开会. (我們每個星期一開會.) (Waw-men may-guh Sheeng-chee ee kye-hway.) (*We have meetings every Monday.*)

>> **Wǒ Xīngqí yī dào Xīngqí wǔ gōngzuò.** 我星期一到星期五工作. (Waw Sheeng-chee ee daow Sheeng-chee woo goong-dzwaw.) (*I work from Monday to Friday.*)

>> **Xiàge Xīngqī sān shì wǒde shēngrì.** 下个星期三是我的生日. (下個星期三是我的生日.) (Shyah-guh Sheeng-chee sahn shir waw-duh shung-ir.) (*Next Wednesday is my birthday.*)

Naming the months

When you know how to count from 1 to 12 (refer to the earlier section "Counting in Chinese"), naming the months in Chinese is really easy. Just think of the cardinal number for each month and put that in front of the word **yuè** 月 (yweh) (*month*). For example, *January* is **Yī yuè** 一月 (Ee yweh), *February* is 二月 **Èr yuè** (Are yweh), and so on. I list the months of the year in Table 5-6. Which month is your **shēngrì** 生日 (shung-ir) (*birthday*)?

Shí'èr yuè, Yī yuè, and **Èr yuè** together make up one of the **sì jì** 四季 (suh-jee) (*four seasons*); check it out with the others in Table 5-7.

Specifying dates

To ask what today's date is, you simply say **Jīntiān jǐ yuè jǐ hào?** 今天几月几号? (今天幾月幾號?) (Jin-tyan jee yweh jee how?) (Literally: *Today is what month and what day?*). To answer that question, remember that the larger unit of the month always comes before the smaller unit of the date in Chinese:

Sān yuè sì hào 三月四号 (三月四號) (Sahn yweh suh how) (*March 4*)

Shí'èr yuè sānshí hào 十二月三十号 (十二月三十號) (Shir-are yweh sahn-shir how) (*December 30*)

Yī yuè èr hào 一月二号 (一月二號) (Ee yweh are how) (*January 2*)

TABLE 5-6

Months of the Year and Other Pertinent Terms

Chinese	Pronunciation	English
Yī yuè 一月	Ee yweh	January
Èr yuè 二月	Are yweh	February
Sān yuè 三月	Sahn yweh	March
Sì yuè 四月	Suh yweh	April
Wǔ yuè 五月	Woo yweh	May
Liù yuè 六月	Lyo yweh	June
Qī yuè 七月	Chee yweh	July
Bā yuè 八月	Bah yweh	August
Jiǔ yuè 九月	Jyo yweh	September
Shí yuè 十月	Shir yweh	October
Shíyī yuè 十一月	Shir-ee yweh	November
Shí'èr yuè 十二月	Shir-are yweh	December
shàng gè yuè 上个月 (上個月)	shahng guh yweh	last month
xià ge yuè 下个月 (下個月)	shyah guh yweh	next month
zhè gè yuè 这个月 (這個月)	jay-guh yweh	this month

TABLE 5-7

The Four Seasons

Chinese	Pronunciation	English
dōngjì 冬季	doong-jee	winter
chūnjì 春季	chwun-jee	spring
xiàjì 夏季	shyah-jee	summer
qiūjì 秋季	chyo-jee	fall

Days don't exist in a vacuum — or even just in a week — and four whole weeks make up one whole month. So if you want to be more specific, you have to say the month before the day, followed by the day of the week:

> **Liù yuè yī hào, Xīngqí yī** 六月一号星期一 (六月一號星期一) (Lyo-yweh ee how, Sheeng-chee ee) *(Monday, June 1)*

Sì yuè èr hào, Xīngqí tiān 四月二号星期天 (四月二號星期天) (Suh-yweh are how, Sheeng-chee tyan) (*Sunday, April 2*)

The same basic idea goes for saying the days of the week. All you have to do is add the number of the day of the week (Monday: Day 1), preceded by the word **lǐbài** 礼拜 (禮拜) (lee-bye) or **xīngqí** 星期 (sheeng-chee), meaning *week*, to say the day you mean. For example, *Monday* is **Xīngqī yī** 星期一 (Sheeng-chee ee) or **Lǐbài yī** 礼拜一 (禮拜一) (Lee-bye ee), *Tuesday* is **Xīngqí'èr** 星期二 (Sheeng-chee are) or **Lǐbài'èr** 礼拜二 (禮拜二) (Lee-bye are), and so on. The only exception is Sunday, when you have to add the word **tiān** 天 (tyan) (*heaven, day*) in place of a number. **Wǒ de tiān!** 我的天! (Waw duh tyan!) (*My heavens!*) Isn't this easy?

GRAMMAR CHAT

You say each month by adding the number of the month in front of the word **yuè**, but if you add the classifier **ge** 个 (個) (guh) between the number and the word **yuè**, you say *one month, two months,* and so on. For example, **Bā yuè** 八月 (bah yweh) means *August* (which is the eighth month), but **bā ge yuè** 八个月 (八個月) (bah guh yweh) means *eight months*.

Talkin' the Talk

Joseph asks Julia about her birthday.

Joseph: **Julia, nǐ de shēngrì shì jǐ yuè jǐ hào?**
Julia, nee duh shung-ir shir jee yweh jee how?
Julia, when's your birthday?

Julia: **Wǒ de shēngrì shì Liù yuè èr hào. Nǐ de ne?**
Waw duh shung-ir shir Lyo yweh are how. Nee duh nuh?
My birthday is June 2. How about yours?

Joseph: **Wǒ de shēngrì shì Wǔ yuè qī hào.**
Waw duh shung-ir shir Woo yweh chee how.
My birthday is May 7.

Julia: **Nàmuh, xià ge Xīngqí yī jiù shì nǐ de shēngrì! Zhù nǐ chà jǐ tiān shēngrì kuàilè!**
Nummuh, shyah guh Sheeng-chee ee jyo shir nee duh shung-ir! Joo nee chah jee tyan shung-ir kwye-luh!
In that case, next Monday is your birthday! Happy almost birthday!

shēngrì dàngāo 生日蛋糕	shung-ir dahn-gaow	birthday cake
shēngrì lǐwù 生日 礼物 (生日禮物)	shung-ir lee-woo	birthday gift
jiéhūn jìniàn rì 结婚纪念日 (結婚紀念日)	jyweh-hwun jee-nyan ir	wedding anniversary

Celebrating Chinese holidays

When was the last time you saw a **wǔshī** 舞狮 (舞獅) (woo-shir) (*lion dance*) in Chinatown? You can catch this colorful (and noisy) dance and all the other festivities during **Nónglì Xīnnián** 农历新年 (農曆新年) (Noong-lee Sheen-nyan) (*the Lunar New Year*), also known as **Chūnjié** 春節 (Chwun-jyeh) (*the Spring Festival*). Just be careful not to get too close to all the **yān huǒ** 烟火 (焰火) (yan hwaw) (*fireworks*).

To extend New Year's greetings, you can say **Xīnnián Kuàilè!** 新年快乐! (新年快樂!) (Shin-nyan Kwye-luh!) (*Happy New Year!*) or, better yet, **Gōngxǐ fācái!** 恭喜发财! (恭喜發財!) (Goong-she fah-tsye!) (*Congratulations, and may you prosper!*). In fact, you can start saying this on **Chúxī** 除夕 (choo-shee) (*Chinese New Year's Eve*), the night when Chinese families get together to share a big, traditional dinner. The next morning children wish their parents a happy New Year and get **hóngbāo** 红包 (紅包) (hoong-baow) (*red envelopes*) with money in them. What a great way to start the year!

TIP

Table 5-8 helps you keep track of which animal year we're in according to the **shēngxiào** 生肖 (shung-shyaow) (*Chinese zodiac*), which runs in 12-year cycles.

TABLE 5-8

Animals of the Chinese Zodiac

Chinese	Pronunciation	English	Year
Shǔ 鼠	Shoo	*Rat*	2008
Niú 牛	Nyo	*Ox*	2009
Hǔ 虎	Hoo	*Tiger*	2010
Tù 兔	Too	*Rabbit*	2011
Lóng 龙(龍)	Loong	*Dragon*	2012
Shé 蛇	Shuh	*Snake*	2013
Mǎ 马 (馬)	Ma	*Horse*	2014

Chinese	Pronunciation	English	Year
Yáng 羊	Yahng	*Goat*	2015
Hóu 猴	Ho	*Monkey*	2016
Jī 鸡 (雞)	Jee	*Rooster*	2017
Gǒu 犬 (狗)	Go	*Dog*	2018
Zhū 猪 (豬)	Joo	*Pig*	2019

CULTURAL WISDOM

Here are some other major Chinese holidays:

>> **Yuánxiāo jié** 元宵节 (元宵節) (Ywan-shyaow jyeh) (*Lantern Festival*): Lantern parades and lion dances help celebrate the first full moon, which marks the end of the Chinese New Year, in either January or February.

>> **Qīngmíng jié** 清明节 (清明節) (Cheeng-meeng jyeh) (Literally: *the Clear and Bright Festival*): This celebration at the beginning of April is actually Tomb Sweeping Day, when families go on spring outings to clean and make offerings at the graves of their ancestors.

>> **Duānwǔ jié** 端午节 (端午節) (Dwan-woo jyeh) (*Dragon Boat Festival*): To commemorate the ancient poet **Qū Yuán** 屈原 (Chew Ywan), who drowned himself to protest government corruption, Chinese people eat **zòngzǐ** 粽子 (dzoong-dzuh) (*glutinous rice dumplings wrapped in lotus leaves*), drink yellow rice wine, and hold dragon boat races on the river. This holiday often falls in late May or early June.

>> **Zhōngqiū jié** 中秋节 (中秋節) (Joong-chyo jyeh) (*Mid-Autumn Festival*): This popular lunar harvest festival celebrates **Cháng'é** 嫦娥 (Chahng-uh), the Chinese goddess of the moon (and of immortality). Red bean and lotus seed pastries called *moon cakes* are eaten, romantic matches are made, and all's right with the world. This holiday usually comes in September.

Sizing Up Weights and Measures

The metric system is standard in both mainland China and Taiwan. The basic unit of weight is the **gōngkè** 公克 (goong-kuh) (*gram*), so you usually buy fruits and vegetables in multiples of that measure. The standard liquid measurement is the **shēng** 升 (shung) (*liter*). One liter equals about 1.06 quarts. Table 5-9 gives you a list of weights and measures.

CULTURAL WISDOM

Although the Chinese use the metric system, more often than not you encounter traditional measurement terms that predate the metric system, such as the words **yīngcùn** for *inch* and **yīngchǐ** for *foot*.

TABLE 5-9

Weights and Measures

Chinese	Pronunciation	English
Volume		
àngsī 盎司	ahng-suh	*ounce*
jiālún 加仑 (加侖)	jyah-lwun	*gallon*
kuā tuō 夸脱 (夸脫)	kwah twaw	*quart*
pǐn tuō 品脱 (品脫)	peen twaw	*pint*
shēng 升	shung	*liter*
Weight/Mass		
bàng 镑 (鎊)	bahng	*pound*
háokè 毫克	how-kuh	*milligram*
gōngkè 公克	goong-kuh	*gram*
jīn; gōngjīn 斤; 公斤	jeen; goong-jeen	*kilogram*
Distance		
gōnglǐ 公里	goong-lee	*kilometer*
límǐ 厘米	lee-mee	*centimeter*
mǎ 码 (碼)	mah	*yard*
mǐ 米	mee	*meter*
yīngchǐ 英尺	eeng-chir	*foot*
yīngcùn 英寸	eeng-tswun	*inch*
yīnglǐ 英里	eeng-lee	*mile*

FUN & GAMES

Count to 10 and then to 100 in multiples of 10 by filling in the blanks with the correct numbers. Turn to Appendix C for the answers.

yī 一

èr 二

sān 三

sì 四

_____

liù 六

_____

bā 八

jiǔ 九

_____

èrshí 二十

_____

sìshí 四十

wǔshí 五十

_____

qīshí 七十

bāshí 八十

_____

yìbǎi 一百

» **Furnishing your new digs**

» **Understanding the importance of fēng shuǐ**

» **Filling your rooms with furniture**

Chapter **6**

Speaking Chinese at Home

f you're one of those people who believes your **jiā** 家 (jyah) (*home*) is your **chéngbǎo** 城堡 (chuhng-baow) (*castle*), then this chapter's for you. Maybe you just transferred to Beijing for a new job, or you're taking a year off to study kung fu in Taipei. Either way, you're going to want to call your new environment home for a while, and what better way to do that than to buy or rent your own place?

Planning on relocating with your spouse and children? Or maybe even your in-laws? All the more reason to make your new digs as comfortable as possible and carry on as if you weren't suddenly halfway around the world. This chapter helps you get settled and be so comfortable that you can start asking for the **yǎokòng qī** 遥控器 (遙控器) (yaow-koong chee) (*remote*) again when you want to change channels.

REMEMBER

You can listen to all the Talkin' the Talk dialogues featured in this chapter. Go to www.dummies.com/go/chinese and click on the dialogue you want to hear.

Hanging Out at Home

Whether you're in the bedroom taking a nap, in the living room watching TV, or in the dining room having dinner, the one thing you want to feel is at home. Want the dog to fetch your slippers? Want the kids to quiet down? Just remember that the character for *family* (家) is the same ideograph used for the word *home*: a pig underneath a roof (as in, domesticated animals). Sometimes the domestication just takes a little longer.

CULTURAL WISDOM

In China, you commonly see **sān dài** 三代 (sahn dye) (*three generations*) living under one roof. It's the ideal Chinese family, in fact, where grandparents are taken care of in old age and children have lots of love and attention all around. Especially in the countryside, **sān dài** live in the same traditional family compound for generations, sharing a common courtyard with a hall in the center to honor the family's ancestors.

Hunting for an Apartment

Are you one of the thousands of people considering making a long-term move to China for business purposes? Starting to think about purchasing some **fángdìchǎn** 房地产 (房地產) (fahng-dee-chahn) (*real estate*) in the form of a **gōngyù fáng** 公寓房 (goong-yew fahng) (*condominium*) or a **hézuò gōngyù** 合作公寓 (huh-dzwaw goong-yew) (*co-op*) in Beijing or Shanghai? Just a few decades ago, contemplating such a purchase of **cáichǎn** 财产 (財產) (tsye-chahn) (*property*) was unthinkable. These days, though, with the enormous influx of foreign investment and joint-venture companies, countless foreigners are beginning to take advantage of the many reputable **fángdìchǎn jīngjì rén** 房地产经纪人 (房地產經紀人) (fahng-dee-chahn jeeng-jee run) (*realtors*) to help them do just that.

And if you've already purchased some **cáichǎn,** you may want to **chūzū** 出租 (choo-dzoo) (*rent*) or **zhuǎn zū** 转租 (轉租) (jwan dzoo) (*sublet*) a **kōng gōngyù fángjiān** 空公寓房间 (空公寓房間) (koong goong-yew fahng-jyan) (*vacant apartment*) to a trustworthy **chéngzū rén** 承租人 (chung-dzoo run) (*tenant*). Here are some terms you may want to know when thinking of buying a place in China:

>> **ànjiē fèi** 按揭费 (按揭費) (ahn-jyeh fay) (*closing costs*)

>> **dàilǐ** 代理 (dye-lee) (*agent*)

>> **dǐyā jīn** 抵押金 (dee-yah jeen) (*mortgage*)

>> **gǔběn** 权益 (goo-bun) (*equity*)

>> **hétóng** 合同 (huh-toong) (*contract*)

>> **jiànzhù guīzé** 建筑规则 (建築規則) (jyan-joo gway-dzuh) (*building code*)

>> **jīngjì rén** 经纪人 (經紀人) (jeeng-jee run) (*broker*)

>> **lìxī** 利息 (lee-she) (*interest*)

» **píngjià** 评价 (評價) (peeng-jya) (*appraisal*)

» **tóubiāo** 投标 (投標) (toe-byaow) (*bid*)

» **tóukuǎn** 头款 (頭款) (toe-kwahn) (*down payment*)

» **xìnyòng bàogào** 信用报告 (信用報告) (sheen-yoong baow-gaow) (*credit report*)

Talkin' the Talk

Fatima contacts a realtor about buying a condo in Shanghai.

Fatima:	**Nǐ hǎo. Wǒ xiǎng zài Shànghǎi mǎi yíge gōngyù fáng.**
	Nee how. Waw shyahng dzye Shahng-hi my ee-guh goong-yew fahng.
	Hi. I'm thinking of buying a condo in Shanghai.
Realtor:	**Méiyǒu wèntǐ. Wǒ jiù shì yí ge fángdìchǎn jīngjì rén. Hěn yuànyì bāngmáng.**
	Mayo one-tee. Waw jyo shir ee guh fahng-dee-chahn jeeng-jee run. Hun ywan-yee bahng-mahng.
	No problem. I'm a real estate broker. I'd be more than happy to help you.
Fatima:	**Nà tài hǎole. Zài něi ge dìqū mǎi fángzi zuì hǎo?**
	Nah tye haow-luh. Dzye nay guh dee-chyew my fahng-dzuh dzway how?
	That's great. Which area do you consider to be the best to buy some property?
Realtor:	**Shànghǎi yǒu hěn duō hěn hǎo de fángdìchǎn. Kěnéng zuì qiǎngshǒu de shì Hóngqiáo hé Jīnqiáo. Hěn duō wàiguó bàngōngshì xiànzài zài Pǔdōng.**
	Shahng-hi yo hun dwaw hun how duh fahng-dee-chahn. Kuh-nung dzway chyahng-show duh shir Hoong-chyaow huh Jeen-chyaow. Hun dwaw why-gwaw bahn-goong shir shyan-dzye dzye Poo-doong.
	Shanghai has many excellent properties. Perhaps the most popular locations are Hongqiao and Jinqiao. Many foreign offices are now in Pudong.

WORDS TO **KNOW**

Bǎ mén suǒ shàng! (把門鎖上!)	Bah mun swaw shahng!	Lock the door!
yàoshi 钥匙 (鑰匙)	yaow-shir	key
jǐngbào xìtǒng 警报系统 (警 報 系 統)	jeeng-baow shee-toong	alarm system

WARNING

Be sure you're using the correct tone when you pronounce the letters **m-a-i** (pronounced my) in Chinese. If you say it with a third (dipping) tone, **mǎi,** it means *to buy.* If you say it with a fourth (falling) tone, however — **mài** — it means *to sell.* If you're not careful, you may end up selling something you had hoped to live in yourself.

GRAMMAR CHAT

The Chinese language is fascinating and incredibly logical. If you put **mǎi** and **mài** together and add the word **zuò** (dzwaw) (*to do*) in front of them, to say **zuò mǎimài** 做买卖 (做買賣) (dzwaw my-my), it means *to do business.* (To buy and to sell . . . get it?)

THE GROWTH OF PUDONG

Pǔdōng 浦东 (浦東) (Poo-doong) is the stretch of land east of the Huangpu River in the city of Shanghai. (**Pǔ** is short for the Huangpu River, and **dōng** means *east.*) Just a decade ago, this area was indistinguishable from many other backwater Chinese villages — just farmland and countryside. Today, it's a city within a city, boasting a population of over 24 million on a piece of real estate larger than the entire country of Singapore. Foreign investment in this part of Shanghai is enormous. In addition to its claim to fame as the fastest growing business area in China, it also boasts Asia's largest department store, its highest TV tower, and, needless to say, the Shanghai Stock Exchange.

Decorating Your New Digs

Whether you've bought a condo or a co-op, have rented an apartment, or are spending a semester in a **sùshè** 宿舍 (soo-shuh) (*dormitory*), you probably want to start buying some **jiājù** 家具 (jyah-jyew) (*furniture*) or to otherwise **zhuāngshì** 装饰 (裝飾) (jwahng-shir) (*decorate*) your new digs and put your individual stamp on the place.

Does your new place have a **hòu yuànzi** 后院子 (後院子) (ho ywan-dzuh) (*backyard*) with a pretty **huāyuán** 花园 (花園) (hwah-ywan) (*garden*), perhaps? How about a **yángtái** 阳台 (陽台) (yahng-tye) (*balcony*) or a more romantic little **zǒuláng** 走廊 (dzoe-lahng) (*veranda*)? You can put some really nice **zhíwù** 植物 (jir-woo) (*plants*) out there, or even some **huā** 花 (hwah) (*flowers*), like **júhuā** 菊花 (jyew-hwah) (*chrysanthemums*) or **lánhuā** 兰花 (蘭花) (lahn-hwah) (*orchids*), or even some **méihuā** 梅花 (may-hwah) (*plum blossoms*). Wouldn't that be nice?

Is there a **lóu shàng** 楼上 (樓上) (low shahng) (*upstairs*) as well as a **lóu xià** 楼下 (樓下) (low shyah) (*downstairs*)? Do you have a grand **ménkǒu** 门口 (門口) (mun-koe) (*entrance*) or at least a **diàntī** 电梯 (電梯) (dyan-tee) (*elevator*) if you're on the top floor? Does the place have lots of floor-to-ceiling **chuānghu** 窗户 (chwahng-hoo) (*windows*) with great views, or do they look straight into an airshaft, forcing you to cover them with **chuānglián** 窗帘 (窗簾) (chwahng-lyan) (*curtains*) the first chance you get? No matter. At least you finally have a place you can call your own.

With all these new things to buy, just try not to run up too much of a **xìnyòng kǎ** 信用卡 (sheen-yoong kah) (*credit card*) bill, or you may regret having made that move from Poughkeepsie to Pudong in the first place.

CULTURAL WISDOM

Wondering what to plant in your new garden? Consider one (or all) of the **suìhán sānyǒu** 岁寒三友 (歲寒三友) (sway-hahn sahn-yo) (*the three friends of winter*): plum, pine, and bamboo. When other plants have long withered away, these three still thrive in the winter months. Representing both resilience and the possibility of renewal, they're often depicted in Chinese literature, painting, and garden design.

Appointing Your Rooms, Fēngshuǐ Style

Literally translated as *wind and water*, the goal of **fēngshuǐ** 风水 (風水) (fuhng-shway) is to create harmony between the flow of **qì** 气 (氣) (chee) (*energy*) in the environment and the good fortune of the person who is in it. Buildings, rooms, and even graves are all built with **fēngshuǐ** principles in mind.

Fēngshuǐ is no joke in Asia. Entire buildings depend on the expert placement and location chosen by **fēngshuǐ** geomancers, and an entire industry is booming as a result. (Not the construction industry, silly; the **fēngshuǐ** consultant industry.) Even U.S. realtors are sure to make houses and apartments they show **fēngshuǐ** friendly. Ideally, the building should have some kind of elevated landscape in back of it and a water feature in the front, like a pond, river, or well.

Check out the rooms that you may need a **fēngshuǐ** master to help you organize in Table 6-1.

TABLE 6-1   ## Areas of the Home

Chinese	Pronunciation	English
chúfáng 厨房 (廚房)	choo-fahng	*kitchen*
dǐnglóu 顶楼 (頂樓)	deeng-low	*attic*
dìxiàshì 地下室	dee-shyah-shir	*basement*
fángjiān 房间 (房間)	fahng-jyan	*room(s)*
fàntīng 饭厅 (飯廳)	fahn-teeng	*dining room*
kètīng 客厅 (客廳)	kuh-teeng	*living room*
kōngfáng 空房	koong-fahng	*spare room*
shūfáng 书房 (書房)	shoo-fahng	*study*
wòshì 卧室	waw-shir	*bedroom*
xiūxishì 休息室	shyo-she-shir	*den*
yùshì 浴室	yew-shir	*bathroom*

According to **fēngshuǐ** principles, color helps balance the energy of a room. So the color of the décor of each room is pretty important. Bathrooms, for example, should reflect **yīn** qualities of peace and seclusion (for self-explanatory reasons).

The Chinese associate colors with one of each of the **wǔxíng** 五行 (woo-sheeng) (*five elements*): wood, water, fire, earth, and metal. Table 6-2 lists each of these elements.

TABLE 6-2
The Five Elements

Chinese	Pronunciation	English
mù 木	moo	*wood*
huǒ 火	hwaw	*fire*
tǔ 土	too	*earth*
jīn 金	gin	*metal*
shuǐ 水	shway	*water*

TIP

You can think of the five elements as different phases of nature. For example, wood creates fire; fire creates earth (ashes); elements from the earth create metal; objects made of metal (such as buckets) carry water; and water nourishes wood, bringing the cycle right back to the first element again.

The bedroom

After you move in and discover how much empty space you really have, you probably want to go out and buy at least the bare bones basics as far as furniture is concerned. How about some of these for the **wòshì** 卧室 (臥室) (waw-shir) (*bedroom*)?

>> **bèizi** 被子 (bay-dzuh) (*quilt*)

>> **chuáng** 床 (chwahng) (*bed*)

>> **chuángdān** 床单 (床單) (chwahng-dahn) (*sheets*)

>> **chuángdiàn** 床垫 (床墊) (chwahng-dyan) (*mattress*)

>> **chuángzhào** 床罩 (chwahng-jaow) (*bedspread*)

>> **tǎnzi** 毯子 (tahn-dzuh) (*blanket*)

>> **yīguì** 衣柜 (衣櫃) (ee-gway) (*chest of drawers*)

>> **zhěntóu** 枕头 (枕頭) (juhn-toe) (*pillow*)

The good news, of course, is that after you've purchased all these items, you can actually collapse on your own new bed. The bad news is that now you have no excuse not to **pūchuáng** 铺床 (鋪床) (poo-chwahng) (*make the bed*) every morning.

Here are three quick **fēngshuǐ** tips for the bedroom:

>> Place the bed as far away from the door as possible for more control over your life.

>> Don't put your bed against a side wall if you want more flexibility in life.

>> Put lots of space between the front of your bed and the rest of the room if you want your life to expand.

And if you have kids, you'll probably want to make sure there's a **shūzhuō** 书桌 (書桌) (shoo-jwaw) (*desk*) somewhere in their bedroom so that they can get some studying in after school. (You don't have to be a **fēngshuǐ** expert to know that.)

The bathroom

Okay, I'll cut to the chase. The bathroom is the one room in the house no one can do without. Here are the basics: You need a **cèsuǒ** 厕所 (廁所) (tsuh-swaw) (*toilet*), a **yùgāng** 浴缸 (yew-gahng) (*bathtub*) or **línyù jiān** 淋浴间 (淋浴間) (leen-yew jyan) (*shower*), and a **shuǐchí** 水池 (shway-chir) (*sink*).

TIP

One last thing you don't want to realize you've forgotten to stock up on before turning in for the night: **wèishēngzhǐ** 卫生纸 (衛生紙) (way-shung-jir) (*toilet paper*). While you're at it, make sure you have some **féizào** 肥皂 (fay-dzaow) (*soap*) on hand in this room, too. Don't say I didn't warn you.

Here are some **fēngshuǐ** tips for the bathroom:

>> To prevent **qì** from escaping, keep the door closed when the room isn't in use. (Actually, keep the door closed when it's in use, too.)

>> Close the toilet lid after you're done.

>> Make sure there are no leaks.

>> Put a potted plant or ceramic bowl with pebbles on the toilet tank. (Using a non-water color or element helps balance out all the water already in the room.)

The kitchen

Now you're cookin'. The kitchen is a room all of us can wrap our minds (or at least our stomachs) around. Aside from the one piece of furniture every kitchen usually needs — a **chúfáng cānzhuō** 厨房餐桌 (廚房餐桌) (choo-fahng tsahn-jwaw) (*kitchen table*) — and basic food prep appliances like a **kǎo lú** 烤炉 (烤爐) (cow loo) (*oven*) and a **diàn bīngxiāng** 电冰箱 (電冰箱) (dyan beeng-shyahng) (*refrigerator*), you may need some dishware and smaller appliances. Here are some things you may want to know how to say:

>> **bēizi** 杯子 (bay-dzuh) (*glasses*)

>> **jiǔ bēi** 酒杯 (jyo bay) (*wine glasses*)

>> **kāfēi bēi** 咖啡杯 (kah-fay bay) (*coffee cups*)

>> **wǎndié** 碗碟 (wahn-dyeh) (*dishes*)

>> **wēibōlú** 微波炉 (微波爐) (way-baw-loo) (*microwave*)

>> **yǐn qì** 银器 (銀器) (yin-chee) (*silverware*)

The best way to **fēngshuǐ** your kitchen is simply to keep it simple. Eliminate the clutter to avoid stagnant energy in your life. Old, stale food has old, stale energy, so clean out the fridge regularly. An unused stove implies untapped resources or ignored opportunities, so start using all the burners on the stove, and use the oven once in a while, too. (It can't hurt. Plus, you'll save a ton of money by not eating in restaurants.)

The living room

Now here's one room where everyone loves to hang out and watch some **diànshì** 电视 (電視) (dyan-shir) (*TV*) in — the **kètīng** 客厅 (客廳) (kuh-teeng) (*living room*). Want to put your feet up on the **cháji** 茶几 (chah-jee) (*coffee table* [Literally: *tea table*]) while you're watching? Don't even think about it. The **cháji** was meant for **kāfēi** 咖啡 (kah-fay) (*coffee*), not **jiǎo** 脚 (腳) (jyaow) (*feet*). (Don't ask me why it's not called a **kāfēijī** rather than a **cháji** — I don't have a clue.) The reality is that you can put coffee, tea, soda, and (when no one else is looking) even your feet on this table. Just don't say I said so.

CULTURAL WISDOM

THE KITCHEN GOD

In Chinese mythology, **Zào Jūn** 灶君 (Dzaow Jewn) (*the Kitchen God* [Literally: *the Master of the Stove,* because you hang his image over the stove]) is the most important deity of the entire home. A week before the Lunar New Year, he goes to the Jade Emperor, who rules the heavens, to report on the family's behavior from the prior year. To ensure that he gives a good report to the Jade Emperor, families smear the Kitchen God's mouth with honey to sweeten his tongue. They then burn his image, and his spirit is sent to the heavens with the good report. On New Year's Eve, each family puts up a new Kitchen God, and thus begins another year of watching over the family.

You almost always find a **shāfā** 沙发 (沙發) (shah-fah) (*sofa*) in the **kètīng,** and possibly a **yáoyǐ** 摇椅 (搖椅) (yaow-ee) (*rocking chair*), too. In fact, some apartments are so small that the **kètīng** doubles as a **fàntīng** 饭厅 (飯廳) (fahn-teeng) (*dining room*). In those cases, you may not have an actual **fàntīng shèbèi** 餐厅设备 (餐廳設備) (fahn-teeng shuh-bay) (*dining room set*) with a big table and chairs, but then again, that's what **chájī** are sometimes for.

Here are some **fēngshuǐ** tips for the living room:

» Keep the living room well lit and clutter-free, and make sure the air quality is good.

» Avoid an L-shaped furniture arrangement because it creates a lack of balance in the room and in your life.

» Don't crowd the living room with too many pieces of furniture, or the **qì** in the room and in your family's life will be blocked.

The basement

Some people find the **dìxiàshì** 地下室 (dee-shyah-shir) (*basement*) pretty scary. In addition to ghosts and spiders, though, it can actually have some really cool things in it. Table 6-3 lists what you may find in a basement.

TABLE 6-3 ### Things You Find in a Basement

Chinese	Pronunciation	English
cúnchǔ kōngjiān 存储空间 (存儲空間)	tswun-choo koong-jyan	*storage space*
guǐ 鬼	gway	*ghosts*
hǒng gān jī 烘干机 (烘乾機)	hoong gahn jee	*dryer*
mùgōng chējiān 木工车间 (木工車間)	moo-goong chuh-jyan	*carpentry workshop*
táiqiú zhuō 台球桌	tye-chyo jwaw	*pool table*
xǐyījī 洗衣机 (洗衣機)	shee-ee-jee	*washing machine*
zhīzhū 蜘蛛	jir-joo	*spiders*

BATS ARE GOOD FORTUNE, AND OTHER TRADITIONS

In Chinese architecture, door gods are placed on doorways to ward off evil and bring good fortune. Because bats actually represent good fortune in China, they can often be found in designs within the home. Another thing you may see in traditional homes is a raised piece of wood that you need to step over to get into each room. These pieces have a serious purpose: to trip the evil spirits, because evil spirits travel only in straight lines. (That's why you see a lot of curved roofs as well.) Similarly, spirit walls are placed in courtyards in front of the doors to the entrance of the house so that evil spirits will have to go around them.

Here are some **fēngshuǐ** tips for the basement:

>> Improve the air quality in normally stuffy basements with plants that purify the air, such as bamboo palm, English ivy, or rubber plants.

>> Make sure the basement has enough light and that you augment this light with brightly colored wall hangings.

The attic

The **gélóu** 阁楼 (閣樓) (guh-low) (*attic*) is another part of the house some people try to avoid. Sure, there are bound to be some **zhīzhū wǎng** 蜘蛛网 (蜘蛛網) (jir-joo wahng) (*spider webs*) up there, but you may also find your grandmother's **jiù yīfú** 旧衣服 (舊衣服) (jyo ee-foo) (*old clothes*) and, if you're lucky, maybe even some **chuánjiābǎo** 传家宝 (傳家寶) (chwan-jyah-baow) (*heirlooms*). Okay, you may also see an occasional **bīngfú** 蝙蝠 (beeng-foo) (*bat*), but in China, those are auspicious creatures.

Here are some **fēngshuǐ** tips for the attic:

>> Attics represent the future in **fēngshuǐ,** so definitely keep this area free of clutter and open to all sorts of possibilities.

>> Consider making the attic into a quiet meditation room instead of a willy-nilly storage space.

>> Use the energy of the attic for reflective pursuits. You may want to make it into a research area or library.

FUN & GAMES

For the following household items, match the English word to the corresponding Chinese word. Check Appendix C for the answers.

yùshì 浴室	*dining room*
wòshì 卧室	*balcony*
fàntīng 饭厅 (飯廳)	*sofa*
tǎnzi 毯子	*desk*
yángtái 阳台 (陽台)	*quilt*
zhěntóu 枕头 (枕頭)	*bedroom*
bèizi 被子	*bathroom*
shūzhuō 书桌 (書桌)	*blanket*
shāfā 沙发 (沙發)	*pillow*

2

Chinese in Action

Chapter **7**

Getting to Know You: Making Small Talk

S mall talk can really break the ice when you're interacting with someone you've just met or barely know. It's how you get to know someone, have a brief chat with the man sitting next to you on the plane, or get acquainted with the folks you'll be working with. This chapter helps you master a few key phrases and questions you can use to establish a relationship.

Xiánliáo 闲聊 (閒聊) (shyan-lyaow) means *small talk* in Chinese. **Xiántán** 闲谈 (閒談) (shyan-tahn) is *to chat*. Either term does the trick.

You can listen to all the Talkin' the Talk dialogues featured in this chapter. Go to www.dummies.com/go/chinese and click on the dialogue you want to hear.

REMEMBER

Establishing a Connection

A surefire way of initiating a conversation is to ask someone a question. Here are some basic question words to keep in mind as you approach the moment of acquaintance:

» **Duō jiǔ?** 多久? (Dwaw jyoe?) (*For how long?*)

» **Shéi?** 谁? (誰?) (Shay?) (*Who?*)

>> **Shénme?** 什么? (甚麼?) (Shummuh?) (*What?*)

>> **Shénme shíhòu?** 什么时候? (甚麼時候?) (Shummuh shir-ho?) (*When?*)

>> **Wèishénme?** 为什么? (為甚麼?) (Way-shummuh?) (*Why?*)

>> **Zài nǎr?** 在哪儿? (在哪兒?) (Dzye nar?) (*Where?*)

>> **Zěnme?** 怎么? (怎麼?) (Dzummuh?) (*How?*)

Here are a few examples of how to use these question words in simple sentences; sometimes you can also use some of the words on their own, just as in English:

Cèsuǒ zài nǎr? 厕所在哪儿? (廁所在哪兒?) (Tsuh-swaw dzye nar?) (*Where's the bathroom?*)

Jǐ diǎn zhōng? 几点钟? (幾點鐘?) (Jee dyan joong?) (*What time is it?*)

Nǐ shénme shíhòu chīfàn? 你什么时候吃饭? (你甚麼時候吃飯?) (Nee shummuh shir-ho chir-fahn?) (*When do you eat?*)

Nǐ wèishénme yào qù Zhōngguó? 你为什么要去中国? (你為甚麼要去中國?) (Nee way-shummuh yaow chyew Joong-gwaw?) (*Why do you want to go to China?*)

Nǐ yào shénme? 你要什么? (你要甚麼?) (Nee yaow shummuh?) (*What would you like?*)

Nǐ zěnme yàng? 你怎么样? (你怎麼樣?) (Nee dzummuh yahng?) (*How's it going?*)

Nǐ yǐjīng zài zhèr duōjiǔle? 你已经在这儿多久了? (你已經在這兒多久了?) (Nee ee-jeeng dzye jar dwaw-jyoe-luh?) (*How long have you been here already?*)

Tā shì shéi? 他/她是谁? (他/她是誰?) (Tah shir shay?) (*Who is he/she?*)

Xiànzài jǐ diǎn zhōng? 现在几点钟? (現在幾點鐘?) (Shyan-dzye jee dyan joong?) (*What time is it now?*)

You can also use the following responses to the questions in the preceding list if someone happens to approach you. These statements are the basics of small talk and really come in handy when you're learning a foreign language:

>> **Duìbùqǐ.** 对不起. (對不起.) (Dway-boo-chee.) (*Excuse me.*)

>> **Hěn bàoqiàn.** 很抱歉. (Hun baow-chyan.) (*I'm so sorry.*)

>> **Wǒ bùdǒng.** 我不懂. (Waw boo-doong.) (*I don't understand.*)

>> **Wǒ bú rènshi tā.** 我不认识他/她. (我不認識他/她.) (Waw boo run-shir tah.) (*I don't know him/her.*)

>> **Wǒ bù zhīdào.** 我不知道. (Waw boo jir-daow.) (*I don't know.*)

Talkin' the Talk

Miriam doesn't have a watch and wants to know what time it is. She asks a man on the street.

Miriam: **Duìbùqǐ. Qǐngwèn, xiànzài jǐ diǎn zhōng?**
Dway-boo-chee. Cheeng-one, shyan-dzye jee dyan joong?
Excuse me. May I ask what time it is?

Oscar: **Xiànzài yī diǎn bàn.**
Shyan-dzye ee dyan bahn.
It's 1:30.

Miriam: **Hǎo. Xièxiè nǐ.**
How. Shyeh-shyeh nee.
Great. Thank you.

Oscar: **Bú kèqì.**
Boo kuh-chee.
You're welcome.

Miriam: **Máfán nǐ, sì lù chēzhàn zài nǎr?**
Mah-fahn nee, suh loo chuh-jahn dzye nar?
Sorry to trouble you again, but where's the #4 bus stop?

Oscar: **Chēzhàn jiù zài nàr.**
Chuh-jahn jyoe dzye nar.
The bus stop is just over there.

Miriam: **Hǎo. Xièxiè.**
How. Shyeh-shyeh.
Okay. Thanks.

Oscar: **Méi wèntí.**
May one-tee.
No problem.

Posing simple introductory questions

The following is a list of simple questions you can use when you meet people. (To find out how to respond, or to talk about yourself, flip to Chapter 4.)

>> **Nǐ huì jiǎng Zhōngwén ma?** 你会讲中文吗? (你會講中文嗎?) (Nee hway jyahng Joong-one mah?) (*Do you speak Chinese?*)

>> **Nǐ jiào shénme míngzi?** 你叫什么名字? (你叫甚麼名字?) (Nee jyaow shummuh meeng-dzuh?) (*What's your name?*)

>> **Nǐ jiéhūnle méiyǒu?** 你结婚了没有? (你結婚了沒有?) (Nee jyeh-hwun-luh mayo?) (*Are you married?*)

>> **Nǐ niánjì duō dà?** 你年纪多大? (你年紀多大?) (Nee nyan-jee dwaw dah?) (*How old are you?*)

>> **Nǐ shénme shíhòu zǒu?** 你什么时候走? (你甚麼時候走?) (Nee shummuh shir-ho dzoe?) (*When are you leaving?*)

>> **Nǐ xǐhuān kàn diànyǐng ma?** 你喜欢看电影吗? (你喜歡看電影嗎?) (Nee she-hwahn kahn dyan-yeeng mah?) (*Do you like to see movies?*)

>> **Nǐ yǒu háizi ma?** 你有孩子吗? (你有孩子嗎?) (Nee yo hi-dzuh mah?) (*Do you have children?*)

>> **Nǐ zhù zài nǎr?** 你住在哪儿? (你主在哪兒?) (Nee joo dzye nar?) (*Where do you live?*)

>> **Nǐ zuò shénme gōngzuò?** 你做什么工作? (你做甚麼工作?) (Nee dzwaw shummuh goong-dzwaw?) (*What kind of work do you do?*)

Chatting about family

If you want to talk about your family when answering questions or making small talk, you need to know these common words:

» **àirén** 爱人 (愛人) (eye-run) (*spouse* [used mostly in mainland China])

» **dìdì** 弟弟 (dee-dee) (*younger brother*)

» **érzi** 儿子 (兒子) (are-dzuh) (*son*)

» **fùmǔ** 父母 (foo-moo) (*parents*)

» **fùqīn** 父亲 (父親) (foo-cheen) (*father*)

» **gēgē** 哥哥 (guh-guh) (*older brother*)

» **háizi** 孩子 (hi-dzuh) (*children*)

» **jiějiě** 姐姐 (jyeh-jyeh) (*older sister*)

» **jiěmèi** 姐妹 (jyeh-may) (*sisters*)

» **mèimèi** 妹妹 (may-may) (*younger sister*)

» **mǔqīn** 母亲 (母親) (moo-cheen) (*mother*)

» **nǚ'ér** 女儿 (女兒) (nyew-are) (*daughter*)

» **qīzi** 妻子 (chee-dzuh) (*wife*)

» **sūnnǚ** 孙女 (swun-nyew) (*granddaughter*)

» **sūnzi** 孙子 (swun-dzuh) (*grandson*)

» **tàitài** 太太 (tye-tye) (*wife* [used mostly in Taiwan])

» **wàigōng** 外公 (wye-goong) (*maternal grandfather*)

» **wàipó** 外婆 (wye-paw) (*maternal grandmother*)

» **xiōngdì** 兄弟 (shyoong-dee) (*brothers*)

» **xiōngdì jiěmèi** 兄弟姐妹 (shyoong-dee jyeh-may) (*siblings*)

» **zhàngfu** 丈夫 (jahng-foo) (*husband*)

» **zǔfù** 祖父 (dzoo-foo) (*paternal grandfather*)

» **zǔmǔ** 祖母 (dzoo-moo) (*paternal grandmother*)

............Talkin' the Talk............

Sammy meets his daughter's classmate, Jasmine, and asks about Jasmine's family.

Sammy: **Jasmine, nǐ yǒu méiyǒu xiōngdì jiěmèi?**
Jasmine, nee yo mayo shyoong-dee jyeh-may?
Jasmine, do you have any brothers or sisters?

Jasmine: **Wǒ yǒu yí ge jiějie.**
Waw yo ee guh jyeh-jyeh.
I have an older sister.

Sammy: **Tā yě huì jiǎng Zhōngwén ma?**
Tah yeah hway jyahng Joong-one mah?
Can she also speak Chinese?

Jasmine: **Búhuì. Tā zhǐ huì Yīngyǔ.**
Boo-hway. Tah jir hway Eeng-yew.
No. She only speaks English.

Sammy: **Nǐ de fùmǔ zhù zài nǎr?**
Nee duh foo-moo joo dzye nar?
Where do your parents live?

Jasmine: **Wǒmen dōu zhù zài Běijīng. Wǒ bàba shì wàijiāo guān.**
Waw-mun doe joo dzye Bay-jeeng. Waw bah-bah shir why-jyaow gwan.
We all live in Beijing. My father is a diplomat.

Sammy: **Nà tài hǎole.**
Nah tye how-luh.
That's great.

....

WORDS TO KNOW

Zěnme yàng? 怎么样? (怎麼樣?)	Dzumma yahng?	What's up?
Mǎmǎ hūhū. 马马虎虎. (馬馬虎虎.)	Ma-ma hoo-hoo.	So-so.
Wán de kāixīn. 玩得开心. (玩得開心.)	Wahn duh kye-sheen.	Have a great time.
Shuì gè hǎo jiào. 睡个好觉. (睡個好覺.)	Shway guh how jyaow.	Sleep well.

Making small talk on the job

The kind of job you have can say plenty about you. It can also be a great topic of conversation or spice up an otherwise dull exchange. To ask someone about his or her **gōngzuò** 工作 (goong-dzwaw) (*work*), you can say **Nǐ zuò shénme gōngzuò?** 你做什么工作? (你做甚麼工作?) (Nee dzwaw shummuh goong-dzwaw?) (*What kind of work do you do?*). You may even try to guess and say, for example, **Nǐ shì lǎoshī ma?** 你是老师吗? (你是老師嗎?) (Nee shir laow-shir mah?) (*Are you a teacher?*).

The following are some occupations you or the person you're talking with may hold:

>> **biānji** 编辑 (編輯) (byan-jee) (*editor*)

>> **cáifeng** 裁缝 (裁縫) (tsye-fung) (*tailor*)

>> **chéngwùyuán** 乘务员 (乘務員) (chuhng-woo-ywan) (*flight attendant*)

>> **chūnàyuán** 出纳员 (出納員) (choo-nah-ywan) (*bank teller*)

>> **diàngōng** 电工 (電工) (dyan-goong) (*electrician*)

>> **fēixíngyuán** 飞行员 (飛行員) (fay-sheeng-ywan) (*pilot*)

>> **hǎiguān guānyuán** 海关官员 (海關官員) (hi-gwan gwan-ywan) (*customs agent*)

>> **hùshì** 护士 (護士) (who-shir) (*nurse*)

>> **jiàoshòu** 教授 (jyaow-show) (*professor*)

>> **jiēxiànyuán** 接线员 (接線員) (jyeh-shyan-ywan) (*telephone operator*)

>> **kèfáng fúwùyuán** 客房服务员 (客房服務員) (kuh-fahng foo-woo-ywan) (*housekeeper*)

>> **kuàiji** 会计 (會計) (kwye-jee) (*accountant*)

>> **lǎoshī** 老师 (老師) (laow-shir) (*teacher*)

» **lièchēyuán** 列车员 (列車員) (lyeh-chuh-ywan) (*train conductor*)

» **lǜshī** 律师 (律師) (lyew-shir) (*lawyer*)

» **qiántái fúwùyuán** 前台服务员 (前台服務員) (chyan-tye foo-woo-ywan) (*receptionist*)

» **shuǐnuǎn gōng** 水暖工 (shway-nwan goong) (*plumber*)

» **yǎnyuán** 演员 (演員) (yan-ywan) (*actor*)

» **yīshēng** 医生 (醫生) (ee-shung) (*doctor*)

» **yóudìyuán** 邮递员 (郵遞員) (yo-dee-ywan) (*mail carrier*)

» **zhǔguǎn** 主管 (joo-gwan) (*CEO*)

The following are some useful job terms and job-related expressions:

» **bànrì gōngzuò** 半日工作 (bahn-ir goong-dzwaw) (*part-time work*)

» **gùyuán** 雇员 (僱員) (goo-ywan) (*employee*)

» **gùzhǔ** 雇主 (goo-joo) (*employer*)

» **jīnglǐ** 经理 (經理) (jeeng-lee) (*manager*)

» **miànshì** 面试 (面試) (myan-shir) (*interview*)

» **quánrì gōngzuò** 全日工作 (chwan-ir goong-dzwaw) (*full-time work*)

» **shīyè** 失业 (失業) (shir-yeh) (*unemployed*)

CULTURAL WISDOM

Since the founding of the People's Republic of China in 1949, right up to the dawn of the twenty-first century, the **dānwèi** 单位 (單位) (dahn-way) (*work unit*) was an integral part of your life. Your **dānwèi** was both your place of work and the group that was responsible for taking care of you. It was also responsible for any missteps you happen to make. In fact, when people ask you to identify yourself over the phone, they still often say **Nǐ nǎr?** 你哪儿? (你哪兒?) (Nee nar?) (Literally: *Where are you from?*) to find out what **dānwèi** you belong to. Through the decades, people were assigned jobs right out of high school and didn't even think of marrying until they knew the location of their assignment. A man could've been given a job in the northern hinterlands of China, and his fiancée could've been sent south — only to see each other once a year during the Chinese New Year. You needed permission from your **dānwèi** to get married and even to have a baby. The **dānwèi** instantly provided people with a **tiě fàn wǎn** 铁饭碗 (鐵飯碗) (tyeh fahn wahn) (*iron rice bowl*) — the equivalent of a "job for life." It guaranteed housing, an income, benefits, and job security. It also enforced government policies, such as the one-child-per-family policy, in force from 1979 right up until 2016. Nowadays you still hear the term **dānwèi,** but it primarily refers to any organization you happen to be working for.

Talkin' the Talk

Yáng and Xiǎo Liú discuss their respective professions, which are quite different from each other. Xiǎo Liú is a nurse in a city located in Henan Province, not far from the famed Shaolin Temple.

Xiǎo Liú: **Yáng, nǐ zuò shénme gōngzuò?**
Yahng, nee dzwaw shummuh goong-dzwaw?
Yang, what kind of work do you do?

Yáng: **Wǒ shì yǎnyuán.**
Waw shir yan-ywan.
I'm an actor.

Xiǎo Liú: **Nà hěn yǒuyìsi.**
Nah hun yo-ee-suh.
That's very interesting.

Yáng: **Nǐ ne?**
Nee nuh?
How about you?

Xiǎo Liú: **Wǒ shì hùshì. Wǒ zài Kāifēng dì yī yīyuàn gōngzuò.**
Waw shir hoo-shir. Waw dzye kye-fung dee ee ee-ywan goong-dzwaw.
I'm a nurse. I work at Kaifeng's No. 1 Hospital.

Yáng: **Nán bùnán?**
Nahn boo-nahn?
Is it difficult?

Xiǎo Liú: **Bùnán. Wǒ hěn xǐhuān wǒ de zhíyè.**
Boo-nahn. Waw hun she-hwahn waw duh jir-yeh.
It's not difficult. I really like my profession.

WORDS TO KNOW

xiūxí 休息	shyo-shee	to rest
Nígū 尼姑	Nee-goo	Buddhist nun
yōusī 幽思 (醫院)	yo-suh	to meditate
lěngjìng 冷静 (冷 靜)	lung-jeeng	calm

Talking about where you live

After folks get to know each other through small talk, they may exchange addresses and phone numbers to keep in touch. That introductory question covered earlier in this chapter, **Nǐ zhù zài nǎr?** 你住在哪儿? (你主在哪兒?) (Nee joo dzye nar?) (*Where do you live?*), may pop up. You may also want to ask a few of these questions:

» **Nǐ de diànhuà hàomǎ duōshǎo?** 你的电话号码多少? (你的電話號碼多少?) (Nee duh dyan-hwah how-mah dwaw-shaow?) (*What's your phone number?*)

» **Nǐ de dìzhǐ shì shénme?** 你的地址是什么? (你的地址是甚麼?) (Nee duh dee-jir shir shummuh?) (*What's your address?*)

» **Nǐ shénme shíhòu zài jiā?** 你什么时侯在家? (你甚麼時候在家?) (Nee shummuh shir-ho dzye jyah?) (*When will you be at home?/When are you home?*)

You may also talk about your home from time to time. These words and phrases can come in handy:

» **Wǒ zhù de shì gōngyù.** 我住的是公寓. (Waw joo duh shir goong-yew.) (*I live in an apartment.*)

» **Wǒmen zhù de shì fángzi.** 我们住的是房子. (我們住的是房子.) (Waw-mun joo duh shir fahng-dzuh.) (*We live in a house.*)

» **Wǒ zhù zài chénglǐ.** 我住在城里. (我住在城裡.) (Waw joo dzye chuhng-lee.) (*I live in the city.*)

» **Wǒ zhù zài jiāowài.** 我住在郊外. (Waw joo dzye jyaow-why.) (*I live in the suburbs.*)

» **Wǒ zhù zài nóngcūn.** 我住在农村. (我住在農村.) (Waw joo dzye noong-tswun.) (*I live in the countryside.*)

In addition to your **diànhuà hàomǎ** 电话号码（電話號碼）(dyan-hwah how-mah) (*phone number*) and your **dìzhǐ** 地址 (dee-jir) (*address*), people now also want to know your **diànzǐ yóuxiāng dìzhǐ** 电子邮箱地址 （電子郵箱地址）(dyan-dzuh yo-shyahng dee-jir) (*email address*). And if you find yourself in a more formal situation, giving someone your **míngpiàn** 名片 (meeng-pyan) (*business card*) may be appropriate. (To find out how to pronounce numbers, refer to Chapter 5.)

FUN & GAMES

Match these people with the words that identify their professions. Check out Appendix C for the answers.

yīshēng 医生 (醫生)   *accountant*

lǎoshī 老师 (老師)   *doctor*

fēixíngyuán 飞行员 (飛行員)   *pilot*

kuàiji 会计 (會計)   *teacher*

Chapter **8**

Dining Out and Shopping for Food

You may think you already know what Chinese food is all about, but if you suddenly find yourself a guest in a Chinese friend's home or the guest of honor at a banquet for your company's new branch in Shanghai, you may want to keep reading. This chapter not only helps you communicate when you're hungry or thirsty, go grocery shopping, and order food in a restaurant, but also gives you some useful tips on how to be both a wonderful guest and a gracious host when you have only one shot at making a good impression.

Feeling hungry yet? Allow me to whet your appetite by inviting you to take a closer look at world-renowned Chinese cuisine. No doubt you're already familiar with a great many Chinese dishes, from chow mein and chop suey to sweet and sour pork to that delicious favorite of all Chinese fare, **dim sum.**

Exploring Chinese food and Chinese eating etiquette is a great way to discover Chinese culture. You can also use what you discover in this chapter to impress your date by ordering in Chinese the next time you eat out.

REMEMBER

You can listen to all the Talkin' the Talk dialogues featured in this chapter. Go to www.dummies.com/go/chinese and click on the dialogue you want to hear.

All about Meals

If you feel hungry when beginning this section, you should stop to **chī** 吃 (chir) (*eat*) **fàn** 饭 (飯) (fahn) (*food*). In fact, **fàn** always comes up when you talk about meals in China. Different meals throughout the day, for example, are called

>> **zǎofàn** 早饭 (早飯) (dzaow-fahn) (*breakfast*)

>> **wǔfàn** 午饭 (午飯) (woo-fahn) (*lunch*)

>> **wǎnfàn** 晚饭 (晚飯) (wahn-fahn) (*dinner*)

For centuries, Chinese people greeted each other not by saying **Nǐ hǎo ma?** 你好吗? (你好嗎?) (Nee how ma?) (*How are you?*) but rather by saying **Nǐ chīfànle méiyǒu?** 你吃饭了没有? (你吃飯了沒有?) (Nee chir-fahn-luh mayo?) (Literally: "*Have you eaten?*")

CULTURAL WISDOM

In China, **fàn** actually means some kind of grain or starch-based staple. You can have **mǐfàn** 米饭 (米飯) (mee-fahn) (*rice*), which can be **chǎofàn** 炒饭 (炒飯) (chaow-fahn) (*fried white rice*) or **bái mǐfàn** 白米饭 (白米飯) (bye mee-fahn) (*boiled white rice*); **miàntiáo** 面条 (面條) (myan-tyaow) (*noodles*); **mántóu** 馒头 (饅頭) (mahn-toe) (*steamed bread*); **bāozi** 包子 (baow-dzuh) (*steamed buns*); or **jiǎozi** 饺子 (餃子) (jyaow-dzuh) (*dumplings*). As you can see, you have many types of **fàn** to choose from.

Satisfying your hunger

If you're hungry, you can say **Wǒ hěn è.** 我很饿. (我很餓.) (Waw hun uh.) (*I'm very hungry.*) and wait for a friend to invite you for a bite to eat. If you're thirsty, just say **Wǒde kǒu hěn gān.** 我的口很干. (Waw-duh ko hun gahn.) (Literally: *My mouth is very dry.*) to hear offers for all sorts of drinks. You may not get a chance to even utter these words, however, because Chinese rules of hospitality dictate offering food and drink to guests right off the bat.

TIP

You have a few subtle ways to get across the idea that you're hungry without appearing too forward. You can say any of the following:

>> **Nǐ è bú è?** 你饿不饿? (你餓不餓?) (Nee uh boo uh?) (*Are you hungry or not?*)

>> **Nǐ è ma?** 你饿吗? (你餓嗎?) (Nee uh mah?) (*Are you hungry?*)

>> **Nǐ hái méi chī wǎnfàn ba.** 你还没吃晚饭吧. (你還沒吃晚飯吧.) (Nee hi may chir wahn-fahn bah.) (*I bet you haven't had dinner yet.*)

By checking to see whether the other person is hungry first, you display the prized Chinese sensibility of consideration for others, and you give yourself a chance to gracefully get out of announcing that you, in fact, are really the one who's dying for some Chinese food. If you want, you can always come right out and say that you're the one who's hungry by substituting **wǒ** 我 (waw) (*I*) for **nǐ** 你 (nee) (*you*).

If you hear the sound **ba** 吧 (bah) at the end of a sentence, you can probably interpret it as *I bet*, as in **Nǐ hái méi chī wǎnfàn ba**, in the previous bulleted list, or as *let's*, as in **Wǒmen qù chīfàn ba.** 我们去吃饭吧. (我們去吃飯吧.) (Waw-men chyew chir-fahn bah.) (*Let's go have dinner.*). One little utterance serves to soften the sound of making a request (or a command).

You can say something like **Nǐ xiān hē jiǔ.** 你先喝酒. (Nee shyan huh jyoe.) (*[You] drink wine first.*), but you sound nicer and friendlier if you say **Nǐ xiān hē jiǔ ba.** 你先喝酒吧. (Nee shyan huh jyoe bah.) (*Better drink some wine first./Why not have some wine first?*).

When an acquaintance invites you over for dinner, he may ask **Nǐ yào chī fàn háishì yào chī miàn?** 你要吃饭还是要吃面? (你要吃飯還是要吃麵?) (Nee yaow chir fahn hi-shir yaow chir myan?) (*Do you want to eat rice or noodles?*). Naturally, your host doesn't just serve you a bowl of rice or noodles; he wants to know what basic staple to prepare before he adds the actual **cài** 菜 (tsye) (*the various dishes that go with the rice or noodles*).

The many varieties of **cài** have made China the envy of the culinary world. Centuries of subsistence-level existence have taught the Chinese not to waste one morsel of an animal, mineral, or vegetable when they can use the morsel as food. Chronic shortages of food at various points in Chinese history have lent credence to the saying "Necessity is the mother of invention." The Chinese say it another way, however: They eat "anything with legs that's not a table and anything with wings that's not an airplane." Either way, you get the idea.

DO YOU PREFER MEAT HÁISHÌ FISH?

When you can choose between more than one item on a Chinese menu, you can use the alternative question structure for interrogative expressions by placing the word **háishì** 还是 (還是) (hi-shir) (*or*) between the two choices. If you use the term *or* in affirmative sentences, however — such as when you say she's arriving either today or tomorrow — you should use the word **huò** 或 (hwaw) or **huò zhe** 或者 (hwaw juh) instead.

Sitting down to eat and practicing proper table manners

After you've chosen what staple you want and it actually sits staring you in the face on the table, you probably want to know what utensils to use in order to eat the meal. Don't be shy about asking for a good old fork and knife, even if you're in a Chinese restaurant. The idea that Chinese people all eat with chopsticks is a myth anyway. Table 8-1 presents a handy list of utensils you need to know how to say at one point or another.

TABLE 8-1 ## Utensils

Chinese	Pronunciation	English
bēizi 杯子	bay-dzuh	*cup*
cānjīnzhǐ 餐巾纸 (餐巾紙)	tsahn-jeen-jir	*napkin*
chāzi 叉子	chah-dzuh	*fork*
dāozi 刀子	daow-dzuh	*knife*
pánzi 盘子 (盤子)	pahn-dzuh	*plate*
tiáogēng 调羹 (調羹)	tyaow-gung	*spoon*
wǎn 碗	wahn	*bowl*
yì shuāng kuàizi 一双筷子 (一雙筷子)	ee shwahng kwye-dzuh	*a pair of chopsticks*

When you receive an invitation to someone's home, always remember to bring a small gift and to toast others before you take a drink yourself during the meal. The Chinese have no problem slurping their soup or belching during or after a meal, by the way, so don't be surprised if you witness both at a perfectly formal gathering. And to remain polite and in good graces, you should always make an attempt to serve someone else before yourself when dining with others; otherwise, you run the risk of appearing rude and self-centered. (Check out Chapter 21 for a list of other etiquette considerations.)

Don't hesitate to use some of these phrases at the table:

>> **Duō chī yìdiǎr ba!** 多吃一点儿吧! (多吃一點兒吧!) (Dwaw chir ee-dyar bah!) (*Have some more!*)

>> **Gānbēi!** 干杯! (幹杯!) (Gahn-bay!) (*Bottoms up!*)

>> **Màn chī!** *or* **màn màn chī!** 慢吃! *or* 慢慢吃! (Mahn chir! *or* Mahn mahn chir!) (*Bon appetite!*) This phrase literally means *Eat slowly,* but it's loosely translated as *Take your time and enjoy your food.*

>> **Wǒ chībǎo le.** 我吃饱了. (我吃飽了.) (Waw chir-baow luh.) (*I'm full.*)

>> **Zìjǐ lái.** 自己来. (自己來.) (Dzuh-jee lye.) (*I'll help myself.*)

CULTURAL WISDOM

Whenever a dining partner begins to serve you food, as is the custom, you must always feign protest with a few mentions of **Zìjǐ lái,** so you don't appear to assume that someone *should* be serving you. In the end, you should permit the person to follow proper etiquette by serving you portions from each dish if you're the guest.

WARNING

And whatever you do, don't use a **yáqiān** 牙签 (牙籤) (yah-chyan) (*toothpick*) without covering your mouth. One of the ultimate dining faux pas is to make your teeth visible during toothpick use.

Getting to Know Chinese Cuisines

CULTURAL WISDOM

You may have already discovered that different regions of China specialize in different types of cuisine. Each province has its own specialties, cooking style, and favorite ingredients. Some corner the market on spicy food, and others showcase rather bland food. But no matter where you go, you're sure to discover a new taste bud or two along the way.

Northern Chinese food, found in places such as Beijing, is famous for all sorts of meat dishes. You find plenty of beef, lamb, and duck (remember Peking Duck?). Garlic and scallions garnish the meat for good measure; otherwise, though, Northern cooking is bland because of the lack of excessive condiments. So don't expect anything overtly salty, sweet, or spicy.

Shanghai dining, as well as that of the neighboring Jiangsu and Zhejiang provinces, represents Eastern cuisine. Because these places are close to the sea and boast many lakes, you can find an infinite variety of seafood in this part of China. Fresh vegetables, different kinds of bamboo, and plenty of soy sauce and sugar are also hallmarks of this region's cuisine.

Food from Sichuan and Hunan provinces is considered Western Chinese cuisine. Western Chinese food is common in Chinese restaurants in the United States. Because this part of China is hot and humid, hot peppers and salt are commonly found here. (The food isn't the only thing considered fiery in these parts; some famous revolutionaries, such as Mao Zedong, have hailed from this region of China.)

Southern Chinese cuisine comes from Guangdong (formerly known as Canton) province, as well as from Fujian and Taiwan. Like Shanghai cuisine, it offers plentiful amounts of seafood, fresh fruits, and vegetables. One of the most famous types of food from Guangdong that you've no doubt heard of is **dim sum** (deem sum), which in standard Mandarin is pronounced **diǎn xīn** 点心 (點心) (dyan sheen). You can read more about this fare in the later section "Dipping into some dim sum."

Dining Out

Breaking bread with friends at home is great, but sometimes you want the Chinese dining experience out on the town. Taking on a menu in a foreign language can be daunting (and even that won't help you find the restroom), so the following sections take you through all sorts of restaurant basics, from sorting through the food options (including checking out **dim sum**) to ordering, paying the bill, and yes, locating the facilities.

REMEMBER

You ask for something politely by saying **Qǐng nǐ gěi wǒ. . .?** 请你给我. . .? (請你給我. . .?) (Cheeng nee gay waw. . .?) (*Would you mind please getting me a. . .?*). You can also say **Máfan nǐ gěi wǒ. . .?** 麻烦你给我. . .? (麻煩你给我. . .?) (Mah-fahn nee gay waw. . .?) (*May I trouble you to please get me a. . .?*).

Flip to Table 8-1 earlier in the chapter for a list of common utensils. Here are a couple of additional items you commonly encounter or need to ask for when dining out:

>> **yíge rè máojīn** 一个热毛巾 (一個熱毛巾) (ee-guh ruh maow-jeen) (*a hot towel*)

>> **yíge shī máojīn** 一个湿毛巾 (一個濕毛巾) (ee-guh shir maow-jeen) (*a wet towel*)

GRAMMAR CHAT

When in doubt, use the measure word **ge** 个 (個) (guh) in front of the noun you want to modify by a numeral or a specifier, such as **zhè** 这 (這) (jay) (*this*) or **nà** 那 (nah) (*that*). The word for "a" always begins with **yī** 一 (ee), meaning the number 1 in Chinese. In between **yī** and the noun is the measure word. For chopsticks, it's **shuāng** 双 (雙) (shwahng), meaning *pair*; for napkin, it's **zhāng** 张 (張) (jahng), used for anything with a flat surface (such as paper, a map, or even a bed); and a toothpick's measuring word is **gēn** 根 (gun), referring to anything resembling a stick, such as rope, a thread, or a blade of grass. Chinese has many different measure words, but **ge** (guh) is by far the most common.

Talkin' the Talk

Audrey and William meet after work in New York and decide where to eat.

William: **Audrey, nǐ hǎo!**
Audrey, nee how!
Audrey, hi!

Audrey: **Nǐ hǎo. Hǎo jiǔ méi jiàn.**
Nee how. How jyoe may jyan.
Hi there. Long time no see.

William: **Nǐ è bú è?**
Nee uh boo uh?
Are you hungry?

Audrey: **Wǒ hěn è. Nǐ ne?**
Waw hun uh. Nee nuh?
Yes, very hungry. How about you?

William: **Wǒ yě hěn è.**
Waw yeah hun uh.
I'm also pretty hungry.

Audrey: **Wǒmen qù Zhōngguó chéng chī Zhōngguó cài, hǎo bùhǎo?**
Waw-men chyew Joong-gwaw chuhng chir Joong-gwaw tsye, how boo how?
Let's go to Chinatown and have Chinese food, okay?

William: **Hǎo. Nǐ zhīdào Zhōngguó chéng nǎ jiā cānguǎn hǎo?**
How. Nee jir-daow joong-waw-chuhng nah jya tsahn-gwahn how?
Okay. Do you know which restaurant in Chinatown is good?

Audrey: **Běijīng kǎoyā diàn hǎoxiàng bú cuò.**
Bay-jeeng cow-ya dyan how-shyang boo tswaw.
The Peking Duck place seems very good.

William: **Hǎo jíle. Wǒmen zǒu ba.**
How jee-luh. Waw-men dzoe bah.
Great. Let's go.

WORDS TO KNOW

Wǒ è sǐle! 我饿死了! (我餓死了!)	Waw uh suh-luh!	I'm starving!
kāiwèi cài 开胃菜 (開胃菜)	kye-way tsye	appetizer
zhǔ cài 主菜	joo tsye	main dish
xiǎo cài 小菜	shyaow tsye	side dish
tián diǎn 甜点 (甜點)	tyan dyan	dessert

REMEMBER

Nǐ hǎo 你好 (Nee how), which appears in the nearby Talkin' the Talk dialogue, can be translated as *Hi, Hello,* or *How are you?*

Understanding what's on the menu

Are you a vegetarian? If so, you want to order **sùcài** 素菜 (soo-tsye) (*vegetable dishes*). If you're a dyed-in-the-wool carnivore, however, you should definitely keep your eye on the kind of **hūncài** 荤菜 (葷菜) (hwun-tsye) (*meat or fish dishes*) listed on the **càidān** 菜单 (菜單) (tsye-dahn) (*menu*). Unlike the rice or noodles you may order, which come in individual bowls for everyone at the table, the **cài** 菜 (tsye) (*dishes*) you order arrive on large plates, which you're expected to share with others.

You should become familiar with the basic types of food on the menu in case you have only Chinese characters and **pīnyīn** Romanization to go on. Having this knowledge allows you to immediately know which section to focus on (or, likewise, to avoid).

Take meat, for example. In English, the words for *pork, beef,* and *mutton* have no hints of the words for the animals themselves, such as **zhū** 猪 (豬) (joo) (*pig*), **niú** 牛 (nyoe) (*cow*), or **yáng** 羊 (yahng) (*lamb*). Chinese is much simpler. Just combine the word for the animal and the word **ròu** 肉 (row), meaning *meat,* such as **zhūròu** 猪肉 (豬肉) (joo-row) (*pork*), **niúròu** 牛肉 (nyoe-row) (*beef*), or **yángròu** 羊肉 (yahng-row) (*mutton*). Voilà! You have the dish.

Table 8-2 shows the typical elements of a Chinese menu.

TABLE 8-2

Typical Sections of a Chinese Menu

Chinese	Pronunciation	English
diǎnxīn 点心 (點心)	dyan-sheen	*dessert*
hǎixiān 海鲜 (海鮮)	hi-shyan	*seafood dishes*
jī lèi 鸡类 (雞類)	jee lay	*poultry dishes*
kāiwèi cài 开胃菜 (開胃菜)	kye-way tsye	*appetizer*
ròu lèi 肉类 (肉類)	row lay	*meat dishes*
sùcài 素菜	soo-tsye	*vegetarian dishes*
tāng 汤 (湯)	tahng	*soup*
yǐnliào 饮料 (飲料)	een-lyaow	*drinks*

Talkin' the Talk

Will, Eli, and Sheldon meet at a restaurant in Shanghai after work, and a host greets them on the way in.

Host: **Jǐ wèi?**
           Jee way?
           How many are in your party?

Will: **Sān wèi.**
           Sahn way.
           There are three of us.

The host shows them to their table. The three must now decide what to order for their meals.

Host: **Qǐng zuò zhèr. Zhè shì càidān.**
           Cheeng dzwaw jar. Jay shir tsye-dahn.
           Please sit here. Here's the menu.

Will: **Nǐ yào chī fàn háishì yào chī miàn?**
           Nee yaow chir fahn hi-shir yaow chir myan?
           Do you want to eat rice or noodles?

Eli:	**Liǎng ge dōu kěyǐ.**
	Lyahng guh doe kuh-yee.
	Either one is fine.

Sheldon:	**Wǒ hěn xǐhuān yāoguǒ jīdīng. Nǐmen ne?**
	Waw hun she-hwan yaow-gwaw jee-deeng. Nee-men nuh?
	I love diced chicken with cashew nuts. How about you guys?

Eli:	**Duìbùqǐ, wǒ chī sù. Wǒmen néng bùnéng diǎn yìdiǎr dòufu?**
	Dway-boo-chee, waw chir soo. Waw-mun nung boo-nung dyan ee-dyar doe-foo?
	Sorry, I'm a vegetarian. Can we order some tofu?

Sheldon:	**Dāngrán kěyǐ.**
	Dahng-rahn kuh-yee.
	Of course we can.

Will:	**Bùguǎn zěnme yàng, wǒmen lái sānpíng píjiǔ, hǎo bù hǎo?**
	Boo-gwahn dzummuh yahng, waw-mun lye san-peeng pee-jyoe, how boo how?
	No matter what, let's get three bottles of beer, okay?

Eli:	**Hěn hǎo!**
	Hun how!
	Very good!

• •

WORDS TO KNOW

Jǐ wèi? 几位? (幾位?)	Jee way?	How many are in your party?
Bù guǎn zěnme yang . . . 不管怎么样 . . . (不管怎麼樣 . . .)	Boo gwahn dzummah yahng . . .	No matter what . . .
hóngjiǔ 红酒 (紅酒)	hoong-jyo	wine
píjiǔ 啤酒	pee-jyo	beer
guǒzhī 果汁	gwaw-jir	juice

Vegetarian's delight

If you're a vegetarian, you may feel lost when looking at a menu filled with mostly pork (the staple meat of China), beef, and fish dishes. Not to worry. As long as you memorize a couple of the terms shown in Table 8-3, you won't go hungry.

TABLE 8-3

Vegetables Commonly Found in Chinese Dishes

Chinese	Pronunciation	English
bōcài 菠菜	baw-tsye	spinach
dòufu 豆腐	doe-foo	bean curd
fānqié 番茄	fahn-chyeh	tomato
gāilán 芥兰 (芥蘭)	gye-lahn	Chinese broccoli
mógū 蘑菇	maw-goo	mushroom
qiézi 茄子	chyeh-dzuh	eggplant
qīngjiāo 青椒	cheeng-jyaow	green pepper
sìjídòu 四季豆	suh-jee-doe	string bean
tǔdòu 土豆	too-doe	potato
xī lánhuā 西兰花 (西蘭花)	she lahn-hwah	broccoli
yángbáicài 洋白菜	yahng-bye-tsye	cabbage
yùmǐ 玉米	yew-me	corn
zhúsǔn 竹笋 (竹筍)	joo-swoon	bamboo shoot

When you have a good understanding of the vegetables that go into Chinese dishes, you, oh proud vegetarian, can start to order specialized vegetarian dishes at all your favorite restaurants. Table 8-4 shows some vegetarian dishes good for a night on the town.

TABLE 8-4

Vegetarian Dishes

Chinese	Pronunciation	English
dànhuā tāng 蛋花汤 (蛋花湯)	dahn-hwah tahng	egg drop soup
gānbiān sìjìdòu 干煸四季豆 (乾煸四季豆)	gahn-byan suh-jee-doe	sautéed string beans
hóngshāo dòufu 红烧豆腐 (紅燒豆腐)	hoong-shaow doe-foo	braised bean curd in soy sauce
suān là tāng 酸辣汤 (酸辣湯)	swan lah tahng	hot-and-sour soup
yúxiāng qiézi 鱼香茄子 (魚香茄子)	yew-shyang chyeh-dzuh	spicy eggplant with garlic

CULTURAL WISDOM

You may be tempted to **chī** 吃 (chir) (*eat*) your soup in a Chinese restaurant, but you should actually **hē** 喝 (huh) (*drink*) it instead. If it tastes really good, you can say the soup is **hěn hǎo hē** 很好喝 (hun how huh) (*very tasty*), just like anything else you may have ordered to drink.

Some favorite Chinese dishes

You may be familiar with many of the following dishes if you've ever been in a Chinese restaurant:

» **Běijīng kǎoyā** 北京烤鸭 (北京烤鴨) (Bay-jeeng cow-yah) (*Peking Duck*)

» **chūnjuǎn** 春卷 (春捲) (chwun-jwan) (*spring roll*)

» **dòufu gān** 豆腐干 (豆腐乾) (doe-foo gahn) (*dried bean curd*)

» **gàilán niúròu** 芥兰牛肉 (芥蘭牛肉) (guy-lahn nyoe-row) (*beef with broccoli*)

» **gong bǎo jī dīng** 宫保鸡丁 (宮保雞丁) (goong baow jee deeng) (*diced chicken with hot peppers*)

» **háoyóu niúròu** 蚝油牛肉 (蠔油牛肉) (how-yo nyoe-row) (*beef with oyster sauce*)

» **húntūn tāng** 馄饨汤 (餛飩湯) (hwun-dwun tahng) (*wonton soup*)

» **shuàn yángròu** 涮羊肉 (shwahn yahng-row) (*Mongolian hot pot*)

» **tángcù yú** 糖醋鱼 (糖醋魚) (tahng-tsoo yew) (*sweet-and-sour fish*)

» **yān huángguā** 腌黄瓜 (醃黃瓜) (yan hwahng-gwah) (*pickled cucumber*)

CULTURAL WISDOM

CHOWING DOWN ON THE CHINESE NEW YEAR

On the eve of the Chinese lunar New Year, known as **chú xī** 除夕 (choo she), the Chinese eat a big **nián yèfàn** 年夜饭 (年夜飯) (nyan yeh-fahn) (*New Year's Eve dinner*). The dinner almost always includes a whole cooked **yú** 鱼 (魚) (yew) (*fish*), because the word for fish rhymes with the word for *abundance* (**yù**), even though the written characters for the words look quite different. In some of the poorer parts of northern China, people often eat **jiǎozi** 饺子 (餃子) (jyaow-dzuh) (*dumplings*) rather than fish because their shape resembles traditional **yuánbāo** 元宝 (元寶) (ywan-baow) (*gold ingots*) used in pre-modern times by people of means. These people hope that the prosperity and abundance of such wealthy families will also come into their lives through the eating of the **jiǎozi.** Southerners often eat **fā cài** 发菜 (fah tsye) (*a kind of stringy black vegetable*), which rhymes with **fā cái** 发财 (發財) (fah tsye), although you pronounce the words in different tones. **Fā cái** means to get wealthy and prosper; in fact, the most common greeting on New Year's day is **Gōngxǐ fācái!** 恭喜发财! (恭喜發財!) (Goong-she fah-tsye!) (*Congratulations, and may you prosper!*).

Sauces and seasonings

The Chinese use all kinds of seasonings and sauces to make their dishes so tasty. Check out *Chinese Cooking For Dummies* by Martin Yan (Wiley) for much more info. Here are just a few of the basics:

>> **cù** 醋 (tsoo) (*vinegar*)

>> **jiāng** 姜 (jyahng) (*ginger*)

>> **jiàngyóu** 酱油 (醬油) (jyahng-yo) (*soy sauce*)

>> **làyóu** 辣油 (lah-yo) (*hot sauce*)

>> **máyóu** 麻油 (mah-yo) (*sesame oil*)

>> **yán** 盐 (鹽) (yan) (*salt*)

Even though Chinese food is so varied and great you could have it three meals a day forever, once in a while you might really find yourself hankering for a good old American hamburger or a stack of French fries. In fact, you may be surprised to find places like McDonald's and Kentucky Fried Chicken in Asia when you least expect to. Table 8-5 lists some items you can order when you're in need of some old-fashioned comfort food, and Table 8-6 lists common beverages.

TABLE 8-5   **Western Food**

Chinese	Pronunciation	English
bǐsābǐng 比萨饼 (比薩餅)	bee-sah-beeng	*pizza*
hànbǎobāo 汉堡包 (漢堡包)	hahn-baow-baow	*hamburger*
kǎo tǔdòu 烤土豆	cow too-doe	*baked potato*
règǒu 热狗 (熱狗)	ruh-go	*hot dog*
sānmíngzhì 三明治	sahn-meeng-jir	*sandwich*
shālā jiàng 沙拉酱 (沙拉醬)	shah-lah jyahng	*salad dressing*
shālā zìzhù guì 沙拉自助柜 (沙拉自助櫃)	shah-lah dzuh-joo gway	*salad bar*
tǔdòu ní 土豆泥	too-doe nee	*mashed potatoes*
yáng pái 羊排	yahng pye	*lamb chops*
Yìdàlì shì miàn tiáo 意大利式面条 (意大利式麵條)	Ee-dah-lee shir myan tyaow	*spaghetti*
zhà jī 炸鸡 (炸雞)	jah jee	*fried chicken*
zhà shǔ tiáo 炸薯条 (炸薯條)	jah shoo tyaow	*French fries*
zhà yáng cōng quān 炸洋葱圈 (炸洋蔥圈)	jah yahng tsoong chwan	*onion rings*
zhūpái 猪排 (豬排)	joo-pye	*pork chops*

TABLE 8-6   **Beverages**

Chinese	Pronunciation	English
chá 茶	chah	*tea*
gān hóng pūtáojiǔ 干红葡萄酒 (干紅葡萄酒)	gahn hoong poo-taow-jyoe	*dry red wine*
guǒzhī 果汁	gwaw-jir	*fruit juice*
kāfēi 咖啡	kah-fay	*coffee*
kělè 可乐 (可樂)	kuh-luh	*soda*
kuāngquán shuǐ 矿泉水 (礦泉水)	kwahng-chwan shway	*mineral water*
níngmén qìshuǐ 柠檬汽水 (檸檬汽水)	neeng-muhn chee-shway	*lemonade*
niúnǎi 牛奶	nyoe-nye	*milk*
píjiǔ 啤酒	pee-jyoe	*beer*

Placing an order and chatting with the waitstaff

CULTURAL WISDOM

I bet you're used to your dining partners ordering one dish for themselves, right? Well, in China, diners almost always share dishes by putting them on common platters smack in the middle of the table where everyone can pick and choose. You get used to ordering with the whole group in mind, not just yourself — just one more example of how the collective is always considered before the individual in Chinese culture.

Chinese table etiquette dictates that everyone decides together what to order. The two main categories you must decide on are the **cài** 菜 (tsye) (*food dishes*) and the **tāng** 汤 (湯) (tahng) (*soup*). Feel free to be the first one to ask **Wǒmen yīnggāi jiào jǐ ge cài jǐ ge tāng?** 我们应该叫几个菜几个汤？(我們應該叫幾個菜幾個湯？) (Waw-men eeng-gye jyaow jee guh tsye jee guh tahng?) (*How many dishes and how many soups should we order?*). Ideally, one of each of the five major tastes should appear in the dishes you choose for your meal to be a "true" Chinese meal: **suān** 酸 (swan) (*sour*), **tián** 甜 (tyan) (*sweet*), **kǔ** 苦 (koo) (*bitter*), **là** 辣 (lah) (*spicy*), and **xián** 咸 (shyan) (*salty*).

I know it can be hard to choose what to eat from all the fantastic choices staring back at you from most any Chinese menu; after all, the Chinese perfected the art of cooking long before the French and Italians appeared on the scene. But when you finally hit on something you like, you have to figure out how to tell the waiter what you want to **chī** 吃 (chir) (*eat*), whether you like spicy food, if you want to avoid **wèijīng** 味精 (way-jeeng) (*MSG*), what kind of beer you want to **hē** 喝 (huh) (*drink*), and that you want to know what kind of **náshǒu cài** 拿手菜 (nah-show tsye) (*house specialty*) the restaurant has going today.

Here are some questions your waiter or waitress is likely to ask you:

>> **Nǐmen yào hē diǎr shénme?** 你们要喝点儿什么？(你們要喝點兒甚麼？) (Nee-men yaow huh dyar shummuh?) (*What would you like to drink?*)

>> **Nǐmen yào shénme cài?** 你们要什么菜？(你們要甚麼菜？) (Nee-men yaow shummuh tsye?) (*What would you like to order?* [Literally: *What kind of food would you like?*])

>> **Yào jǐ píng píjiǔ?** 要几瓶啤酒？(要幾瓶啤酒？) (Yaow jee peeng pee-jyoe?) (*How many bottles of beer do you want?*)

When addressing waiters or waitresses, you can call them by the same name: **fúwùyuán** 服务员 (服務員) (foo–woo–ywan) (*service personnel*). In fact, *he, she,* and *it* all share the same Chinese word, too: **tā** 他/她/它 (tah). Isn't that easy to remember? Here are some questions, requests, and statements that may come in handy:

» **Dà shīfu náshǒu cài shì shénme?** 大师傅拿手菜是什么? (大師傅拿手菜是甚麼?) (Dah shir-foo nah-show tsye shir shummuh?) (*What's the chef's specialty?*)

» **Nǐ gěi wǒmen jièshào cài, hǎo ma?** 你给我们介绍菜, 好吗? (你給我們介紹菜, 好嗎?) (Nee gay waw-men jyeh-shaow tsye how ma?) (*Can you recommend some dishes?*)

» **Nǐmen yǒu kuàngquán shuǐ ma?** 你们有矿泉水吗? (你們有礦泉水嗎?) (Nee-men yo kwahng-chwan shway mah?) (*Do you have any mineral water?*)

» **Qǐng bǎ yǐnliào sòng lái.** 请把饮料送来. (請把飲料送來.) (Cheeng bah yin-lyaow soong lye.) (*Please bring our drinks.*)

» **Qǐng bié fàng wèijīng, wǒ guòmǐn.** 请别放味精, 我过敏. (請別放味精, 我過敏.) (Cheeng byeh fahng way-jeeng, waw gwaw-meen.) (*Please don't use any MSG, I'm allergic.*)

» **Qǐng cā zhuōzi.** 请擦桌子. (請擦桌子.) (Cheeng tsah jwaw-dzuh.) (*Please wipe off the table.*)

» **Qǐng gěi wǒ càidān.** 请给我菜单. (請給我菜單.) (Cheeng gay waw tsye-dahn.) (*Please give me the menu.*)

» **Wǒ bù chī zhūròu.** 我不吃猪肉. (我不吃豬肉.) (Waw boo chir joo-row.) (*I don't eat pork.*)

» **Wǒ bùnéng chī yǒu táng de cài.** 我不能吃有糖的菜. (Waw boo-nuhng chir yo tahng duh tsye.) (*I can't eat anything made with sugar.*)

» **Wǒ búyào là de cài.** 我不要辣的菜. (Waw boo-yaow lah duh tsye.) (*I don't want anything spicy.*)

» **Wǒ bú yuànyì chī hǎishēn.** 我不愿意吃海参. (我不願意吃海参.) (Waw boo ywan-yee chir hi-shun.) (*I don't want to try sea slugs.*)

» **Wǒ méi diǎn zhèige.** 我没点这个. (我没点這個.) (Waw may dyan jay-guh.) (*I didn't order this.*)

» **Wǒmen yào yíge suān là tāng.** 我们要一个酸辣汤. (我們要一個酸辣湯.) (Waw-men yaow ee-guh swan lah tahng.) (*We'd like a hot-and-sour soup.*)

» **Yú xīnxiān ma?** 鱼新鲜吗? (魚新鮮嗎?) (Yew shin-shyan mah?) (*Is the fish fresh?*)

Regular nouns in Chinese make no distinction between singular and plural. Whether you want to talk about one **pínɡɡuǒ** 苹果 (蘋果) (peeng-gwaw) (*apple*), two **júzi** 桔子 (jyew-dzuh) (*oranges*), or both **pínɡɡuǒ hé júzi** 苹果和桔子 (peeng-gwaw huh jyew-dzuh) (*apples and oranges*), the fruits always sound the same in Chinese. On the other hand, if you want to refer to human beings, you can always add the suffix **men** 们 (們) (mun). The word for *I* or *me* is **wǒ** 我 (waw), but *we* becomes **wǒmen** 我们 (我們) (waw-mun). The same goes for **nǐ** 你 (nee) (*you*) and **tā** 他/她/它 (tah) (*he/she/it*). *Both of you* or *all of you* becomes **nǐmen** 你们 (你們) (nee-mun) and *both of them* or *all of them* becomes **tāmen** 他们 他們) / 她们 (她們) / 它们 (它們) (tah-mun). If you want to refer to a specific number of apples, however, you don't use **men** as a suffix. You can either say **pínɡɡuǒ** for *apple* (or *apples*) or **liǎnɡ ɡe pínɡɡuǒ** 两个苹果 (兩個蘋果) (lyahng guh peeng-gwaw), meaning *two apples*. How do you like them apples?

Dipping into some dim sum

Dim sum is probably the most popular food of Chinese folks in the United States and of people in Guangdong province and all over Hong Kong, where you can find it served for breakfast, lunch, and sometimes dinner. Vendors even sell dim sum snacks in subway stations.

The dish's main claim to fame is that it takes the shape of mini portions, and it's often served with tea to help cut through the oil and grease afterward. You have to signal the waiters when you want a dish of whatever is on the dim sum cart they push in the restaurant, however, or they just pass on by. Dim sum restaurants are typically crowded and noisy, which only adds to the fun.

Part of the allure of dim sum is that you get to sample a whole range of different tastes while you catch up with old friends. Dim sum meals can last for hours, which is why most Chinese people choose the weekends to have dim sum. No problem lingering on a Saturday or Sunday.

Because dim sum portions are so small, your waiter often tallies the total by the number of plates left on your table. You can tell the waiter you want a specific kind of dim sum by saying **Qǐng lái yì dié**_____. 请来一碟 _____. (請來一碟 _____.) (Cheeng lye ee dyeh _____.) (*Please give me a plate of* _____.). Fill in the blank with one of the tasty choices I list in Table 8-7.

TABLE 8-7 **Common Dim Sum Dishes**

Chinese	Pronunciation	English
chūnjuǎn 春卷 (春捲)	chwun-jwan	spring rolls
dàntǎ 蛋挞 (蛋撻)	dahn-tah	egg tarts
dòushā bāo 豆沙包	doe-shah baow	sweet bean buns
guō tiē 锅贴 (鍋貼)	gwaw tyeh	fried pork dumplings
luóbō gāo 萝卜糕 (蘿蔔糕)	law-baw gaow	turnip cake
niàng qīngjiāo 酿青椒 (釀青椒)	nyahng cheeng-jyaow	stuffed peppers
niúròu wán 牛肉丸	nyoe-row wahn	beef balls
xiā jiǎo 虾饺 (蝦餃)	shyah jyaow	shrimp dumplings
xiǎolóng bāo 小笼包 (小籠包)	shyaow-loong baow	steamed pork buns
xiā wán 虾丸 (蝦丸)	shyah wahn	shrimp balls
yù jiǎo 芋饺 (芋餃)	yew jyaow	deep fried taro root

GRAMMAR
CHAT

Have you ever used the particle **guò** 过 (過) (gwaw)? If you want to ask whether someone has ever done something, use this word directly after the verb to get your point across:

> **Nǐ qùguò Měiguó méiyǒu?** 你去过美国没有? (你去過美國沒有?) (Nee chew-gwaw May-gwaw mayo?) (*Have you ever been to America?*)

> **Nǐ chīguò Yìdàlì fàn ma?** 你吃过意大利饭吗? (你吃過意大利飯嗎?) (Nee chir-gwaw Ee-dah-lee fahn ma?) (*Have you ever eaten Italian food?*)

Finding the restrooms

After you have a bite to eat, you may be in need of a restroom. The need may be dire if you're smack in the middle of a 12-course banquet in Beijing and already have a couple of glasses of **máotái** 茅台 (maow-tye), the stiffest of all Chinese drinks, under your belt.

Now all you have to do is garner the energy to ask *Where's the restroom?* **Cèsuǒ zài nǎr?** 厕所在哪儿? (廁所在哪兒?) (Tsuh-swaw dzye nar?) if you're in mainland China or **Cèsuǒ zài nǎlǐ?** 厕所在哪里? (廁所在哪理?) (Tsuh-swaw dzye nah-lee?) if you're in Taiwan. You can also ask **Nǎlǐ kěyǐ xǐshǒu?** 哪里可以洗手? (哪裡可以洗手?) (Nah-lee kuh-yee she-show?) (*Where can I wash my hands?*).

CULTURAL WISDOM

If you're in mainland China, don't forget to take some toilet paper with you before you leave the hotel, because many public restrooms don't supply it there. In most cases, the pictures on the bathroom doors are self-explanatory, but you may also see 男, the **pīnyīn** for **nán** (nahn) (*male*) and 女, the **pīnyīn** for **nǔ** (nyew) (*female*) before the word **cèsuǒ**. Those are the words you want to pay attention to above all else.

TIP

You can also find the word **cèsuǒ** in the term for graffiti: **cèsuǒ wénxué** 厕所文学 (廁所文學) (tsuh-swaw one-shweh) (Literally: *bathroom literature*). How apropos.

Finishing your meal and paying the bill

After you're through sampling all possible permutations of Chinese cuisine (or French or Italian, for that matter), you won't be able to just slink away unnoticed out the front door and into the sunset. Time to pay the bill, my friend. Hopefully it was worth the expense. Here are some phrases you should know when the time comes:

>> **Bāokuò fúwùfèi.** 包括服务费. (包括服務費.) (Baow-kwaw foo-woo-fay.) (*The tip is included.*)

>> **fēnkāi suàn** 分开算 (分開算) (fun-kye swahn) (*to go Dutch*)

>> **jiézhàng** 结账 (結賬) (jyeh-jahng) (*to pay the bill*)

>> **Qǐng jiézhàng.** 请结账. (請結賬.) (Cheeng jyeh-jahng.) (*The check, please.*)

>> **Qǐng kāi shōujù.** 请开收据. (請開收據.) (Cheeng kye show-jyew.) (*Please give me the receipt.*)

>> **Wǒ kěyǐ yòng xìnyòngkǎ ma?** 我可以用信用卡吗? (我可以用信用卡嗎?) (Waw kuh-yee yoong sheen-young-kah mah?) (*May I use a credit card?*)

>> **Wǒ qǐngkè.** 我请客. (我請客.) (Waw cheeng-kuh.) (*It's on me.*)

>> **Zhàngdān yǒu cuò.** 账单有错. (賬單有錯.) (Jahng-dahn yo tswaw.) (*The bill is incorrect.*)

All the Tea in China

You encounter about as many different kinds of tea as you do Chinese dialects. Hundreds, in fact. To make ordering or buying this beverage easier, however, you really need to know only the most common kinds of tea:

>> **Lǜ chá** 绿茶 (綠茶) (Lyew chah) (*Green tea*): Green tea is the oldest of all the teas in China, with many unfermented sub-varieties. The most famous kind of Green tea is called **Lóngjǐng chá** 龙井茶 (龍井茶) (loong-jeeng chah), meaning *Dragon Well tea*. You can find it near the famous West Lake region in Hangzhou, but people in the south generally prefer this kind of tea.

>> **Hóng chá** 红茶 (紅茶) (Hoong chah) (*Black tea*): Even though **hóng** means *red* in Chinese, you translate this phrase as *Black tea* instead. Unlike Green tea, Black teas are fermented; they're enjoyed primarily by people in Fujian province.

>> **Wūlóng chá** 乌龙茶 (烏龍茶) (Oo-loong chah) (*Black Dragon tea*): This kind of tea is semi-fermented. It's a favorite in Guangdong and Fujian provinces in the South, and in Taiwan.

>> **Mòlìhuā chá** 茉莉花茶 (茉莉花茶) (Maw-lee-hwah chah) (*Jasmine*): This kind of tea is made up of a combination of Black, Green, and Wūlóng teas in addition to some fragrant flowers such as jasmine or magnolia thrown in for good measure. Most northerners are partial to Jasmine tea, probably because the north is cold and this type of tea raises the body's temperature.

CULTURAL WISDOM

Tea is always offered to guests the minute they enter a Chinese home. The hosts aren't just being polite; the offering of tea shows respect to the guest and presents a way to share something that all parties can enjoy together. It may be considered rude not to at least take a sip. Chinese custom says that a host only fills the teacup to 70 percent of its capacity. The other 30 percent is supposed to contain friendship and affection. Isn't that a nice concept?

GRAMMAR CHAT

You often use the adjective **hǎo** 好 (how) (*good*) with a verb to create an adjective that means *good to*. Here are a few examples:

hǎochī 好吃 (how-chir) (*tasty* [Literally: *good to eat*])

hǎohē 好喝 (how-huh) (*tasty* [Literally: *good to drink*])

hǎokàn 好看 (how-kahn) (*pretty, interesting* [Literally: *good to look at or watch*]). This designation can apply to people or even movies.

hǎowán 好玩 (how-wahn) (*fun, interesting* [Literally: *good to play*])

THE CHINESE NIGHT MARKET

Night markets are great places to stroll, shop, eat, and otherwise hang out with family and friends. Vendors hawk their wares from clothes to **xiǎo chī** 小吃 (shyaow chir) (*snacks* [Literally: *small eats*]) of every kind in noisy, crowded stalls in what can only be described as a carnival-like atmosphere. The most famous night market in Taiwan is in the **Shìlín** 士林 (Shir-leen) district of Taipei, which closes well after midnight. In mainland China, don't miss the **Kāifēng yèshì** 开封夜市 (開封夜市) (Kye-fuhng yeh-shir) (*Kaifeng night market*), in northern China's Henan province. At night, Kaifeng's streets turn into veritable restaurants, with the specialty being northern-style dumplings.

Taking Your Chinese to Go

Restaurants are great, but once in a while you may want to mingle with the masses as people go about buying food for a home-cooked family dinner. Outdoor food markets abound in China and are great places to see how the locals shop and what they buy. And what better way to try out your Chinese? You can always point to what you want and discover the correct term for it from the vendor.

In addition to clothes, books, and kitchen utensils, outdoor markets may offer all sorts of food items:

>> **ròu** 肉 (row) (*meat*): **niúròu** 牛肉 (nyoe-row) (*beef*), **yángròu** 羊肉 (yahng-row) (*lamb*), or **jīròu** 鸡肉 (雞肉) (jee-row) (*chicken*)

>> **shuǐguǒ** 水果 (shway-gwaw) (*fruit*): **píngguǒ** 苹果 (蘋果) (peeng-gwaw) (*apples*) or **júzi** 桔子 (jyew-dzuh) (*oranges*)

>> **yú** 鱼 (魚) (yew) (*fish*): **xiā** 虾 (蝦) (shyah) (*shrimp*), **pángxiè** 螃蟹 (pahng-shyeh) (*crab*), **lóngxiā** 龙虾 (龍蝦) (loong-shyah) (*lobster*), or **yóuyú** 鱿鱼 (魷魚) (yo-yew) (*squid*)

Chinese people generally don't eat any raw food. The idea of a raw salad bar is truly foreign to them. In fact, **shēngcài** 生菜 (shung-tsye) (*lettuce*) literally translates as raw food, and the Chinese generally consider it fit only for farm animals.

Making comparisons

When you want to compare people or objects, you generally put the word **bǐ** 比 (bee) (*compared to*) between two nouns, followed by an adjective: A **bǐ** B (adjective). This construction means *A is more _____ than B*.

Here are a few examples:

Píngguǒ bǐ júzi hǎochī. 苹果比桔子好吃。(蘋果比橘子好吃。) (Peeng-gwaw bee jyew-dzuh how-chir.) (*Apples are tastier than oranges.*)

Tā bǐ nǐ niánqīng. 她比你年轻。(他比你年輕。) (Tah bee nee nyan-cheeng.) (*She's younger than you.*)

Zhèige fànguǎr bǐ nèige fànguǎr guì. 这个饭馆比那个饭馆贵。(這個飯館比那個飯館貴。) (Jay-guh fahn-gwar bee nay-guh fahng-gwar gway.) (*This restaurant is more expensive than that one.*)

How much is that thousand-year-old egg?

When you're ready to buy some foodstuffs, here are two simple ways to ask how much the products cost:

» **Duōshǎo qián?** 多少钱? (多少錢?) (Dwaw-shaow chyan?) (*How much money is it?*)

» **Jǐ kuài qián?** 几块钱? (幾塊錢?) (Jee kwye chyan?) (Literally: *How many dollars does it cost?*)

The only difference between the two questions is the implied amount of the cost. If you use the question word **duōshǎo** 多少 (dwaw–shaow), you want to inquire about something that's most likely more than $10. If you use **jǐ** 几 (幾) (jee) in front of **kuài** 块 (塊) (kwye) (*dollars*), you assume the product costs less than $10. (You can also use **jǐ** in front of **suì** 岁 (歲) (sway) (*years*) when you want to know how old a child under 10 is.)

Talkin' the Talk

At the local open-air market in Kaifeng, Margaret and Emmanuel eye some vegetables and discuss the price with the older man selling them in his stall.

Margaret: **Shīfu, qǐng wèn, nǐ yǒu méiyǒu bōcài?**
Shir-foo, cheeng one, nee yo may-yo baw-tsye?
Sir, may I ask, do you have any spinach?

Shīfu: **Dāngrán. Yào jǐ jīn?**
Dahng-rahn. Yaow jee jeen?
Of course. How many kilograms would you like?

Emmanuel:	**Wǒmen mǎi sān jīn, hǎo bùhǎo?** Waw-men my sahn jeen, how boo-how? *Let's get three kilograms, okay?*
Margaret:	**Hǎo. Sān jīn ba.** How. Sahn jeen bah. *Okay. It'll be three kilograms then.*
Shīfu:	**Méi wèntǐ. Yì jīn sān kuài qián. Nàmme, yígòng jiǔ kuài.** May one-tee. Ee jeen sahn kwye chyan. Nummuh, ee-goong jyoe kwye. *No problem. It's $3 a kilogram. So that will be $9 all together.*
Emmanuel:	**Děng yíxià. Bōcài bǐ gàilán guì duōle. Wǒmen mǎi gàilán ba.** Dung ee-shyah. Baw-tsye bee guy-lahn gway dwaw-luh. Waw-mun my guy-lahn bah. *Wait a minute. Spinach is more expensive than Chinese broccoli. Let's buy Chinese broccoli then.*
Shīfu:	**Hǎo. Gàilán liǎng kuài yì jīn. Hái yào sān jīn ma?** How. Guy-lahn lyahng kwye ee jeen. Hi yaow sahn jeen mah? *Okay. Chinese broccoli is $2 a kilogram. Do you still want three kilograms?*
Margaret:	**Shì de.** Shir duh. *Yes.*
Shīfu:	**Nà, sān jīn yígòng liù kuài.** Nah, sahn jeen ee-goong lyo kwye. *In that case, three kilograms will be $6.*
Emmanuel:	**Hǎo. Zhè shì liù kuài.** How. Juh shir lyoe kwye. *Okay. Here's $6.*
Shīfu:	**Xièxiè.** Shyeh-shyeh. *Thank you.*

Emmanuel:	**Xièxiè. Zàijiàn.**
	Shyeh-shyeh. Dzye-jyan.
	Thanks. Goodbye.
Shīfu:	**Zàijiàn.**
	Dzye-jyan.
	Goodbye.

WORDS TO KNOW

qīngzhēn ròu 清真肉	cheeng-juhn roe	halal meat
yóutài shíwù 犹太食物	yo-tye shir-woo	kosher food
chún sùshí 纯素食 (純素食)	chwun soo-shir	vegetarian food

CULTURAL
WISDOM

Shīfu 师傅 (師傅) (shir-foo) is a term used to indicate someone providing a service; it shows more respect due to age than the term **fúwùyuán** 服务员 (服務員) (foo-woo-ywan), which indicates any kind of attendant, does.

FUN & GAMES

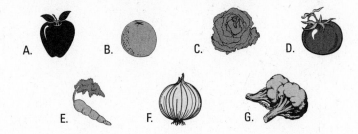

A.   B.   C.   D.

E.   F.   G.

Identify these fruits and vegetables and write their Chinese names below. Check out Appendix C for the answers.

A. _____

B. _____

C. _____

D. _____

E. _____

F. _____

G. _____

What's your favorite dish? Choose from Tables 8-5 and 8-7 to get some ideas.

I love diced chicken with cashew nuts. How about you?

Wǒ hěn xǐhuān <u>yāoguǒ jīdīng</u>. Nǐ ne?

Waw hun she-hwan yaow-gwaw jee-deeng. Nee nuh?

I love _____. How about you?

Wǒ hěn xǐhuān _____. Nǐ ne?

Waw hun she-hwan _____. Nee nuh?

I love _____. How about you?

Wǒ hěn xǐhuān _____. Nǐ ne?

Waw hun she-hwan _____. Nee nuh?

» **Looking for clothes and other items**

» **Bargaining for a better price**

Chapter 9

Shopping Made Easy

E ver dreamed of shopping till you dropped in a foreign country where the rate of exchange is really great? Or in faraway lands where lively outdoor night markets abound? This chapter helps you navigate both small shops and fancy department stores; get a handle on prices, colors, and merchandise; and in general negotiate the best deal wherever possible.

To **mǎi dōngxi** 买东西(買東西) (my doong-she) (*buy things*) is one of the most enjoyable pastimes for people the world over. Whether you're just going **guàng shāngdiàn** 逛商店 (gwahng shahng-dyan) (*window shopping*) or actually about to **mǎi dōngxi** doesn't matter. You can still enjoy looking at all the **shāngpǐn** 商品 (shahng-peen) (*merchandise*), fantasizing about buying that **zuànshí jièzhi** 钻石戒指 (鑽石戒指) (dzwan-shir jye-jir) (*diamond ring*), and haggling over the **jiàgé** 价格 (價格) (jyah-guh) (*price*).

REMEMBER

You can listen to all the Talkin' the Talk dialogues featured in this chapter. Go to www.dummies.com/go/chinese and click on the dialogue you want to hear.

Going to Stores

You can find all sorts of stores to meet your shopping needs throughout China. Table 9-1 presents some common store options.

TABLE 9-1   Kinds of Stores

Chinese	Pronunciation	English
bǎihuò shāngdiàn 百货商店 (百貨商店)	bye-hwaw shahng-dyan	*department store*
cài shìchǎng 菜市场 (菜市場)	tsye shir-chahng	*food market*
chàngpiàn diàn 唱片店	chahng-pyan dyan	*record store*
chāojí shìchǎng 超级市场 (超級市場)	chow-jee shir-chahng	*supermarket*
fúzhuāng diàn 服装店 (服裝店)	foo-jwahng dyan	*clothing store*
lǐpǐn diàn 礼品店 (禮品店)	lee-peen dyan	*gift shop*
shūdiàn 书店 (書店)	shoo-dyan	*bookstore*
wánjù diàn 玩具店	wahn-jyew dyan	*toy store*
wǔjīn diàn 五金店	woo-jeen dyan	*hardware store*
xié diàn 鞋店	shyeh dyan	*shoe store*
yàofáng 药房 (藥房)	yaow-fahng	*drugstore*
zhūbǎo diàn 珠宝店	joo-baow dyan	*jewelry store*

Here are some things you can find in various stores:

» **Zài yí ge shūdiàn nǐ kéyǐ mǎi shū, zázhì hé bàozhǐ.** 在一个书店你可以买书, 杂志和报纸. (在一個書店你可以買書, 雜誌和報紙.) (Dzye ee guh shoo-dyan nee kuh-yee my shoo, dzah-jir huh baow-jir.) (*In a bookstore, you can buy books, magazines, and newspapers.*)

» **Zài yí ge wǔjīn diàn nǐ kéyǐ mǎi zhuǎn jiē qì, chātóu hé yānwù bàojǐng qì.** 在一个五金店你可以买转接器, 插头和烟雾报警器. (在一個五金店你可以買轉接器, 插頭和煙霧報警器.) (Dzye ee guh woo-jeen dyan nee kuh-yee my jwan jyeh chee, chah-toe huh yan-woo baow-jeeng chee.) (*In a hardware store, you can buy adaptors, plugs, and smoke detectors.*)

» **Zài yíge zhūbǎo diàn nǐ kéyǐ mǎi shǒuzhuó, ěrhuán, xiàngliàn, xiōngzhēn hé jièzhi.** 在一个珠宝店你可以买手镯, 耳环, 项链, 胸针和戒指. (在一個珠寶店你可以買手鐲, 耳環, 項鍊, 胸針和戒指.) (Dzye ee-guh joo-baow dyan nee kuh-yee my show-jwaw, are-hwahn, shyahng-lyan, shyoong-juhn huh jyeh-jir.) (*In a jewelry store, you can buy bracelets, earrings, necklaces, pins, and rings.*)

When you finally make up your mind about what to shop for, you may want to call ahead to check out the store's hours. Here are some questions that can help:

» **Nǐmen wǔdiǎn zhōng yǐhòu hái kāi ma?** 你们五点钟以后还开吗? (你們五點鐘以後還開嗎?) (Nee-men woo-dyan joong ee-hoe hi kye mah?) (*Are you open after 5:00 p.m.?*)

» **Nǐmen Xīngqī tiān kāi bùkāi?** 你们星期天开不开? (你們星期天開不開?) (Nee-mun Sheeng-chee tyan kye boo-kye?) (*Are you open on Sundays?*)

» **Nín jǐdiǎn zhōng kāi/guānmén?** 您几点钟开/关门? (您幾點鐘開/關門?) (Neen jee-dyan joong kye/gwahn-mun?) (*What time do you open/close?*)

CULTURAL WISDOM

Most stores in China are open quite early, around 8:00 a.m., and don't close until 8:00 p.m. or even later. If you want a less harried shopping experience, avoid shopping on the weekends, when seemingly a quarter of humanity is out doing the same thing.

·············· Talkin' the Talk ··············

Margot and Charles discuss going shopping for the day. Here's how they start out.

Margot: **Wǒ jīntiān xiǎng qù mǎi dōngxi.**
Waw jin-tyan shyahng chyew my doong-she.
I want to go shopping today.

Charles: **Nǐ qù nǎr mǎi dōngxi?**
Nee chyew nar my doong-she?
Where will you go to shop?

Margot: **Wǒ yào qù bǎihuò shāngdiàn mǎi yīfu.**
Waw yaow chyew bye-hwaw shahng-dyan my ee-foo.
I want to go to the department store to buy some clothes.

Charles: **Tīngshuō zài zhège chénglǐ dōngxi dōu hěn guì.**
Teeng-shwaw dzye jay-guh chuhng-lee doong-she doe hun gway.
I've heard that everything's very expensive in this city.

Margot:	**Nà bùyídìng. Kàn shì shénme diàn. Yǒu de hěn guì, yǒu de yìdiǎn dōu búguì.**
	Nah boo-ee-deeng. Kahn shir shummuh dyan. Yo duh hun gway, yo duh ee-dyan doe boo-gway.
	Not necessarily. It depends on the store. Some are really expensive, and some aren't expensive at all.
Charles:	**Hǎo ba. Wǒmen zǒu ba. Wǒmen qù mǎi yīfu.**
	How bah. Waw-mun dzoe bah. Waw-mun chyew my ee-foo.
	Great. Let's go. Let's buy some clothes.

• •

WORDS TO KNOW

máoyī 毛衣	maow-ee	sweater
yùndòng shān 运动衫	yoon-doong shahn	sweatshirt
niúzǎikù 牛仔裤 (牛仔褲)	nyo-dzye-koo	jeans
bèixīn 背心	bay-sheen	tank top
yùndòng xié 运动鞋	yoon-doong shyeh	sneakers

GRAMMAR CHAT

Whenever you see the words **yìdiǎn dōu bú** 一点都不 (一點都不) (ee-dyan doe boo) before an adjective, it means *not at all (adjective)*. This construction is a great way to emphasize something. You can say something like **Wǒ yìdiǎn dōu búlèi.** 我一点都不累. (我一點都不累.) (Waw ee-dyan doe boo-lay.) (*I'm not tired in the least.*) or **Tā yìdiǎn dōu búpiàoliàng.** 她一点都不漂亮. (她一點都不漂亮.) (Tah ee-dyan doe boo-pyaow-lyahng.) (*She's not at all pretty.*) to get your point across.

Getting What You Want at a Department Store

If you don't have a clue how to begin shopping in China, much less what you want to buy, you may want to start off at one of the many luxury department stores that have sprouted up throughout China in the last decade. Here, you can get almost any name-brand thing you're looking for, from **zhūbǎo** 珠宝 (joo-baow) (*jewelry*) and **huāpíng** 花瓶 (hwah-peeng) (*vases*) to **yīfu** 衣服 (ee-foo) (*clothing*) and **yuèqì** 乐器 (樂器) (yweh-chee) (*musical instruments*).

Department stores aren't the only places you can shop, but they're certainly the easiest because everything is right there within walking distance and you can browse without fighting off vendors trying to push their wares.

CULTURAL WISDOM

Even though traditional alley markets and shop fronts still exist in China, Western-style shopping malls are quickly putting their imprint on places like Beijing and Shanghai. You can still get the best prices, though, at the many open-air markets and street vendors, which sell traditional arts and crafts and other specialties. Beijing's number-one shopping area isn't far from **Tiān'ānmén Square** 天安门 (天安門) (Tyan-ahn-mun Square) on **Wángfǔjǐng** 王府井 (Wahng-foo-jeeng) and **Dōngdān** 东单 (東單) (Doong-dahn) streets. Or on **Jiànguó mén wài Dàjiē** 建国门外大街 (建國門外大街) (Jyan-gwaw mun why Dah-jyeh) Avenue.

Just browsing

You may want to call ahead of time to see when the biggest department store in town opens before you decide to stroll on over. It's a nice day outside, you're in a mellow mood, all's right with the world, and all you want to do is just window shop — inside the store. You start out on the **dì yī céng** 第一层 (第一層) (dee ee tsuhng) (*first floor*), take the **zìdòng lóutī** 自动楼梯 (自動樓梯) (dzuh-doong low-tee) (*escalator*) all the way up to the **dì sān céng** 第三层 (第三層) (dee sahn tsuhng) (*third floor*), and enjoy checking out tons of **shāngpǐn** 商品 (shahng-peen) (*merchandise*) quietly by yourself, when all of a sudden a **shòuhuò yuán** 售货员 (售貨員) (show-hwaw ywan) (*salesperson*) sneaks up behind you and says **Nǐ xiǎng mǎi shénme?** 你想买什么? (你想買甚麼?) (Nee shyahng my shummuh?) (*What would you like to buy?*).

At this point, you really just want to be left alone, so you say **Wǒ zhǐ shì kànkàn. Xièxiè.** 我只是看看. 谢谢. (我只是看看. 謝謝.) (Waw jir shir kahn-kahn. Shyeh-shyeh.) (*I'm just looking. Thanks.*).

Asking for help

But what if you really do want help? First, you'd better look around for that salesperson you just told to go away. You may not find too many others nearby when you finally need them. If your luck holds, though, here are some questions you may want to ask:

» **Nǎr yǒu wàitào?** 哪儿有外套? (哪兒有外套?) (Nar yo why-taow?) (*Where are the jackets?*)

» **Néng bùnéng bāngmáng?** 能不能帮忙? (能不能幫忙?) (Nung boo-nung bahng-mahng?) (*Can you help me?*)

» **Nǐ yǒu méiyǒu Yīngwén de shū?** 你有没有英文的书? (你有沒有英文的書?) (Nee yo mayo Eeng-one duh shoo?) (*Do you have any books in English?*)

» **Nǐmen mài búmài guāngpán?** 你们卖不卖光盘? (你們賣不賣光盤?) (Nee-mun my boo-my gwahng-pahn?) (*Do you sell CDs?*)

» **Qǐng nǐ gěi wǒ kànkàn nǐ de xīzhuāng.** 请你给我看看你的西装. (請你給我看看你的西裝.) (Cheeng nee gay waw kahn-kahn nee duh she-jwahng.) (*Please show me your [Western] suits.*)

» **Wǒ zhǎo yì běn yǒu guān Zhōngguó lìshǐ de shū.** 我找一本有关中国历史的书. (我找一本有關中國歷史的書.) (Waw jaow ee bun yo gwan Joong-gwaw lee-shir duh shoo.) (*I'm looking for a book about Chinese history.*)

Talkin' the Talk

Tania is in a clothing store. She tries to get a fúwùyuán (foo-woo-ywan) (attendant) to help her locate dresses in her size.

Tania: **Xiǎojiě! Nǐ néng bāng wǒ ma?**
Shyaow-jyeh! Nee nung bahng waw mah?
Miss! Can you help me?

Fúwùyuán: **Kéyǐ. Qǐng děng yíxià.**
Kuh-yee. Cheeng dung ee-shyah.
Yes. Just a moment.

After the store attendant puts some boxes away, she returns to help Tania.

Fúwùyuán: **Hǎo. Nǐ yào mǎi shénme?**
How. Nee yaow my shummuh?
Okay. What did you want to buy?

Tania: **Nǎr yǒu qúnzi?**
Nar yo chwun-dzuh?
Where are the skirts?

Fúwùyuán: **Qúnzi jiù zài nàr.**
Chwun-dzuh jyo dzye nar.
The skirts are just over there.

WORDS TO KNOW

Nǐ kàn qǐlái hěn bàng! 你看起来很棒!	Nee kahn chee-lye hun bahng!	You look great!
Nǐ kàn qǐlái hěn zāogāo! 你看起来很糟糕!	Nee kahn chee-lye hun dzaow-gaow!	You look terrible!
Wǒ méiyǒu shénme kě chuān de. 我没有什么可穿的.	Waw may-yo shummuh kuh chwan duh.	I have nothing to wear.

Shopping for Clothes

Going shopping for clothes is an art — one requiring lots of patience and fortitude, not to mention lots of new vocabulary if you're going to do it in Chinese. You need to know how to ask for your own size, how to see whether something is available in a different color or fabric, and in general how to compare apples and oranges (or at least skirts and shirts).

What's your size?

If you ask for clothing in the **dàxiǎo** 大小 (dah–shyaow) (*size*) you're used to quoting in the United States when you're in Taiwan or mainland China, you're in for a surprise. The numbers you generally throw out when talking to salespeople in the United States are vastly different from the ones you have to get used to using when dealing with Chinese sizes.

Here are some useful phrases you may want to know:

>> **Dàxiǎo búduì.** 大小不对. (大小不對.) (Dah-shyaow boo-dway.) (*It's the wrong size.*)

>> **Hěn héshēn.** 很合身. (Hun huh-shun.) (*It fits really well.*)

>> **Nín chuān duō dà hào?** 您穿多大号? (您穿多大號?) (Neen chwan dwaw dah how?) (*What size are you?*)

>> **Zài Měiguó wǒde chǐcùn shì wǔ hào.** 在美国我的尺寸是五号. (在美國我的尺寸是五號.) (Dzye May-gwaw waw-duh chir-tswun shir woo how.) (*In America, I wear a size 5.*)

Instead of using the word **dàxiǎo**, you can say things like the following:

» **Nín chuān jǐ hào de chènshān?** 您穿几号的衬衫? (您穿幾號的襯衫?) (Neen chwahn jee how duh chun-shahn?) (*What size shirt do you wear?*)

» **Wǒ chuān sānshíqī hào.** 我穿三十七号. (我穿三十七號.) (Waw chwahn sahn-shir-chee how.) (*I wear a size 37.*)

» **Wǒ chuān xiǎohào.** 我穿小号. (我穿小號.) (Waw chwahn shyaow-how.) (*I wear a size small.*)

Of course, you can always guess your approximate size just by indicating you want to see something in one of the following categories:

» **xiǎo** 小 (shyaow) (*small*)

» **zhōng** 中 (joong) (*medium*)

» **dà** 大 (dah) (*large*)

Talkin' the Talk

Kathryn approaches a salesperson at a department store in Beijing. She's unsure of what size to ask for because the measurement systems are different in China than they are in the United States.

Kathryn:	**Xiǎojiě!**
	Shyaow-jyeh!
	Miss!

Fúwùyuán:	**Nǐ hǎo. Xiǎng mǎi shénme?**
	Nee how. Shyahng my shummuh?
	Hello. What would you like to buy?

Kathryn:	**Wǒ xiǎng mǎi yíjiàn jiákè.**
	Waw shyahng my ee-jyan jyah-kuh.
	I'm looking for a jacket.

Fúwùyuán:	**Hǎo ba. Nǐ chuān jǐ hào?**
	How bah. Nee chwahn jee how?
	Very well. What size are you?

Kathryn:	**Wǒ bùzhīdào. Měiguó de hàomǎ hé Zhōngguó de hàomǎ hěn bùyíyàng.**
	Waw boo-jir-daow. May-gwaw duh how-ma huh Joong-gwaw duh how-ma hun boo-ee-yahng.
	I don't know. American sizes are quite different from Chinese sizes.

Fúwùyuán:	**Wǒ gūjì nǐ chuān xiǎohào.**
	Waw goo-jee nee chwahn shyaow-how.
	I would estimate you wear a size small.

Kathryn:	**Hǎo ba. Nà, máfán nǐ gěi wǒ kànkàn xiǎohào de jiákè. Xièxiè.**
	How bah. Nah, mah-fahn nee gay waw kahn-kahn shyaow-how duh jyah-kuh. Shyeh-shyeh.
	That sounds about right. Would you mind showing me the small-size jackets, then? Thank you.

WORDS TO KNOW

liángxié 凉鞋 (涼鞋)	lyahng-shyeh	sandals
gāogēnxié 高跟鞋	gaow-gun-shyeh	high heels
xuēzi 靴子	shweh-dzuh	boots

Comparing quality: Good, better, best

When you want to let loose with a superlative in order to say something is absolutely the best — or, for that matter, the worst —always keep this one little word in mind: **zuì** 最 (dzway), which means *the most* (it's the equivalent of the suffix *–est*).

Zuì is a word just waiting for something to follow it; otherwise, it doesn't have much meaning. Here are some superlatives you may need to use from time to time:

>> **zuì hǎo** 最好 (dzway how) (*best*)

>> **zuì lèi** 最累 (dzway lay) (*the most tired*)

>> **zuì màn** 最慢 (dzway mahn) (*the slowest*)

>> **zuì máng** 最忙 (dzway mahng) (*the busiest*)

» **zuì qíguài** 最奇怪 (dzway chee-gwye) (*the strangest*)

» **zuì yǒumíng** 最有名 (dzway yo-meeng) (*the most famous*)

» **zuì yǒuqián** 最有钱 (最有錢) (dzway yo-chyan) (*the richest*)

If you just want to say that something is better than something else, or more something (not necessarily the best), you use the word **gèng** 更 (guhng) before an adjective. You can consider these the equivalent of the suffix *-er*. Another word that has the meaning of *more* or *-er* is **yìdiǎn** 一点 (一點) (ee-dyan). Although the term **gèng** comes before an adjective, the term **yìdiǎn** must appear after the adjective. Instead of saying **gèng kuài** 更快 (gung kwye) (*faster*), for example, you'd say **kuài yìdiǎn** 快一点 (快一點) (kwye ee-dyan) to mean *faster*.

Here are some examples:

gèng cōngmíng 更聪明 (更聰明) (guhng tsoong-meeng) (*smarter*)

gèng hǎo 更好 (guhng how) (*better*)

gèng guì 更贵 (更貴) (guhng gway) (*more expensive*)

gèng piányi 更便宜 (gung pyan-yee) (*cheaper*)

piányi yìdiǎn 便宜一点 (便宜一點) (pyan-yee ee-dyan) (*cheaper*)

gèng kuài 更快 (guhng kwye) (*faster*)

gèng màn 更慢 (guhng mahn) (*slower*)

duǎn yìdiǎn 短一点 (短一點) (dwahn ee-dyan) (*shorter*)

cháng yìdiǎn 长一点 (長一點) (chahng ee-dyan) (*longer*)

xiǎo yìdiǎn 小一点 (小一點) (shyaow ee-dyan) (*smaller*)

dà yìdiǎn 大一点 (大一點) (dah ee-dyan) (*larger*)

Comparing two items

The simplest way to compare two items is by using the *coverb* (the part of speech akin to a preposition) **bǐ** 比 (bee) (*compared with*) between the two things you're comparing, followed by an adjective. If you say **A bǐ B hǎo.** A 比 B 好. (A bee B how.), you're saying *A is better than B*.

Here are some ways to make comparisons with **bǐ**:

Hóngde bǐ huángde hǎo. 红的比黄的好. (紅的比黃的好. (Hoong-duh bee hwahng-duh how.) (*The red one is better than the yellow one.*)

Tā bǐ wǒ lǎo. 她比我老. (Tah bee waw laow.) (*She's older than me.*)

Zhèige wūzi bǐ nèige dà. 这个屋子比那个大. (這個屋子比那個大.) (Jay-guh woo-dzuh bee nay-guh dah.) (*This room is bigger than that one.*)

One way to convey similarity between two things is to use the coverbs **gēn** 跟 (gun) or **hé** 和 (huh) between the two things being compared, followed by the word **yíyàng** 一样 (一樣) (ee-yahng) (*the same*) and then the adjective. So if you say **A gēn B yíyàng dà.** A 跟 B 一样大. (A 跟 B 一樣大.) (A gun B ee-yahng dah.), you're saying that A and B are equally large or are as big as each other. You can also just say **A gēn B yíyàng,** meaning *A and B are the same.* Here are some other things you can say with this sentence pattern:

» **Gēge hé dìdi yíyàng gāo.** 哥哥和弟弟一样高. (哥哥和弟弟一樣高.) (Guh-guh huh dee-dee ee-yahng gaow.) (*My older brother is as tall as my younger brother.*)

» **Māo gēn gǒu yíyàng tiáopí.** 猫跟狗一样调皮. (貓跟狗一樣調皮.) (Maow gun go ee-yahng tyaow-pee.) (*Cats are just as naughty as dogs.*)

» **Wǒ gēn nǐ yíyàng dà.** 我跟你一样大. (我跟你一樣大.) (Waw gun nee ee-yahng dah.) (*You and I are the same age.*)

So what if you want to make a negative comparison, such as *I'm not as tall as him?* For that, you have to use the following sentence pattern: **A méiyǒu B nàme (adjective).** A 没有 B 那么 (那麼) (adjective). (A mayo B nah-muh [adjective].) (*A isn't as [adjective] as B.*). You can see this pattern in action in the following sentences:

Shāyú méiyǒu jīnyú nàme kě'ài. 鲨鱼没有金鱼那么可爱. (鯊魚沒有金魚那麼可愛.) (Shah-yew mayo jeen-yew nah-muh kuh-eye.) (*Sharks aren't as cute as goldfish.*)

Yīngwén méiyǒu Zhōngwén nàme nán. 英文没有中文那么难. (英文沒有中文那麼難.) (Eeng-one mayo Joong-one nah-muh nahn.) (*English isn't as difficult as Chinese.*)

Māo de wěiba méiyǒu tùzi de wěiba nàme cū. 猫的尾巴没有兔子的尾巴那么粗. (猫的尾巴没有兔子的尾巴那么粗.) (Maow duh way-bah mayo too-dzuh duh way-bah nah-muh tsoo.) (*Cats' tails aren't as thick as the tails of rabbits.*)

Talkin' the Talk

Olivia and Lěiléi go shopping and check out some traditional Chinese women's dresses known as **qípáo** (chee-paow). Those are the ankle-length dresses with high necks and a high slit up the side of one leg.

Olivia: **Zhèi jiàn qípáo zěnme yàng?**
           Jay jyan chee-paow dzummuh yahng?
           What do you think of this traditional Chinese dress?

Lěiléi: **Wǒ juéde hěn hǎo.**
           Waw jweh-duh hun how.
           I think it looks great.

Olivia: **Zhēnde ma?**
           Jun-duh mah?
           Really?

Lěiléi: **Zhēnde. Kěshì jīnsè de méiyǒu hóng de nàme piàoliàng.**
           Jun-duh. Kuh-shir jeen-suh duh mayo hoong-duh nah-muh pyaow-lyahng.
           Really. But the gold one isn't as pretty as the red one.

Olivia: **Jīnsè de hé hóng de yíyàng guì ma?**
           Jeen-suh duh huh hoong duh ee-yahng gway mah?
           Are the gold one and the red one the same price?

Lěiléi: **Méiyǒu. Jīnsè de bǐ hóng de piányi.**
           Mayo. Jeen-suh duh bee hoong duh pyan-yee.
           No. The gold one is less expensive than the red one.

Olivia: **Nà, wǒ jiù mǎi jīnsè de.**
           Nah, waw jyoe my jeen-suh duh.
           In that case, I'll buy the gold one.

GRAMMAR CHAT

You can use two classifiers when it comes to clothing: **jiàn** and **tiáo.** *Classifiers* are the words used between a number or the words *this* or *that* and the clothing you're talking about. You use **jiàn** when you're talking about clothing worn on the upper part of the body and **tiáo** for clothes worn on the lower part. So you say **yíjiàn chènshān** 一件衬衫（一件襯衫）(ee-jyan chun-shahn) (*one shirt*) or **sāntiáo kùzi** 三条裤子（三條褲子）(sahn-tyaow koo-dzuh) (*three pairs of pants*).

What are you wearing? Chuān versus dài

Dài 戴 (dye) and **chuān** 穿 (chwan) both mean *to wear*, but they're used for different types of things you put on your body. In English, you can say you're wearing everything from hats to socks to skirts to even a necklace. In Chinese, though, you can only **dài** things like **màozi** 帽子 (maow–dzuh) (*hats*), **yǎnjìng** 眼镜 (镜) (yan-jeeng) (*glasses*), and **wéi jīn** 围巾 (圍巾) (way jeen) (*scarf*) — in other words, articles more akin to accessories than to actual clothing. However, you **chuān** things like **qúnzi** 裙子 (chewn–dzuh) (*skirts*), **dàyī** 大衣 (dah–ee) (*coats*), and **xiézi** 鞋子 (shyeh–dzuh) (*shoes*).

Here are some things you can **chuān**:

>> **bèixīn** 背心 (bay-sheen) (*vest*)

>> **cháng kù** 长裤 (長褲) (chahng koo) (*pants*)

>> **cháng xiù** 长袖 (長袖) (chahng shyow) (*long-sleeved shirt*)

>> **chènshān** 衬衫 (襯衫) (chun-shahn) (*blouse*)

>> **dàyī** 大衣 (dah-ee) (*coat*)

>> **duǎnkù** 短裤 (短褲) (dwan-koo) (*shorts*)

>> **duǎn xiù** 短袖 (dwahn shyow) (*short-sleeved shirt*)

>> **gāogēnxiě** 高跟鞋 (gaow-gun-shyeh) (*high heels*)

>> **jiákè** 夹克 (夾克) (jyah-kuh) (*jacket*)

>> **kùzi** 裤子 (褲子) (koo-dzuh) (*pants*)

>> **nèiyī** 内衣 (nay-ee) (*underwear*)

>> **niúzǎikù** 牛仔裤 (牛仔褲) (nyo-dzye-koo) (*blue jeans*)

>> **qúnzi** 裙子 (chewn-dzuh) (*skirt*)

>> **tuōxié** 拖鞋 (twaw-shyeh) (*slippers*)

>> **wàzi** 袜子 (襪子) (wah-dzuh) (*socks*)

>> **yǔyī** 雨衣 (yew-ee) (*raincoat*)

Here are some things you can **dài** but not **chuān**:

>> **lǐngdài** 领带 (領帶) (leen-dye) (*necktie*)

>> **shǒubiǎo** 手表 (show-byaow) (*wristwatch*)

» **shǒutào** 手套 (show-taow) (*gloves*)

» **zhūbǎo** 珠宝 (joo-baow) (*jewelry*)

Asking about the color and material

When you go shopping for clothes, you have a chance to compare all the different **yánsè** 颜色 (顏色) (yan-suh) (*colors*) they come in and choose the one that looks the best on you. Do you generally prefer **dān sè** 单色 (單色) (dahn-suh) (*solid colors*) or **huā** 花 (hwah) (*patterned*) shirts? What about a **shēn yìdiǎn** 深一点 (深一點) (shun ee-dyan) (*darker*) or **dàn yìdiǎn** 淡一点 (淡一點) (dahn ee-dyan) (*lighter*) shade? Whatever your clothing preferences are, after you know how to express your heart's desire with the correct word, you can be sure to ask for what you like.

The following is a list of handy words to use the next time you go shopping either for clothes or for material to create your own. **Shénme yánsè** 什么颜色 (甚麼顏色) (shummuh yan-suh) (*what color*) is your favorite from the following list? Don't be shy to speak up about your preferences. If someone wants you to wear pink with purple polka dots to a wedding, you can always politely just say **Yánsè búduì.** 颜色不对. (顏色不對.) (Yan-suh boo-dway.) (*The color is wrong.*) and leave it at that.

» **bái** 白 (bye) (*white*)

» **fēnhóng** 粉红 (粉紅) (fun-hoong) (*pink*)

» **hēi** 黑 (hey) (*black*)

» **hóng** 红 (紅) (hoong) (*red*)

» **huáng** 黄 (hwahng) (*yellow*)

» **júhóng** 橘红 (橘紅) (jyew-hoong) (*orange*)

» **lán** 蓝 (藍) (lahn) (*blue*)

» **zǐ** 紫 (dzuh) (*purple*)

Liàozi 料子 (lyaow-dzuh) (*fabric*) is another important consideration when you're picking out clothes. Check out these terms for common clothing materials:

» **duànzi** 缎子 (緞子) (dwahn-dzuh) (*satin*)

» **kāisīmǐ** 开司米 (開司米) (kye-suh-mee) (*cashmere*)

» **sīchóu** 丝绸 (絲綢) (suh-cho) (*silk*)

» **yángmáo** 羊毛 (yahng-maow) (*wool*)

Talkin' the Talk

Selena goes shopping for sweaters with her friend Laurie and asks her to weigh in on which color looks best on her.

Selena: **Zhèi jiàn máoyī nǐ juéde zěnmeyàng?**
Jay jyan maow-ee nee jweh-duh dzummuh-yahng?
What do you think of this sweater?

Laurie: **Nèi jiàn máoyī tài xiǎo. Yánsè yě búpiàoliàng.**
Nay jyan maow-ee tye shyaow. Yan-suh yeh boo-pyaow-lyahng.
That sweater is too small. The color doesn't look good either.

Selena: **Nǐ xǐhuān shénme yánsè?**
Nee she-hwahn shummuh yan-suh?
What color do you like?

Laurie: **Wǒ xǐhuān hóngde. Búyào nèige hēi de.**
Waw she-hwahn hoong-duh. Boo-yaow nay-guh hey duh.
I like the red one. You shouldn't get the black one.

Selena: **Hǎole. Nà, wǒ jiù mǎi hóng de ba.**
How-luh. Nah, waw jyo my hoong duh bah.
Okay. In that case, I'll buy the red one.

GRAMMAR CHAT

When the possessive particle **de** is attached to an adjective and there's no noun following it, it can be translated as *the one that is (adjective)*, as in **hóng de** 红的 (紅的) (hoong duh) (*the red one*), **dà de** 大的 (dah–duh) (*the big one*), **tián de** 甜的 (tyan duh) (*the sweet one*), and so on.

Shopping for Other Items

Of course, clothes aren't the only things in the world to shop for (although I know some would beg to differ with me). How about some antiques or high-tech toys? The possibilities are endless in this consumer–oriented world.

Hunting for antiques

One of the best places in the world to go searching for **gǔdǒng** 古董 (goo-doong) (*antiques*) is — you guessed it — China. **Gǔdǒng diàn** 古董店 (goo-doong dyan) (*antique shops*) abound in major cities near large stores and in small alleyways. You can buy everything from 200-year-old **diāokè pǐn** 雕刻品 (dyaow-kuh peen) (*carved objects*) to 100-year-old **bíyān hú** 鼻烟壶 (鼻煙壺) (bee-yan who) (*snuff bottles*). You can find all sorts of rare things.

After you find the perfect antique item, though, you need to deal with all the possible export restrictions, like for porcelain that is older than 200 years or some types of rare wood products. You have to have a red wax seal put on the item in order to legally take it out of China. The cultural artifacts bureau of the city in which you buy the item must apply the seal.

CULTURAL WISDOM

Slightly southwest of **Tiān'ānmén Square** in **Beijing** lies **Liúlì chǎng** 琉璃厂 (琉璃廠) (Lyoe-lee chahng), an area considered the best in the city for antiques and other traditional arts and crafts. In **Shanghai**, the **Dōngtái** 东台 (東台) (Doong-tye) antiques market is the one to look for, not far from **Huáihǎi Lù** 淮海路 (Hwye-hi Loo). You can even find a Ghost Market in the Old Town Bazaar where folks go for weekend antique shopping. The Ghost Market is so named because of the ungodly hour the vendors begin setting up shop — a time before sunrise when only ghosts can check out what's on sale. Even though you're dealing with antiques, you're still allowed to haggle over the price, so don't be shy trying to get the best deal possible.

Here are some words and phrases that come in handy when you're hunting for antiques:

>> **dēnglóng** 灯笼 (燈籠) (dung-loong) (*lantern*)

>> **fóxiàng** 佛像 (faw-shyahng) (*Buddhas*)

>> **gǔdǒng jiājù** 古董家具 (goo-doong jyah-jyew) (*antique furniture*)

>> **gùizi** 柜子 (櫃子) (gway-dzuh) (*chest*)

>> **jìbài yòng de zhuōzi** 祭拜用的桌子 (jee-bye yoong duh jwaw-dzuh) (*altar table*)

>> **jǐngtàilán** 景泰蓝 (景泰藍) (jeeng-tye-lahn) (*cloisonné*)

>> **píngfēng** 屏风 (屏風) (peeng-fung) (*screen*)

>> **shénxiàng** 神像 (shun-shyahng) (*idol*)

>> **shūfǎ** 书法 (書法) (shoo-fah) (*calligraphy*)

» **xiōngzhēn** 胸针 (胸針) (shyoong-juhn) (*brooch*)

» **xiùhuā zhìpǐn** 绣花制品 (繡花製品) (shyow-hwah jir-peen) (*embroidery*)

» **yù** 玉 (yew) (*jade*)

These sentences can help you find precisely what you're looking for and avoid surprises when you try to take your treasures home:

» **Kéyǐ bù kéyǐ jiā zhúnxǔ chūguó de huò qī yìn?** 可以不可以加准许出国的货器印? (可以不可以加准許出國的貨器印?) (Kuh-yee boo kuh-yee jyah jwun-shyew choo-gwaw duh hwaw chee yeen?) (*Can you put the export seal on it?*)

» **Něi ge cháodài de?** 哪个朝代的? (哪個朝代的?) (Nay guh chaow-dye duh?) (*Which dynasty is it from?*)

» **Néng dài chūguó ma?** 能带出国吗? (能帶出國嗎?) (Nung dye choo-gwaw mah?) (*Can it be taken out of China?*)

» **Nǐ de gǔdǒng dìtǎn zài nǎr?** 你的古董地毯在哪儿? (你的古董地毯在哪兒?) (Nee duh goo-doong dee-tahn dzye nar?) (*Where are your antique carpets?*)

» **Zhège duōshǎo nián?** 这个多少年? (這個多少年?) (Jay-guh dwaw-shaow nyan?) (*How old is this?*)

» **Zhèi shì něige cháodài de?** 这是哪个朝代的? (這是哪個朝代的?) (Jay shir nay-guh chaow-dye duh?) (*Which dynasty is this from?*)

Getting a Good Price and Paying

Folks the world over want to get good deals on their purchases. At least they should. This section helps you discover the joys (and pitfalls) of haggling in Chinese.

Negotiating prices at the night market

One of the fun things to do in Taiwan and mainland China is to visit one of the lively night markets that abound. There, you can find anything from clothing and jewelry to antiques and food. Because the Chinese love to shop and **tǎojià huánjià** 讨价还价 (討價還價) (taow–jyah hwahn–jyah) (*haggle*), you have plenty of company on your sojourns.

You should always assume that prices are negotiable in an open air market. You can always ask one of the following and see what happens:

» **Néng bùnéng piányì yìdiǎr?** 能不能便宜一点儿? (能不能便宜一點兒?) (Nung boo-nung pyan-yee ee-dyar?) (*Can you sell it more cheaply?*)

» **Néng bùnéng shǎo yìdiǎr?** 能不能少一点儿? (能不能少一點兒?) (Nung boo-nung shaow ee-dyar?) (*Can you lower the price?*)

Or you can always play hardball and say something like **Zěnme zhème guì ah?** 怎么这么贵啊? (怎麼這麼貴啊?) (Dzuh-muh juh-muh gway ah?) (*Why is this so expensive?*) in an exasperated voice, start walking away, and see what happens. (Bet they come back with a lower price.)

These haggling-related phrases are also worth knowing:

» **Dǎzhé, hǎo bùhǎo?** 打折, 好不好? (Dah-juh, how boo-how?) (*How about giving me a discount?*)

» **Kéyǐ jiǎngjià ma?** 可以讲价吗? (可以講價嗎?) (Kuh-yee jyahng-jyah mah?) (*Can we negotiate the price?*)

» **Nǐmen yào búyào Měiyuán?** 你们要不要美元? (你們要不要美元?) (Nee-men yaow boo-yaow May-ywan?) (*Do you want U.S. dollars?*)

» **Zhèige duōshǎo qián?** 这个多少钱? (這個多少錢?) (Jay-guh dwaw-shaow chyan?) (*How much is this?*)

CULTURAL WISDOM

If you see something called a **Yǒuyí Shāngdiàn** 友谊商店 (友誼商店) (Yo-ee Shahng-dyan) (*Friendship Store*), be aware that it's one of the ubiquitous state-run stores in China, so prices are generally fixed. However, bargaining is the norm everywhere else. Beware of goods with no prices marked on them! If you ask about them, you'll probably be quoted a price far different than that charged to the locals. Often, you can get 5 to 10 percent taken off any price quoted verbally, so try to practice bargaining before you set foot in a street market.

Paying for your purchase (or demanding a refund)

When you finish checking out all the merchandise, haggling (or not) over the price, and deciding on just what to buy, you probably start reaching for your **qiánbāo** 钱包 (錢包) (chyan-baow) (*wallet*) to see whether you should take out your **xìnyòngkǎ** 信用卡 (sheen-yoong-kah) (*credit card*) or some **xiànqián** 现钱 (現錢) (shyan-chyan) (*cash*) or, if you got a really good deal, just some **língqián** 零钱 (零錢)

(leeng-chyan) (*small change*). When you **fùqián** 付钱 (付錢) (foo-chyan) (*pay*), you may also want to get a **shōujù** 收据 (收據) (show-jyew) (*receipt*).

If you end up being **bùyúkuài** 不愉快 (boo-yew-kwye) (*unhappy*) about your purchase, you try to **tuì huí** 退回 (tway hway) (*return*) your merchandise by saying: **Duì wǒ bù héshēn.** 对我不合身. (對我不合身.) (Dway waw boo huh-shun.) (*It doesn't fit me.*)

>> **Qǐng nǐ bǎ qián jìrù wǒ de xìnyòngkǎ.** 请你把钱计入我的信用卡. (請你把錢计入我的信用卡.) (Cheeng nee bah chyan jee-roo waw duh sheen-yoong-kah.) (*Please refund my credit card.*)

>> **Wǒ néng bùnéng jiàn zǒngjīnglǐ?** 我能不能见总经理? (我能不能見總經理?) (Waw nung boo-nung jyan dzoong-jeeng-lee?) (*May I see the manager?*)

>> **Wǒ yào tuìkuǎn.** 我要求退款. (Waw yaow tway-kwahn.) (*I want a refund.*)

>> **Wǒ yào tuìhuò.** 我要退货 (我要退貨) (Waw yaow tway-hwaw.) (*I would like to return this.*)

Here's how you ask for change:

Nǐ yǒu méiyǒu yí kuài qián de língqián? 你有没有一块钱的零钱? (你有没有一塊錢的零錢?) (Nee yo mayo ee kwye chyan duh leeng-chyan?) (*Do you have change for a dollar?*)

FUN & GAMES

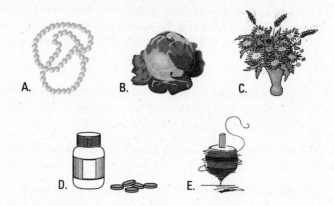

A.   B.   C.

D.   E.

Take a look at the illustrations. In what type of store would you find these items? Choose from among the following: yàofáng, cài shìchǎng, zhūbǎo diàn, huā diàn, wánjù diàn, yàofáng. The answers are in Appendix C.

A. _____

B. _____

C. _____

D. _____

E. _____

You absolutely MUST go somewhere today. Where will it be? If it was me, I'd say: **Wǒ děi qù fúzhuāng diàn.** 我得去服装店。(我得去服装店。) (Waw day chyew foo-jwahng dyan.) (*I must go to the clothing store.*) How about you? Let the world know by filling in the blanks below.

Wǒ děi qù _____. **Waw day chyew** _____.

Wǒ děi qù _____. **Waw day chyew** _____.

You are the busiest person in the world! **Nǐ shì quán shìjiè zuì máng de rén!** 你是全世界最忙的人! (你是全世界最忙的人!) (Nee shir chwan shir-jieh dzway mahng duh run.) Now tell me what I am!

Nǐ shì quán shìjiè zuì ____ de rén! (Nee shir chwan shir-jieh dzway _____ duh run.) (*You are the most ____ person!*)

Nǐ shì quán shìjiè zuì ____ de rén!

Nǐ shì quán shìjiè zuì ____ de rén!

Chapter **10**
Exploring the Town

Don't even think of staying around your hotel or house on a beautiful sunny day — especially if you're about to explore a new **chéngshì** 城市 (chuhng-shir) (*city*) in China. You have so much to see and do. You may want to check out a performance of Peking Opera or head over to the nearest museum to take in an art exhibit. Or perhaps a movie or concert and a nightcap are more your style. However you want to spend your time in town, this chapter gives you the vocab you need.

REMEMBER

You can listen to all the Talkin' the Talk dialogues featured in this chapter. Go to www.dummies.com/go/chinese and click on the dialogue you want to hear.

Attending a Performance

Plan on taking in a few **yǎnchū** 演出 (yan-choo) (*shows*) in the near future? You have so much to choose from nowadays. You can check out some **gējù** 歌剧 (歌劇) (guh-jyew) (*operas*), or, if you prefer, a **bāléiwú** 芭蕾舞 (bah-lay-woo) (*ballet*) or a **yīnyuè huì** 音乐会 (音樂會) (een-yweh hway) (*music concert*).

CULTURAL WISDOM

Shanghai in particular is pretty famous for its **zájì tuán** 杂技团 (雜技團) (dzah-jee twahn) (*acrobatics troupes*).

The following sections help you talk about all sorts of performances, from naming your favorite kind of music to getting your tickets and chatting about others' experiences.

Exploring different types of music

You often hear that the language of music crosses international boundaries. If you're feeling a bit exhausted after practicing Chinese, you can head to a musical event in the evening where you can relax. Let the music transport you to another mental space.

Here are some terms to help you talk about music and performances:

>> **dài wèi yuán** 带位员 (帶位員) (dye way ywan) (*usher*)

>> **gēchàng huì** 歌唱会 (歌唱會) (guh-chahng hway) (*choral recital*)

>> **gǔdiǎn yīnyuè** 古典音乐 (古典音樂) (goo-dyan een-yweh) (*classical music*)

>> **jiāoxiǎng yuè** 交响乐 (交響樂) (jyaow-shyahng yweh) (*symphonic music*)

>> **jiémù dān** 节目单 (節目單) (jyeh-moo-dahn) (*program*)

>> **jùchǎng** 剧场 (劇場) (jyew-chahng) (*theatre*)

>> **juéshì yīnyuè** 爵士音乐 (爵士音樂) (jyweh-shir een-yweh) (*jazz music*)

>> **lǐtáng** 礼堂 (禮堂) (lee-tahng) (*auditorium*)

>> **míngē** 民歌 (meen-guh) (*folk song*)

>> **mùjiān xiūxi** 幕间休息 (幕間休息) (moo-jyan shyo-she) (*intermission*)

>> **péngkè yáogǔn yīnyuè** 朋克摇滚音乐 (朋克搖滾音樂) (pung-kuh yaow-gwun een-yweh) (*punk rock*)

>> **qìyuè** 器乐 (器樂) (chee yweh) (*instrumental music*)

>> **shìnèi yuè** 室内乐 (室內樂) (shir-nay yweh) (*chamber music*)

>> **shuōchàng yīnyuè** 说唱音乐 (說唱音乐) (shwaw-chahng een-yweh) (*rap music*)

>> **yáogǔnyuè** 摇滚乐 (搖滾樂) (yaow-gun-yweh) (*rock 'n' roll*)

>> **Zhōngguó gǔdiǎn yīnyuè** 中国古典音乐 (中國古典音樂) (Joong-gwaw goo-dyan een-yweh) (*classical Chinese music*)

CULTURAL WISDOM

At the end of a concert in China, you don't hear anyone yelling "Encore!" What you do hear is **Zài lái yíge, zài lái yíge!** 再来一个! (再來一個!) (Dzye lye ee-guh, dzye lye ee-guh!) (*Bring on one more!*).

Talkin' the Talk

Wendy and Michael discuss what kind of concert to attend this weekend.

Michael: **Wǒmen zhèige zhōumò qù yīnyuè tīng tīng Zhōngguó gǔdiǎn yīnyuè ba.**
Waw-men jay-guh joe-maw chyew een-yweh teeng teeng Joong-gwaw goo-dyan een-yweh bah.
Let's go to the concert hall to hear a classical Chinese music concert this weekend.

Wendy: **Wǒ bùxǐhuān Zhōngguó gǔdiǎn yīnyuè. Wǒ gèng xǐhuān juéshì yīnyuè.**
Waw boo-she-hwahn Joong-gwaw goo-dyan yeen-yweh. Waw gung she-hwahn jyweh-shir een-yweh.
I don't like classical Chinese music. I prefer jazz.

Michael: **Juéshì yīnyuè tài qíguài. Yáogǔn yuè yě bùxǐhuān.**
Jyweh-shir een-yweh tye chee-gwye. Yaow-gwun yweh yeh boo-she-hwahn.
Jazz is too strange. I also don't like rock 'n' roll.

Wendy: **Nǐ dàgài zhǐ xǐhuān jiāoxiǎng yuè nèi lèi de yīnyuè ba.**
Nee dah-gye jir she-hwahn jyaow-shyahng yweh nay lay duh een-yweh bah.
You probably only like symphonic music and that sort of thing.

Michael: **Duì le.**
Dway luh.
Yup.

WORDS TO KNOW

Jīngjù 京剧 (京劇)	Jeeng-jyew	Peking Opera
shuōchàng 说唱 (說唱)	shwaw-chahng	rap music
jiézòu lándiào 节奏蓝调 (節奏藍調)	jyeh-dzoe lahn-dyaow	rhythm and blues
mínjiān yīnyuè 民间音乐 (民間音樂)	meen-jyan yeen-yweh	folk music

Buying a ticket

Before you can attend any performances, however, you have to buy a **piào** 票 (pyaow) (*ticket*) or two. The following phrases should help you get what you want, or at least understand what you're being told:

>> **Duìbùqǐ, jīntiān wǎnshàng de piào dōu màiwán le.** 对不起, 今天晚上的票 都卖完了. (對不起, 今天晚上的票都賣完了.) (Dway-boo-chee, jin-tyan wahn-shahng duh pyaow doe my-wahn luh.) (*I'm sorry, tickets for tonight are all sold out.*)

>> **Shénme shíhòu kāiyǎn?** 什么时侯开演? (甚麼時候開演?) (Shummuh shir-ho kye-yan?) (*What time does the show begin?*)

>> **Shénme shíhòu yǎn wán?** 什么时侯演完? (甚麼時候演完?) (Shummuh shir-ho yan wahn?) (*What time does the show end?*)

>> **Wǒ yào mǎi yì zhāng dàrén piào, liǎng zhāng értóng piào.** 我要买一张大人 票, 两张儿童票. (我要買一張大人票, 兩張兒童票.) (Waw yaow my ee jahng dah-run pyaow, lyahng jahng are-toong pyaow.) (*I'd like to buy one adult ticket and two kid's tickets.*)

>> **Yǒu méiyǒu jīntiān wǎnshàng yǎnchū de piào?** 有没有今天晚上演出的票? (Yo may-yo jin-tyan wahn-shahng yan-choo duh pyaow?) (*Are there any tickets to tonight's performance?*)

>> **Zài nǎr kéyǐ mǎi dào piào?** 在哪儿可以买到票? (在哪兒可以買到票?) (Dzye nar kuh-yee my daow pyaow?) (*Where can I buy tickets?*)

Asking whether someone has done something

CULTURAL WISDOM

If you're thinking of going out on the town with a new date, and you want to ask that person whether he or she has ever done something so you can plan something special, just add the particle **–guò** 过 (過) (gwaw) to the verb and use the question word **ma** 吗 (嗎) (mah) or **méiyǒu** 没有 (mayo) at the end. Here are some examples:

Nǐ kànguò Jīngjù ma? 你看过京剧吗? (你看過京劇嗎?) (Nee kahn-gwaw Jeeng-jyew mah?) (*Have you ever seen Peking Opera?*)

Nǐ chīguò xiā méiyǒu? 你吃过虾没有? (你吃過蝦沒有?) (Nee chir-gwaw shyah mayo?) (*Have you ever eaten shrimp?*)

Nǐ qùguò Měiguó ma? 你去过美国吗? (你去過美國嗎?) (Nee chyew-gwaw May-gwaw mah?) (*Have you ever been to America?*)

TAKING A PEEK AT PEKING OPERA

Have you ever been to **Jīngjù** (Jeeng-jyew) (*Peking Opera*)? This Chinese opera is one of the most beloved art forms in China, with a history of over 200 years. The opera is a great spectacle of music, song, and acrobatics, telling and retelling great works of Chinese history and literature. Performances abound, especially during the traditional festivals when everyone is off work.

Even though its title is Peking (Beijing) Opera, it actually originated in the Anhui and Hubei provinces. Originally staged for the royal family, it came to Beijing in 1790 and later became familiar to the general public. Thousands of local branches of Chinese Opera exist (including Peking), each with a unique dialect. Opera is the one art form in a country of over 1 billion people that appeals to every level of society.

To answer any of these questions, you can repeat the verb plus **guò** if the answer is yes, or simply say **méiyǒu,** meaning *No, I haven't.* You can also say **méiyǒu** [verb] **guò** if you want.

If you happen to do something **chángcháng** 常常 (chahng-chahng) (*often*) or just **yǒu de shíhòu** 有的时侯 (yo duh shir-ho) (*sometimes*), don't be shy about saying so. You can use these adverbs in both the questions and the answers.

Exploring Museums and Galleries

Theatre shows and live musical performances aren't the only forms of entertainment you can see to get your fill of **wénhuà** 文化 (one-hwah) (*culture*). One of the nicest, calmest activities to do at your own pace is to visit a **bówùguǎn** 博物馆 (博物館) (baw-woo-gwahn) (*museum*) or **huàláng** 画廊 (畫廊) (hwah-lahng) (*gallery*).

You can check out anything from **gǔdài de yìshù pǐn** 古代的艺术品 (古代的藝術品) (goo-dye duh ee-shoo peen) (*ancient artifacts*) to **shānshuǐ huà** 山水画 (山水畫) (shahn-shway hwah) (*landscape painting*) to **xiàndài yìshù** 现代艺术 (現代藝術) (shyan-dye ee-shoo) (*modern art*). Sometimes the best reason to go to a **bówùguǎn** is to buy some **lǐwù** 礼物 (禮物) (lee-woo) (*gifts*) and some cool **zhāo tiē** 招贴 (招貼) (jaow tyeh) (*posters*) for yourself.

Here are some questions you may want to ask in a museum or gallery:

>> **Bówùguǎn jǐdiǎn zhōng kāimén?** 博物馆几点钟开门? (博物館幾點鐘開門?) (Baw-woo-gwahn jee-dyan joong kye-mun?) (*What time does the museum open?*)

>> **Lǐpǐn shāngdiàn shénme shíhòu guānmén?** 礼品商店什么时侯关门? (禮品商店甚麼時候關門?) (Lee-peeng shahng-dyan shummuh shir-ho gwahn-mun?) (*What time does the gift shop close?*)

>> **Nǐmen mài búmài zhāotiē?** 你们卖不卖招贴? (你們賣不賣招貼?) (Nee-mun my boo-my jaow-tyeh?) (*Do you sell posters?*)

Talkin' the Talk

George arrives at the local art museum pretty late in the day, so he approaches the clerk to ask some questions.

George: **Qǐng wèn, nǐmen jǐ diǎn zhōng guanmén?**
Cheeng one, nee-mun jee dyan joong gwahnmun?
Excuse me, what time do you close?

Clerk: **Zhèige bówùguǎn wǎnshàng liù diǎn zhōng guānmén.**
Jay-guh baw-woo-gwahn wahn-shahng lyo dyan joong gwahn-mun.
This museum closes at 6:00 p.m.

George: **Xiànzài yǐjīng wǔ diǎn duōle. Wǒ néng bùnéng miǎnfèi jìnqù?**
Shyan-dzye ee-jeeng woo dyan dwaw-luh. Waw nung boo-nung myan-fay jeen-chyew?
It's now already after 5:00. May I enter for free?

Clerk: **Bùxíng. Hái yào fù qián. Shí kuài yì zhāng.**
Boo-sheeng. Hi yaow foo chyan. Shir kwye ee jahng.
No. You still have to pay. It's $10 a ticket.

George: **Nà, wǒ míngtiān zài lái, duō huā yìdiǎr shíjiān zài zhèr. Xièxiè.**
Nah, waw meeng-tyan dzye lye, dwaw hwah ee-dyar shir-jyan dzye jar. Shyeh-shyeh.
In that case, I'll come back tomorrow to spend a little more time here. Thanks.

WORDS TO KNOW		
Qǐng wèn? 请问? (請問?)	Cheeng-one?	May I ask?
bówùguǎn 博物馆 (博物館)	baw-woo-gwahn	museum
miǎnfèi 免费 (免費)	myan-fay	free of charge

Visiting Historical Sites

Make sure to take at least one well-coordinated trip to a historical site if you visit China, even if you have only a week for business. Take the **Cháng Chéng** 长城 (長城) (Chahng Chung) (*Great Wall*), for example. Just north of Beijing, the wall is one of the greatest man-made objects on earth.

And while you're on your way to the Great Wall, you may want to stop off at the **Míng shísān líng** 明十三陵 (Meeng shir-sahn leeng) (*Ming Tombs*), which contain the mausoleums of 13 **Ming** dynasty (1368–1644) emperors guarded by stone animals and warrior statues.

By far the easiest way to see the major historical sites in China is to join a tour. Here are some phrases that may come in handy:

» **Bàntiān duōshǎo qián?** 半天多少钱? (半天多少錢?) (Bahn-tyan dwaw-shaow chyan?) (*How much for half a day?*)

» **Lǚxíngshè zài nǎr?** 旅行社在哪儿? (旅行社在哪兒?) (Lyew-sheeng-shuh dzye nar?) (*Where's the travel agency?*)

» **Nǐ yǒu méiyǒu lǚyóu shǒucè?** 你有没有旅游手册? (你有沒有旅遊手冊?) (Nee yo mayo lyew-yo show-tsuh?) (*Do you have a travel guidebook?*)

» **Yǒu méiyǒu shuō Yīngwén de dǎoyóu?** 有没有说英文的导游? (有沒有說英文的導遊?) (Yo mayo shwaw Eeng-one duh daow-yo?) (*Are there any English-speaking guides?*)

CULTURAL WISDOM

Some of China's most-visited historical sites include the Great Wall, the Forbidden City in Beijing, and the terra-cotta warriors of Xi'an, where an army of over 6,000 carved warriors and horses stands guard over the tomb of China's first Emperor, **Qín Shǐhuáng** (Chin Shir-hwahng), who dates back to the third century BCE.

Talkin' the Talk

Sammy hires a taxi and takes his two children to the Jade Buddha Temple in Shanghai, where he tries to get entrance tickets from the clerk. He's eager to show his children the temple's Song dynasty (960–1279 CE) architecture.

Sammy: **Qǐngwèn, zài nǎr kéyǐ mǎi piào?**
           Cheeng-one, dzye nar kuh-yee my pyaow?
           Excuse me, where can I buy tickets for admission?

Clerk: **Jiù zài zhèr.**
           Jyo dzye jar.
           You can buy them here.

Sammy: **Hǎo jíle. Piào jià duōshǎo?**
           How jee-luh. Pyaow jyah dwaw-shaow?
           Great. How much is the ticket price?

Clerk: **Yìzhāng shí kuài.**
           Ee-jahng shir kwye.
           Tickets are $10 each.

Sammy: **Xiǎo háizi miǎnfèi ma?**
           Shyaow hi-dzuh myan-fay mah?
           Do children get in free?

Clerk: **Bù miǎnfèi, kěshì xiǎo háizi bàn piào.**
           Boo myan-fay, kuh-shir shyaow hi-dzuh bahn pyaow.
           No, but they're half price.

Sammy: **Wǒmen kě bù kěyǐ zhàoxiàng?**
           Waw-mun kuh boo kuh-yee jaow-shyahng?
           May we take pictures?

Clerk: **Dāngrán kěyǐ. Méiyǒu wèntí.**
           Dahng-rahn kuh-yee. Mayo one-tee.
           Of course you can. No problem.

WORDS TO KNOW

Yǐjīng mài guāngle ma? 已经卖光了吗? (已經賣光了嗎?)	Ee-jeeng mye gwahng-luh mah?	Is it already sold out?
Hái yǒu piào ma? 还有票吗? (還有票嗎?)	Hye yo pyaow mah?	Are there any tickets left?
Shénme shíhòu kāishǐ? 什么时候开始? (什麼時候開始?)	Summah shir-hoe kye-shir?	What time does it start?

Going to the Movies

After a full day of sightseeing, you may want to relax, kick back, and take in a **diànyǐng** 电影 (電影) (dyan-yeeng) (*movie*). At the movies you can sit and watch what's on the **yínmù** 银幕 (銀幕) (yeen-moo) (*screen*) without walking or talking. But what to do when the lights dim and you suddenly realize the film is completely in **Zhōngwén** 中文 (Joong-one) (*Chinese*), without any **Yīngwén zìmù** 英文字幕 (Eeng-one dzuh-moo) (*English subtitles*) whatsoever? You read this book, of course!

What kind of movie do you want to see? Table 10-1 gives you a few genres to choose from:

TABLE 10-1 ## Movie Genres

Chinese	Pronunciation	English
àiqíng piān 爱情片 (愛情片)	eye-cheeng pyan	*romance*
dònghuà piān 动画片 (動畫片)	doong-hwah pyan	*cartoon*
dòngzuò piān 动作片 (動作片)	doong-dzwaw pyan	*action*
gùshi piān 故事片	goo-shir pyan	*drama*
jìlù piān 纪录片 (紀錄片)	jee-loo pyan	*documentary*
kǒngbù piān 恐怖片	koong-boo pyan	*horror*
wàiguó piān 外国片 (外國片)	wye-gwaw pyan	*foreign film*
wǔxiá piān 武侠片 (武俠片)	woo-shyah pyan	*kung-fu*
xǐjù piān 喜剧片 (喜劇片)	she-jyew pyan	*comedy*

Talkin' the Talk

Wendy and Elly decide to go to the movies tonight.

Wendy: **Wǒmen jīntiān wǎnshàng qù kàn yíbù diànyǐng ba.**
Waw-men jin-tyan wahn-shahng chyew kahn ee-boo dyan-yeeng bah.
Let's go see a movie tonight.

Elly: **Jīntiān yǎn shénme?**
Jin-tyan yan shummuh?
What's playing today?

Wendy: **Yíge Zhāng Yìmóu dǎoyǎn de piānzi. Wǒ wàngle nèige míngzi.**
Ee-guh Jahng Ee-moe daow-yan duh pyan-dzuh. Waw wahng-luh nay-guh meeng-dzuh.
A film directed by Zhang Yimou. I forget the name.

Elly: **Shì shuō Yīngwén de ma?**
Shir shwaw Eeng-one duh mah?
Is it in English?

Wendy: **Búshì, kěshì yǒu Yīngwén zìmù.**
Boo-shir, kuh-shir yo Eeng-one dzuh-moo.
No, but there are English subtitles.

WORDS TO KNOW

yǎnyuán (演員)	yan ywan	actor/actress
gēshǒu (歌手)	guh sho	singer
yīnyuè jiā (音樂家)	een-yweh jyah	musician

Hopping Around Bars and Clubs

Are you a night owl who, after a full day of sightseeing and even an evening concert, still has the energy to go barhopping and carousing around fun clubs? If so, you need to know some common bar speak, especially when you're on vacation in a toddlin' town like Shanghai — or Chicago, for that matter. After all, not everyone you meet or go out with may be fluent in English. The following phrases may come in handy when you're out exploring the local pubs and dance halls:

>> **Nǐ jīngcháng lái zhèr ma?** 你经常来这儿吗? (你經常來這兒嗎?) (Nee jeeng-chahng lye jar mah?) *(Do you come here often?)*

>> **Nǐ xiǎng gēn wǒ tiàowǔ ma?** 你想跟我跳舞吗? (你想根我跳舞嗎?) (Nee shyahng gun waw tyaow-woo mah?) *(Would you like to dance?)*

>> **Qǐng lái yìpíng píjiǔ.** 请来一瓶啤酒 (請來一瓶啤酒) (Cheeng lye ee-peeng pee-jyoe.) *(Please bring me a bottle of beer.)*

>> **Wǒmen dào nǎr qù tiàowǔ?** 我们到哪儿去跳舞? (我們到哪兒去跳舞?) (Waw-men daow nar chyew tyaow-woo?) *(Where can we go to dance?)*

>> **Wǒ néng bùnéng qǐng nǐ hē jiǔ?** 我能不能请你喝酒? (我能不能請你喝酒?) (Waw nung boo-nung cheeng nee huh jyoe?) *(May I get you a drink?)*

>> **Yǒu méiyǒu rùchǎng fèi?** 有没有入场费? (有沒有入場費?) (Yo may-yo roo-chahng fay?) *(Is there a cover charge?)*

When you go to a bar with friends, you may ask for some **bīngzhèn de píjiǔ** 冰镇的啤酒 (冰鎮的啤酒) (beeng-juhn duh pee-jyoe) *(cold beer)* or maybe some **hóng** 红 (紅) (hoong) *(red)* or **bái** 白 (bye) *(white)* **pútáo jiǔ** 葡萄酒 (poo-taow jyoe) *(wine)*. And don't forget to ask for some **huāshēng mǐ** 花生米 (hwah-shung mee) *(peanuts)* or **tǔdòu piàn** 土豆片 (too-doe pyan) *(potato chips)* so you don't get too sloshed with all that **píjiǔ.**

FUN & GAMES

Match the English term on the left with the corresponding Chinese term on the right. You can find the answers in Appendix C.

1. *movie theatre*   a. **yīnyuè huì** 音乐会 (音樂會)

2. *concert hall*   b. **Jīngjù** 京剧 (京劇)

3. *museum*   c. **yìshù** 艺术 (藝術)

4. *art*   d. **bówùguǎn** 博物馆 (博物館)

5. *concert*   e. **yīnyuè tīng** 音乐厅 (音樂廳)

6. *Peking opera*   f. **diànyǐngyuàn** 电影院 (電影院)

Choose your favorite movie genre and put one of your new words in the spaces below:

Nǐ xǐhuān kàn kǒngbù piān ma? 你喜欢看恐怖片吗?(你喜歡看恐怖片嗎?) (Nee shee-hwahn kahn koong-boo pyan mah? (*Do you like to watch horror films?*)

Nǐ xǐhuān kàn _____ **piān ma?** 你喜欢看_____吗?你喜歡看_____嗎?) (Nee shee-hwahn kahn _____ pyan mah?) (*Do you like to watch _____ movies?*)

Nǐ xǐhuān kàn _____ **piān ma?** 你喜欢看_____吗?(你喜歡看_____嗎?) (Nee shee-hwahn kahn _____ pyan mah?) (*Do you like to watch _____ movies?*)

Chapter **11**

Taking Care of Telecommunications

lthough email may be the preferred method of communication these days, you can't duplicate hearing your loved one's **shēngyīn** 声音 (聲音) (shung-yeen) (*voice*) on the other end of the line or reaching just the right person you need to begin discussing a **hébìng** 合并 (合併) (huh-beeng) (*merger*) through the computer. All the more reason to know how to use the telephone in addition to **shàngwǎng** 上网 (上網) (shahng wahng) (*going online*).

The art of making a phone call in another language, and even in another country, is just that — an art. To master it, you have to feel comfortable with such basics as using the telephone in the first place. What do you actually say when someone picks up on the other end? This chapter helps you navigate the communication terrain, whether you're in Boise or Beijing.

Getting Familiar with Telephone Terms

Before even going near a **diànhuà** 电话 (電話) (dyan-hwah) (*telephone*), you may want to become familiar with some common Chinese words and phrases connected to using one. In fact, you see so many different kinds of phones nowadays that you shouldn't have a problem finding out which one best suits your needs. The only kind you probably won't see no matter how hard you look is the **gōngyòng diànhuà** 公用电话 (公用電話) (goong-yoong dyan-hwah) (*public telephone*), which at this point has gone the way of the **kǒnglóng** 恐龙 (恐龍) (koong-long) (*dinosaur*). Nine times out of ten you'll use one of these to **dǎ diànhuà** 打电话 (打電話) (dah dyan-hwah) (*to make a phone call*):

>> **zuò jī** 座机 (座機) (dzwaw jee) (*land line*)

>> **shǒujī** 手机 (手機) (sho-jee) (*cellphone*)

>> **píngguǒ shǒujī** 苹果手机 (蘋果手機) (peeng-gwaw sho-jee) (*iPhone*)

>> **wúxiàn diànhuà** 无线电话 (無線電話) (woo-shyan dyan-hwah) (*cordless phone*)

And these are some basic terms you need to know before you call for a **wēnquán** 温泉 (溫泉) (wun chwan) (*spa*) appointment or two:

>> **diànhuà hàomǎ** 电话号码 (電話號碼) (dyan-hwah how-mah) (*telephone number*)

>> **diànhuàkǎ** 电话卡 (電話卡) (dyan-hwah-kah) (*phone card*)

>> **chá diànhuà hàomǎ** 查电话号码 (查電話號碼) (chah dyan-hwah how-mah) (*look up a phone number*)

And don't forget your **chōngdiàn qì** 充电器 (充電器) (choong-dyan chee) (*charger*) or you won't be able to call in the first place.

Be sure to check out a few things beforehand, like what **dìqū hàomǎ** 地区号码 (地區號碼) (dee-chyew how-mah) (*area code*) and **diànhuà hàomǎ** 电话号码 (電話號碼) (dyan-hwah how-mah) (*telephone number*) to **bō** 拨 (撥) (baw) (*dial*). Sometimes you need the help of a **jiēxiànyuán** 接线员 (接線員) (jyeh-shyan-ywan) (*operator*) for some of the following kinds of calls, but others you can take care of on your own:

>> **běnshì diànhuà** 本市电话 (本市電話) (bun-shir dyan-hwah) (*local call*)

>> **chángtú diànhuà** 长途电话 (長途電話) (chahng-too dyan-hwah) (*long-distance call*)

>> **duìfāng fùfèi diànhuà** 对方付费电话 (對方付費電話) (dway-fahng foo-fay dyan-hwah) (*collect call*)

>> **guójì diànhuà** 国际电话 (國際電話) (gwaw-jee dyan-hwah) (*international phone calls*)

If you're like me, you need to ask plenty of basic questions before you figure out what you're doing with a telephone overseas. Here are a few questions that may come in handy:

» **Běnshì diànhuà shōufèi duōshǎo qián?** 本市电话收费多少钱? (本市電話收費多少錢?) (Bun-shir dyan-hwah show-fay dwaw-shaow chyan?) (*How much is a local phone call?*)

» **Zài nǎr kéyǐ dǎ diànhuà?** 在哪儿可以打电话? (在哪兒可以打電話?) (Dzye nar kuh-yee dah dyan-hwah?) (*Where can I make a call?*)

» **Zěnme dǎ diànhuà?** 怎么打电话? (怎麼打電話?) (Dzummuh dah dyan-hwah?) (*How can I place a phone call?*)

And don't forget to ask your service provider if there are any **guójì mànyóu fèi** 国际漫游费 (國際漫遊費) (*international roaming charges*) before you go, or you may be in for a big surprise when you get the bill.

As of 2018, China's key **kuāndài** 宽带 (寬帶) (kwahn dye) (*broadband*) and **yídòng hùliánwǎng tígōng shāng** 移动互联网提供商 (移動互聯網提供商) (ee-doong hoo-lyan-wahng tee-goong shahng) (*mobile Internet providers*) are

» **Zhōngguó liántōng** 中国联通 (Joong-gwaw lyan-toong) (*China Telecom*)

» **Zhōngguó diànxìn** 中国电信 (中國電信) (Joong-gwaw dyan-sheen) (*China Unicom*)

» **Zhōngguó yídòng** 中国移动 (中國移動) (Joong-gwaw ee-doong) (*China Mobile*)

Going Mobile with a Cellphone

The majority of folks in the world don't have telephones in their homes. Can you imagine? That goes for mainland China as well, where almost a quarter of humanity resides. You can find phones everywhere in Taiwan, however, as well as in Singapore and Hong Kong. In big cities across the globe, you're apt to see a million people (sometimes literally millions in places like Shanghai) on the street with their **shǒujī** 手机 (手機) (sho-jee) (*cellphone*) in tow . . . or, rather, in hand, right next to their **zuǐbā** 嘴巴 (dzway-bah) (*mouth*), yakking away. It's the preferred mode of communication these days, so most people you meet have a **shǒujī hàomǎ** 手机号码 (手機號碼) (sho-jee how-mah) (*cellphone number*).

Although the more well-known cellphone brands have tried to make their marks on the vast Chinese market of cellphone users, home-grown brands such as **Huáwèi**华为(華為) (Hwah-way) and **Xiǎomǐ** 小米 (Shyaow-mee) corner the market on their home turf nowadays.

Cellphones have become so wildly popular that even as recently as 2016, there were over 1.3 billion mobile phone numbers in China. Middle and high school students risk having their cellphones confiscated, smashed, or dunked in water, though, in keeping with a zero tolerance policy for students using cellphones in class.

Making a Phone Call

Wéi? 喂 (餵) (Way?) (*Hello?*). You hear this word spoken in the second (or rising) tone a lot on the other end of the line when you make a phone call. It's kind of like testing the waters to see if someone is there. You can reply with the same word in the fourth (or falling) tone so you sound like you're making a statement, or you can just get right to asking whether the person you want to speak with is in at the moment. (For more about the four tones, refer to Chapter 1.)

A phrase you may hear on the other end of the line in mainland China is **Nǐ nǎr?** 你哪儿? (你哪兒?) (Nee nar?) (Literally: *Where are you?*). It asks what **dānwèi** 单位 (單位) (dahn-way) (*work unit*) you're attached to. After these first little questions, you may finally be ready to ask for the person you intended to call in the first place.

For decades after Communist rule took over mainland China in 1949, all Chinese people were assigned a **dānwèi**, which pretty much regulated every aspect of their lives — from where they lived to when they married and even when they had children. Even though that particular system has largely fallen by the wayside, asking about a person's **dānwèi** is still pretty common when answering the phone.

Here are some things you can do before, during, or after your call:

>> **náqǐ diànhuà** 拿起电话 (拿起電話) (nah-chee dyan-hwah) (*pick up the phone*)

>> **dǎ diànhuà** 打电话 (打電話) (dah dyan-hwah) (*make a phone call*)

>> **shōudào diànhuà** 收到电话 (收到電話) (show-daow dyan-hwah) (*receive a phone call*)

>> **jiē diànhuà** 接电话 (接電話) (jyeh dyan-hwah) (*answer a phone call*)

>> **huí diànhuà** 回电话 (回電話) (hway dyan-hwah) (*return a phone call*)

>> **liú yíge huà** 留一个话 (留一個話) (lyo ee-guh hwah) (*leave a message*)

>> **guà diànhuà** 挂电话 (掛電話) (gwah dyan-hwah) (*hang up*)

Calling your friends

Feel like getting in touch with a friend or co-worker to **liáotiān** 聊天 (lyaow–tyan) (*chat*) after class or work? Want to confer with your classmate about tomorrow's exam? Maybe you two are planning a party over the weekend and you need to confer about the details. To get the party started, you have to pick up that phone and start talking.

Talkin' the Talk

Mary calls to see whether her best friend Luò Chéng is at home and speaks with his father.

Mr. Luò: **Wéi?**
             Way?
             Hello?

Mary: **Qǐngwèn, Luò Chéng zài ma?**
             Cheeng-one, Law Chung dzye mah?
             May I please speak to Luo Cheng?

Mr. Luò: **Qǐngwèn, nín shì nǎ yí wèi?**
             Cheeng-one, neen shir nah ee way?
             May I ask who's calling?

Mary: **Wǒ shì tāde tóngxué Mary.**
             Waw shir tah-duh toong-shweh Mary.
             I'm his classmate Mary.

Mr. Luò: **Hǎo. Shāoděng. Wǒ qù jiào tā.**
             How. Shaow-dung. Waw chyew jyao tah.
             Okay. Just a moment. I'll go get him.

WORDS TO KNOW

yùfù fèi diànhuàkǎ 预付费电话卡 (預付費電話卡)	yew-foo fay dyan-hwah-kah	pre-paid phone card
Fèiyòng yǒu bāohán xìnxī fèi ma? 费用有包含信息费吗? (費用有包含信息費嗎?)	Fay-yoong yo baow-hahn sheen-shee fay mah?	Is data included in the rate?
Zhànxiàn 占线 (佔線)	Jahn-shyan.	The line is busy.
Wǒmen de diànhuà gānggāng duànle. 我们的电话刚刚断了. (我們的電話剛剛斷了.)	Waw-men duh dyan-hwah gahng-gahng dwan-luh.	We just got disconnected.

Ringing hotels and places of business

Calling places of business may be a bit different from the more informal call to a friend or co-worker. When you call a **lǚguǎn** 旅馆 (旅館) (lyew-gwahn) (*hotel*), **shāngdiàn** 商店 (shahng-dyan) (*store*), or a particular **gōngsī** 公司 (goong-suh) (*company*), you may be asked what **fēnjī hàomǎ** 分机号码 (分機號碼) (fun-jee how-mah) (*extension*) you want. If you don't know, you can ask for the same: **Qǐngwèn, fēnjī hàomǎ shì duōshǎo?** 请问, 分机号码是多少? (請問, 分機號碼是多少?) (Cheeng-one, fun-jee how-mah shir dwaw-shaow?) (*May I ask what the extension is?*).

After you figure out the extension, the operator will hopefully say **Wǒ xiànzài jiù gěi nǐ jiē hào.** 我现在就给你接号. (我現在就給你接號.) (Waw shyan-dzye jyo gay nee jyeh how.) (*I'll transfer you now.*).

Even after all your work thus far, you may find that you **jiē bù tōng** 接不通 (jyeh boo toong) (*can't connect*) or that **méiyǒu rén jiē** 没有人接 (may-yo run jyeh) (*no one answers*). Maybe **diànhuàxiàn duànle** 电话线断了 (電話線斷了) (dyan-hwah-shyan dwahn-luh) (*the line has been disconnected*). That's really **máfan** 麻烦 (麻煩) (mah-fahn) (*annoying*), isn't it? Here are some other **máfan** problems you may encounter while trying to make a phone call:

>> **děnghòu** 等候 (dung-ho) (*be on hold*)

>> **diànhuà huàile** 电话坏了 (電話壞了) (dyan-hwah hwye-luh) (*the phone is broken*)

>> **méiyǒu bōhào yīn** 没有拨号音 (沒有撥號音) (may-yo baw-how yeen) (*no dial tone*)

» **nǐ bōcuò hàomǎ le** 你拨错号码了 (你駁錯號碼了) (nee baw-tswaw how-mah luh) (*you dialed the wrong number*)

» **záyīn** 杂音 (雜音) (dzah-yeen) (*static*)

» **zhànxiàn** 占线 (佔線) (jahn-shyan) (*the line is busy*)

If you finally do get through to an employee's office only to discover the person isn't there, you can always leave a **yǒu shēng yóujiàn** 有声邮件 (有聲郵件) (yo shung yo-jyan) (*voice mail*). Flip to the later section "Sorry, I Can't Take Your Call Right Now . . ." for the ins and outs of leaving and receiving messages.

Phoning a client

If you want to reach your **kèhù** 客户 (kuh-hoo) (*client*) or your **shengyì huǒbàn** 生意伙伴 (生意夥伴) (shuhng-yee hwaw-ban) (*business partner*) in today's business world, you just have to pick up that phone. Personally connecting with a phone call is a good way to maintain good business relationships. It's the next best thing to being there.

Sometimes you need a little help from the **mìshū** 秘书 (秘書) (mee-shoo) (*secretary*) or **xíngzhèng zhùlǐ** 行政助理 (sheeng-juhng joo-lee) (*administrative assistant*) to connect to the person you want to reach.

Talkin' the Talk

Jacob enlists the help of Liú Xiǎojiě (Miss Liu), his trusty administrative assistant in Taipei, to help him make a call.

Jacob: **Liú Xiǎojiě, zěnme jiē wàixiàn?**
Lyo Shyaow-jyeh, dzummuh jyeh why-shyan?
Miss Liu, how can I get an outside line?

Liú Xiǎojiě: **Méi wèntí. Wǒ bāng nǐ dǎ zhèige hàomǎ.**
May one-tee. Waw bahng nee dah jay-guh how-mah.
Don't worry. I'll help you dial the number.

Jacob: **Xièxiè.**
Shyeh-shyeh.
Thanks.

Miss Liu gets through and speaks to Mr. Wang's **zhùlǐ** 助理 (joo-lee) (*assistant*).

Liú Xiǎojiě:	**Wéi? Zhè shì Wáng Xiānshēng de bàngōngshì ma?** Way? Jay shir Wahng Shyan-shung duh bahn-goong-shir ma? *Hello? Do I have the office of Mr. Wang?*
Assistant:	**Duì le. Jiù shì.** Dway luh. Jyo shir. *Yes it is.*
Liú Xiǎojiě:	**Kéyǐ gěi wǒ jiē tā ma?** Kuh-yee gay waw jyeh tah mah? *Can you connect me with him, please?*
Assistant:	**Duìbùqǐ, tā xiànzài kāihuì. Nǐ yào liúyán ma?** Dway-boo-chee, tah shyan-dzye kye-hway. Nee yaow lyo-yan mah? *I'm sorry, he's in a meeting at the moment. Would you like to leave a message?*
Liú Xiǎojiě:	**Máfan nǐ gàosù tā ABC gōngsī de jīnglǐ Jacob Smith gěi ta dǎ diànhuà le?** Mah-fahn nee gaow-soo tah ABC goong-suh duh jeeng-lee Jacob Smith gay tah dah dyan-hwah luh? *May I trouble you to tell him that Jacob Smith, the manager of ABC Company, called him?*

WORDS TO KNOW

diànhuà huìyì 电话会议 (電話會議)	dyan-hwah hway-ee	conference call
zàixiàn huìyì 在线会议 (在線會議)	dzye-shyan hway-ee	online meeting
fēi zhèngshì huìyì 非正式会议 (非正式會議)	fay juhng-shir hway-ee	informal meeting
chūbù huìyì 初步会议 (初步會議)	choo-boo hway-ee	preliminary meeting

Sorry, I Can't Take Your Call Right Now . . .

Because people lead such busy lives, you often can't get ahold of them directly when you try to **gěi tāmen dǎ diànhuà** 给他们打电话 (給他們打電話) (gay tah-mun dah dyan-hwah) (*give them a call*). Even though business people all have cellphones, if they can't pick up the call immediately, you have no choice but to **liúhuà** 留话 (留話) (lyo-hwah) (*leave a message*). You can always try to leave a **xìnxī** 信息 (sheen-she) (*message*) with a real person, too. In the following sections, I give you the lowdown on listening to and leaving messages.

Listening to messages that people leave you

If you've been working nonstop all day and haven't had a second to even check your messages 'til now, you'll likely discover that many callers have **liúle huà** 留了话 (留了話) (lyo-luh hwah) (*left messages*) for you. You may be tempted to **tīng** 听 (聽) (teeng) (*listen to*) them right away rather than **bùlǐ** 不理 (boo-lee) (*ignore*) them. Relax. Take a Zen moment to unwind and decompress. Have a glass of wine while you cook dinner. After a break, you'll be ready to tackle all the voice mails that barraged your cellphone throughout the day.

Here's what a typical message sounds like:

Wéi? William, zhè shì Catherine. Zhèige zhōumò wǒmen yìqǐ qù nèige wǎnhuì, hǎo bùhǎo? Yīnggāi hěn bàng. Yǒu kōng gěi wǒ dǎ diànhuà. Wǒde shǒujī hàomǎ shì 212-939-9991. Xièxiè.

Way? William, jay shir Catherine. Jay-guh joe-maw waw-men ee-chee chyew nay-guh wahn-hway, how boo-how? Eeng-guy hun bahng. Yo koong gay waw dah dyan-hwah. Waw-duh show-jee how-mah shir are ee are, jyo sahn jyo, jyo jyo jyo ee. Shyeh-shyeh.

Hello? William, this is Catherine. Want to go to that party together this weekend? It should be awesome. When you get a chance, give me a call. My cell number is 212-939-9991. Thanks.

Recording and understanding greeting messages

Here are some common greetings you may hear if your call goes straight to voice mail:

>> **"Zhè shì Michael Ian."** 这是 Michael Ian. (這是 Michael Ian.) (Jay shir Michael Ian.) (*You've reached Michael Ian.*)

» **Wǒ xiànzài búzài.** 我现在不在. (我現在不在.) (Waw shyan-dzye boo-dzye.) (*I'm not in at the moment./I'm away from my desk.*)

» **Sān yuè sì hào zhīqián wǒ zài dùjià.** 三月四号之前我在度假. (三月四號之前我在度假.) (Sahn yweh suh how jir-chyan waw dzye doo-jyah.) (*I'm on vacation until March 4th.*)

» **Nín rúguǒ xiǎng gēn wǒde zhùshǒu tōnghuà, qǐng bō fēnjī 108.** 您如果想跟我的助手通话, 请拨分机一零八. (您如果想跟我的助手通話, 請撥分機一零八.) (Neen roo-gwaw shyahng gun waw-duh joo-show toong-hwah, cheeng baw fun-jee yaow leeng bah.) (*If you'd like to speak with my assistant, please dial extension 108.*)

» **Qǐng liú xià nínde míngzi, diànhuà hàomǎ hé jiǎnduǎn de liúyán. Wǒ huì gěi nín huí diànhuà.** 请留下您的名字, 电话号码和简短的留言. 我会给你回电话. (請留下您的名字, 電話號碼和簡短的留言. 我會給你回電話.) (Cheeng lyo shyah neen-duh meeng-dzuh, dyan-hwah how-mah huh jyan-dwahn duh lyo-yan. Waw hway gay neen hway dyan-hwah.) (*Please leave your name, number, and a brief message. I'll get back to you.*)

REMEMBER

Sometimes you have to press the **jǐng hào jiàn** 井号键 (井號鍵) (jeeng how jyan) (*pound key*) before leaving a message. In that case, you have to recognize the **jǐng zìhào** 井字号 (井字號) (jeeng dzuh–how) (*pound sign*): #. When dealing with voice mail, you may have to deal with the following kinds of instructions on a recorded message:

» **Nín rúguǒ shǐyòng ànjiàn shì diànhuà jī, qǐng àn 3.** 您如果使用按键式电话机, 请按三. (您如果使用按鍵式電話機, 請按三.) (Neen roo-gwaw shir-yoong ahn-jyan shir dyan-hwah jee, cheeng ahn sahn.) (*If you have a touch-tone phone, please press 3 now.*)

» **Yào huí dào zhǔ mùlù qǐng àn jǐng zìhào.** 要回到主目录请按井字号. (要回到主目錄請按井字號.) (Yaow hway daow joo moo-loo cheeng ahn jeeng dzuh-how.) (*If you want to return to the main menu, please press pound now.*)

Leaving messages

When you leave a message, be sure to give clear instructions about what you want the person to do:

» **Bié wàngle huí wǒde diànhuà.** 别忘了回我的电话. (別忘了回我的電話.) (Byeh wahng-luh hway waw-duh dyan-hwah.) (*Don't forget to return my call.*)

» **Qǐng gěi wǒ dǎ diànhuà.** 请给我打电话. (請給我打電話.) (Cheeng gay waw dah dyan-hwah.) (*Please give me a call.*)

>> **Wǒ zài gěi nǐ dǎ diànhuà.** 我再给你打电话. (我再給你打電話.) (Waw dzye gay nee dah dyan-hwah.) (*I'll call back again.*)

If a live person answers and you have to leave a message, be sure to be polite. Here are some good phrases to keep in mind:

>> **Máfan nǐ qǐng tā huí wǒde diànhuà?** 麻烦你请他回我的电话? (麻煩你請他 回我的電話?) (Mah-fahn nee cheeng tah hway waw-duh dyan-hwah?) (*May I trouble you to please have him return my call?*)

>> **Qǐng gàosù tā wǒ gěi tā dǎ diànhuà le.** 请告诉她我给她打电话了. (請告訴 她我給她打電話了.) (Cheeng gaow-soo tah waw gay tah dah dyan-hwah luh.) (*Please tell her I called.*)

>> **Qǐng gàosù tā wǒ huì wǎn yìdiǎr lái.** 请告诉他我会晚一点儿来. (請告訴他我 會晚一點兒來.) (Cheeng gaow-soo tah waw hway wahn ee-dyar lye.) (*Please let him know I'll be a little late.*)

>> **Qǐng gěi wǒ zhuǎn tāde liúyán jī?** 请给我转他的留言机? (請給我轉他的留言機?) (Cheeng gay waw jwan tah-duh lyo-yan jee?) (*Could you please transfer me to his voice mail?*)

Talkin' the Talk

George calls Susan and discovers she's not home. He has to leave a message with her mother.

Susan's mom:	**Wéi?**
	Way?
	Hello?

George:	**Qǐngwèn, Susan zài ma?**
	Cheeng-one, Susan dzye mah?
	Hello, is Susan there?

Susan's mom:	**Tā búzài. Tā qù yóujú le. Qǐngwèn, nín shì nǎ yí wèi?**
	Tah boo-dzye. Tah chyew yo-jyew luh. Cheeng-one, neen shir nah ee way?
	She's not home. She went to the post office. May I ask who this is?

George:	**Wǒ shì George, tāde tóngbān tóngxué. Máfan nǐ qǐng gàosù tā wǒ gěi tā dǎ diànhuà le.**
	Waw shir George, tah-duh toong-bahn toong-shweh. Mah-fahn nee cheeng gaow-soo tah waw gay tah dah dyan-hwah luh.
	I'm George, her classmate. May I trouble you to please tell her I called?
Susan's mom:	**Yídìng.**
	Ee-deeng.
	Certainly.

. . . .

Checking Your Email

Your **diànzǐ yóuxiāng dìzhǐ** 电子邮箱地址 (電子郵箱地址) (dyan-dzuh yo-shyahng dee-jir) (*email address*) is as important as your **míngzi** 名字 (meeng-dzuh) (*name*) and your **diànhuà hàomǎ** 电话号码 (電話號碼) (dyan-hwah how-mah) (*phone number*) when it comes to keeping in touch. Email is indispensable if you want to do business from Taipei to Timbuktu. Just check your **shōu xìnxiāng** 收信箱 (show sheen-shyahng) (*inbox*) on your **táishì diànnǎo** 台式电脑 (台式電腦) (tye-shir dyan-now) (*desktop*), and you'll probably have received a few more **diànzǐ yóujiàn** 电子邮件 (電子郵件) (dyan-dzuh yo-jyan) (*emails*) while reading this section alone.

Here are some things you can do with email once you have your own account:

» **bǎ wénjiàn fùjiā zài diànzǐ yóujiàn** 把文件附加在电子邮件 (把文件附加在電子郵件) (bah wun-jyan foo-jyah dzye dyan-dzuh yo-jyan) (*attach a file to an email*)

» **fā diànzǐ yóujiàn** 发电子邮件 (發電子郵件) (fah dyan-dzuh yo-jyan) (*send an email*)

» **sòng wénjiàn** 送文件 (soong wun-jyan) (*send a file*)

» **zhuǎnfā xìnxī** 转发信息 (轉發信息) (jwan-fah sheen-she) (*forward a message*)

Talkin' the Talk

Arlene shows Jo how to email her grandchildren. This is Jo's first time using a computer, and she's pretty nervous about the basics.

Jo: **Zěnme fā yíge diànzǐ yóujiàn ne?**
         Dzummuh fah ee-guh dyan-dzuh yo-jyan nuh?
         So how do you send an email?

Arlene: **Shǒuxiān nǐ děi dǎkāi "xīn yóujiàn."**
         Show-shyan nee day dah-kye "sheen yo-jyan."
         First you have to open up "new mail."

Jo: **Ránhòu ne?**
         Rahn-ho nuh?
         And then?

Arlene: **Ránhòu tiánhǎo shōujiànrén de diànzǐ yóuxiāng dìzhǐ hé yóujiàn de tímù. Xiěhǎo xìn, jiù kěyǐ fā le.**
         Rahn-ho tyan-how show-jyan-run duh dyan-dzuh yo-shyahng dee-jir huh yo-jyan duh tee-moo. Shyeh-how sheen, jyo kuh-yee fah luh.
         After that, you have to fill in the recipient's email address and type in the subject. After you're finished writing the message, you can finally send it.

Jo: **Tài bàngle! Xièxiè.**
         Tye bahng luh! Shyeh-shyeh.
         That's fantastic. Thanks.

WORDS TO KNOW

fā yīgè duǎnxìn 发一个短信 (發一個短信)	fah ee-guh dwan-sheen	send a text
yìngyòng 应用 (應用)	eeng-yoong	app
xià zǎi yīgè yìngyòng chéngxù 下载一个应用程序 (下載一個應用程序)	shyah dzye ee-guh eeng-yoong chung-shyew	download an app
jíshí tōngxùn 即时通讯 (即時通訊)	jee-shir toong-shewn	instant messaging

Going Online

Thanks to the **wànwéiwǎng** 万维网 (萬維網) (wahn-way-wahng) (*World Wide Web*), the whole world is now connected in **diànzǐ kōngjiān** 电子空间 (電子空間) (dyan-dzuh koong-jyan) (*cyberspace*). With **bǐjìběn diànnǎo** 笔记本电脑 (筆記本電腦) (bee-jee-bun dyan-naow) (*laptops*) and multiple **jiǎnsuǒ yǐnqíng** 检索引擎 (檢索引擎) (jyan-swaw yeen-cheeng) (*search engines*), you can find just about anything you're looking for, whether you're sitting in the privacy of your own home or with a million strangers having a coffee.

Not sure what you're doing with computers? Forget your **mìmǎ** 密码 (密碼) (mee-mah) (*password*)? **Jìshù fúwù** 技术服务 (技術服務) (jee-shoo foo-woo) (*technical support*) is only a phone call away. Here are some basic things you need to know how to do before you even **shàngwǎng** 上网 (上網) (shahng-wahng) (*go online*):

» **dǎkāi diànnǎo** 打开电脑 (打開電腦) (dah-kye dyan-now) (*turn on the computer*)

» **guāndiào diànnǎo** 关掉电脑 (關掉電腦) (gwahn-dyaow dyan-now) (*turn off the computer*)

» **jìn rù** 进入 (進入) (gin roo) (*log on*)

» **tuì chū** 退出 (tway choo) (*log off*)

» **ānzhuāng tiáozhìjiětiáoqì** 安装调制解调器 (安裝調製解調器) (ahn-jwahng tyaow-jir-jyeh-tyaow-chee) (*install a modem*)

» **xuǎnzé yìjiā wǎngshàng fúwù tígōng shāng** 选择一家网上服务提供商 (選擇一家網上服務提供商) (shwan-dzuh ee-jya wahng-shahng foo-woo tee-goong shahng) (*choose an Internet service provider*)

» **xuǎnzé yīgè liúlǎn qì** 选择一个浏览器 (選擇一個瀏覽器) (shwan-dzuh ee-guh lyo-lahn chee) (*choose a browser*)

Hopefully, you won't need too much help learning how to **xiàzài wénjiàn** 下载 文件 (下載文件) (shyah-dzye wun-jyan) (*download a file*), **ānzhuāng tiáozhìjiětiáoqì** (ahn-jwahng tyaow-jir-jyeh-tyaow-chee) (*install a modem*), or **chóngxīn kāijī** 重新开机 (重新開機) (choong-sheen kye-jee) (*reboot*) a computer.

And if you do need help, you can always call your handy **xìnxī jìshù rényuán** 信息 技术人员 (信息技術人員) (sheen-shee jee-shoo run-ywan) (*IT guy or gal*) or **wǎngluò guǎnlǐ yuán** 网络管理员 (網絡管理員) (wahng-lwaw gwan-lee ywan) (*network administrator*).

CULTURAL WISDOM

China is home to almost 750 million Internet users today — almost half its population.

WORDS TO KNOW		
wǎngchóng 网虫(網蟲)	wahng-choong	Internet geek; netter
wǎnggòu 网购 (網購)	wahng-go	online shopping
wǎngshàng zhīfù 网上支付 (網上支付)	wahng-shahng jir-foo	online payment
wǎngyè shèjì shī 网页设计师 (網頁設計師)	wahng-yeh shuh-jee shir	web designer

The Great Wall . . . Firewall, That Is

Once you get hooked up, you're ready to get friendly with things like **sōusuǒ yǐnqíng** 搜索引擎 (搜索引擎) (so-swaw een-cheeng) (*search engines*) and **wǎngluò liúlǎn qì** 网络浏览器 (網絡瀏覽器) (wahng-lwaw lyo-lahn chee) (*browsers*). I think you'll do just fine . . . fine until you hear about things like **shēnfèn dàoyòng** 身份 盗用 (身份盗用) (shun-fun daow-yoong) (*identity theft*), or even **wǎngluò kǒngbù zhǔyì** 网络恐怖主义 (網絡恐怖主義) (wahng-lwaw koong-boo joo-ee) (*cyber terrorism*) that lurk beneath the surface of the **wǎngluò shìjiè** 网络世界 (網絡世界) (wahng-lwaw shir-jyeh) (*cyberworld*) that you are now a part of. Good to keep your **tiānxiàn** 天线 (天線) (tyan-shyan) (*antenna*) up, even though the likelihood of these things happening to you is the same as your chances of being hit by a **shǎndiàn** 闪电 (閃電) (shahn-dyan) (*lightning bolt*).

When your plane touches down and you're just dying to **Gǔgē** 谷歌 (*Google*) your new Chinese city, you're in for a rude awakening. Ditto when you go to post that cutesy photo of yourself jogging along the Great Wall on your **Yèmiàn** 页面 (頁面) (Yeh-myan) (*Facebook page*).

You won't find Google, and you sure as heck won't find Facebook. In fact, as of 2017, you won't even find the BBC. Congratulations! You've just met the **wěidà de fánghuǒqiáng** 伟大的防火墙 (偉大的防火牆) (way-dah duh fahng-hwaw-chyahng) (*The Great Chinese Firewall*).

CULTURAL
WISDOM

As of 2018, China is ranked 176th out of 180 countries when it comes to freedom of the press. Only Syria, North Korea, Turkmenistan, and Eritrea have worse track records in this regard.

China has successfully blocked all sorts of foreign websites, but **jiǎnsuǒ yīntèwǎng** 检索因特网 (檢索因特網) (jyan-swaw een-tuh-wahng) (*searching the Internet*) is still one of the favorite pastimes of a billion people. Just make sure you have an **ānquán fúwùqì** 安全服务器 (安全服務器) ahn-chwan foo-woo-chee) (*secure server*) after you **jiànlì yíge zhànghù** 建立一个账户 (建立一個賬戶) (jyan-lee ee-guh jahng-hoo) (*set up an account*) while there. Your mother will **fàngxīnle** 放心了 (fahng-sheen-luh) (*breathe a sigh of relief*).

Talkin' the Talk

Dick and Dean discuss the wonders of the Internet.

Dick: **Yīntèwǎng dàodǐ shì shénme dōngxi?**
Een-tuh-wahng daow-dee shir shummuh doong-she?
Just what exactly is the Internet?

Dean: **Yīntèwǎng shì yìzhǒng diànnǎo de guójì hùlián wǎng. Tā tígòng xìnxī fúwù.**
Een-tuh-wahng shir ee-joong dyan-now duh gwaw-jee hoo-lyan wahng. Tah tee-goong sheen-she foo-woo.
The Internet is a kind of interconnected international network. It provides information.

Dick: **Tīngshuō wànwéiwǎng shénme dōu yǒu.**
Teeng-shwaw wahn-way-wahng shummuh doe yo.
I've heard that the World Wide Web has everything.

Dean: **Duì le. Nǐ yī shàngwǎng jiù kěyǐ liúlǎn hěn duō bùtóng de wǎngzhàn.**
Dway luh. Nee ee shahng-wahng jyo kuh-yee lyo-lahn hun dwaw boo-toong duh wahng-jahng.
That's correct. The minute you go online, you can browse all sorts of different websites.

WORDS TO KNOW

diànzǐ yóujiàn 电子邮件 (電子郵件)	dyan-dzuh yo-jyan	email
diànzǐ yóujiàn dìzhǐ 电子邮件地址 (電子郵件地址)	dyan-dzuh yo-jyan dee-jir	email address
wǎngluò ānquánxìng 网络安全性 (網絡安全性)	wahng-lwaw ahn-chwan-sheeng	network security
wǎngjì xiéyì 网际协议 (網際協議)	wahng-jee shyeh-ee	Internet protocol
wǎngsù 网速 (網速)	wahng-soo	Internet connection speed
wǎngzhàn 网站 (網站)	wahng-jahn	website

One thing everyone wants to do whether he's in Hong Kong or Hangzhou is go shopping. And if you're the techie type, you want to come back with techie things.

New electronic gadgets appear on the market every two minutes these days, or so it seems. Just when you think you've gotten the latest model of something, another one comes out with great fanfare. Following is a list of the most commonly used (and most commonly bought) items you may need while you're in China — even while reading *Chinese For Dummies*.

>> **bǐjìběn diànnǎo** 笔记本电脑 (筆記本電) (bee-jee-bun dyan-naow) (*laptop*)

>> **diànshì jī** 电视机 (電視機) (dyan-shir jee) (*TV*)

>> **guāngpán** 光盘 (光盤) (gwahng-pahn) (*CD*)

>> **kǎlā'ōukè jī** 卡拉欧克机 (卡拉歐克機) (kah-lah-o-kuh jee) (*karaoke machine*)

>> **MP3 bōfàngqì** MP3 播放器 (MP3 baw-fahng-chee) (*MP3 player*)

>> **shèxiàng jī** 摄像机 (攝像機) (shuh-shyahng jee) (*camcorder*)

>> **shìpín yóuxì** 视频游戏 (視頻遊戲) (shir-peen yo-shee) (*video games*)

>> **xiǎo píngbǎn diànnǎo** 小平板电脑 (小平板電腦) (shyaow peeng-bahn dyan-naow) (*small tablet PC*)

>> **zàixiàn yóuxì** 在线游戏 (在線遊戲) (dzye-shyan yo-shee) (*online gaming*)

>> **zǔhé yīnxiǎng** 组合音响 (組合音嚮) (dzoo-huh yeen-shyahng) (*stereo system*)

Now you know how to ask for what you want when you walk in that store, and how to chill out and kick back with the **yáokòng qì** 遥控器 (遙控器) (yaow–koong chee) (*remote*). You're going to love it.

FUN & GAMES

Match each of the Chinese phrases to the correct English phrase. Turn to Appendix C for the answers.

Just a moment.

Is she at home?

Hello?

Sorry, you dialed the wrong number.

Please leave a message.

Wéi? 喂?

Duìbùqǐ, nǐ bōcuò hàomǎle. 对不起, 你拨错号码了. (對不起, 你撥錯號碼了.)

Shāoděng. 稍等.

Qǐng nǐ liú yíge huà. 请你留一个话. (請你留一個話.)

Tā zài ma? 她在吗? (她在嗎?)

» Keeping your office supplied

» Conducting business meetings

» Hosting banquets — Chinese style

Chapter 12

Chinese at School and Work

Time to get down to **shēngyì** 生意 (shuhng-yee) (*business*). Your **shēngyi,** that is. Want to know how to manage that job in Jiangsu or how to deal with the head honcho in Hangzhou? This chapter helps you do business in Chinese — everything from making a business appointment to conducting a meeting to hosting a farewell banquet — Chinese style.

Because China has the fastest-growing economy in the world, it's no wonder you gravitated to this chapter. Think of it. China is the fastest-growing source of international profits for U.S. companies, with over a billion potential customers. The United States is China's second largest trading partner (after the European Union) and has hundreds of satellite offices everywhere from Shanghai to Shenzhen. With hundreds of billions (that's right, billions) of dollars in exports throughout the world, China is most decidedly making its mark.

Before you get that job in Wuhan, though, you need to get a good education. This chapter helps you navigate the academic side of things, from kindergarten through college and beyond.

Going to School

You may get out of it for the first five or six years of life, but eventually we all have to **shàngxué** 上学 (上學) (shahng-shweh) (*go to school*) for about 12 years or so. The following sections break down everything you need to know about school-related terms.

Schools and supplies

Table 12-1 lists all the different kinds of **xuéxiào** 学校 (學校) (shweh-shyaow) (*school*) you or your children may be ready to attend.

TABLE 12-1   Schools

Chinese	Pronunciation	English
rìjiān zhàogù zhōngxīn 日间照顾中心 (日間照顧中心)	ir-jyan jaow-goo joong-sheen	*day-care center*
yōu'ér yuán 幼儿园 (幼兒園)	yo-are ywan	*kindergarten*
xiǎoxué 小学 (小學)	shyaow-shweh	*elementary school*
zhōngxué 中学 (中學)	joong-shweh	*middle school*
gāo zhōngxué 高中学 (高中學)	gaow-joong shweh	*high school*
zhuānyè xuéxiào 专业学校 (專業學校)	jwan-yeh shweh-shyaow	*vocational school*
dàxué 大学 (大學)	dah-shweh	*college*
wǎng shàng kèchéng 网上课程 (網上課程)	wahng shahng kuh-chuhng	*online courses*
yánjiū yuàn 研究院	yan-jyo ywan	*graduate school*
yī xuéyuàn 医学院 (醫學院)	ee shweh-ywan	*medical school*
fǎ xuéyuàn 法学院 (法學院)	fah shweh-ywan	*law school*
shāng xuéyuàn 商学院 (商學院)	shahng shweh-ywan	*business school*

Say you've applied for **dàxué** and gotten into the one that was (lucky you) your **shǒuxuǎn**首选 (首選) (show-shwan) (*first choice*). By the end of the first day of class, you need to buy **kèběn** 课本 (課本) (kuh-bun) (*textbooks*) and **yòngpǐn** 用品 (yoong-peen) (*supplies*). Here are some supplies you may need, depending on the **kè** 课 (課) (kuh) (*classes*) you register for:

>> **bǐjìběn** 笔记本 (筆記本) (bee-jee-bun) (*notebook*)

>> **bǐjìběn diànnǎo** 笔记本电脑 (筆記本電腦) (bee-jee-bun dyan-naow) (*laptop*)

- » **gāngbǐ** 钢笔 (鋼筆) (gahng-bee) (*ballpoint pens*)
- » **jìsuàn qì** 计算器 (計算器) (jee-swan chee) (*calculator*)
- » **mùtān lābǐ** 木炭蜡笔 (木炭蠟筆) (moo-tahn lah-bee) (*charcoal crayons*)
- » **qiānbǐ** 铅笔 (鉛筆) (chyan-bee) (*pencils*)
- » **sùmiǎo diàn** 素描垫 (素描墊) (soo-myaow dyan) (*sketch pad*)
- » **táishì diànnǎo** 台式电脑 (台式電腦 (tye-shir dyan-naow) (*desktop computer*)

CULTURAL WISDOM

The Children's Palace in Shanghai is one of the most prestigious after-school arts programs for gifted children in all of China. Built in 1918 as a private villa by the Iraqi Jewish Kadoorie family, who came to Shanghai in the late 1800s, the palace's ornate features; large fireplaces; huge, winding staircase; and marble hallways lent themselves to its original name: Marble Hall. Tourists often come here to see the children perform as one of the highlights of a trip to Shanghai.

Teachers and subjects

Remember your favorite **xiǎoxué lǎoshī** 小学老师 (小學老師) (shyaow-shweh laow-shir) (*elementary school teacher*)? Remember how great it felt to learn how to **yuèdú** 阅读 (閱讀) (yweh-doo) (*read*)? Well, soon enough **yuèdú** turns into **xuéxí** 学习 (學習) (shweh-shee) (*studying*) and maybe even some serious academic or scientific **yánjiū** 研究 (yan-jyo) (*research*), and you really have to hunker down. Table 12-2 lists all sorts of subjects you may study with a **lǎoshī** 老师 (老師) (laow-shir) (*teacher*) or **jiàoshòu** 教授 (jyaow show) (*professor*).

TABLE 12-2   **Academic Subjects**

Chinese	Pronunciation	English
dài shùxué 代数学 (代數學)	dye shoo-shweh	*algebra*
Fǎyǔ 法语 (法語)	Fah-yew	*French*
guójì guānxì 国际关系 (國際關係)	gwaw-jee gwan-shee	*international relations*
huàxué 化学 (化學)	hwah-shweh	*chemistry*
jǐhé xué 几何学 (幾何學)	jee-huh shweh	*geometry*
jīngjì xué 经济学 (經濟學)	jeeng-jee shweh	*economics*
lìshǐ 历史 (歷史)	lee-shir	*history*
shēngwù xué 生物学 (生物學)	shung-woo shweh	*biology*

(continued)

TABLE 12-2 *(continued)*

Chinese	Pronunciation	English
shùxué 数学 (數學)	shoo-shweh	*mathematics*
wénxué 文学 (文學)	wuhn-shweh	*literature*
wǔdǎo 舞蹈	woo-daow	*dance*
wùlǐ 物理	woo-lee	*physics*
Xībānyá yǔ 西班牙语 (西班牙語)	Shee-bahn-yah yew	*Spanish*
xìjù 戏剧 (戲劇)	shee-jyew	*drama*
Yìdàlì yǔ 意大利语 (意大利語)	Ee-dah-lee yew	*Italian*
Yīngyǔ 英语 (英語)	Eeng-yew	*English*
yìshù 艺术 (藝術)	ee-shoo	*art*
zhèngzhì xué 政治学 (政治學)	juhng-jir shweh	*political science*
zhéxué 哲学 (哲學)	juh-shweh	*philosophy*

Here are some class-related phrases:

>> **Nǐ xué shénme?** 你学什么? (你學甚麼?) (Nee shweh shummah?) (*What are you studying?*)

>> **shàng kè** 上课 (上課) (shahng kuh) (*to go to class*)

>> **xué** 学 (學) (shweh) (*to study*)

Exams and semesters

After you get into the swing of the **xuéqí** 学期 (學期) (shweh-chee) (*semester*), you begin to realize your time isn't your own. You have classes to attend, **kèwài huódòng** 课外活动 (課外活動) (kuh-wye hwaw-doong) (*extracurricular activities*) to participate in, and a whole bunch of **kǎoshì** 考试 (考試) (*exams*) to take. These words and phrases come in handy during the school year:

>> **qīmò kǎo** 期末考 (chee-maw kaow) (*final exam*)

>> **qīzhōng kǎo** 期中考 (chee-joong kaow) (*midterm*)

» **suí táng cèyàn** 随堂测验 (隨堂測驗) (sway tahng tsuh-yan) (*pop quiz*)

» **wénzhāng** 文章 (wuhn-jahng) (*essay*)

» **Wǒ děi xiě yìpiān wénzhāng.** 我得写一篇文章. (我得寫一篇文章) (Waw day shyeh ee-pyan wuhn-jahng.) (*I have to write an essay.*)

» **zuìhòu qíxiàn** 最后期限 (最後期限) (dzway-hoe chee-shyan) (*deadline*)

After you've studied hard and taken that **kǎoshì,** you may want to ask your **tóngxué** 同学 (同學) (toong-shweh) (*classmate*) one of these questions:

» **Nǐ déle jǐfēn?** 你得了几分? (你得了幾分?) (Nee duh-luh jee-fun?) (*What [grade] did you get?*)

» **Nǐ kǎo bù jígé ma?** 你考不及格吗? (你考不及格嗎?) (Nee kaow boo jee-guh mah?) (*Did you fail?*)

» **Nǐ kǎo de jígé ma?** 你考得及格吗? (你考得及格嗎?) (Nee kaow duh jee-guh mah?) (*Did you pass?*)

Degrees and diplomas

When you're finally done with all the **xuéxí** 学习 (學習) (shweh-shee) (*studying*) and you're ready to **bìyè** 毕业 (畢業) (bee-yeh) (*graduate*), it's a great day. All that hard work has paid off and you're ready to get your **gāozhōng bìyè wénpíng** 高中毕业文凭 (高中畢業文憑) (gaow-joong bee-yeh wuhn-peen) (*high school diploma*) or a **dàxué xuéwèi** 大学学位 (大學學位) (dah-shweh shweh-way) (*college degree*); you can rest assured that everyone's very proud of you. Here are some of the degrees you may be getting:

» **Bóshì xuéwèi** 博士学位 (博士學位) (Baw-shir shweh-way) (*Doctorate*)

» **Fǎxué bóshì** 法学博士 (法學博士) (Fah-shweh baw-shir) (*Juris Doctor*)

» **Suòshì xuéwèi** 硕士学位 (碩士學位) (Swaw-shir shweh-way) (*Master's degree*)

» **Xuéshì xuéwèi** 学士学位 (學士學位) (Shweh-shir shweh-way) (*Bachelor's degree*)

» **Yīxué bóshì** 医学博士 (醫學博士) (Ee-shweh baw-shir) (*Medical Doctor*)

Settling into Your Office Digs

Whether you're a **mìshū** 秘书 (秘書) (mee-shoo) (*secretary*) or the **zhǔxí** 主席 (joo-she) (*chairman*) of the board, the atmosphere and physical environment of your **bàngōngshì** 办公室 (辦公室) (bahn-goong-shir) (*office*) is pretty important. It can even help get you through an otherwise tough day. May as well make it as comfortable as possible. Why not put a photo of the family dog on your **bàngōng zhuō** 办公桌 (辦公桌) (bahn-goong jwaw) (*desk*) for starters? That should put a smile on your face as you start the day.

The first thing you may look around for when you get to work in the morning is the **kāfēi jī** 咖啡机 (咖啡機) (kah-fay jee) (*coffee machine*). In fact, the one part of the day you may look forward to the most is the **xiūxi** 休息 (shyo-she) (*coffee break*).

As you look around your **xiǎo gé jiān** 小隔间 (小隔間) (shyaow guh jyan) (*cubicle*), I bet you can find all these things:

>> **bǐjìběn** 笔记本 (筆記本) (bee-jee-bun) (*notebook*)

>> **dàng'àn** 档案 (檔案) (dahng-ahn) (*file*)

>> **ding shū jī** 钉书机 (訂書機) (deeng shoo jee) (*stapler*)

>> **gāngbǐ** 钢笔 (鋼筆) (gahng-bee) (*pen*)

>> **huí wén zhēn** 回纹针 (回紋針) (hway one jun) (*paper clip*)

>> **jiāodài** 胶带 (膠帶) (jyaow-dye) (*transparent tape*)

>> **jìsuàn qī** 计算器 (計算器) (jee-swan chee) (*calculator*)

>> **qiānbǐ** 铅笔 (鉛筆) (chyan-bee) (*pencil*)

>> **ruǎnmù sāi bǎn** 软木塞板 (**軟木塞板**) (rwan moo sye bahn) (*cork board*)

>> **xiàngpíjīn** 橡皮筋 (shyahng-pee-jeen) (*rubber band*)

These days you don't even have to get up out of your **yǐzi** 椅子 (ee-dzuh) (*chair*) to notice all the basic office equipment you need to get the job done all around you. Things like:

>> **chuánzhēnjī** 传真机 (傳真機) (chwan-jun-jee) (*fax machine*)

>> **dǎyìnjī** 打印机 (打印機) (dah-een-jee) (*printer*)

» **diànhuà** 电话 (電話) (dyan-hwah) (*telephone*)

» **fùyìnjī** 复印机 (復印機) (foo-een-jee) (*copier*)

» **sǎomiáoyí** 扫描仪 (掃描儀) (saow-myaow-ee) (*scanner*)

If you're working from a **táishì diànnǎo** 台式电脑 (台式電腦) (*desktop computer*), you'll have to know something about all of these:

» **diànnǎo** 电脑 (電腦) (dyan-now) (*computer*)

» **diànnǎo shèbèi** 电脑设备 (電腦設備) (dyan-now shuh-bay) (*computer equipment*)

» **gèrén diànnǎo** 个人电脑 (個人電腦) (guh-run dyan-now) (*PC*)

» **jiànpán** 键盘 (鍵盤) (jyan-pahn) (*keyboard*)

» **ruǎnjiàn** 软件 (軟件) (rwahn-jyan) (*software*)

» **shǔbiāo** 鼠标 (鼠標) (shoo-byaow) (*mouse*)

» **xiǎnshìqì** 显示器 (顯示器) (shyan-shir-chee) (*monitor*)

» **yìngjiàn** 硬件 (eeng-jyan) (*computer hardware*)

And if you're on the go, by land, sea, or air, you can whip out your trusty **bǐjìběn diànnǎo** 笔记本电脑 (筆記本電腦) (*bee-jee-bun dyan-naow*) (laptop) or **píngguǒ shǒujī** 苹果手机 (蘋果手機) (peeng-gwaw sho-jee) (*iPhone*) to **yuǎnchéng gōngzuò** 远程工作 (遠程工作) (ywan-chung goong-dzwaw) (*work remotely*). Just don't forget your **mìmǎ** 密码 (密碼) (*password*), so you can log on to your computer or iPhone in the first place.

REMEMBER

If you can't find some indispensable item just when you need it, you can always ask someone in the next **xiǎo gé jiān** 小隔间 (小隔間) (shyaow guh jyan) (*cubicle*). The simplest way to ask is by using the phrase **Nǐ yǒu méiyǒu _____?** 你有没有 _____? (Nee yo mayo _____?) (*Do you have any _____?*) Use that phrase as often as you like. Just make sure you can reciprocate whenever your **tóngshì** 同事 (toong-shir) (*co-worker*) needs something as well.

Nǐ yǒu méiyǒu ding shū jī? 你有没有钉书机? (你有没有訂書機?) (Nee yo mayo deeng shoo jee?) (*Do you have a stapler?*)

Nǐ yǒu méiyǒu gāngbǐ? 你有没有钢笔? (你有没有鋼筆?) (Nee yo mayo gahng-bee?) (*Do you have a pen?*)

Talkin' the Talk

Ollie and Tommy are co-workers in Xi'an. Ollie is about to go into a meeting but is horrified that he can't find something as basic as his laptop. He quickly checks with Tommy in the next cubicle.

Ollie: **Tommy! Wǒ jíde yào mìng! Kuài yào kāihuì le, kěshì zhǎobúdào wǒde bǐjìběn diànnǎo.**
Tommy! Waw jee-duh yaow meeng! Kwye yaow kye-hway luh, kuh-shir jaow-boo-daow waw-duh bee-jee-bun dyan-naow.
Tommy! I'm in such a hurry! We're about to have a meeting, and I can't find my laptop.

Tommy: **Wǒ yǒu bǐjìběn diànnǎo. Jiè gěi nǐ.**
Waw yo bee-jee-bun dyan-naow. Jyeh gay nee.
I have a laptop. I'll loan it to you.

Ollie: **Tài hǎo le! Xièxiè.**
Tye how luh! Shyeh-shyeh.
That's great! Thanks.

WORDS TO KNOW

jiǎn qiè 剪切	jyan chyeh	cut
zhāntiē 粘贴 (粘貼)	jahn-tyeh	paste
fùzhì 复制 (複製)	foo-jir	copy
shuāxīn 刷新	shwah-sheen	refresh
bǎocún 保存	baow-tswuhn	save
dǎyìn 打印	dah-een	print
diǎnjī 点击 (點擊)	dyan-jee	click
shuāngjī 双击 (雙擊)	shwahng-jee	double-click

GRAMMAR CHAT

Whenever you add -**de yàomìng** 得要命 (duh yaow-meeng) right after a verb, you add a touch of drama and emphasize whatever the verb is. For example, if you say you're **lèi** 累 (lay), that means you're tired. But if you say you're **lèi de yàomìng** 累得要命 (lay duh yaow-meeng), that means you're absolutely exhausted. If you're not just **máng** 忙 (mahng) (*busy*) but rather **máng de yàomìng** 忙得要命 (mahng duh yaow-meeng), you're extremely busy, running around like a chicken without a head. Here are some useful phrases to compare:

Wǒ lěng. 我冷. (Waw lung.) (*I'm cold.*)

Wǒ lěng de yàomìng. 我冷得要命. (Waw lung duh yaow-meeng.) (*I'm freezing.*)

Jīntiān hěn rè. 今天很热. (今天很熱.) (Jeen-tyan hun ruh.) (*It's very hot today.*)

Jīntiān rè de yào mìng. 今天热得要命. (今天熱得要命.) (Jeen-tyan ruh duh yaow-meeng.) (*It's a real scorcher today.*)

REMEMBER

If you're going to emphasize a verb by adding -**de yào mìng** after it, you can't also use **hěn** 很 (hun) (*very*) in the same breath. It just makes your statement redundant. (Wait a minute. Did I say that already?)

Conducting a Meeting

Congratulations! You've finally set up shop in your new office in Beijing or welcomed your business partners from Taiwan and are all set to have your first business meeting. But just what is the purpose of your **huìyì** 会议(會議) (hway-ee) (*meeting*)? Is it to **yǎnshì** 演示 (yan-shir) (*give a presentation*) about a new **chǎnpǐn** 产品 (產品) (chahn-peen) (*product*)? Is it to **tánpàn** 谈判 (談判) (tahn-pahn) (*negotiate*) a **hétóng** 合同 (huh-toong) (*contract*)? How about **shòuxùn** 受训 (受訓) (show-shwun) (*training*) — either you or your Chinese colleagues? Do you have a specific **yìchéng** 议程 (議程) (ee-chung) (*agenda*) in mind already? I hope so. You definitely don't want to look unprepared.

Scheduling and planning a meeting

You may be one of those people who needs to **ānpái huìyì yìchéng** 安排会议议程 (安排會議議程) (ahn-pye hway-ee ee-chung) (*schedule a meeting*) just to prepare for another meeting. Here are some things you may want to do at such a preliminary meeting:

>> **jiějué wèntí** 解决问题 (解決問題) (jyeh-jweh one-tee) (*solve problems*)

>> **tǎolùn wèntí** 讨论问题 (討論問題) (taow-lwun one-tee) (*discuss problems*)

>> **tuánduì jiànshè** 团队建设 (團隊建設) (twan-dway jyan-shuh) (*team-building*)

>> **zhìdìng huìyì yìchéng** 制定会议议程 (制定會議議程) (jir-deeng hway-ee ee-chung) (*set an agenda*)

What is your role at these meetings? Are you the one to **zhǔchí huìyì** 主持会议 (主持會議) (joo–chir hway-ee) (*lead the meeting*) or just to **cānjiā huìyì** 参加会议 (參加會議) (tsahn–jya hway-ee) (*participate in the meeting*)? Are you the **xiétiáo rén** 协调人 (協調人) (shyeh–tyaow run) (*facilitator*) of the meeting, trying to elicit as much **fǎnkuì** 反馈 (反饋) (fahn–kway) (*feedback*) as possible? Or do you always have the unenviable task of contacting everyone to **qǔxiāo huìyì** 取消会议 (取消會議) (chyew–shyaow hway-ee) (*cancel the meeting*)?

Suppose you're the one who's leading the meeting and you want to make sure everyone has a say in matters. Here are some phrases you can use to try to include everyone in the process:

>> **Jack, nǐ hái yǒu shénme xūyào bǔchōng ma?** Jack, 你还有什么需要补充吗? (Jack, 你還有什麼需要補充嗎?) (Jack, nee hi yo shummuh shyew-yaow boo-choong mah?) (*Jack, do you have anything else to add?*)

>> **Shéi hái yǒu shénme yìjiàn huòzhě wèntí?** 谁还有什么意见或者问题? (誰還有甚麼意見或者問題?) (Shay hi yo shummuh ee-jyan hwaw-juh one-tee?) (*Who still has any comments or questions?*)

>> **Wǒmen xūyào duì zhèige xiàngmù biǎojué ma?** 我们需要对这个项目表决吗? (我們需要對這個項目表決嗎?) (Waw-men shyew-yaow dway jay-guh shyahng-moo byaow-jweh mah?) (*Do we need to vote on this item?*)

Making the initial greeting

Suppose you've already had some contacts with your business counterparts on the phone or via email but have never actually met them until now. A mere "nice to meet you" may not suffice, especially if you want to emphasize how very glad you are to finally be speaking face to face. Here are a couple of phrases you can use:

>> **Hěn gāoxìng jiàn dào nín běnrén.** 很高兴见到您本人. (很高興見到您本人.) (Hun gaow-sheeng jyan daow neen bun-run.) (*I'm glad to meet you in person.*)

>> **Zǒngsuàn jiàn dào nín le, shízài ràng wǒ hěn gāoxìng.** 总算见到您了, 实在让我很高兴. (總算見到您了, 實在讓我很高興.) (Dzoong-swan jyan daow neen luh, shir-dzye rahng waw hun gaow-sheeng.) (*It's a pleasure to finally meet you.*)

Always greet the person who holds the highest rank first before saying hello to others. Hierarchy is important to the Chinese, so try to always be conscious of this convention, or you may unintentionally cause someone to lose face by not acknowledging his or her importance in the overall scheme of things. This consideration goes for your side of the equation as well. The leader of your team should enter the room first and then wait to be seated by the host of the meeting.

The people you meet with may have one of the following titles:

- » **chǎngzhǎng** 厂长 (廠長) (chahng-jahng) (*factory director*)

- » **dǒngshì** 董事 (doong-shir) (*director of the board*)

- » **fù zǒngcái** 副总裁 (副总裁) (foo dzoong-tsye) (*vice president*)

- » **jīnglǐ** 经理 (經理) (jeeng-lee) (*manager*)

- » **shǒuxí kuàijì** 首席会计 (首席會計) (show-she kwye-jee) (*chief financial officer*)

- » **zhǔrèn** 主任 (joo-run) (*director of a department*)

- » **zhǔxí** 主席 (joo-she) (*chairman*)

- » **zǒngcái** 总裁 (總裁) (dzoong-tsye) (*president*)

- » **zǔzhǎng** 组长 (組長) (dzoo-jahng) (*team leader*)

In Chinese, last names always come first. When addressing someone with a title, always say the last name first, followed by the title. So if you know someone's name is **Lǐ Pēijié** (Lee Pay-jyeh) (**Lǐ** being the surname), and he's the director of the company, you address him as **Lǐ Zhǔrèn** (Lee Joo-run) (*Director Li*).

Try to get a list of the names of your Chinese counterparts in advance so you can practice pronouncing them correctly. That's sure to win a few brownie points right there.

Be sure you have business cards ready (preferably in Chinese as well as English) to give out when you go to China. You should always hand and receive each business card with two hands. Feel free to place the cards you receive in the same order as those seated (for example, from left to right as people seat themselves across from you), so you'll remember who is who.

Before you even step in that **huìyì shì** 会议室 (會議室) (hway-ee shir) (*conference room*) door, make sure you're up on a couple of key cultural do's and don'ts when you do business in China, so you don't put the proverbial **jiǎoyāzi** 脚丫子 (腳丫子) (jyaow-yah-dzuh) (*foot*) in your proverbial mouth. Here are the top three:

Rule #1: Never take "**bù**" 不 (boo) (*no*) for an answer. At least not the final answer. The Chinese value harmony and avoid confrontation at all costs. When an

American hears "no," he figures "end of story." Finito. We're done here. To the Chinese, "no" is just the beginning of the negotiations. It means "make me another offer . . ."

Rule #2: Always cultivate **guānxì**关系 (關係) (gwahn-shee) (*relationships; connections*). Business, as well as life itself, is driven by relationships in China. Strong ones. **Guānxì** based on **xiānghù xìnrèn** 相互信任 (shyahng-hoo sheen-run) (*mutual trust*) is, as Humphrey Bogart once said, "the beginning of a beautiful relationship." Contracts don't just formalize a business agreement, they formalize a new relationship based on trust and respect.

Rule #3: Always come bearing **lǐwù** 礼物 (禮物) (lee-woo) (*gifts*). Just don't bear any clocks, or they'll think their time is up. And at all costs, avoid even the appearance of **shòuhuì** 受贿 (受賄) (sho-hway) (*bribery*) with gifts like a new **Bēnchí** 奔驰 (奔馳) Bbun-chir) (*Mercedes Benz*) or a **biéshù** 别墅 (byeh-shoo) (*villa*) in the South of France. That would probably raise some **méimáo** 眉毛 (may-maow) (*eyebrows*).

Starting the meeting

Here are some things to say when you're ready to get the business meeting started:

>> **Huānyíng nín dào wǒmen de bàngōngshì.** 欢迎您到我们的办公室. (歡迎您到我們的辦公室.) (Hwahn-eeng neen daow waw-mun duh bahn-goong-shir.) (*Welcome to our office.*)

>> **Wǒ xiǎng jièshào yíxià huìyì de cānjiāzhě.** 我想介绍一下会议的参加者. (我想介绍一下會議的參加者.) (Waw shyahng jyeh-shaow ee-shyah hway-ee duh tsahn-jya-juh.) (*I'd like to introduce the conference participants.*)

>> **Zài kāihuì yǐqián, ràng wǒmen zuò yíge zìwǒ jièshào.** 在开会以前, 让我们做一个自我介绍. (在開會以前, 讓我們做一個自我介紹.) (Dzye kye-hway ee-chyan, rahng waw-men dzwaw yee-guh dzuh-waw jyeh-shaow.) (*Before the meeting begins, let's introduce ourselves.*)

>> **Zánmen kāishǐ ba.** 咱们开始吧 (咱們開始吧.) (Dzah-mun kye-shir bah.) (*Let's begin.*)

>> **Zǎoshàng hǎo.** 早上好. (Dzaow-shahng how.) (*Good morning.*)

Making a presentation

When you want to give a presentation during the meeting, here are some words that you may want to use:

» **bǎnzi** 板子 (bahn-dzuh) (*board*)

» **biǎogé** 表格 (byaow-guh) (*charts*)

» **cǎibǐ** 彩笔 (彩筆) (tsye-bee) (*marker*)

» **caí liào** 材料 (tsye-lyaow) (*handouts*)

» **chātú** 插图 (插圖) (chah-too) (*illustrations*)

» **fěnbǐ** 粉笔 (粉筆) (fun-bee) (*chalk*)

» **guàtú** 挂图 (掛圖) (gwah-too) (*flip chart*)

» **huàbǎn** 画板 (畫板) (hwah-bahn) (*easel*)

» **túbiāo** 图表 (圖表) (too-byaow) (*diagrams*)

Planning to go high-tech instead? In that case, you may want one of these:

» **huàndēngjī** 幻灯机 (幻燈機) (hwahn-dung-jee) (*slide projector*)

» **jīguāng bǐ** 激光笔 (激光筆) (jee-gwahng bee) (*laser pointer*)

» **píngmù** 屏幕 (peeng-moo) (*screen*)

» **PowerPoint yǎnshì** PPT 演示 (PPT yan-shir) (*PowerPoint presentation*)

» **tòu yǐngpiàn** 透影片 (toe yeeng-pyan) (*transparency*)

» **wǎngluò shèxiàngjī** 网络摄像机 (wahng-lwaw shuh-shyahng-jee) *web cam*

» **zhìnéng zhǔbǎn** 智能主板 (jir-nung joo-bahn) (*smart board*)

If you plan on videotaping your presentation, you need a **lùxiàngjī** 录像机 (錄像機) (loo-shyahng-jee) (*video recorder*), or better yet, a **shè lù yītǐ jī** 摄录一体机 (攝錄一體機) (shuh loo ee-tee jee) (*camcorder*). And if the room is pretty big, you may also want to use a **màikèfēng** 麦克风 (麥克風) (my-kuh-fung) (*microphone*).

Ending the meeting

Here are some phrases that may come in handy at the conclusion of the meeting:

» **Gǎnxiè dàjiā jīntiān chūxí huìyì.** 感谢大家今天出席会议. (感謝大家今天出席會議.) (Gahn-shyeh dah-jyah jeen-tyan choo-she hway-ee.) (*Thank you, everyone, for participating in today's meeting.*)

» **Wǒmen xūyào zài kāihuì tǎolùn zhè jiàn shìqíng ma?** 我们需要再开会讨论 这件事情吗? (我們需要再開會討論這件事情嗎?) (Waw-men shyew-yaow dzye kye-hway taow-lwun jay jyan shir-cheeng mah?) (*Do we need another meeting to continue the discussion?*)

» **Zài líkāi zhīqián, wǒmen bǎ xià cì huìyì de rìqī dìng xiàlái ba.** 在离开之前, 我们把下次会议的日期定下来吧。(在離開之前, 我們把下次會議 的日期定下來吧。) (Dzye lee-kye jir-chyan, waw-mun bah shyah tsuh hway-ee duh er-chee deeng shyah-lye bah.) (*Before we leave, let's confirm a date for the next meeting.*)

Talkin' the Talk

Cynthia and Pete have introduced themselves to their Chinese counterparts at the ABC Company in Shenzhen. They plan to give a presentation on their new software product a little later on.

Cynthia: **Dàjiā hǎo. Zhè cì huìyì de mùdì shì gěi nǐmen jièshào ABC gōngsī de xīn chǎnpǐn, yīzhǒng bào biǎo de ruǎnjiàn.**
Dah-jyah how. Jay tsuh hway-ee duh moo-dee shir gay nee-men jyeh-shaow ABC goong-suh duh sheen chahn-peen, ee-joong baow byaow duh rwahn-jyan.
Hello everyone. The purpose of this meeting is to introduce you all to ABC Company's new product, a type of spreadsheet software.

Pete: **Měi gè rén dōu yǒu huìyì yìchéng ma?**
May guh run doe yo hway-ee ee-chung mah?
Does everyone have a copy of the agenda?

Cynthia: **Xièxiè, Pete. Duì le. Dàjiā dōu yǐjīng nádào zīliào le ma?**
Shyeh-shyeh, Pete. Dway luh. Dah-jyah doe ee-jeeng nah-daow dzuh-lyaow luh mah?
Thank you, Pete. Yes, has everyone already received the materials?

WORDS TO KNOW

běndì huà shēngchǎn 本地化生产 (本地化生產)	bun-dee hwah shung-chahn	local production
chǎnwù 产物 (產物)	chahn-woo	product
chūkǒu jiégòu 出口结构 (出口結構)	choo-ko jyeh-go	export structure
dìnghuò chéngbàn 订货承办 (訂貨承辦)	deeng-hwaw chung-bahn	ordering and processing
duōbiān màoyì 多边贸易 (多邊貿易)	dwaw-byan maow-ee	multilateral trade
fēngxiǎn tóuzī 风险投资 (風險投資)	fung-shyan toe-dzuh	venture capital
gǔdōng 股东 (股東)	goo-doong	shareholder

Discussing Business and Industry

Because China has opened up to the world so quickly since the death of Mao Zedong in 1976 (the same year the United States established diplomatic relations with China) and within the last ten years has burst on the international economic scene, U.S. businesses have set up shop throughout the country. Whether your company has an office in mainland China, Taiwan, Singapore, or Hong Kong, you're sure to find one or more of the industries listed in Table 12-3 represented in those places.

Regardless of what industry you're in, here are some things you can do to help you decide how to advertise your company and its products or services or to determine how it's going:

» **diàntái yú diànshì guǎnggào** 电台与电视广告 (電台與電視廣告) (dyan-tye yew dyan-shir gwahng-gaow) (*radio and television ads*)

» **dīngdāng** 叮当 (叮噹) (deeng-dahng) (*jingle*)

» **guǎnggào xuānchuán** 广告宣传 (廣告宣傳) (gwahng-gaow shwan-chwan) (*ad campaign*)

» **pǐnpái tuīguǎng** 品牌推广 (品牌推广) (peen-pye tway-gwahng) (*brand-name promotion*)

TABLE 12-3   Industries

Chinese	Pronunciation	English
bǎoxiǎn 保险 (保險)	baow-shyan	*insurance*
cǎikuǎng yú shíyóu 采矿与石油 (採礦與石油)	tsye-kwahng yew shir-yo	*mining and petroleum*
chūbǎn 出版	choo-bahn	*publishing*
diànnǎo 电脑 (電腦)	dyan-now	*computers*
fángdìchǎn 房地产 (房地產)	fahng-dee-chahn	*real estate*
gōngchéng 工程	goong-chung	*engineering*
gōngguān 公关 (公關)	goong-gwan	*public relations*
guǎnggào 广告 (廣告)	gwahng-gaow	*advertising*
guǎnlǐ zīxún 管理咨询 (管理咨詢)	gwahn-lee dzuh-shwun	*management consulting*
jiànzào 建造 (建造)	jyan-dzaow	*construction*
qìchē 汽车 (汽車)	chee-chuh	*automotive*
shízhuāng 时装 (時裝)	shir-jwahng	*fashion*
xīnwén 新闻 (新聞)	sheen-one	*journalism*
yínháng yǔ cáiwù 银行与财务 (銀行與財物)	yeen-hahng yew tsye-woo	*banking and finance*
yúlè 娱乐 (娛樂)	yew-luh	*entertainment*
yùnshū 运输 (運輸)	yewn-shoo	*shipping*
zhìyào 制药 (製藥)	jir-yaow	*pharmaceuticals*

>> **shìchǎng yánjiū** 市场研究 (市場研究) (shir-chahng yan-jyo) (*market research*)

>> **xiāofèizhě yánjiū** 消费者研究 (消費者研究) (shyaow-fay-juh yan-jyo) (*consumer research*)

>> **xìnxī guǎnggào** 信息广告 (信息廣告) (sheen-she gwahng-gaow) (*infomercial*)

>> **zhíxiāo yùndòng** 直销运动 (直銷運動) (jir-shyaow yoon-doong) (*direct marketing campaign*)

And here are some things you should have on hand in meetings or at that **màoyì zhǎnxiāohuì** 贸易展销会 (貿易展銷會) (maow-ee jahn-shyaow-hway) (*trade show*):

>> **chǎnpǐn mùlù** 产品目录 (產品目錄) (chahn-peen moo-loo) (*catalogue*)

>> **túbiāo** 图标 (圖標) (too-byaow) (*logo*)

>> **xiǎocèzǐ** 小册子 (小冊子) (shyaow-tsuh-dzuh) (*brochure*)

Of course, if your product is so good it virtually sells itself, your greatest source of business is undoubtedly going to come from good ol' **kǒuchuán guǎnggào** 口传广告 (口傳廣告) (ko-chwan gwahng-gaow) (*word-of-mouth advertising*).

Still, in this age of the **shèjiāo wǎngluò** 社交网络 (社交網絡) (*social network*), you can't rely solely on others to spread the word. You need to get to know key Chinese social media and marketing platforms already in place, which can reach the proverbial billion customers out there from Xi'an to Xinjiang.

Whether you're ready to burst onto the **diànzǐ gōnggào pái** 电子公告牌 (電子公告牌) (dyan-dzuh goong-gaow pye) (*e-commerce*) scene, or want to promote a very laudable **huánbǎo de jìhuà** 环保的计划 (環保的計劃) (hwahn-baow duh jee-hwah) (*eco-friendly project*) through a **bókè** 博客 (baw-kuh) (*blog*), you'll have to do it the Chinese way — through its search engines, its social media, and its language.

You'd be hard-pressed to find even one Western media platform on the Chinese net. No Google, no Facebook, no Twitter, no Instagram. Zero. Zilch. Nada. And all those **Míngjiào** 鸣叫 (鳴叫) (Meeng-jyaow) (*Tweets*) flying around the U.S. these days? Gone. Nowhere to be found. The reason? The Great Firewall of China . . . Internet censorship, Chinese-style. See Table 12-4 for a list of Chinese equivalents to popular Western social media sites and search engines.

To go around The Great Firewall, you'll have to use **xūnǐ zhuānyòng wǎngluò** 虚拟专用网络 (擬專用網絡) (shwun-nee jwan-yoong wahng-lwaw) (*Virtual Private Network [VPN] services*), if you want to be safe and secure out there in cyberspace.

CULTURAL WISDOM

The Great Firewall is the term used for the filters the Chinese government has put on the Internet, which limit what people in China both say and see online.

CULTURAL WISDOM

As of 2018, China had the largest e-commerce market in the world, with almost 50 percent of its population connected to the Internet.

TABLE 12-4 ## Western Social Media and Search Engines and Their Chinese Counterparts

Western Social Media and Search Engines	Chinese Counterparts
Amazon	**Ālǐbābā** 阿里巴巴 (Ah-lee-bah-bah) (*Alibaba*)
Facebook	**RénRén wǎng** 人人网 (人人網) (Ren Ren wahng); **Téngxùn** 腾讯 (騰訊) (Tuhng-shyewn) (*Tencent*)
Google	**Bǎidù** 百度 (Bye-doo) (*Baidu*); **Sōuhú** 搜狐 (So-hoo) (*Sohu*)
Instagram	**Hǎo zàn** 好赞 (好贊) (Haow dzahn) (*Nice*)
Instant Messaging	**QQ** (The Chinese use the English letters, and there's no separate English translation.) **Wēixìn** 微信 (Way-sheen) (*WeChat*)
Twitter	**Xīnlàng wēi bó** 新浪微博 (Sheen-lahng way baw) (*Sina Weibo*)
YouTube	**Yōukù tǔdòu** 优酷土豆 (優酷土豆) (Yo-koo Too-doe) (*Youku-Tudou*); **Ài qí yì** 爱奇艺 (愛奇藝) (eye Chee ee) (*iQiyi*)

Talkin' the Talk

William and Douglas, two salesmen, visit Guangdong to see whether the Flying Peacock Company wants to buy their product. They're in a meeting with the Flying Peacock Company president, where they've already gone through the preliminary introductions and small talk.

William: **Zhèlǐ shì wǒmen chǎnpǐn de yīgè móxíng. Tā shì àn bǐlì de.**
Jay-lee shir waw-men chahn-peen duh ee-guh maw-sheng. Tah shir ahn bee-lee duh.
Here's a model of our product. It is built to scale.

Douglas: **Wǒmen de chǎnpǐn shì yóu wǒmen zìjǐ de zhuānjiā shèjì de, érqiě zhèngmíng shì mǎn chénggōng de.**
Waw-men duh chahn-peen shir yo waw-men dzuh-jee duh jwan-jyah shuh-jee duh, are-chyeh jung-meeng shir mahn chung-goong duh.
Our product was designed by our own experts and has proven to be quite successful.

William: **Duì le, kěshì wǒmen yě kéyǐ gēnjù nǐde guīgé lái shèjì chǎnpǐn.**

Dway luh, kuh-shir waw-men yeah kuh-yee gun-jyew nee-duh gway-guh lye shuh-jee chahn-peen.

That's correct, but we can also tailor the product to meet your specifications.

Douglas: **Wǒmen de jiàgé yě hěn yǒu jìngzhēnglì.**

Waw-men duh jyah-guh yeah hun yo jeeng-juhng-lee.

Our prices are also quite competitive.

WORDS TO KNOW

diànnǎo ruǎnjiàn 电脑软件 (電腦軟件)	dyan-naow rwan-jyan	computer software
yīntèwǎng 因特网 (因特網)	een-tuh-wahng	Internet
diànnǎo chéngxù 电脑程序 (電腦程序)	dyan-naow chung-shyew	computer program
Shìchuāng 视窗 (視窗)	Shir-chwahng	Windows
Píngguǒ (diànnǎo) 苹果 (电脑)	Peeng-gwaw (dyan-naow)	Mac (computer)
Píngguǒ (gōngsī) 苹果 (蘋果) (公司)	Peeng-gwaw (goong suh)	Apple (company)
Wēiruǎn 微软 (微軟)	Way-rwan	Microsoft
Gǔgē 谷歌	Goo-guh	Google

FUN & GAMES

Match each of the Chinese words to the correct English translation. Turn to Appendix C for the answers.

1. *Internet*

2. *public relations*

3. *e-commerce*

4. *venture capital*

5. *Let's begin.*

a. **gōngguān** 公关 (公關)

b. **Yīntèwǎng** 因特网 (因特網)

c. **fēngxiǎn tóuzī** 风险投资 (風險投資)

d. **diànzǐ gōnggào pái** 电子公告牌 (電子公告牌)

e. **Zánmen kāishǐ ba.** 咱们开始吧. (咱們開始吧.)

Chapter **13**

Recreation and Outdoor Activities

After a hard day at work, most people are ready to kick back and relax. But where to begin? Do you feel so consumed by your **gōngzuò** 工作 (goong-dzwaw) (*work*) that you can't seem to switch gears? Get a life! Better yet, get a **yèyú àihào** 业余爱好 (業餘愛好) (yeh-yew eye-how) (*hobby*). Play some **yīnyuè** 音乐 (音樂) (yeen-yweh) (*music*) on your **xiǎotíqín** 小提琴 (shyaow-tee-cheen) (*violin*). Paint a **huà** 画 (畫) (hwah) (*picture*). Kick a **zúqiú** 足球 (dzoo-chyo) (*football*) around. Do whatever it takes to make you relax and have some fun. Your outside interests make you more interesting to be around, and you make new friends at the same time — especially if you join a **duì** 队 (隊) (dway) (*team*).

And if you're into **lánqiú** 篮球 (籃球) (lahn-chyo) (*basketball*), just utter the name **Yáo Míng** 姚明 (yaow meeng); you'll instantly discover hordes of potential language exchange partners from among the many fans of this 7-foot-6-inch Shanghai native who made it big as a Houston Rockets superstar.

REMEMBER

You can listen to all the Talkin' the Talk dialogues featured in this chapter. Go to www.dummies.com/go/chinese and click on the dialogue you want to hear.

Naming Your Hobbies

Are you someone who likes to collect stamps, play chess, or watch birds in the park? Whatever you enjoy doing, your hobbies are always a good conversation piece. Having at least one **yèyú àihào** is always a good thing. How about getting involved in some of the following?

>> **diàoyú** 钓鱼 (釣魚) (dyaow-yew) (*fishing*)

>> **guān niǎo** 观鸟 (觀鳥) (gwan-nyaow) (*birdwatching*)

>> **jí yóu** 集邮 (集郵) (jee yo) (*stamp collecting*)

>> **kàn shū** 看书 (看書) (kahn shoo) (*reading*)

>> **pēngtiáo** 烹调 (烹調) (pung-tyaow) (*cooking*)

>> **yuányì** 园艺 (園藝) (ywan-ee) (*gardening*)

A common verb associated with many hobbies is **dǎ** 打 (dah) (*to do or play with* [Literally: *to strike, hit, or beat*]). You can use it to talk about partaking in hobbies such as **tàijí quán** 太极拳 (太極拳) (tye-jee chwan) (*a slow form of martial arts commonly referred to just as Tai Ji*) and playing **pūkè** 扑克 (撲克) (poo-kuh) (*cards*), **májiàng** 麻将 (麻將) (mah-jyahng) (*mah-jong*), and **guójì xiàngqí** 国际象棋 (國際象棋) (gwaw-jee shyahng-chee) (*chess*). Here are some quick questions with the verb **dǎ** that can help get a conversation started:

>> **Nǐ huì búhuì dǎ tàijí quán?** 你会不会打太极拳? (你會不會打太極拳?) (Nee hway boo-hway dah tye-jee chwahn?) (*Do you know how to do Tai Ji?*)

>> **Nǐ dǎ májiàng ma?** 你打麻将吗? (你打麻將嗎?) (Nee dah mah-jyahng mah?) (*Do you play mah-jong?*)

Both **tàijí quán** and **májiàng** are quintessential Chinese pastimes. In addition to **tàijí quán,** everyone is familiar with other forms of **wǔshù** 武术 (武術) (woo-shoo) (*martial arts*), including **gōngfū** 功夫 (goong foo) (*kung fu*) — a martial art practiced since the **Táng** 唐 (tahng) dynasty back in the eighth century. In fact, you can still see **kung fu** masters practicing at the Shaolin Temple in Zhengzhou, Henan province — one great reason for making a trip off the beaten path if you ever visit China.

Tàijí quán is considered a martial art which focuses on one's internal, spiritual energy which manifests externally as physical strength. It is the most widely practiced form of martial arts throughout the world. The term **tàijí** (*the Great Ultimate*) refers to the interplay between opposing yet complementary forces in the universe — yin and yang — as the basis of creation. **Quán** means *fist*, emphasizing that this art is a kind of unarmed combat. Very early every morning in China, hundreds of people flock to local parks to practice this slow-motion form of exercise together.

Talkin' the Talk

Donald and Helga discuss their knowledge of taiji quan with each other.

Donald: **Nǐ huì búhuì dǎ tàijí quán?**
Nee hway boo-hway dah tye-jee chwan?
Do you know how to do Tai Ji?

Helga: **Búhuì. Kěshì wǒ zhīdào tàijí quán shì yì zhǒng hěn liúxíng de jiànshēn yùndòng.**
Boo-hway. Kuh-shir waw jir-daow tye-jee chwan shir ee joong hun lyo-sheeng duh jyan-shun yoon-doong.
No, but I know that Tai Ji is a very popular kind of exercise.

Donald: **Duìle. Měitiān zǎoshàng hěn zǎo hěn duō rén yìqǐ dǎ tàijí quán.**
Dway-luh. May-tyan dzaow-shahng hun dzaow hun dwaw run ee-chee dah tye-jee chwan.
That's right. Very early every morning, lots of people practice Tai Ji together.

Helga: **Tàijí quán de dòngzuò kànqǐlái hěn màn.**
Tye-jee chwan duh doong-dzwaw kahn-chee-lye hun mahn.
Tai Ji movements look very slow.

Donald: **Yòu shuō duìle! Shēntǐ zǒngshì yào wěndìng. Dòngzuò zǒngshì yào xiétiáo.**
Yo shwaw dway-luh! Shun-tee dzoong-shir yaow one-deeng. Doong-dzwaw dzoong-shir yaow shyeh-tyaow.
Right again! The body should always be stable, and the movements should always be well coordinated.

WORDS TO KNOW

dǎpái 打牌	dah-pye	to play cards
dǎ májiàng 打麻将 (打麻將)	dah mah-jyahng	to play mah-jong
dǎ wǎngqiú 打网球 (打網球)	dah wahng-chyo	to play tennis

Exploring Nature

If you're working overseas in China and want to get really far from the madding crowds, or even just far enough away from your **bàngōngshì** 办公室 (辦公室) (bahn-goong-shir) (*office*) to feel refreshed, try going to one of China's many sacred mountains or a beautiful beach to take in the **shānshuǐ** 山水 (shahn-shway) (*landscape*). You may want to **qù lùyíng** 去露营 (去露營) (chyew lyew-eeng) (*go camping*) or set up camp on the beach and have a **yěcān** 野餐 (yeh-tsahn) (*picnic*) before you **pá shān** 爬山 (pah shahn) (*climb a mountain*).

CULTURAL WISDOM

Traveling through the Chinese countryside is a great way to escape city life. Check out these sights along the way:

- » **bǎotǎ** 宝塔 (寶塔) (baow-tah) (*pagoda*)
- » **Dào miào** 道庙 (道廟) (Daow-meow) (*Daoist temple*)
- » **dàotián** 稻田 (Daow-tyan) (*rice paddies*)
- » **Fó miào** 佛庙 (佛廟) (Faw-meow) (*Buddhist temple*)
- » **Kǒng miào** 孔庙 (孔廟) (Koong-meow) (*Confucian temple*)
- » **miào** 庙 (廟) (meow) (*temple*)
- » **nóngmín** 农民 (農民) (noong-meen) (*farmers*)

If you're ever exploring **dà zìrán** 大自然 (dah dzuh-rahn) (*nature*) with a friend who speaks Chinese, a few of these words may come in handy:

- » **àn** 岸 (ahn) (*shore*)
- » **chítáng** 池塘 (chir-tahng) (*pond*)
- » **hǎi** 海 (hi) (*ocean*)
- » **hǎitān** 海滩 (海灘) (hi-tahn) (*beach*)
- » **hé** 河 (huh) (*river*)
- » **hú** 湖 (hoo) (*lake*)
- » **niǎo** 鸟 (鳥) (nyaow) (*birds*)
- » **shāmò** 沙漠 (shah-maw) (*desert*)
- » **shān** 山 (shahn) (*mountains*)

CULTURAL WISDOM

CHINA'S SACRED MOUNTAINS

Both Buddhists and Daoists have traditionally built monasteries high on quiet mountaintops or deep inside lush forests to meditate. Some of China's **shān** 山 (shahn) (*mountains*) — five Daoist and four Buddhist — are still considered sacred today, and they all remain sites of pilgrimage. **Huáng Shān** 黄山 (Hwahng Shahn) (*Yellow Mountain*) is perhaps China's most famous sacred mountain; it's distinguished by rare pine trees, unusual rock formations, and hot springs, and is surrounded by lakes and waterfalls.

>> **shāndòng** 山洞 (shahn-doong) (*cave*)

>> **shù** 树 (樹) (shoo) (*trees*)

>> **xiǎo shān** 小山 (shyaow-shahn) (*hills*)

>> **yún** 云 (雲) (yewn) (*clouds*)

Talkin' the Talk

Herman and Serena discover the beauty of the seaside resort of Běidàihé (Bay-dye-huh) in northern China.

Herman: **Nǐ kàn! Zhèr de fēngjǐng duōme piàoliàng!**
            Nee kahn! Jar duh fung-jeeng dwaw-muh pyaow-lyahng!
            Look! The scenery here is gorgeous!

Serena: **Nǐ shuō duìle. Zhēn piàoliàng.**
            Nee shwaw dway-luh. Jun pyaow-lyahng.
            You're right. It's truly beautiful.

Herman: **Shénme dōu yǒu: shān, shēn lán de hǎi, qīng lán de tiān.**
            Shummuh doe yo: shahn, shun lahn duh hi, cheeng lahn duh tyan.
            It has everything: mountains, deep blue ocean, and clear sky.

Serena: **Nǐ shuō duìle. Xiàng tiāntáng yíyàng.**
            Nee shwaw dway-luh. Shyahng tyan-tahng ee-yahng.
            You're right. It's like paradise.

WORDS TO KNOW

qímǎ 骑马 (騎馬)	chee-mah	horsebackriding
hángxíng 航行	hahng-sheeng	sailing
fú qiǎn 浮潜 (浮潛)	foo chyan	snorkeling
shuǐ fèi qiánshuǐ 水肺潜水 (水肺潛水)	shway fay chyan-shway	scuba diving

GRAMMAR CHAT

To indicate a similarity between two ideas or objects, as in the last line of the Talkin' the Talk involving Serena and Herman, use the phrase **xiàng . . . yíyàng** 像 . . . 一样 (像 . . . 一樣) (shyahng . . . ee yahng). Here are some examples:

xiàng nǐ dìdì yíyàng 像你弟弟一样 (像你弟弟一樣) (shyahng nee dee-dee ee-yahng) (*like your younger brother*)

xiàng qīngwā yíyàng 像青蛙一样 (像青蛙一樣) (shyahng cheeng-wah ee-yahng) (*like a frog*)

xiàng fēngzi yíyàng 像疯子一样 (像瘋子一樣) (shyahng fung-dzuh ee-yahng) (*like a crazy person*)

CULTURAL WISDOM

Today you can find such activities as hot-air ballooning and gliding in Anyang. Kind of amazing when you discover Anyang was the capital of China's very first dynasty, almost two millennia before the Common Era. You can even hook up with a hot-air balloon tour of the Great Wall and the Silk Road. These pursuits certainly present a good way to cover such great distances without requiring you to have been a Hun on horseback. Speaking of which, if camel treks are your thing, Chinese travel agencies can now even arrange for you to ride with the Mongols, those horsemen who've perfected the art of riding over the centuries.

CULTURAL WISDOM

THE SHANGHAI CHILDREN'S PALACE

If you ever visit Shanghai, make time for a visit to the **Shàoniángōng** 少年宫 (shaow-nyan-goong) (*the Children's Palace*), where gifted children take part in an assortment of extracurricular activities in areas such as music, art, dance, and science. Founded in 1953 by Song Qingling (whose husband, Dr. Sun Yat-sen, established the Republic of China, or Taiwan), the Children's Palace is in a grand old building originally known as Marble Hall. It was built by the Baghdadi Jewish tycoon Elly Kadoorie in 1924 and still boasts grand marble hallways, winding staircases, ornate fireplaces, chandeliers, and French windows.

Tapping into Your Artistic Side

You may pride yourself on having been the biggest jock, but I bet you still get teary-eyed when you see a beautiful painting or listen to Beethoven. It's okay; just admit it. You're a regular Renaissance man, and you can't help it. No more apologies.

Okay, now you're ready to tap into your more sensitive, artistic side in Chinese. Don't be afraid of expressing your **gǎnqíng** 感情 (gahn-cheeng) (emotions). The Chinese will appreciate your sensitivity to a **shānshuǐ huà** 山水画 (山水畫) (shahn-shway hwah) (landscape painting) from the **Sòng** 宋 (Soong) dynasty (960–1279) or to the beauty of a **cíqì** 瓷器 (tsuh-chee) (porcelain) from the **Míng** 明 (Meeng) dynasty (1368–1644).

I bet you have tons of **chuàngzàoxìng** 创造性 (創造性) (chwahng-dzaow-sheeng) (creativity). If so, try your hand at one of these fine arts:

>> **diāokè** 雕刻 (雕刻) (dyaow-kuh) (sculpting)

>> **huà** 画 (畫) (hwah) (painting)

>> **shūfǎ** 书法 (書法) (shoo-fah) (calligraphy)

>> **shuǐcǎi huà** 水彩画 (水彩畫) (shway-tsye hwah) (watercolor)

>> **sùmiáo huà** 素描画 (素描畫) (soo-meow hwah) (drawing)

>> **táoqì** 陶器 (taow-chee) (pottery)

Striking Up the Band

Do you play a **yuèqì** 乐器 (樂器) (yweh-chee) (musical instrument)? It's never too late to learn, you know. Like kids all over the world, lots of Chinese children take **xiǎotíqín** 小提琴 (shyaow-tee-cheen) (violin) and **gāngqín** 钢琴 (鋼琴) (gahng-cheen) (piano) classes — often under duress. They appreciate the forced lessons when they get older, though, and have their own kids.

You don't have to become a professional **yīnyuè jiā** 音乐家 (音樂家) (een-yweh jyah) (musician) to enjoy playing an instrument. How about trying your hand (or mouth) at one of these?

>> **chángdí** 长笛 (長笛) (chahng-dee) (flute)

>> **cháng hào** 长号 (長號) (chahng how) (trombone)

- » **dà hào** 大号 (大號) (dah how) (*tuba*)

- » **dà tíqín** 大提琴 (dah tee-cheen) (*cello*)

- » **dānhuángguǎn** 单簧管 (單簧管) (dahn-hwahng-gwan) (*clarinet*)

- » **gāngqín** 钢琴 (鋼琴) (gahng-cheen) (*piano*)

- » **gǔ** 鼓 (goo) (*drums*)

- » **lǎbā** 喇叭 (lah-bah) (*trumpet*)

- » **liùxiánqín** 六弦琴 (lyo-shyan-cheen) (*guitar*)

- » **nán dīyīn** 男低音 (nahn dee-een) (*double bass*)

- » **sākèsī guǎn** 萨克斯管 (薩克斯管) (sah-kuh-suh gwahn) (*saxophone*)

- » **shuānghuángguǎn** 双簧管 (雙簧管) (shwahng-hwahng-gwan) (*oboe*)

- » **shùqín** 竖琴 (豎琴) (shoo-cheen) (*harp*)

- » **xiǎotíqín** 小提琴 (shyaow-tee-cheen) (*violin*)

- » **zhōngtíqín** 中提琴 (joong-tee-cheen) (*viola*)

GRAMMAR CHAT

The Chinese language has a few different verbs that you can use to indicate the practice of various instruments. People who play stringed instruments should use the verb **lā** 拉 (lah) (*to draw* [as in draw a bow]) before the name of the instrument. For example, you can say that you **lā zhōngtíqín** 拉中提琴 (lah joong–tee–cheen) (*play the viola*), but you can only **tán** (tahn) (*play*) a piano. For wind instruments, you have to **chuī** 吹 (chway) (*blow*) them.

CULTURAL WISDOM

TRADITIONAL CHINESE INSTRUMENTS

If you've heard any traditional Chinese music at a concert or on a recording, you've probably heard one of these Chinese **yuèqì** 乐器 (樂器) (yweh-chee) (*musical instruments*) at one point or another:

- **èrhú** 二胡 (are-hoo): A two-stringed, bowed instrument

- **gǔzhēng** 古筝 (古箏) (goo-juhng): A long, plucked string instrument that rests on a large stand in front of you

- **pípā** 琵琶 (pee-pah): A plucked string instrument with a fretted fingerboard that sits on your lap

Playing on a Team

No matter where you go in the world, you'll find a national pastime. In America, it's baseball. In most of Europe, it's soccer. And in China, it's ping–pong, although since Yao Ming came on the scene, basketball has gotten some attention as well. Here are the Chinese terms for these and many other popular sports:

» **bàngqiú** 棒球 (bahng-chyo) (*baseball*)

» **bīngqiú** 冰球 (beeng-chyo) (*hockey*)

» **lánqiú** 篮球 (籃球) (lahn-chyo) (*basketball*)

» **lěiqiú** 垒球 (壘球) (lay-chyo) (*softball*)

» **páiqiú** 排球 (pye-chyo) (*volleyball*)

» **pīngpāng qiú** 乒乓球 (peeng-pahng chyo) (*ping-pong*)

» **shǒuqiú** 手球 (show-chyo) (*handball*)

» **tǐcāo** 体操 (體操) (tee-tsaow) (*gymnastics*)

» **wǎngqiú** 网球 (網球) (wahng-chyo) (*tennis*)

» **yīngshì zúqiú** 英式足球 (eeng-shir dzoo-chyo) (*soccer* [Literally: *English-style football*])

» **yóuyǒng** 游泳 (yo-yoong) (*swimming*)

» **yǔmáoqiú** 羽毛球 (yew-maow-chyo) (*badminton*)

» **zúqiú** 足球 (dzoo-chyo) (*football*)

Some sports, such as gymnastics and swimming, actually involve multiple events. Here are the common components of these two sports:

» **ānmǎ** 鞍马 (鞍馬) (ahn-mah) (*pommell horse*)

» **dāngàng** 单杠 (單槓) (dahn-gahng) (*high bar*)

» **gāodīgàng** 高低杠 (高低槓) (gaow-dee-gahng) (*uneven bars*)

» **shuānggàng** 双杠 (雙槓) (shwahng-gahng) (*parallel bars*)

» **zìyóu tǐcāo** 自由体操 (自由體操) (dzuh-yo tee-tsaow) (*floor exercise*)

» **cè yǒng** 侧泳 (側泳) (tsuh yoong) (*sidestroke*)

» **diéyǒng** 蝶泳 (dyeh-yoong) (*butterfly stroke*)

» **wāyǒng** 蛙泳 (wah-yoong) (*frog-style or breast stroke*)

>> **yǎngyǒng** 仰泳 (yahng-yoong) (*backstroke*)

>> **zìyóuyǒng** 自由泳 (dzuh-yo-yoong) (*freestyle*)

And if you're a **tiàoshuǐ yùndòngyuán** 跳水运动员 (跳水運動員) (tyaow-shway yewn-doong-ywan) (*diver*), you'd better not **pà gāo** 怕高 (pah gaow) (*be scared of heights*).

GRAMMAR CHAT

You can use the verb **dǎ** 打 (dah) (*to hit*) to talk about playing sports that use your arm or hands (ping-pong, basketball, tennis . . .) as well as pursuing other hobbies (check out the earlier section "Naming Your Hobbies"). You can use the verb **tī** (踢) to talk about sports that are played with your feet (football, soccer . . .). But you can also **wán** 玩 (wahn) (*play*) ball games as well.

REMEMBER

Some games require the use of **pīngpāng qiúpāi** 乒乓球拍 (peeng-pahng chyo-pye) (*ping-pong paddles*), **wǎngqiú pāi** 网球拍 (網球拍) (wahng-chyo pye) (*tennis rackets*), or **qiú** 球 (chyo) (*balls*). All games, however, require a sense of **gōngpíng jìngzhēng** 公平竞争 (公平競爭) (goong-peeng jeeng-jung) (*fair play*).

CULTURAL WISDOM

Soccer season in Beijing is from May to October, but in southern China it goes year-round. As in Europe, soccer is the spectator sport of preference throughout the country. And just as in Europe, passionate fans sometimes boil over into brawling hordes. If you ever find yourself in Shanghai, check out the game at the Hongkou Stadium. In Beijing, try the Workers' Stadium near the City Hotel.

Here are some useful phrases to know, whether you're an amateur or a professional athlete. At one time or another, you've certainly heard (or said) them all.

>> **Nǐ shūle.** 你输了. (你輸了.) (Nee shoo-luh.) (*You lost.*)

>> **Wǒ dǎ de bú tài hǎo.** 我打得不太好. (Waw dah duh boo tye how.) (*I don't play very well.*)

>> **Wǒ yíngle.** 我赢了. (我贏了.) (Waw yeeng-luh.) (*I won.*)

>> **Wǒ zhēn xūyào liànxí.** 我真需要练习. (我真需要練習.) (Waw jun shyew-yaow lyan-she.) (*I really need to practice.*)

If you prefer to spectate from the stands (or from your couch), here's a list of terms and phrases you need to know if you want to follow the action:

>> **bǐfēn duōshǎo?** 比分多少? (Bee-fun dwaw-shaow?) (*What's the score?*)

>> **chuī shàozi** 吹哨子 (chway shaow-dzuh) (*to blow a whistle*)

>> **dǎngzhù qiú** 挡住球 (擋住球) (dahng-joo chyo) (*to block the ball*)

>> **dé yì fēn** 得一分 (duh ee fun) (*to score a point*)

>> **fā qiú** 发球 (發球) (fah chyo) (*to serve the ball*)

» **Něixiē duì cānjiā bǐsài?** 哪些队参加比赛? (哪些隊參加比賽?) (Nay-shyeh dway tsahn-jya bee-sye?) (*Which teams are playing?*)

» **tī jìn yì qiú** 踢进一球 (踢進一球) (tee jeen ee chyo) (*to make a goal*)

» **Wǒ xiǎng qù kàn qiúsài.** 我想去看球赛. (我想去看球賽.) (Waw shyahng chyew kahn chyo-sye.) (*I want to see a ballgame.*)

Talkin' the Talk

Ernest and Cecilia go to a basketball game together.

Ernest: **Bǐsài shénme shíhòu kāishǐ?**
Bee-sye shummuh shir-ho kye-shir?
When does the game begin?

Cecilia: **Kuài yào kāishǐle.**
Kwye yaow kye-shir-luh.
It's going to start soon.

A few minutes later, the game finally begins.

Ernest: **Wà! Tā méi tóuzhòng!**
Wah! Tah may toe-joong!
Wow! He missed the shot!

Cecilia: **Méi guānxi. Lìngwài nèige duìyuán gāng gāng kòulán défēn.**
May gwahn-she. Leeng-why nay-guh dway-ywan gahng gahng ko-lahn duh-fun.
It doesn't matter. That other player just scored with a slam dunk.

WORDS TO KNOW

Wǒ yíngle. 我赢了.	Waw eeng-luh.	I won.
Nǐ shūle. 你输了.	Nee shoo-luh.	You lost.
jiàoliàn 教练 (教練)	jyaow lyan	coach (Noun)
yùndòngyuán 运动员 (運動員)	yoon-doong-ywan	athlete

FUN & GAMES

A.

B.

C.

D.

E.

What are the people in the pictures doing? Use the correct verb in your response. (See Appendix C for the answers.)

A. _____

B. _____

C. _____

D. _____

E. _____

Imagine two of your ideal environments and describe what they are like in the spaces below:

Xiàng tiāntáng yíyàng. 像天堂一样. (像天堂一樣.) (Shyahng tyan-tahng ee-yahng.) (*It's like paradise.*)

Xiàng ____ yíyàng. 像____一样. (像____一樣.) (Shyahng _____ ee-yahng.) (*It's like _____.*)

Xiàng ____ yíyàng. 像____一样. (像____一樣.) (Shyahng _____ ee-yahng.) (*It's like _____.*)

Chinese on
the Go

Chapter **14**

Planning a Trip

areful planning is the key to a successful vacation or business trip. You have to keep in mind not only where you want to go but also the best time to travel. This chapter tells you how to prepare for a trip abroad and how to choose the exact day, date, and year you want to travel. When it comes to making sure your **hùzhào** 护照 (護照) (hoo-jaow) (*passport*) is still valid and your **qiānzhèng** 签证 (簽證) (chyan-juhng) (*visa*) is in order, however, you're on your own. **Yí lù píng ān!** 一路平安! (Ee loo peeng ahn!) (*Have a good trip!*).

Talking about When You Want to Travel

The time of year you choose to travel can make all the difference in the world for a great (or lousy) vacation. A trip to Beijing during March, just when the dust storms are blowing in from the Gobi Desert, for example, is quite different from a trip during May or October, when pollution is at a minimum and sunny skies are at a maximum. Of course, May and October are peak seasons to travel to China for exactly these reasons, which means hotel prices are also at their peak. Paris in the spring is just as great (and just as expensive) for the same reason. Can't do much to help you there. For more on all things related to dates and seasons, head to Chapter 5.

Want to find out when friends plan to leave on their vacation? Just ask them one of these basic questions:

>> **Nǐ jǐ yuè jǐ hào zǒu?** 你几月几号走? (你幾月幾號走?) (Nee jee yweh jee how dzoe?) (*When are you leaving?* [Literally: *What month and day are you leaving?*])

>> **Nǐ jǐ yuè jǐ hào qù Zhōngguó?** 你几月几号去中国? (你幾月幾號去中國?) (Nee jee yweh jee how chyew joong-gwaw?) (*When will you be going to China? [Literally: What month and day will you be going to China?]*)

If you have to answer the preceding questions, just fill in the number of the month and the number of the day you plan on leaving and put those words in place of each "**jǐ**". Here are some examples:

Wǒ wǔ yuè sānshí hào zǒu. 我五月三十号走. (我五月三十號走.) (Waw woo yweh sahn shir how dzoe.) (*I'm leaving on May 30.*)

Wǒ sān yuè yī hào qù Zhōngguó. 我三月一号去中国. (我三月一號去中國.) (Waw sahn yweh ee how chyew Joong-gwaw.) (*I'm going to China on March 1.*)

Bet you can't wait to start making those travel plans now!

Celebrating the Chinese Holidays

If you travel to China during 2018, you arrive during **Gǒu Nián** 狗年 (Go Nyan) (*Year of the Dog*). Want to travel in later years instead?

>> 2019: **Zhū Nián** 猪年 (豬年) Joo Nyan) (*Year of the Pig*)

>> 2020: **Shǔ Nián** 鼠年 (Shoo Nyan) (*Year of the Rat*)

After the rat, the following animals come calling: **niú** 牛 (nyo) (*ox*), **hǔ** 虎 (hoo) (*tiger*), **tù** 兔 (too) (*rabbit*), **lóng** 龙 (龍) (loong) (*dragon*), **shé** 蛇 (shuh) (*snake*), **mǎ** 马 (馬)(mah) (*horse*), **yáng** 羊 (yahng) (*goat*), **hóu** 猴 (ho) (*monkey*), **jī** 鸡 (雞) (jee) (*rooster*), **gǒu** 狗 (狗) (go) (*dog*), and the **zhū** 猪 (豬) (joo) (*pig*), before the rat comes around again. It's the rat, in fact, which starts the whole new 12-year cycle.

You may want to time your trip to mainland China, Taiwan, or Hong Kong to coincide with certain holidays — or, just as important, to avoid certain days and weeks.

First, you celebrate **xīnnián** 新年 (shin-nyan) (*New Year's Day*), also known as **yuándàn** 元旦 (ywan-dahn), on January 1. That's separate from a three-day celebration coinciding with the lunar New Year known as **Chūnjié** 春节 (春節) (Chwun-jyeh) (*Spring Festival; Chinese New Year*). Every year, the dates for **Chūnjié** change because — you guessed it — it follows the **yīnlì** 阴历 (陰曆) (yeen-lee) (*lunar calendar*) rather than the **yánglì** 阳历 (陽曆) (yahng-lee) (*solar calendar*). **Chūnjié** always occurs sometime in January or February.

In mainland China, **Láodòng jié** 劳动节 (勞動節) (Laow-doong jyeh) (*Labor Day*) is celebrated on May 1, and **Guóqìng jié** 国庆节 (國慶節) (Gwaw-cheeng jyeh) (*National Day*) is celebrated on October 1 in commemoration of the day Mao Zedong and the Chinese Communist Party declared the founding of **Zhōnghuá rénmín gònghé guó** 中华人民共和国 (中華人民共和國) (Joong-hwah run-meen goong-huh gwaw) (*the People's Republic of China*) in 1949. In Taiwan, **Guóqìng jié** is celebrated on October 10 to commemorate the day in 1911 when China's long dynastic history ended and a new era of **Zhōnghuá mínguó** 中华民国 (中華民國) (Joong-hwah meen-gwaw) (*the Republic of China* [another name for Taiwan]) began, under the leadership of Dr. Sun Yat-sen. National Day in Taiwan is often referred to as **Shuāng shí jié** 双十节 (雙十節) (Shwahng shir jyeh) (Literally: *Double 10 day*), because it occurs on the 10th day of the 10th month.

CULTURAL WISDOM

In Taiwan, you often see years written out that seem to be 11 years short of what you think is correct. That's because the founding of the Republic of China in 1911 is considered the base line for all future years. So 1921 is listed as **Mínguó shí nián** 民国十年 (民國十年) (Meen-gwaw shir nyan); **Mínguó** is the abbreviation for **Zhōnghuá mínguó,** and **shí nián,** meaning *10 years,* refers to 10 years following the founding of the Republic of China.

REMEMBER

In addition to the major public holidays worthy of closing down businesses, you may want to experience some of the other fun and interesting Chinese holidays firsthand. Refer to Chapter 5 for more on Chinese holidays.

TIP

All sorts of folk festivals take place in villages throughout mainland China and Taiwan when you least expect them, so if you suddenly find yourself surrounded by a throng of jovial, clapping, and singing people, just follow the crowd and see where the action takes you. You won't be disappointed. Even funeral processions can be the most fascinating and musical of events, with mourners dressed in white sackcloth playing all manner of wind and percussion instruments.

Where To? Deciding on a Destination

Nǐ xiǎng dào nǎr qù? 你想到哪儿去? (你想到哪兒去?) (Nee shyahng daow nar chyew?) (*Where do you want to go?*) Planning a trip to **Yàzhōu** 亚洲 (亞洲) (Yah-joe) (*Asia*), **Fēizhōu** 非洲 (Fay-joe) (*Africa*), **Ōuzhōu** 欧洲 (歐洲) (Oh-joe) (*Europe*), or **Měizhōu** 美洲 (May-joe) (*the Americas*)? Will your voyage be **zài guónèi** 在国内 (在國內) (dzye gwaw-nay) (*within the country/domestic*) or **zài guówài** 在国外 (在國外) (dzye gwaw-why) (*outside the country*)? Table 14-1 shows some countries you may choose to visit.

TABLE 14-1 ### Places to Visit around the Globe

Chinese	Pronunciation	English
Àiěrlán 爱尔兰 (愛爾蘭)	Eye-are-lahn	Ireland
Déguó 德国 (德國)	Duh-gwaw	Germany
Éguó 俄国 (俄國)	Uh-gwaw	Russia
Fǎguó 法国 (法國)	Fah-gwaw	France
Jiānádà 加拿大	Jah-nah-dah	Canada
Mòxīgē 墨西哥	Maw-she-guh	Mexico
Nánfēi 南非	Nahn-fay	South Africa
Rìběn 日本	Ir-bun	Japan
Ruìdiǎn 瑞典	Rway-dyan	Sweden
Ruìshì 瑞士	Rway-shir	Switzerland
Táiwān 台湾 (台灣)	Tye-wahn	Taiwan
Tǎnsāngníyà 坦桑尼亚 (坦桑尼亞)	Tahn-sahng-nee-yah	Tanzania
Xiānggǎng 香港	Shyahng-gahng	Hong Kong
Xiōngyálì 匈牙利	Shyoong-yah-lee	Hungary
Yǐsèliè 以色列	Ee-suh-lyeh	Israel
Yuènán 越南	Yweh-nahn	Vietnam
Zāyiěr 扎伊尔 (扎伊爾)	Zah-ee-are	Zaire
Zhōngguó dàlù 中国大陆 (中國大陸)	Joong-gwaw dah-loo	Mainland China

Depending on the type of activities you enjoy doing when you **fàngjià** 放假 (fahng-jyah) (*take a vacation*), you may want to consider traveling to a place that has plenty of the following features (or at least one special one to make it well worth the trip) so that you can **yóulǎn** 游览 (遊覽) (yo-lahn) (*sightsee*):

>> **Fú miào** 佛庙 (佛廟) (Foo myaow) (*Buddhist temple*)

>> **gǔdǒng diàn** 古董店 (goo-doong dyan) (*antique shop*)

>> **hǎitān** 海滩 (海灘) (hi-tahn) (*beach*)

>> **měishù guǎn** 美术馆 (美術館) (may-shoo gwahn) (*art gallery*)

>> **mótiān dàlóu** 摩天大楼 (摩天大樓) (maw-tyan dah-lo) (*skyscraper*)

>> **shāmò** 沙漠 (shah-maw) (*desert*)

>> **shān** 山 (shahn) (*mountain*)

>> **tǎ** 塔 (tah) (*pagoda*)

>> **xióngmāo** 熊猫 (熊貓) (shyoong-maow) (*pandas*)

>> **xìyuàn** 剧院 (劇院) (she-ywan) (*theatre*)

>> **yóuliè** 游猎 (遊獵) (yo-lyeh) (*safari*)

>> **zhíwùyuán** 植物园 (植物園) (jir-woo-ywan) (*botanical gardens*)

Unless you're the type who thrives on danger and excitement (or works for a relief agency), try to avoid places where the following natural phenomena occur:

>> **dìzhèn** 地震 (dee-juhn) (*earthquake*)

>> **hànzāi** 旱灾 (旱災) (hahn-dzye) (*drought*)

>> **huǒzāi** 火灾 (火災) (hwaw-dzye) (*fire*)

>> **shuǐzāi** 水灾 (水災) (shway-dzye) (*flood*)

>> **táifēng** 台风 (颱風) (tye-fung) (*typhoon*)

>> **yǔjì** 雨季 (yew-jee) (*rainy season*)

GRAMMAR CHAT

Planning to travel **cóng Xiōngyálì** 从 (從) 匈牙利 (tsoong Shyoong-yah-lee) (*from Hungary*) **dào Xiānggǎng** 到香港 (daow Shyahng-gahng) (*to Hong Kong*) anytime soon? How about **cóng Rìběn** 从日本 (從日本) (tsoong Ir-bun) (*from Japan*) **dào Mòxīgē** 到墨西哥 (daow Maw-she-guh) (*to Mexico*) instead? Wherever you travel, you always go **cóng** (tsoong) (*from*) one place **dào** (daow) (*to*) another. Here are some good phrases to know when you tell people about your upcoming travel plans, using the **cóng . . . dào** pattern:

Cóng Nánfēi dào Zāyǐěr 扎伊尔 (扎伊爾) **duō cháng shíjiān?** 从南非到扎伊尔多长时间？(從南非到扎伊爾多長時間?) (Tsoong nahn-fay daow Zah-ee-are dwaw chahng shir-jyan?) (*How long does it take to get from South Africa to Zaire?*)

Nǐmen shénme shíhòu cóng Zhōngguó dào zhèr lái? 你们什么时候从中国到这儿来? (你們甚麼時候從中國到這兒來?) (Nee-mun shummuh shir-ho tsoong Joong-gwaw daow jar lye?) (*When are you all coming here from China?*)

Tā míngtiān cóng Yǐsèliè dào Ruìdiǎn qù. 她明天从以色列到瑞典去. (她明天從以色列到瑞典去.) (Tah meeng-tyan tsoong Ee-suh-lyeh daow Rway-dyan chyew.) (*She's going from Israel to Sweden tomorrow.*)

Wǒ cóng Niǔyuē dào Jiāzhōu qù. 我从纽约到加州去. (我從紐約到加州去.) (Waw tsoong Nyo-yweh daow Jyah-joe chyew.) (*I'm going from New York to California.*)

Talkin' the Talk

Páng Lǎoshī (Pahng Laow-shir) (*Professor Pang*) asks his American student, Wendy, where she plans to go during the upcoming winter vacation. She has already been in Tianjin studying Chinese for four months.

Páng Lǎoshī: **Wendy, nǐ hán jià de shíhòu xiǎng qù nǎr?**
Wendy, nee hahn jyah duh shir-ho shyahng chyew nar?
Wendy, where do you plan on going during the winter vacation?

Wendy: **Yīnwèi wǒ yǐjīng zài Tiānjīn sì ge yuè le, suǒyǐ wǒ xiǎng zhōngyú qù Fēizhōu kànkàn.**
Een-way waw ee-jeeng dzye Tyan-jeen suh guh yweh luh, swaw-yee waw shyahng joong-yew chyew Fay-joe kahn-kahn.
Because I've already been in Tianjin for four months, I'd like to finally go to Africa to have a look.

Páng Lǎoshī: **Fēizhōu! Nàme yuǎn. Wèishénme yào qù nàr?**
Fay-joe! Nah-muh ywan. Way-shummuh yaow chyew nar?
Africa! So far away. Why do you want to go there?

Wendy: **Yīnwèi dōngtiān de shíhòu Tiānjīn tài lěng. Érqiě zài Fēizhōu kěyǐ cānjiā yóuliè!**
Een-way doong-tyan duh shir-ho Tyan-jeen tye lung. Are-chyeh dzye Fay-joe kuh-yee tsahn-jyah yo-lyeh!
Because winters in Tianjin are too cold. What's more, in Africa I can take part in a safari!

Páng Lǎoshī:	**Cóng Yàzhōu dào Fēizhōu zuò fēijī jǐge xiǎoshí?**
	Tsoong Yah-joe daow Fay-joe dzwaw fay-jee jee-guh shyaow-shir?
	How many hours is it from Asia to Africa by plane?
Wendy:	**Cóng Tiānjīn dào Tǎnsāngníyà yào chàbùduō shísān ge xiǎoshí.**
	Tsoong Tyan-jeen daow Tahn-sahng-nee-yah yaow chah-boo-dwaw shir-sahn guh shyaow-shir.
	From Tianjin to Tanzania, it takes about 13 hours.
Páng Lǎoshī:	**Qǐng dài huílái hěn duō xiàngpiàn gěi wǒ kànkàn.**
	Cheeng dye hway-lye hun dwaw shyahng-pyan gay waw kahn-kahn.
	Please bring back lots of pictures to show me.
Wendy:	**Yídìng huì.**
	Ee-deeng hway.
	I certainly will.

· ·

WORDS TO KNOW

pìnqǐng dǎoyóu 聘请导游 (聘請導遊)	peen-cheeng daow-yo	to hire a guide
bāshì lǚyóu 巴士旅游 (巴士旅遊)	bah-shir lyew-yo	bus tour
lìshǐ yōujiǔ de dìqū 历史悠久的 地区 (歷史悠久的地區)	lee-shir yo-jyo dee-chyew	historic district

Passports and Visas: Don't Leave Home without 'Em

Surprise! Actually, the fact that you need a valid **hùzhào** 护照 (護照) (hoo–jaow) (*passport*) and a **qiānzhèng** 签证 (簽證) (chyan–juhng) (*visa*) if you want to enter mainland China or Taiwan should come as no surprise. And if you plan on visiting a couple of different countries in the region for any length of time, you may need a couple of different **qiānzhèng** to go with each destination. Check to see what regulations apply before you board your **fēijī** 飞机 (飛機) (fay-jee) (*airplane*), or you may have the shortest vacation experience of your life.

In the course of securing a visa or two, you'll probably have to locate, navigate, deal with, or ask for the following:

» **B xíng gānyán yìmiǎo** B型肝炎疫苗 (B sheeng gahn-yan ee-myaow) (*Hepatitis B shot*)

» **dāncí rùjìng qiānzhèng** 单次入境签证 (單次入境簽證) (dahn-tsuh roo-jeeng chyan-juhng) (*single-entry visa*)

» **dàshǐ guǎn** 大使馆 (大使館) (dah-shir gwan) (*embassy*)

» **duōcí rùjìng qiānzhèng** 多次入境签证 (多次入境簽證) (dwaw-tsuh roo-jeeng chyan-juhng) (*multiple-entry visa*)

» **guānliǎo zhǔyì** 官僚主义 (官僚主義) (gwan-lyaow joo-ee) (*bureaucracy*)

» **jiànkāng zhèngshū** 健康证书 (健康證書) (jyan-kahng juhng-shoo) (*health certificate*)

» **línshìguǎn** 领事馆 (領事館) (leen-shir-gwan) (*consulate*)

» **páiduì** 排队 (排隊) (pye-dway) (*to stand in line*)

» **qiānzhèng chù** 签证处 (簽證處) (chyan-juhng choo) (*visa section*)

Packing for Your Trip

Are you the type who likes to **zhuāngrù** 装入 (jwahng-roo) (*pack*) everything under the sun in three different pieces of oversized **xíngli** 行李 (sheeng-lee) (*luggage*) before a trip? Or are you more the **bēibāo** 背包 (bay-baow) (*backpack*) type, content to take only the bare essentials? Either way, you have to prepare your bags in advance if you want to qualify them as **shǒutí xíngli** 手提行李 (show-tee sheeng-lee) (*carry-on luggage*) or **tuōyùn xíngli** 托运行李 (托運行李) (twaw-yewn sheeng-lee) (*checked luggage*).

What kind of clothes to pack depends on where you're going; Chapter 9 gives you the lowdown on various items of clothing. No matter where you plan to go, you should pack some of these items:

» **chúchòu jì** 除臭剂 (除臭劑) (choo-cho jee) (*deodorant*)

» **féizào** 肥皂 (fay-dzaow) (*soap*)

- **guālián dāo** 刮脸刀 (刮臉刀) (gwah-lyan daow) (*razor*)

- **huàzhuāng pǐn** 化妆品 (hwah-jwahng peen) (*makeup*)

- **nào zhōng** 闹钟 (鬧鐘) (naow joong) (*alarm clock*)

- **shuāzi** 刷子 (shwah-dzuh) (*brush*)

- **shùkǒu shuǐ** 漱口水 (shoo-ko shway) (*mouthwash*)

- **tàiyáng yǎnjìng** 太阳眼镜 (太陽眼鏡) (tye-yahng yan-jeeng) (*sunglasses*)

- **wèishēng jīn** 卫生巾 (衛生巾) (way-shung jeen) (*sanitary napkins*)

- **yágāo** 牙膏 (yah-gaow) (*toothpaste*)

- **yáshuā** 牙刷 (yah-shwah) (*toothbrush*)

- **yuèjīng yòng miánsāi** 月经用棉塞 (月經用棉塞) (yweh-jeeng yoong myan-sye) (*tampons*)

- **yùndǒu** 熨斗 (yewn-doe) (*iron*)

- **yǔsǎn** 雨伞 (雨傘) (yew-sahn) (*umbrella*)

- **zhàoxiàng jī** 照相机 (照相機) (jaow-shyahng jee) (*camera*)

- **zhuǎnjiē qì** 转接器 (轉接器) (jwahn-jyeh chee) (*adaptor*)

GRAMMAR CHAT

The sentence structure for the verb **zhuāng** 装 (裝) (jwahng) (*to pack*) is **bǎ A zhuāngrù B** 把 A 装入 B (bah A jwahng–roo B), which translates into *pack A into B*, even though the word for *pack* comes between what you're packing (*A*) and what you pack it into (*B*).

Enlisting the Help of a Travel Agency

Think you can handle traipsing around the world without an advance plan or hotel reservations? Think again. China, for example, is one country you should travel to as part of a **guānguāng tuán** 观光团 (觀光團) (gwahn-gwahng twahn) (*tour group*). If you don't like the idea of group travel, you should at least make advance reservations for hotels and domestic travel and even for your own private **dǎoyóu** 导游 (導遊) (daow-yo) (*tour guide*) through a **lǚxíngshè** 旅行社 (lyew-sheeng-shuh) (*travel agency*). Remember, you generally hear no **Yīngyǔ** 英语 (英語) (Eeng-yew) (*English*) spoken anywhere in China, so having someone who knows the ropes help you iron out the details ahead of time (including arranging an English-speaking tour guide) can help avoid headaches when you're there.

Talkin' the Talk

Daisy and Michael discuss their travel plans with a local travel agent, Miss Lǐ, in Hong Kong.

Miss Lǐ: **Nǐmen hǎo. Wǒ néng bāng shénme máng?**
Nee-men how. Waw nung bahng shummuh mahng?
Hello. How may I be of help?

Daisy: **Wǒmen hěn xiǎng qù Zhōngguó dàlù. Néng bùnéng yùdìng yíge lǚguǎn?**
Waw-men hun shyahng chyew Joong-gwaw dah loo. Nung boo-nung yew-deeng ee-guh lyew-gwahn?
We're very interested in traveling to mainland China. Would you be able to reserve hotels for us in advance?

Miss Lǐ: **Méiyǒu wèntí. Nǐmen shénme shíhòu yào zǒu?**
Mayo one-tee. Nee-mun shummuh shir-ho yaow dzoe?
No problem. When would you like to go?

Michael: **Tīngshuō wǔ yuèfèn de tiānqì zuì hǎo.**
Teeng-shwaw woo yweh-fun duh tyan-chee dzway how.
I've heard the weather in May is the best.

Miss Lǐ: **Duì le. Wǒ yě jiànyì nǐmen gēn yíge guānguāng tuán yíkuàr qù.**
Dway luh. Waw yeah jyan-ee nee-mun gun ee-guh gwahn-gwahng twan ee-kwar chyew.
That's correct. I also suggest you go with a tour group.

Daisy: **Wèishénme?**
Way-shummuh?
Why?

Miss Lǐ: **Guānguāng tuán yǒu shuō Yīngyǔ de dǎoyóu hé yóulǎnchē. Nà zuì fāngbiàn.**
Gwahn-gwahng twahn yo shwaw Eeng-yew duh daow-yo huh yo-lahn-chuh. Nah dzway fahng-byan.
Tour groups have an English-speaking tour guide and a sight-seeing bus. That's the most convenient way to go.

Michael: **Hǎo. Juédìng le.**
How. Jweh-deeng luh.
Okay. It's decided.

WORDS TO KNOW

Wǒ xūyào yùdìng ma? 我需要预订吗? (我需要預訂嗎?)	Waw shyew-yaow yew-deeng mah?	Do I need a reservation?
Wǒ yǒu yùdìng. 我有预订. (我有預訂.)	Waw yo yew-deeng.	I have a reservation.
Wǒ kěyǐ gēnggǎi wǒ de yùdìng ma? 我可以更改我的预订吗? (我可以更改我的預訂嗎?)	Waw kuh-yee gung-gye waw duh yew-deeng mah?	Can I change my reservation?
Wǒ xiǎng qǔxiāo wǒ de dìng wèi. 我想取消我的订位. (我想取消我的訂位.)	Waw shyahng chyew-shyaow waw duh deeng way.	I want to cancel my reservation.
shǔjià 暑假	shoo jyah	summer vacation
hánjià 寒假	hahn jyah	winter vacation
chūnjià 春假	chwun jyah	spring break

FUN & GAMES

Fill in the missing words with one of the three possible answers. See Appendix C for the answers.

1. **Wǒmen jīnnián qù _____.** 我们今年去_____. (我們今年去
   _____.) (*This year we're going to Ireland.*)

   a. **Àiěrlán** 爱尔兰. (愛爾蘭.)

   b. **Éguó** 俄国. (俄國.)

   c. **Nánfēi** 南非.

2. **Tāmen _____ zǒu.** 他们_____走. (他們_____走.) (*They're leaving on June 8.*)

   a. **Sì yuè wǔ hào** 四月五号 (四月五號)

   b. **Wǔ yuè jiǔ hào** 五月九号 (五月九號)

   c. **Liù yuè bā hào** 六月八号 (六月八號)

3. **Wǒmen yídìng yào kàn _____.** 我们一定要看_____. (我們一定要看
   _____.) (*We definitely want to see Buddhist temples.*)

   a. **xióngmāo** 熊猫. (熊貓.)

   b. **fó miào** 佛庙. (佛廟.)

   c. **yóuliè** 游猎. (遊獵.)

4. **Bié wàngle zhuāngrù _____.** 别忘了装入_____. (別忘了裝入_____.)
   (*Don't forget to pack a toothbrush.*)

   a. **yáshuā** 牙刷.

   b. **yágāo** 牙膏.

   c. **huàzhuāng pǐn** 化妆品. (化妝品.)

5. **Méiyǒu wèntí. _____.** 没有问题_____. (沒有問題_____.)
   (*No problem. Just kidding.*)

   a. **Juédìng le.** 决定了. (決定了.)

   b. **Kāi wán xiào.** 开玩笑. (開玩笑.)

   c. **Jiù wán le.** 就完了.

Chapter **15**
Making Cents of Money

Qián 钱 (錢) (chyan) (*money*) makes the world go 'round. People make their money in all sorts of ways. Most ways are legitimate. (If you've attained yours through nefarious means, I'm not sure I want to know, so don't tell me!) You may be one of those lucky people who win the lottery or receive a large inheritance you use to traipse to the other side of the world. Or perhaps you have a modest amount saved up from working hard and paying your bills on time, and you hope to make it go a long way. However you get your money, you find out how to change it (and then save it or spend it) with the help of this chapter.

Of course, family and friends are priceless, but you can't very well support yourself or help those you love, much less donate to a charity of your choice, unless you have something to give. And that's what life is really all about. (Unless, of course, your main goal in life is to buy a sports car, acquire rare works of art, and live in the south of France . . . in which case you need a lot of **qián.** All the more reason to read this chapter.)

In this chapter, I share with you important words and phrases for acquiring and spending money — things you can easily do nowadays all over the world. I give you some banking terms to help you deal with everything from live tellers to inanimate ATMs. I even give you tips on tipping.

You can listen to all the Talkin' the Talk dialogues featured in this chapter. Go to www.dummies.com/go/chinese and click on the dialogue you want to hear.

REMEMBER

Staying Current with Chinese Currency

Depending on where in Asia (or any place where Chinese is spoken) you live, work, or visit, you have to get used to dealing with different types of **huòbì** 货币 (貨幣) (hwaw-bee) (*currency*), each with its own **duìhuànlǜ** 兑换率 (兑换率) (dway-hwahn-lyew) (*rate of exchange*). See Table 15-1 for the Chinese versions of international currency and the following sections for the main forms of Chinese **huòbì**. I delve into currency exchange in the later section "Exchanging Money."

TABLE 15-1

International Currencies

Chinese	Pronunciation	English
Gǎngbì 港币 (港幣)	Gahng-bee	Hong Kong dollar
Měiyuán 美元	May-ywan	U.S. dollar
Ōuyuán 欧元 (歐元)	Oh-ywan	Euro
rénmínbì 人民币 (人民幣)	run-meen-bee	(mainland) Chinese dollar
Rì yuán 日元	Ir ywan	Japanese dollar
Xīnjiāpō yuán 新加坡元	Sheen-jyah-paw ywan	Singapore dollar
Xīn Táibì 新台币 (新臺幣)	Shin Tye-bee	Taiwan dollar

Rénmínbì (RMB) in the PRC

In the People's Republic of China (PRC), the equivalent of the U.S. dollar is the **yuán** 元 (ywan), also known as **rénmínbì** 人民币 (人民幣) (run-meen-bee) (*[mainland] Chinese dollars* [Literally: *the people's money*]) or RMB. More than 1 billion people around the globe currently use this currency. As of January 2018, 1 U.S. dollar is equivalent to about 6.33 (mainland) Chinese dollars. Here's how you say that in Chinese:

Yī Měiyuán huàn liù diǎn sān bā yuán rénmínbì. 一美元换六点三八元人民币. (一美元換六點三八元人民幣.) (Ee May-ywan hwahn lyo dyan sahn ba ywan run-meen-bee.) (*One U.S. dollar is 6.33 [mainland] Chinese dollars.*)

The Chinese **yuán**, which is a paper bill, comes in denominations of 1, 2, 5, 10, 20, 50, and 100 in rénmínbì. One **yuán** is the equivalent of 10 **máo** 毛 (maow), which may also be referred to as **jiǎo** 角 (jyaow) — the equivalent of 10 cents. Each **máo** is the equivalent of 100 **fēn** 分 (fun), which compare to American pennies. Paper bills, in addition to the **yuán**, also come in denominations of 2 and 5 **jiǎo**. Coins come in denominations of 1, 2, and 5 **fēn**; 1, 2, and 5 **jiǎo**; and 1, 2, and 5 **yuán**.

GRAMMAR CHAT

In addition to saying you have **yì yuán**, you can say you have **yí kuài qián** 一块钱 (一塊錢) (ee kwye chyan), which means the exact same thing — one Chinese dollar. The difference between **yuán** and **kuài**, and between **jiǎo** and **máo**, is that **yuán** and **jiǎo** are formal, written ways of saying those denominations and **kuài** and **máo** are the more colloquial forms.

Want to know how much money I have right now in my pocket, Nosy? Why not just ask me?

>> **Nǐ yǒu jǐ kuài qián?** 你有几块钱? (你有幾塊錢?) (Nee yo jee kwye chyan?) (*How much money do you have?*)

Use this phrase if you assume the amount is less than $10.

>> **Nǐ yǒu duōshǎo qián?** 你有多少钱? (你有多少錢?) (Nee yo dwaw-shaow chyan?) (*How much money do you have?*)

Use this phrase if you assume the amount is greater than $10.

Xīn Táibì in the ROC

As of January 2018, in Taiwan, also known as the Republic of China, or ROC, 1 U.S. dollar equals about 30 **Xīn Táibì** 新台币 (新臺幣) (Shin Tye-bee) (*New Taiwan dollars*). Here's how you say that in Chinese:

Yì Měiyuán huàn sānshí yuán Xīn Táibì. 一美元 换三十元新台币. (一美元 换三十元新臺幣.) (Ee May-ywan hwahn sahn-shir ywan Shin Tye-bee.) (*One U.S. dollar is 30 New Taiwan dollars.*)

You see bills in denominations of 50, 100, 500, and 1,000 and coins in denominations of 1, 5, 10, and 50 cents. Taiwanese coins are particularly beautiful — they have all sorts of flowers etched into them — so you may want to save a few to bring back to show friends (or just to have). Just make sure you keep enough **língqián** 零钱 (零錢) (leeng-chyan) (*small change*) on hand for all the great items you can buy cheaply at the wonderful night markets.

Hong Kong dollars

Hong Kong, the longtime financial dynamo of Asia, uses the Hong Kong dollar, or the **Găngbì** 港币 (港幣) (Gahng–bee). Currently, in 2018, 1 U.S. dollar is equivalent to 7.8 Hong Kong dollars. Here's how you say that in Chinese:

Yì Měiyuán huàn qī diǎn bā yuán Găngbì. 一美元换七点八元港币. (一美元换七點八元港幣.) (Ee Měi yuán hwahn chee dyan bah ywan Găngbì.) (*One U.S. dollar is 7.8 Hong Kong dollars.*)

Singapore dollars

Singapore is a Mandarin-speaking country in Asia. Its dollars are called Xīnjiāpō yuán 新加坡元 (Shin–jyah–paw ywan) and come in denominations of 2, 5, 10, 50, and 100. You can find coins in denominations of 1 cent, 5 cents, 10 cents, 20 cents, 50 cents, and 1 dollar. (One U.S. dollar is 1.34 Singapore dollars.)

GRAMMAR CHAT

In Singapore, if you want to say $1.25, you don't use the number **wǔ** 五 (woo) (*five*) to refer to the final 5 cents in the amount. You use the term **bàn** 半 (bahn), which means *half*: **yí kuài liǎng máo bàn** 一块两毛半 (一塊兩毛半) (ee kwye lyahng maow bahn) rather than **yí kuài liǎng máo wǔ** 一块两毛五 (一塊兩毛五) (ee kwye lyahng maow woo). You can definitely use the number **wǔ** in Taiwan, Hong Kong, or mainland China, however.

Exchanging Money

You can always **huàn qián** 换钱 (換錢) (hwahn chyan) (*exchange money*) the minute you arrive at the airport at the many **duìhuàn chù** 兑换处 (兌換處) (dway-hwahn choo) (*exchange bureaus*), or you can wait until you get to a major bank or check in at your hotel.

The following phrases come in handy when you're ready to **huàn qián**:

» **Jīntiān de duìhuàn lǜ shì shénme?** 今天的兑换率是什么? (今天的兑换率是甚麼?) (Jin-tyan duh dway-hwahn lyew shir shummuh?) (*What's today's exchange rate?*)

» **Nǐmen shōu duōshǎo qián shǒuxù fèi?** 你们收多少钱手续费? (你們收多少錢手續費?) (Nee-men show dwaw-shaow chyan show-shyew fay?) (*How much commission do you charge?*)

» **Qǐng nǐ gěi wǒ sì zhāng wǔshí yuán de.** 请你给我四张五十元的. (請妳給我四张五十元的) (Cheeng nee gay waw suh jahng woo-shir ywan duh.) (*Please give me four 50-yuan bills.*)

» **Qǐngwèn, yínháng zài nǎr?** 请问, 银行在哪儿? (請問, 銀行在哪兒?) (Cheeng-one, een-hahng dzye nar?) (*Excuse me, where is the bank?*)

» **Qǐngwèn, zài nǎr kěyǐ huàn qián?** 请问, 在哪儿可以换钱? (請問, 在哪兒可以換錢?) (Cheeng-one, dzye nar kuh-yee hwahn chyan?) (*Excuse me, where can I change money?*)

» **Wǒ yào huàn yì bǎi Měiyuán.** 我要换一百美元. (我要换一百美元.) (Waw yaow hwahn ee bye May-ywan.) (*I'd like to change $100.*)

TIP

No matter where you get money or how much money you plan to convert into local currency, you may have to show your **hùzhào** 护照 (護照) (hoo–jaow) (*passport*), so always have that ready to whip out.

.... Talkin' the Talk ....

Jasmine arrives at the airport in Beijing and needs to change some money. She asks a **xínglǐ yuán** (sheeng-lee ywan) (*porter*) where she can find a place to exchange money.

Jasmine: **Qǐngwèn, zài nǎr kěyǐ huàn qián?**
Cheeng-one, dzye nar kuh-yee hwahn chyan?
Excuse me, where can I change money?

Xíngliyuán: **Duìhuàn chù jiù zài nàr.**
Dway-hwahn choo jyoe dzye nar.
The exchange bureau is just over there.

Jasmine: **Xièxiè.**
Shyeh-shyeh.
Thank you.

Jasmine goes to the money exchange counter to change some U.S. dollars into Chinese **yuán** with the help of the **chūnà yuán** (choo-nah-ywan) (*cashier*).

Jasmine: **Nǐ hǎo. Wǒ yào huàn yì bǎi Měiyuán de rénmínbì.**
Nee how. Waw yaow hwahn ee bye May-ywan duh run-meen-bee.
Hello. I'd like to change USD $100 into (mainland) Chinese dollars.

Chūnà yuán:	**Méiyǒu wèntí.**
	Mayo one-tee.
	No problem.

Jasmine:	**Jīntiān de duìhuàn lǜ shì duōshǎo?**
	Jin-tyan duh dway-hwahn lyew shir dwaw-shaow?
	What's today's exchange rate?

Chūnà yuán:	**Yì Měiyuán huàn liù diǎn sān bā yuán rénmínbì.**
	Ee May-ywan hwahn lyo dyan sahn ba ywan
	run-meen-bee.
	One U.S. dollar is 6.38 (mainland) Chinese dollars.

Jasmine:	**Hǎo. Qǐng gěi wǒ liǎng zhāng wǔshí yuán de.**
	How. Cheeng gay waw lyahng jahng woo-shir ywan duh.
	Great. Please give me two 50-yuán bills.

Chūnà yuán:	**Méiyǒu wèntí. Qǐng gěi wǒ kànkàn nǐde hùzhào.**
	Mayo one-tee. Cheeng gay waw kahn-kahn nee-duh
	hoo-jaow.
	No problem. Please show me your passport.

WORDS TO KNOW

zìdòng qǔkuǎn jī 自动取款机 (自動取款機)	dzuh-doong chyew-kwahn jee	ATM machine
yínháng 银行 (銀行)	een-hahng	bank
Xīn Táibì 新台币	Sheen Tye bee	New Taiwan dollar
Gǎngbì 港币 (港幣)	Gahng-bee	Hong Kong dollar
Xīnjiāpō yuán 新加坡元	sheen-jyah-paw ywan	Singapore dollar
duìhuàn lǜ 兑换率 (兌換率)	dway-hwahn lyew	exchange rate
Qǐng gěi wǒ kànkàn nǐde hùzhào. 请给我看看你的护照. (請給我看看你的護照.)	Cheeng gay waw kahn-kahn nee-duh hoo-jaow.	Please show me your passport.

Spending Money

I don't think I'll have trouble selling you on (no pun intended) the thought of spending money. Whenever you see something you want, whether in a store, on the street, or at a night market, you may as well give in to temptation and buy it, as long as you have enough **qián**. It's as easy as that. Have money, will travel. Or, rather, have money, will spend.

When you're ready to buy something, you can do it with cash, check, or credit card. And when traveling overseas, you often use traveler's checks.

GRAMMAR CHAT

If you end up buying so many items that you can barely hold them all with both hands, here's one adverb you should remember. It comes in handy when you start adding up the cost of everything before you fork over all your money: I'm speaking of **yígòng** 一共 (ee-goong) (*altogether*), as in "How much are these 20 toys and 80 sweaters altogether?"

You may overhear the following conversation in a store:

> **Zhèige hé nèige yígòng duōshǎo qián?** 这个和那个一共多少钱? (這個和那個一共多少錢?) (Jay-guh huh nay-guh ee-goong dwaw-shaow chyan?) (*How much are this and that altogether?*)

> **Zhèige sān kuài liǎng máo wǔ, nèige yí kuài liǎng máo, suǒyǐ yígòng sì kuài sì máo wǔ.** 这个三块两毛五, 那个一块两毛, 所以一共四块四毛五. (這個三塊兩毛五, 那個一塊兩毛, 所以一共四塊四毛五.) (Jay-guh sahn kwye lyahng maow woo, nay-guh ee kwye lyahng maow, swaw-yee ee-goong suh kwye suh maow woo.) (*This is $3.25, and that is $1.20, so altogether that will be $4.45.*)

Before you decide to **mǎi dōngxi** 买东西 (買東西) (my doong-she) (*buy things*), be sure you have enough money **yígòng** to buy everything you want so you don't feel disappointed after spending many hours in your favorite store.

GRAMMAR CHAT

The term **dōngxi** 东西 (東西) (doong-she) (*things*) is literally a combination of **dōng** 东 (東) (*east*) and **xī** 西 (西) (*west*). The Chinese language often combines two such opposite words to come up with various concepts. **Dōngxi** always refers to physical objects.

CULTURAL WISDOM

Overseas, many places accept American Express. Closer to America, businesses may only accept MasterCard or Visa. In some out-of-the-way parts of China, you can't use plastic at all, so have plenty of cash or traveler's checks on hand, just in case.

Using cash

I don't care what anybody tries to tell you, **xiànjīn** 现金 (現金) (shyan-jin) (*cash*) in local currency is always useful, no matter where you are and what time of day it is. Sometimes you can buy things and go places with **xiànjīn** that you can't swing with a credit card. For example, if your kid hears the ice cream truck coming down the street, you can't just whip out your **xìnyòngkǎ** to buy him an ice cream cone when the truck stops in front of your house. You can't even try to convince the ice cream guy to take a **zhīpiào** 支票 (紙票) (jir-pyaow) (*check*). For times like these, my friend, you need cold, hard **xiànjīn**. You can use it to buy everything from ice cream on the street to a movie ticket at the theater. Just make sure you put your money in a sturdy **qiánbāo** 钱包 (錢包) (chyan-baow) (*wallet*) and keep it in your front pocket so a thief can't easily steal it.

GRAMMAR CHAT

When you talk about how much something costs, you put the numerical value before the word for bill or coin. For example, you can call a dollar **yí kuài** 一块 (一塊) (ee kwye) (*one dollar*) or **sān kuài** 三块 (三塊) (sahn kwye) (*three dollars*). You translate 10 cents, literally, as one 10-cent coin — **yì máo** 一毛 (ee maow) — or 30 cents, literally, as three 10-cent coins — **sān máo** 三毛 (sahn maow).

Here's how you speak of increasing amounts of money. You mention the larger units before the smaller units, just like in English:

> **sān kuài** 三块 (三塊) (sahn kwye) (*$3.00*)
>
> **sān kuài yì máo** 三块一毛 (三塊一毛) (sahn kwye ee maow) (*$3.10*)
>
> **sān kuài yì máo wǔ** 三块一毛五 (三塊一毛五) (sahn kwye ee maow woo) (*$3.15*)

As useful and convenient as **xiànjīn** is, you really have to pay with **zhīpiào** for some things. Take your rent and electricity bills, for example. Can't use cash for these expenses, that's for sure. And when you travel overseas, everyone knows the safest way to carry money is in the form of **lǚxíng zhīpiào** 旅行支票 (lyew-sheeng jir-pyaow) (*traveler's checks*), so you can replace them if they get lost or stolen.

REMEMBER

The basic elements of all Chinese currency are the **yuán** (colloquially referred to as a **kuài**), which you can think of as a dollar, the **jiǎo** (colloquially referred to as the **máo**), which is the equivalent of a dime, and the **fēn** 分, which is equivalent to the penny. You can read more about the various types of Chinese currency earlier in the chapter.

Talkin' the Talk

Mary goes shopping in Taipei and finds something she likes. She asks the clerk how much it is.

Mary: **Qǐngwèn, zhè jiàn yīfu duōshǎo qián?**
Cheeng-one, jay jyan ee-foo dwaw-shaow chyan?
Excuse me, how much is this piece of clothing?

Clerk: **Èrshíwǔ kuài.**
Are-shir-woo kwye.
It's $25.

Mary: **Nǐmen shōu bù shōu zhīpiào?**
Nee-men show boo show jir-pyaow?
Do you take checks?

Clerk: **Lǚxíng zhīpiào kěyǐ. Xìnyòng kǎ yě kěyǐ.**
Lyew-sheeng jir-pyaow kuh-yee. Sheen-yoong kah yeah kuh-yee.
Traveler's checks are okay. Credit cards are also okay.

WORDS TO KNOW		
piányí 便宜	pyan-yee	cheap
gèng piányí 更便宜	gung pyan-yee	cheaper
zhékòu 折扣	juh-ko	discount
huíkòu 回扣	hway-ko	rebate

Paying with plastic

The **xìnyòng kǎ** 信用卡 (sheen-yoong kah) (*credit card*) may be the greatest invention of the twentieth century — for credit card companies, that is. Everyone else is often stuck paying all kinds of potentially exorbitant **lìlǜ** 利率 (lee-lyew) (*interest rates*) if he's not careful. Still, credit cards do make paying for things much more convenient, don't you agree?

To find out whether a store accepts credit cards, all you have to say is

Nǐmen shōu bù shōu xìnyòng kǎ? 你们收不收信用卡? (你們收不收信用卡?) (Nee-men show boo show sheen-yoong kah?) (*Do you accept credit cards?*)

Whether the **jiàgé** 价格 (價格) (jyah-guh) (*price*) of the items you want to buy is **guì** 贵 (貴) (gway) (*expensive*) or **piányì** 便宜 (pyan-yee) (*cheap*), the **xìnyòng kǎ** comes in handy.

Read on for a list of credit-card-related terms:

» **shēzhàng de zuì gāo é** 赊帐的最高额 (賒帳的最高額) (shuh-jahng duh dzway gaow uh) (*credit line*)

» **shōu** 收 (show) (*accept*)

» **xìnyòng** 信用 (sheen-yoong) (*credit*)

» **xìnyòng xiàn'é** 信用限额 (信用限額) (sheen-yoong shyan-uh) (*credit limit*)

Doing Your Banking

If you plan on staying in Asia for an extended time or you want to continue doing business with a Chinese company, you may want to open a **huóqī zhànghù** 活期账户 (活期賬戶) (hwaw-chee jahng-hoo) (*checking account*) where you can both **cún qián** 存钱 (存錢) (tswun chyan) (*deposit money*) and **qǔ qián** 取钱 (取錢) (chyew chyan) (*withdraw money*). If you stay long enough, you should open a **dìngqī cúnkuǎn hùtóu** 定期存款户头 (定期存款戶頭) (deeng-chee tswun-kwan hoo-toe) (*savings account*) so you can start earning some **lìxī** 利息 (lee-she) (*interest*). Sure beats stuffing large bills under your mattress for years.

How about trying to make your money work for you by investing in one of the following?

» **chǔxù cúnkuǎn** 储蓄存款 (儲蓄存款) (choo-shyew tswun-kwan) (*certificate of deposit/CD*)

» **guókù quàn** 国库券 (國庫券) (gwaw-koo chwan) (*treasury bond*)

» **gǔpiào** 股票 (goo-pyaow) (*stock*)

» **hùzhù jījīn** 互助基金 (hoo-joo jee-jeen) (*mutual fund*)

» duìchōng **jījīn** 对冲基金 (對沖基金) (dway-choong jee-jeen) (*hedge fund*)

» **zhàiquàn** 债券 (債券) (jye-chwan) (*bond*)

CULTURAL WISDOM

Larger bank branches in the PRC are generally open seven days a week from 9:00 a.m. to 5:00 p.m., but some close between 12:00 p.m. and 2:00 p.m. In Taiwan, banks close at 3:30 p.m., and in Hong Kong they're usually open from 9:00 a.m. to 4:30 p.m. during the week and from 9:00 a.m. to 12:00 p.m. on Saturdays.

Making withdrawals and deposits

Whether you need to **cún qián** 存钱 (存錢) (tswun chyan) (*deposit money*) or **qǔ qián** 取钱 (取錢) (chyew chyan) (*withdraw money*), you need to make sure you have enough **qián** in the first place to do so. One way to ensure you don't overextend is to make sure you know what your **jiéyú** 结余 (結餘) (jyeh–yew) (*account balance*) is at any given moment. Sometimes you can check your available balance if you go online to see which checks may have already cleared. If someone gives you an **yínháng běnpiào** 银行本票 (銀行本票) (een–hahng bun–pyaow) (*cashier's check*), however, it cashes immediately. Lucky you!

If you plan to cash some checks along with your deposits, here are a couple of useful phrases to know:

» **Wǒ yào duìxiàn zhèi zhāng zhīpiào.** 我要兑现这张支票. (我要兑現這張支票.) (Waw yaow dway-shyan jay jahng jir-pyaow.) (*I'd like to cash this check.*)

» **Bèimiàn qiān zì xiě zài nǎr?** 背面签字写在哪儿? (背面簽字寫在哪兒?) (Bay-myan chyan dzuh shyeh dzye nar?) (*Where shall I endorse it?*)

Talkin' the Talk

Ian decides to open a savings account in Hong Kong. He enters a bank and approaches the teller.

Ian: **Nín hǎo. Wǒ xiǎng kāi yíge dìngqī cúnkuǎn hùtóu.**
Neen how. Waw shyahng kye ee-guh deeng-chee tswun-kwan hoo-toe.
Hello. I'd like to open a savings account.

Teller: **Méiyǒu wèntí. Nín yào xiān cún duōshǎo qián?**
Mayo one-tee. Neen yaow shyan tswun dwaw-shaow chyan?
No problem. How much would you like to deposit initially?

Ian: **Wǒ yào cún yìbǎi kuài qián.**
Waw yaow tswun ee-bye kwye chyan.
I'd like to deposit $100.

Teller: **Hǎo. Qǐng tián zhèige biǎo. Wǒ yě xūyào kànkàn nínde hùzhào.**
How. Cheeng tyan jay-guh byaow. Waw yeah shyew-yaow kahn-kahn neen-duh hoo-jaow.
Fine. Please fill out this form. I will also need to see your passport.

WORDS TO KNOW

liánghǎo de xìnyù 良好的信誉 (良好的信譽)	lyahng-haow duh sheen-yew	good credit
bùliáng xìnyòng 不良信用	boo-lyahng sheen-yoong	bad credit
xìnyòng píngfēn 信用评分 (信用評分)	sheen-yoong peeng-fun	credit score
yǒu zīgé huòdé dàikuǎn 有资格获得贷款 (有資格獲得貸款)	yo dzuh-guh hwaw-duh dye-kwan	to qualify for a loan

Accessing an ATM

One of the most convenient ways to access some quick cash is to go to the nearest **zìdòng tíkuǎnjī** 自动提款机 (自動提款機) (dzuh-doong tee-kwan-jee) (*ATM*). ATMs are truly ubiquitous these days. Wherever you turn, there they are, on every other street corner. Sometimes I wonder how we ever survived without them. (Same goes for the personal computer . . . but I digress.)

In order to use a **zìdòng tíkuǎnjī,** you need a **zìdòng tíkuǎn kǎ** 自动提款卡 (自動提款卡) (dzuh-doong tee-kwan kah) (*ATM card*) to find out your account balance or to deposit or withdraw money. And you definitely need to know your **mìmǎ** 密码 (密碼) (mee-mah) (*PIN*); otherwise, the **zìdòng tíkuǎnjī** is useless. Just remember: Make sure you don't let anyone else know your **mìmǎ.** It's a **mìmì** 秘密 (mee-mee) (*secret*).

Tips on Tipping

Usually in the United States, a 15–20 percent tip is customary at restaurants, and you often give a 10 percent tip to taxi drivers. Giving **xiǎofèi** 小费 (小費) (shyaow-fay) (*tips*) is expected pretty much everywhere from here to Timbuktu. In some instances, you should even give **xiǎofèi** to people setting up towels in the public bathroom. Better to know in advance of your trip how much (or how little) is expected of you so you don't embarrass yourself (and by extension, your country folk).

Here are some general tipping conventions for various Chinese-speaking countries:

» In Taiwan, **xiǎofèi** are generally included in restaurant bills. If not, 10 percent is standard. You can **gěi** 给 (給) (gay) (*give*) bellboys and porters a dollar (USD) per bag.

» In Hong Kong, most restaurants automatically include a 10 percent tip, but feel free to give an additional 5 percent if the **fúwù** 服务 (服務) (foo-woo) (*service*) is good. Small tips are also okay for taxi drivers, bellboys, and washroom attendants.

» Tipping in mainland China used to be rare, but the idea is finally catching on, especially now that service with a scowl rather than a smile is fast becoming a thing of the past. (For the longest time, workers simply had no incentive to work harder or with a more pleasant demeanor after the Cultural Revolution. Can you blame workers for having no reason to perform their duties with the idea of customer service in mind?) A 5 percent tip is standard in restaurants (still low compared to Taiwan and Hong Kong). Bellboys and room service attendants typically expect a dollar or two (USD). Tipping in U.S. currency is still very much appreciated, because it's worth about six times as much as the Chinese dollar.

If you get a bill and can't make heads or tails of it, you can always ask the following question to find out whether the tip is included:

Zhàngdān bāokuò fúwùfēi ma? 账单包括服务费吗？(賬單包括服務費嗎？) (Jahng-dahn baow-kwaw foo-woo-fay mah?) (*Does the bill include a service charge/tip?*)

In English, when you say *15 percent*, you mean 15 percent out of a total of 100. The way to express **bǎifēnbǐ** 百分比 (bye-fun-bee) (*percentages*) in Chinese is to start with the larger denomination of **bǎi** 百 (bye) (*100*) first and then work your way backward with the percentage of that amount. Here are some examples:

bǎifēn zhī bǎi 百分之百 (bye-fun jir bye) (*100 percent* [Literally: *100 out of 100 parts*])

bǎifēn zhī bāshíwǔ 百分之八十五 (bye-fun jir bah-shir-woo) (*85 percent* [Literally: *85 out of 100 parts*])

bǎifēn zhī shíwǔ 百分之十五 (bye-fun jir shir-woo) (*15 percent* [Literally: *15 out of 100 parts*])

bǎifēn zhī sān 百分之三 (bye-fun jir sahn) (*3 percent* [Literally: *3 out of 100 parts*])

bǎifēn zhī líng diǎn sān 百分之零点三 (百分只零點三) (bye-fun jir leeng dyan sahn) (*0.3 percent* [Literally: *0.3 out of 100 parts*])

For more information on numbers, head to Chapter 5.

Talkin' the Talk

Denzel and Pauletta are in a restaurant. They get their bill and discuss how much of a tip to leave.

Denzel: **Wǒmen de zhàngdān yígòng sānshí kuài qián. Xiǎofèi yīnggāi duōshǎo?**
Waw-men duh jahng-dahn ee-goong sahn-shir kwye chyan. Shyaow-fay eeng-guy dwaw-shaow?
Our bill comes to $30 altogether. How much should the tip be?

Pauletta: **Yīnwèi fúwù hěn hǎo, suǒyǐ xiǎofèi kěyǐ bǎifēn zhī èrshí. Nǐ tóngyì ma?**
Een-way foo-woo hun how, swaw-yee shyaow-fay kuh-yee bai-fun jir are-shir. Nee toong-ee mah?
Because the service was really good, I think we can leave a 20 percent tip. Do you agree?

Denzel: **Tóngyì.**
Toong-ee.
I agree.

WORDS TO KNOW

Qǐng nǐ gěi wǒ zhàngdān. 请你给我账单. (請你給我賬單.)	Cheeng nee gay waw jahng-dahn.	Check, please.
Wǒ xiǎng zhège zhàngdān shì bùduì. 我想这个账单不对. (我想這個賬單不對.)	Waw shyahng jay-guh jahng-dahn boo-dway.	I think the bill is incorrect.
Wǒ néng bùnéng yàu yī zhāng shōu jù? 我能不能要一张收据? (我能不能要一張收據?)	Waw nung boo-nung yaow ee jahng sho jyew?	May I have a receipt?
Shèng xià lái de wǒ kěyǐ dài zǒu ma? 剩下来的我可以带走吗? (剩下來的我可以帶走嗎?)	Shung shyah lye duh waw kuh-yee dye dzo mah?	Can I get the rest to go?
dǎbāo dài 打包袋	dah-baow dye	doggie bag

FUN & GAMES

Name the Chinese equivalent of the following U.S. coins. See Appendix C for the correct answers.

1. dollar   _____

2. dime   _____

3. penny   _____

Identify what the following illustrations depict in Chinese. See Appendix C for the correct answers.

A.

B.

C.

D.

E.

F.

A.   _____

B.   _____

C.   _____

D.   _____

E.   _____

F.   _____

Change $100 of your favorite new currencies in the spaces below:

Wǒ yào huàn yì bǎi Měiyuán.
Waw yaow hwahn ee bye <u>May-ywan</u>.
I'd like to change $100 <u>U.S. dollars</u>.

Wǒ yào huàn yì bǎi _____.
Waw yaow hwahn ee bye _____.
I'd like to change $100 _____.

Wǒ yào huàn yì bǎi _____.
Waw yaow hwahn ee bye _____.
I'd like to change $100 _____.

Chapter **16**

Getting Around

Traveling halfway around the world to **Zhōngguó** 中国 (中國) (Joong-gwaw) (*China*) can be a long haul. Knowing the magic traveling words and phrases in Chinese can make your journey as efficient and comfortable as possible. This chapter helps you make your way around the airport and the airplane, survive the customs experience, and board different types of transportation after you reach your destination.

Flying Around the Airport

Consider yourself a veteran traveler just because you've been all through Europe and the Americas? Well, my friend, you're in for a rude awakening. When it comes to finding your way around China, English (or any other Western language) does you little good. You spend a lot of unproductive time trying to interpret the signs to get some sense of which line to stand in and where to go next at the **fēijī chǎng** 飞机场 (飛機場) (fay-jee chahng) (*airport*). You need to at least know the **pīnyīn** 拼音 (pin-yin) (Literally: *spelled the way it sounds*) Romanization system, if not Chinese characters themselves. If you don't, you'll be up a creek without a paddle. You may end up following the guy next to you, even if it takes you to the bathroom rather than baggage claims. (See Chapter 1 for more about the **pīnyīn** system of spelling Chinese words.)

Good move to get a head start by reading *Chinese For Dummies* in advance of your trip. You can bone up on some essential words and phrases before the whole airport experience makes you want to get right back on the next plane bound for home.

Making it past the check-in counter

Ready to **bànlǐ dēngjī shǒuxù** 办理登记手续 (辦理登記手續) (bahn-lee duhng-jee show-shyew) (*check in*)? After lugging your bags up to this point, you finally get to **tuōyùn** 托运 (托運) (twaw-yewn) (*check*) your **xíngli** 行李 (sheeng-lee) (*luggage*). You receive a **dēng jī pái** 登机牌 (登機牌) (duhng jee pye) (*boarding pass*) at the check-in counter, at which point you're ready to make your way to the appropriate **chūkǒu** 出口 (choo-ko) (*gate*), taking only your **shǒutí xínglǐ** 手提行李 (show-tee sheeng-lee) (*carry-on luggage*).

All sorts of questions may be running through your mind about now. Here are some basic phrases that may come in handy during check-in:

» **Fēijī jǐ diǎn qǐfēi?** 飞机几点起飞? (飛機幾點起飛?) (Fay-jee jee dyan chee-fay?) (*What time does your flight leave?*)

» **Wǒde hángbān hào shì duōshǎo?** 我的航班号是多少? (我的航班號是多少?) (Waw-duh hahng-bahn how shir dwaw-shaow?) (*What's my flight number?*)

» **Wǒ xiǎng tuōyùn xínglǐ.** 我想托运行李. (我想托運行李.) (Waw shyahng twaw-yewn sheeng-lee.) (*I'd like to check my luggage.*)

» **Wǒ xiǎng yào kào chuāng de wèizi.** 我想要靠窗的位子. (Waw shyahng yaow cow chwahng duh way-dzuh.) (*I'd like a window seat.*)

» **Wǒ xiǎng yào kào guòdào de wèizi.** 我想要靠过道的位子. (我想要靠過道的位子.) (Waw shyahng yaow cow gwaw-daow duh way-dzuh.) (*I'd like an aisle seat.*)

» **Zài jǐ hào mén hòujī?** 在几号门候机? (在幾號門候機?) (Dzye jee how mun ho-jee?) (*Which gate do we leave from?*)

» **Zhè shì wǒde hùzhào.** 这是我的护照. (這是我的護照.) (Jay shir waw-duh hoo-jaow.) (*Here's my passport.*)

After you check in, you may encounter all sorts of unpleasant surprises. Perhaps the plane can't **zhèngdiǎn qǐfēi** 正点起飞 (正點起飛) (juhng-dyan chee-fay) (*depart on time*) after all, and the airline must **tuīchí** 推迟 (推遲) (tway-chir) (*postpone*) your departure or **qǔxiāo** 取消 (chyew-shyaow) (*cancel*) it altogether. Maybe the **tiānqì** 天气 (天氣) (tyan-chee) (*weather*) is causing the problems.

Talkin' the Talk

Shí Píng is checking in at the airport in New York for a business trip to Beijing. She shows her ticket and passport to the **zhíyuán** (jir-ywan) (*agent*) and checks her luggage.

Zhíyuán:	**Nín hǎo. Qǐng chūshì nínde jīpiào.** Neen how. Cheeng choo-shir neen-duh jee-pyaow. *Hello. Your ticket, please.*
Shí Píng:	**Zài zhèr.** Dzye jar. *Here it is.*
Zhíyuán:	**Nín shì bú shì qù Běijīng? Néng kànkàn nínde hùzhào ma?** Neen shir boo shir chyew Bay-jeeng? Nuhng kahn-kahn neen-duh hoo-jaow mah? *Are you going to Beijing? May I see your passport?*
Shí Píng:	**Kěyǐ.** Kkuh-yee. *Here you are.*
Zhíyuán:	**Yǒu jǐ jiàn xíngli?** Yo jee jyan sheeng-lee? *How many suitcases do you have?*
Shí Píng:	**Wǒ yǒu sānge xiāngzi.** Waw yo sahn-guh shyahng-dzuh. *I have three suitcases.*
Zhíyuán:	**Yǒu méiyǒu shǒutí xínglǐ?** Yo mayo show-tee sheeng-lee? *Do you have any carry-on luggage?*
Shí Píng:	**Wǒ zhǐ yǒu yíge gōngwénbāo.** Waw jir yo ee-guh goong-one-baow. *I have only one briefcase.*
Zhíyuán:	**Hǎo. Nín yào kào guòdào de wèizi háishì yào kào chuāng de wèizi?** How. Neen yow cow gwaw-daow duh way-dzuh hi-shir yaow cow chwahng duh way-dzuh? *All right. Would you like an aisle or a window seat?*

Shí Píng:	**Wǒ xiǎng yào kào guòdào de wèizi.** Waw shyahng yaow cow gwaw-daow duh way-dzuh. *I'd like an aisle seat.*
Zhíyuán:	**Hǎo. Zhèi shì nínde dēngjīpái. Qù Běijīng de 108 cì bānjī, 19 pái, B zuò.** How. Jay shir neen-duh duhng-jee-pye. Chyew Bay-jeeng duh ee-bye-leeng-bah tsuh bahn-jee, shir-jyo pye, B dzwaw. *Fine. Here's your boarding pass. Flight 108 to Beijing, Row 19, Seat B.*
Shí Píng:	**Xièxiè.** Shyeh-shyeh. *Thanks.*
Zhíyuán:	**Zhè shì nínde xínglǐ lǐngqǔdān. Dàole Běijīng yǐhòu kěyǐ lǐngqǔ nínde xíngli.** Jay shir neen-duh sheeng-lee leeng-chyew-dahn. Dow-luh Bay-jeeng ee-ho kuh-yee leeng-chyew neen-duh sheeng-lee. *Here are your luggage claim tags. After you arrive in Beijing, you can claim your luggage.*
Shí Píng:	**Xièxiè.** Shyeh-shyeh. *Thanks.*
Zhíyuán:	**Zhù nín yílù píng'ān.** Joo neen ee-loo peeng-ahn. *Have a nice trip.*

WORDS TO KNOW

dānchéng piào 单程票 (單程票)	dahn-chung pyaow	one-way ticket
wǎngfǎn piào 往返票 (往返票)	wahng-fahn pyaow	round-trip ticket
shāngwù cāng 商务舱 (商務艙)	shahng-woo tsahng	business class
jīngjì cāng 经济舱 (經濟艙)	jeeng-jee tsahng	economy/coach
tóuděng cāng 头等舱 (頭等艙)	toe-dung tsahng	first-class

Boarding your flight

Okay! You're all set to board the **fēijī** 飞机 (飛機) (fay-jee) (*airplane*). Are you lucky enough to sit in the **tóuděng cāng** 头等舱 (頭等艙) (toe-duhng tsahng) (*first class*) section, or do you have to sit in **jīngjì cāng** 经济舱 (經濟艙) (jeeng-jee tsahng) (*economy class*) the whole time? Either way, here are some people you see get on the plane (at least I hope you do):

» **chéngwùyuán** 乘务员 (乘務員) (chung-woo-ywan) (*flight attendants*)

» **jiàshǐ yuán** 驾驶员 (駕駛員) (jyah-shih ywan) (*pilot*)

» **jīzǔ** 机组 (機組) (jee-dzoo) (*crew*)

And if you're like me, you get worried about some things as the plane begins to taxi down the runway:

» **qǐfēi** 起飞 (起飛) (chee-fay) (*takeoff*)

» **qìliú** 气流 (氣流) (chee-lyo) (*turbulence*)

» **zhuólù** 着陆 (著陸) (jwaw-loo) (*landing*)

Aaah! I get nervous just thinking about them. It's okay, though. The **chéngwù yuán** are on to people like you and me. That's why they make sure to tell you before takeoff where the **jiùshēngyī** 救生衣 (jyo-shung-ee) (*life vests*) and **jǐnjí chūkǒu** 紧急出口 (緊急出口) (jin-jee choo-ko) (*emergency exits*) are located. You may also hear them bark out the following instructions, if you haven't already managed to tune everything out:

» **Bǎ tuōpán cānzhuō shōu qǐlái.** 把托盘餐桌收起来. (把托盤餐桌收起來.) (Bah twaw-pahn tsahn-jwaw show chee-lye.) (*Put your tray table back.*)

» **Bǎ nǐ de zuòwèi fàng zài zhílì de wèizhì.** 把你的座位放在直立的位置. (Bah nee duh dzwaw-way fahng dzye jir-lee duh way-jir.) (*Put your seat back to the upright position.*)

» **Bù zhǔn chōuyān.** 不准抽烟. (不准抽煙.) (Boo jwun cho-yan.) (*No smoking permitted.*)

» **Jìjǐn nǐde ānquándài.** 系紧你的安全带. (繫紧你的安全带.) (Jee-jin nee-duh ahn-chwan-dye.) (*Fasten your seat belt.*)

» **Rúguǒ kōngqì yā yālì yǒu biànhuà, yǎngqì zhào huì zìdòng luòxià.** 如果空气压压力有变化, 氧气罩会自动落下. (如果空氣壓壓力有變化, 氧氣罩會自動落下.) (Roo-gwaw koong-chee yah yah-lee yo byan-hwah, yahng-chee jaow hway dzuh-doong lwaw-shyah.) (*If there's any change in air pressure, the oxygen mask will automatically drop down.*)

GRAMMAR CHAT

You use the coverb **bǎ** 把 (bah) when you want to put the object right up front before you state the verb that tells what you did or will do with the object. (See Chapter 18 for more on this unique coverb.)

If you're not a nervous flyer, you'll probably spend all your time listening to music through the **ěrjī** 耳机 (耳機) (are-jee) (*headset*), flipping dials on the radio or channels on the television, or trying to sleep. Hopefully the flight is showing a good **diànyǐng** 电影 (電影) (dyan-yeeng) (*movie*) on such a long trip.

Going through customs

If you survive all the turbulence and the boring movie on your long flight without having a breakdown, good for you! The next test you have to get through is the **hǎiguān** 海关 (海關) (hi-gwahn) (*customs*) experience. After you get to customs, you see many **hǎiguān guān yuán** 海关关员 (海關關員) (hi-gwahn gwahn ywan) (*customs officers*), none of whom may understand English. Table 16-1 lists the items you need to have ready at customs. The following phrases should come in handy, too:

>> **Nǐ dǒng Yīngyǔ ma?** 你懂英语吗? (你懂英語嗎?) (Nee doong Eeng-yew mah?) (*Do you understand English?*)

>> **Wǒ shì Jiānádà rén.** 我是加拿大人. (Waw shir Jyah-nah-dah run.) (*I'm Canadian.*)

>> **Wǒ shì Měiguó rén.** 我是美国人. (我是美國人.) (Waw shir May-gwaw run.) (*I'm American.*)

>> **Wǒ shì Yīngguó rén.** 我是英国人. (我是英國人.) (Waw shir Eeng-gwaw run.) (*I'm British.*)

>> **Xǐshǒujiān zài nǎr?** 洗手间在哪儿? (洗手間在哪兒?) (She-show-jyan dzye nar?) (*Where are the restrooms?*)

TABLE 16-1

Items to Have Ready at Customs

Chinese	Pronunciation	English
bāo 包	baow	*bag*
chūjìng dēngjì kǎ 出境登记卡 (出境登記卡)	choo-jeeng duhng-jee kah	*departure card*
jiànkāng zhèng 健康证 (健康證)	jyan-kahng jung	*health certificate*
jiǔ 酒	jyo	*alcohol* (to declare)

Chinese	Pronunciation	English
rùjìng dēngjì kǎ 入境登记卡 (入境登記卡)	roo-jeeng duhng-jee kah	*arrival card*
shēnbào de wùpǐn 申报的物品 (申報的物品)	shun-baow duh woo-peen	*articles to declare*
xiāngyān 香烟 (香煙)	shyahng-yan	*cigarettes* (to declare)
xiāngzi 箱子	shyahng-dzuh	*suitcase*
xínglǐ 行李	sheeng-lee	*luggage*

The **hǎiguān guān yuán** may ask you a couple of these important questions:

>> **Nǐ dǎsuàn zài zhèr dāi duōjiǔ?** 你打算在这儿待多久? (你打算在這兒待多久?) (Nee dah-swan dzye jar dye dwaw-jyo?) (*How long do you plan on staying?*)

>> **Nǐ lái zhèr shì bàn gōngwù háishì lǚyóu?** 你来这儿是办公务还是旅游? (你來這兒是辦公務還是旅遊?) (Nee lye jar shir bahn goong-woo hi-shir lyew-yo?) (*Are you here on business or as a tourist?*)

>> **Nǐ yǒu méiyǒu yào shēnbào de wùpǐn?** 你有没有要申报的物品? (你有沒有要申報的物品?) (Nee yo may-yo yaow shun-baow duh woo-peen?) (*Do you have anything you want to declare?*)

>> **Qǐng gěi wǒ kànkàn nǐde hǎiguān shēnbào dān.** 请给我看看你的海关申报单. (請給我看看你的海關申報單.) (Cheeng gay waw kahn-kahn nee-duh hi-gwan shun-baow dahn.) (*Please show me your customs declaration form.*)

>> **Qǐng gěi wǒ kànkàn nǐde hùzhào.** 请给我看看你的护照. (請給我看看你的護照.) (Cheeng gay waw kahn-kahn nee-duh hoo-jaow.) (*Please show me your passport.*)

Customs agents aren't the only people with questions to ask. You may have some questions you want to try out yourself:

>> **Wǒ yào fù shuì ma?** 我要付税吗? (我要付稅嗎?) (Waw yaow foo shway mah?) (*Must I pay duty?*)

>> **X guāng huì sǔnhuài wǒde jiāojuǎn ma?** X光会损坏我的胶卷吗? (X光會損壞我的膠卷嗎?) (X gwahng hway swuhn-hwye waw-duh jyaow-jwan mah?) (*Will the X-ray damage my film?*)

>> **Xínglǐ kéyǐ shōu qǐlái ma?** 行李可以收起来吗? (行李可以收起來嗎?) (Sheeng-lee kuh-yee show chee-lye mah?) (*May I close my suitcases now?*)

>> **Xínglǐ yào dǎkāi ma?** 行李要打开吗? (行李要打開嗎?) Sheeng-lee yaow dah-kye mah?) (*Should I open my luggage?*)

Talkin' the Talk

Rose gets off her plane in Shanghai and begins the customs process by approaching an agent.

Agent: **Qǐng gěi wǒ kànkàn nǐde hùzhào.**
            Cheeng gay waw kahn-kahn nee-duh hoo-jaow.
            Please show me your passport.

Rose shows him her passport, and the agent asks her some important questions.

Agent: **Měiguórén. Nǐ yǒu méiyǒu yào shēnbào de wùpǐn?**
            May-gwaw-run. Nee yo may-yo yaow shun-baow duh
            woo-peen?
            American. Do you have anything you'd like to declare?

Rose: **Méiyǒu. Wǒ zhǐ yǒu yìtiáo xiāngyān.**
            May-yo. Waw jir yo ee-tyaow shyahng-yan.
            No. I have only a carton of cigarettes.

Agent: **Nǐ lái zhèr shì bàn gōngwù háishì lǚyóu?**
            Nee lye jar shir bahn goong-woo hi-shir lyew-yo?
            Are you here on business or as a tourist?

Rose: **Wǒ lái zuò shēngyì.**
            Waw lye dzwaw shung-ee.
            I've come on business.

Agent: **Nǐ kéyǐ zǒu le.**
            Nee kuh-yee dzoe luh.
            You may go.

WORDS TO KNOW

miǎnshuì 免税 (免稅)	myan-shway	duty free
jìn pǐn 禁品	jeen peen	contraband
dúpǐn zǒusī fàn 毒品走私犯	doo-peen dzo-suh fahn	drug smuggler
Rúguǒ nǐ kàn dào shénme, jìu gàosu yǒuguān rén yuán. 如果你看到什么, 就告诉有关人员. (如果你看到什麼, 就告訴有關人員.)	Roo-gwaw nee kahn daow shummah, jyo gaow-soo you-gwan run-ywan.	If you see something, say something.

Navigating Around Town

It's Friday night, and you just had a pretty successful day doing business with your Chinese counterparts. You've finally mustered the courage to venture out of your hotel room for a night on the town. You decide to check out a popular dance hall, and you begin to determine what mode of transport can best get you there.

CULTURAL WISDOM

Renting a car is virtually impossible in China. Cars just aren't available. And even if you can find a rental, you may not want to get one, given the bureaucracy and driving conditions. Signs aren't printed in English, which is probably the main reason you shouldn't even attempt driving. Just think of the upside. You don't have to suddenly learn how to use a stick shift or purchase any extra car insurance. Let someone else worry about how to get you from point A to point B.

No matter what form of **jiāotōng** 交通 (jyaow-toong) (*transportation*) you end up taking, here are a few crucial words and phrases to know:

>> **fāngxiàng** 方向 (fahng-shyahng) (*directions*)

>> **dìtú** 地图 (地圖) (dee-too) (*map*)

>> **Wǒ mílù le.** 我迷路了. (Waw mee-loo luh.) (*I'm lost.*)

Hailing a cab

Although **zìxíngchē** 自行车 （自行車） (dzuh-sheeng-chuh) (*bicycles*), **mótuōchē** 摩托车 （摩托車） (maw-twaw-chuh) (*motorcycles*), **mǎchē** 马车 （馬車） (mah-chuh) (*horse-drawn carts*), and even **niú** 牛 (nyo) (*cows*) are still the main forms of transportation for the average individual in some parts of mainland China, most foreigners take taxis wherever they go. You can easily find taxis around hotels, and cabs are certainly more comfortable and convenient than having to deal with nonexistent rules of the road; breathing in air pollution while bicycling; finding your way through a maze of old alleyways; or, depending on the time of year, leaving yourself to the mercy of the natural elements.

Here's what you say to the hotel door attendant if you want help hailing a cab: **Wǒ yào jiào jìchéngchē.** 我要叫计程车. （我要叫計程車.） (Waw yaow jyaow jee-chung-chuh.) (*I'd like a taxi.*)

After you're safely ensconced in the cab, you need to know how to say the following phrases:

>> **Nǐ kéyǐ děng jǐ fēnzhōng ma?** 你可以等几分钟吗? (你可以等幾分鐘嗎?) Nee kuh-yee duhng jee fun-joong mah?) (*Can you wait a few minutes?*)

>> **Qǐng dǎ biǎo.** 请打表. (請打表.) (Cheeng dah byaow.) (*Please turn on the meter.*)

>> **Qǐng dài wǒ dào zhèige dìzhǐ.** 请带我到这个地址. (請带我到這個地址.) (Cheeng dye waw daow jay-guh dee-jir.) (*Please take me to this address.*)

>> **Qǐng kāi kuài yìdiǎr.** 请开快一点儿. (請開快一點兒.) (Cheeng kye kwye ee-dyar.) (*Please drive a little faster.*)

>> **Qǐng kāi màn yìdiǎr.** 请开慢一点儿. (請開慢一點兒.) (Cheeng kye mahn ee-dyar.) (*Please drive a little slower.*)

>> **Qǐng zǒu fēngjǐng hǎo de lù.** 请走风景好的路. (請走風景好的路.) (Cheeng dzoe fung-jeeng how duh loo.) (*Please take a scenic route.*)

>> **Wǒ děi gǎn shíjiān.** 我得赶时间. (我得趕時間.) (Waw day gahn shir-jyan.) (*I'm in a hurry.*)

>> **Zài zhè'er guǎiwān er.** 在这儿拐弯儿. (在這兒拐彎兒.) (Dzye jar gwye wahr.) (*Turn here.*)

Oh, and one more thing. As you set off with your taxi **sījī** 司机 (司機) (suh-jee) (*driver*), make sure you put on your **ānquán dài** 安全带 (ahn-chwan dye) (*seat belt*).

Finally, before you get out of the cab, these phrases may come in handy for price negotiations:

>> **Bié qīpiàn wǒ.** 别欺骗我. (別欺騙我.) (Byeh chee-pyan waw.) (*Don't cheat me.*)

>> **Búyòng zhǎole.** 不用找了. (Boo-yoong jaow-luh.) (*Keep the change.*)

>> **Kāiwánxiào! Wǒ jùjué fù zhèmme duō qián.** 开玩笑! 我拒绝付这么多钱. (開玩笑! 我拒絕付這麼多錢.) (Kye-wahn-shyaow! Waw jyew-jweh foo juhmmuh dwaw chyan.) (*You've got to be kidding! I refuse to pay so much.*)

>> **Qǐng gěi wǒ shōujù.** 请给我收据. (請給我收據.) (Cheeng gay waw show-jyew.) (*Please give me a receipt.*)

>> **Wǒ gāi gěi nǐ duōshǎo qián?** 我该给你多少钱? (我該給你多少錢?) (Waw guy gay nee dwaw-shaow chyan?) (*How much do I owe you?*)

>> **Wǒ huì àn biǎo fù kuǎn.** 我会按表付款. (我會按表付款.) (Waw hway ahn byaow foo kwahn.) (*I'll pay what the meter says.*)

TIP

Because most people in China don't speak English, always remember to take a hotel card when you leave your hotel. Your card has the name and address in English and Chinese. You can always show the card to a taxi driver when you want to get back. If you're walking around town, you may want to take a map that shows local landmarks such as pagodas or train stations near your hotel.

Talkin' the Talk

Bill ventures out for a night on the town and needs a cab. He enlists the help of his hotel doorman.

Bill:	**Wǒ yào jiào jìchéngchē.** Waw yaow jyaow jee-chung-chuh. *I'd like a taxi.*
Doorman:	**Hǎo.** How. *Certainly.*

Bill enters the cab and shows the driver a card with the name and address of a local nightclub.

Bill:	**Qǐng dài wǒ dào zhèige yèzǒnghuì.** Cheeng dye waw daow jay-guh yeh-dzoong-hway. *Please take me to this nightclub.*
Driver:	**Méiyǒu wèntí.** Mayo one-tee. *No problem.*
Bill:	**Wǒ bù jí. Qǐng kāi màn yìdiǎr.** Waw boo jee. Cheeng kye mahn ee-dyar. *I'm not in a hurry. Please drive a little slower.*

Bill finally reaches the nightclub after his scenic cab drive.

Bill:	**Wǒ gāi gěi nǐ duōshǎo qián?** Waw guy gay nee dwaw-shaow chyan? *How much do I owe you?*
Driver:	**Shí kuài liǎng máo wǔ.** Shir kwye lyahng maow woo. *That will be $10.25.*

Bill hands the driver $15.

Bill: **Qǐng gěi wǒ shōujù. Bú yòng zhǎo le.**
             Cheeng gay waw show-jyew. Boo yoong jaow luh.
             Please give me a receipt. Keep the change.

Driver: **Hǎo. Xièxiè.**
             How. Shyeh-shyeh.
             Okay. Thanks.

WORDS TO KNOW

Qǐng nǐ bǎ nuǎnqì tiáo gāo yīdiǎr. 请你把暖气调高一点儿. (請你把暖氣調高一點兒.)	Cheeng nee bah nwahn chee tyaow gaow ee dyar.	Please turn on the heater.
Qǐng nǐ bǎ kōngtiáo tiáo gāo yīdiǎn'er. 请你把空调调高一点儿. (請你把暖氣調高一點兒.)	Cheeng nee bah koong-tyaow tyaow gaow ee-dyar.	Please turn on the air conditioner.
Wǒmen yǐjīng dàole ma? 我们已经到了吗? (我們已經到了嗎?)	Waw-mun ee-jeeng daow-luh mah?	Are we there yet?

Hopping on the bus

Gōnggòng qìchē 公共汽车 (公共汽車) (goong-goong chee-chuh) (*buses*) are almost as common as bicycles in China. They also cost much less than taxis. But here's the catch: Bus drivers usually don't speak a word of English, signs are only in Chinese, and the buses are always super crowded. Still, if you're game for a unique travel experience and you don't mind killing time waiting for the bus, put these phrases in your carry-on bag:

» **Chē piào duōshǎo qián?** 车票多少钱? (車票多少錢?) (Chuh pyaow dwaw-shaow chyan?) (*How much is the fare?*)

» **Duōjiǔ lái yítàng?** 多久来一趟? (多久來一趟?) (Dwaw-jyo lye ee-tahng?) (*How often does it come?*)

» **Gōnggòng qìchē zhàn zài nǎr?** 公共汽车站在哪儿? (公共汽車站在哪兒?) (Goong-goong chee-chuh jahn dzye nar?) (*Where's the bus station?*)

» **Qǐng gàosù wǒ zài nǎr xià chē.** 请告诉我在哪儿下车. (請告訴我在哪兒下車.) (Cheeng gaow-soo waw dzye na'er shyah chuh.) (*Please let me know where to get off.*)

>> **Yīnggāi zuò jǐ lù chē?** 应该坐几路车? (應該坐幾路車?) (Eeng-guy dzwaw jee loo chuh?) (*Which [number] bus should I take?*)

Talkin' the Talk

Charlie is walking along the street, trying to find a bus that can take him to the famous Shilin night market in Taiwan. He sees his old friend Louise, and after saying hello, he asks her for help.

Charlie: **Qù Shílín yīnggāi zuò jǐ lù gōnggòng qìchē?**
Chyew Shir-leen eeng-guy dzwaw jee loo goong-goong chee-chuh?
Which bus should I take to go to Shilin?

Louise: **Yīnggāi zuò sān lù chē. Nèige gōnggòng qìchē zhàn jiù zài zhèr.**
Eeeng-guy dzwaw sahn loo chuh. Nay-guh goong-goong chee-chuh jahn jyo dzye jar.
You should take the number 3 bus. That bus stop is right here.

Charlie: **Tài hǎo le. Duōjiǔ lái yítàng?**
Tye how luh. Dwaw-jyo lye ee-tahng?
That's great. How often does it come?

Louise: **Měi sānshí fēn zhōng. Hái hǎo.**
May sahn-shir fun joong. Hi how.
Every 30 minutes. That's not too bad.

Charlie: **Xièxiè nǐ.**
Shyeh-shyeh nee.
Thank you.

WORDS TO KNOW		
gōngchē sījī 公车司机 (公車司機)	goong-chuh suh-jee	bus driver
bào tāi 爆胎	baow tye	flat tire
chēpiào 车票 (車票)	chuh-pyaow	bus ticket
ānquán dài 安全带 (安全帶)	ahn-chwan dye	seat belt

Riding the rails

If you want to get where you need to go really quickly, especially in Hong Kong or New York, the fastest way to get there may take you below the ground — to the **dìtiě** 地铁 (地鐵) (dee-tyeh) (*subway*). Most **dìtiě zhàn** 地铁站 (地鐵站) (dee-tyeh jahn) (*subway stations*) are pretty easy to navigate.

As of 2015, mainland China had subway lines in 25 cities. Fourteen more lines are set to open in 2018 alone. In fact, Shanghai and Beijing alone have the world's first and second busiest subways in the world. (No big surprise here, with over a billion potential strap-hangers throughout the country.) Above-ground **huǒchē** 火车 (火車) (hwaw-chuh) (*train*) travel is still the tried and true go-to mode of transportation — especially because China is such a huge place and distances between cities are so great. Unlike the number of subway stations, you can find plenty of **huǒchē zhàn** 火车站 (火車站) (hwaw-chuh jahn) (*train stations*) in China. They even come equipped with waiting rooms.

TIP

If you plan to travel a long distance, be sure to book a soft sleeper — or at least ask for a soft seat — because they're the more comfortable accommodations and not as jam-packed as other parts of the train. Trust me. Soft sleepers are worth the extra cost. For more on the types of seats in trains, see Table 16-2.

TABLE 16-2

Seating Accommodations on Trains

Chinese	Pronunciation	English
ruǎnwò 软卧 (軟臥)	rwahn-waw	*soft sleeper*
ruǎnzuò 软座 (軟座)	rwan-dzwaw	*soft seat*
shàngpù 上铺 (上舖)	shahng-poo	*upper berth*
xiàpù 下铺 (下舖)	shyah-poo	*lower berth*
yìngwò 硬卧	eeng-waw	*hard sleeper*
yìngzuò 硬座	eeng-dzwaw	*hard seat*

CULTURAL WISDOM

TAKING THE SUBWAY AROUND CHINA

Hong Kong constantly upgrades and extends its subway system, making it quite reliable. Taipei also has an excellent and efficient subway system. In Shanghai, China's major commercial center of Pudong has a subway that connects the east and west sides of the Huangpu River. And in Beijing, the 2008 Olympics prompted extensive subway expansion in preparation for the hordes that descended into its metro system. It now has 21 lines (up from 15, barely a decade ago), and close to 200 stations.

REMEMBER

February is a particularly risky month to attempt long-distance train travel, because the shortest month often features the Chinese New Year, and you're bound to meet what seems like the entire country traveling from one part of China to another. Make sure you consult a **shíkè biǎo** 时刻表 (時刻表) (shir-kuh byaow) (*time schedule*) in advance and note the correct **dàodá shíjiān** 到达时间 (到達時間) (daow-dah shir-jyan) (*arrival time*) and **kāichē shíjiān** 开车时间 (開車時間) (key-chuh shir-jyan) (*departure time*) of your train.

Before you **shàngchē** 上车 (上車) (shahng-chuh) (*board the train*) to enjoy your comfy, soft seat, you need to go to the **shòupiào chù** 售票处 (售票處) (show-pyaow choo) (*ticket office*) to buy your ticket. You use the following words and phrases to get the job done:

» **dānchéng piào** 单程票 (單程票) (dahn-chuhng pyaow) (*one-way ticket*)

» **láihuí piào** 来回票 (來回票) (lye-hway pyaow) (*round-trip ticket*)

» **mànchē** 慢车 (慢車) (mahn-chuh) (*local train*)

» **piào** 票 (pyaow) (*ticket*)

» **piào jià** 票价 (票價) (pyaow jyah) (*fare*)

» **tèkuài** 特快 (tuh-kwye) (*express train*)

The following may come in handy at the train station:

» **Huǒchē cóng něige zhàntái kāi?** 火车从哪个站台开? (火車從哪個站台開?) (Hwaw-chuh tsoong nay-guh jahn-tye kye?) (*Which gate does the train leave from?*)

» **Piàofáng zài nǎr?** 票房在哪儿? (票房在哪兒?) (Pyaow-fahng dzye nar?) (*Where's the ticket office?*)

TIP

Notice the different way of saying *ticket office* in this question. Options abound in the Chinese language.

» **Wǒ yào yìzhāng yìngwò piào.** 我要一张硬卧票. (我要一張硬臥票.) (Waw yow ee-jahng eeng-waw pyaow.) (*I'd like a hard-sleeper ticket.*)

And when you finally hear the **lièchē yuán** 列车员 (列車員) (lyeh-chuh ywan) (*conductor*) say **Shàng chē le!** 上车了! (上車了!) Shahng chuh luh!) (*All aboard!*), you can board and ask the following questions:

» **Cānchē zài nǎr?** 餐车在哪儿? (餐車在哪兒?) (Tsahn-chuh dzye nar?) (*Where's the dining car?*)

» **Zhèige zuòwèi yǒu rén ma?** 这个座位有人吗? (這個座位有人嗎?) (Jay-guh dzwaw-way yo run mah?) (*Is this seat taken?*)

Talkin' the Talk

Fatima is at the Beijing train station to buy a round-trip ticket to Shanghai for tomorrow. She approaches a ticket agent to purchase her ticket.

Fatima: **Qǐngwèn, yǒu méiyǒu míngtiān qù Shànghǎi de huǒchē piào?**
Cheeng-one, yo mayo meeng-tyan chyew Shahng-hi duh hwaw-chuh pyaow?
Excuse me, do you have any train tickets to Shanghai for tomorrow?

Ticket agent: **Yǒu. Yào jǐ zhāng?**
Yo. Yaow jee jahng?
Yes. How many would you like?

Fatima: **Zhǐ yì zhāng láihuí piào. Xiàge lǐbàiyī yào huílái.**
Jir ee jahng lye-hway pyaow. Shyah-guh lee-bye-ee yaow hway-lye.
Just one round-trip ticket. I'd like to return next Monday.

Ticket agent: **Hǎo. Yào yìngwò, ruǎnwò, háishì ruǎnzuò?**
How. Yaow eeng-waw, rwahn-waw, hi-shir rwahn-dzwaw?
Okay. Would you like a hard sleeper, a soft sleeper, or a soft seat?

Fatima: **Wǒ yào yì zhāng ruǎnwò. Xièxiè.**
Waw yaow ee jahng rwahn-waw. Shyeh-shyeh.
I'd like a soft sleeper. Thanks.

WORDS TO KNOW

Wǒ yào gǎi wǒ de piào. 我要改我的票. (我要改我的票.)	Waw yaow gye waw duh pyaow.	I would like to change my ticket.
Wǒ xūyào tuìhuán wǒ de piào. 我需要退我的票. (我需要退我的票.)	Waw shyew yaow tway-hwan waw duh pyaow.	I need to return my ticket.
Wǒ bǎ wǒ de piào nòng diūle. 我把我的票弄丢了.	Waw bah waw duh pyaow noong dyo luh.	I lost my ticket.

FUN & GAMES

How do you say these types of transportation in Chinese? (Flip to Appendix C for the answers.)

A. _____

B. _____

C. _____

D. _____

E. _____

You just arrived huffing and puffing at the airport. Suddenly, the airport worker asks you: **Nǐ yǒu méiyǒu chūjìng dēngjì kǎ?** (Nee yo may-yo choo-jeeng dung-jee kah?), and you answer:

Wǒ yǒu chūjìng dēngjì kǎ. (Waw yo choo-jeeng duhng-jee kah.) (*I have a departure card.*)

Wǒ yǒu _____. (Waw yo _____.) (*I have a _____.*)

Wǒ yǒu _____. (Waw yo _____.) (*I have a _____.*)

There you are at the train station, trying valiantly to get your favorite kind of seat (or sleeper car) to go all the way from Beijing to Xinjiang Province — a trip of over a day. You tell the train station clerk that you want a hard seat ticket. Fill in the blanks with other possible answers, depending on the kind of experience you want to have on the train in China.

Wǒ xiǎng yào yīgè yìngzuò piào. (Waw shyahng yaow ee guh eeng dzwaw pyaow.) (*I want a hard seat ticket.*)

Wǒ xiǎng yào yīgè _____ piào. (Waw shyahng yaow ee guh _____ pyaow.) (*I want a _____ ticket.*)

Wǒ xiǎng yào yīgè _____ piào. (Waw shyahng yaow ee guh _____ pyaow.) (*I want a _____ ticket.*)

» Covering time and distances

» Picking out specific spots with ordinal numbers

» Pointing the way with directional coverbs

Chapter **17**

Asking for Directions

Everyone (yes, even you) has to ask for **fāngxiàng** 方向 (fahng-shyahng) (*directions*) at some time or another. Even if you just need to find the bathroom — when you've got to go, you'd better know.

You may find yourself baffled by the boulevards in Beihai or dumbfounded by directions in Dalian. This chapter helps you figure out exactly how to ask for directions before you ever **mílù** 迷路 (mee-loo) (*get lost*). Whether you lose your bearings in Beijing or wander off the path in Luoyang, this chapter gives you helpful tips that make it easier to find your way back home. Or at least back to your hotel.

REMEMBER

You definitely need to know how to ask where certain places are in mainland China, where most people don't speak English. You have a greater likelihood of hailing an English-speaking cabbie in Taipei or Kowloon to take you where you need to go than you do in one of the cities or towns in mainland China, but you can't bank on that.

Avoiding 20 Questions: Just Ask "Where?"

Okay, so you're searching for the closest post office to mail a package home before your mother's birthday next week. A passerby tells you to go right down the street, but for the life of you, all you see are a couple of bookstores and an occasional subway station. Time to ask for directions. But how?

The easiest way to ask where something is in Chinese is to use the question word **nǎr** 哪儿 (哪兒) (nar) (*where*). But you can't just say **nǎr**, or folks still won't know what you're talking about. You have to use the coverb **zài** 在 (dzye), which can be translated as *in* or *at*, in front of **nǎr** (**zài nǎr**). (A *coverb* is officially a verb but functions as a preposition.) Just put the name of whatever you're looking for before the word **zài** to create a complete question:

> **Nǐ zài nǎr?** 你在哪儿? (你在哪兒?) (Nee dzye nar?) (*Where are you?*)

> **Shūdiàn zài nǎr?** 书店在哪儿? (書店在哪兒?) (Shoo-dyan dzye nar?) (*Where's the bookstore?*)

> **Yóujú zài nǎr?** 邮局在哪儿? (郵局在哪兒?) (Yo-jyew dzye nar?) (*Where's the post office?*)

Here are some places you may be looking for when you lose your way:

» **cèsuǒ** 厕所 (廁所) (tsuh-swaw) (*bathroom*)

» **chūzū qìchē zhàn** 出租汽车站 (出租汽車站) (choo-dzoo chee-chuh jahn) (*taxi stand*)

» **dìtiě zhàn** 地铁站 (地鐵站) (dee-tyeh jahn) (*subway station*)

» **fànguǎn** 饭馆 (飯館) (fahn-gwahn) (*restaurant*)

» **gōnggòng qìchē zhàn** 公共汽车站 (公共汽車站) (goong-goong chee-chuh jahn) (*bus stop*)

» **huǒchē zhàn** 火车站 (火車站) (hwaw-chuh-jahn) (*train station*)

» **jiēdào** 街道 (jyeh-daow) (*street*)

» **jízhěn shì** 急诊室 (急診室) (jee-juhn shir) (*emergency room*)

» **Měiguó dàshǐguǎn** 美国大使馆 (美國大使館) (May-gwaw dah-shir-gwahn) (*American embassy*)

» **piàofáng** 票房 (票房) (pyaow-fahng) (*ticket office*)

» **shūdiàn** 书店 (書店) (shoo-dyan) (*bookstore*)

» **xuéxiào** 学校 (學校) (shweh-shyaow) (*school*)

» **yínháng** 银行 (銀行) (een-hahng) (*bank*)

» **yóujú** 邮局 (郵局) (yo-jyew) (*post office*)

When you travel in unknown areas, you may need to determine whether you can walk or if you need to take a bus or taxi to reach your destination:

>> **Hěn jìn ma?** 很近吗? (很進嗎?) (Hun jeen mah?) (*Is it near?*)

>> **Hěn yuǎn ma?** 很远吗? (很遠嗎?) (Hun ywan mah?) (*Is it far?*)

Chapter 16 has the lowdown on all sorts of transportation.

Different strokes for different folks: Saying năr versus saying nălĭ

GRAMMAR CHAT

Chinese people immediately know where you're from, where you've studied, or at least where your Chinese language teacher is from by the way you say the word *where*. If you say **năr** 哪儿 (哪兒) (nahr) with an *r* sound at the end of the word, you represent a northern Chinese accent commonly found in Beijing. If you say it with a *lee* sound at the end rather than an *r* sound, as in **nălĭ** 哪里 (哪裡) (nah–lee), that indicates you've probably lived or studied in Taiwan.

WARNING

The word **năr** spoken with a third (low falling and then rising) tone means *where*, but the same word said with a fourth (falling) tone, **nàr**, means *there*, so be particularly careful which tone you use when you ask for directions. The person you ask may think you're making a statement, not asking a question.

Talkin' the Talk

Elizabeth is about to leave her hotel in Beijing to head for the American embassy to renew her passport. She's not sure where to find it, so she asks a hotel attendant how to get there.

Elizabeth: **Qǐngwèn, Měiguó dàshǐguǎn zài năr?**
Cheeng-one, May-gwaw dah-shir-gwahn dzye nar?
Excuse me, where's the American embassy?

Attendant: **Měiguó dàshǐguǎn zài Xiùshuǐ Běi Jiē.**
May-gwaw dah-shir-gwahn dzye Shyow-shway Bay Jyeh.
The American embassy is on Xiushui Bei Street.

Elizabeth: **Hěn yuǎn ma?**
Hun ywan mah?
Is it far?

Attendant:	Hěn yuǎn. Nǐ zuì hǎo zuò chūzū qìchē qù.	
	Hun ywan. Nee dzway how zwaw choo-dzoo chee-chuh chyew.	
	Yes, it's quite far. You'd best take a taxi.	
Elizabeth:	**Xièxiè.**	
	Shyeh-shyeh.	
	Thanks.	

WORDS TO KNOW

Yīngguó lǐngshì guǎn 英国领事馆 (英國領事館)	Eeng-gwaw leen-shir gwan	British Consulate
dà jiē 大街	dah jyeh	avenue
Qǐng zuǒ zhuǎn. 请左转. (請左轉.)	Cheeng dzwaw jwahn.	Please turn left.
Qǐng yòu zhuǎn. 请右转. (請右轉.)	Cheeng yo jwahn.	Please turn right.

Getting direction about directions

Knowing how to ask where you can find a particular place is the first step, but you also need to know how to get there. (Otherwise, why would you ask where it is in the first place, right?) Here's the simplest way to find out: **Qù _____ zěnme zǒu?** 去 _____ 怎么走? (去 _____ 怎麼走?) (Chyew _____ dzummuh dzoe?) (*How do I get to_____?*)

Here are some examples of how to use this question pattern:

Qù fēijī chǎng zěnme zǒu? 去飞机场怎么走? (去飛機場怎麼走?) (Chyew fay-jee chahng dzummuh dzoe?) (*How do I get to the airport?*)

Qù túshūguǎn zěnme zǒu? 去图书馆怎么走? (去圖書館怎麼走?) (Chyew too-shoo-gwahn dzummuh dzoe?) (*How do I get to the library?*)

Qù xuéxiào zěnme zǒu? 去学校怎么走? (去學校怎麼走?) (Chyew shweh-shyaow dzummuh dzoe?) (*How do I get to the school?*)

CULTURAL WISDOM

If you get lost in any city in mainland China, you can often get back on track by asking where **Zhōngshān Lù** 中山路 (Joong-shahn Loo) or **Jiěfàng Lù** 解放路 (Jyeh-fahng Loo) is. **Zhōngshān,** which literally means *the middle mountain,* refers to the birthplace of Dr. Sun Yat-sen, founder of the modern Chinese Republic (Taiwan) in 1911. **Jiěfàng,** on the other hand, means *liberation* and refers to the "liberation" of the mainland by the Communists in 1949. **Lù** just means *road.* Generally, these streets are located in the middle of town. They serve as the Chinese equivalent of Main Street in Anytown, USA. Always a safe bet.

Understanding the answers to "where" questions

Short of using international sign language with a pantomime act, you may want to get a handle on some basic terms that indicate direction and location. Read on for a quick list:

- » **duìmiàn** 对面 (對面) (dway-myan) (*opposite*)
- » **fùjìn** 附近 (foo-jeen) (*near*)
- » **hòu** 后 (後) (ho) (*back*)
- » **kàojìn** 靠近 (kaow-jeen) (*next to*)
- » **lǐ** 里 (裡) (lee) (*inside*)
- » **qián** 前 (chyan) (*front*)
- » **shàng** 上 (shahng) (*above*)
- » **sìzhōu** 四周 (suh-joe) (*around*)
- » **wài** 外 (why) (*outside*)
- » **xià** 下 (shyah) (*below*)
- » **yòu** 右 (yo) (*right*)
- » **yòu zhuǎn** 右转 (右轉) (yo jwan) (*turn right*)
- » **zhí zǒu** 直走 (jir dzoe) (*go straight ahead*)
- » **zhuǎn wān** 转弯 (轉彎) (jwan wahn) (*turn around*)
- » **zuǒ** 左 (dzwaw) (*left*)
- » **zuǒ zhuǎn** 左转 (左轉) (dzwaw jwan) (*turn left*)

REMEMBER

Three different, completely interchangeable word endings work with any of the location words:

>> **biān** 边 (邊) (byan)

>> **miàn** 面 (myan)

>> **tóu** 头 (頭) (toe)

So, for example, to tell you that the bus stop is outside, someone may say any of the following sentences:

Chūzū qìchē zhàn zài wàibiān. 出租汽车站在外边. (出租汽車站在外邊.) (Choo-dzoo chee-chuh jahn dzye why-byan.) (*The bus stop is outside.*)

Chūzū qìchē zhàn zài wàimiàn. 出租汽车站在外面. (出租汽車站在外面.) (Choo-dzoo chee-chuh jahn dzye why-myan.) (*The bus stop is outside.*)

Chūzū qìchē zhàn zài wàitóu. 出租汽车站在外头. (出租汽車站在外頭.) (Choo-dzoo chee-chuh jahn dzye why-toe.) (*The bus stop is outside.*)

Sometimes the situation may require a more complex location expression, such as when your friendly direction–giver doesn't want to simply note where something is. Perhaps your helper wants to tell you where a certain action should take place. For example, if he or she wants to say *Please turn left in front of the school*, here's what you'll hear:

Qǐng nǐ zài xuéxiào qiánbiān wǎng zuǒ zhuǎn. 请你在学校前边往左转. (請你在學校前邊往左轉.) (Cheeng nee dzye shweh-shyaow chyan-byan wahng dzaw jwan.) (*Please turn left in front of the school.*)

Qǐng nǐ zài xuéxiào qiánmiàn wǎng zuǒ zhuǎn. 请你在学校前面往左转. (請你在學校前面往左轉.) (Cheeng nee dzye shweh-shyaow chyan-myan wahng dzaw jwan.) (*Please turn left in front of the school.*)

Qǐng nǐ zài xuéxiào qiántóu wǎng zuǒ zhuǎn. 请你在学校前头往左转. (請你在學校前頭往左轉.) (Cheeng nee dzye shweh-shyaow chyan-toe wahng dzaw jwan.) (*Please turn left in front of the school.*)

In such cases, the verb **děng** 等 (dung) (*to wait*) comes after the specified location (**xuéxiào qiánmiàn**). Here are some other examples:

Zài túshūguǎn qiántóu děng. 在图书馆前头等. (在圖書館前頭等.) (Dzye too-shoo-gwahn chyan-toe dung.) (*Wait in front of the library.*)

Zài wūzi lǐ wàibiān děng. 在屋子里外边等. (在屋子理外邊等.) (Dzye woo-dzuh lee why-byan dung.) (*Wait outside the room.*)

Zài xuéxiào hòumiàn děng. 在学校后面等. (在學校後面等.) (Dzye shweh-shyaow ho-myan dung.) (*Wait in back of the school.*)

Talkin' the Talk

Jay asks Melody for directions in Tainan. He wants to get to the post office.

Jay:	**Qǐngwèn, Melody, yóujú zài nǎr?**
	Cheeng-one, Melody, yo-jyew dzye nar?
	Excuse me, Melody, where's the post office?
Melody:	**Yóujú jiù zài yínháng duìmiàn. Guò liǎng tiáo lù jiù shì.**
	Yo-jyew jyo dzye een-hahng dway-myan. Gwaw lyahng tyaow loo jyo shir.
	The post office is right opposite the bank. If you go two more blocks, it's right there.
Jay:	**Xièxiè. Qù yóujú zěnme zǒu?**
	Shyeh-shyeh. Chyew yo-jyew dzummuh dzoe?
	Thank you. How should I walk to the post office?
Melody:	**Wàng nán zǒu. Yìzhí zǒu jiù dào le.**
	Wahng nahn dzoe. Ee-jir dzoe jyoe daow luh.
	Walk south. Go straight, and you'll see it.

WORDS TO KNOW

zài yèzǒnghuì duìmiàn (在夜總會對面)	dzye yeh-dzoong-hway dway-myan	opposite the nightclub
zǒu (zǒulù) 走路	dzoe (dzoe-loo)	to walk
chéng dìtiě 乘地铁 (乘地鐵)	chung dee-tyeh	take the subway

Expressing Distances (Time and Space) with Lí

Even though you can use the **cóng . . . dào** pattern to literally say *from here to there* (**cóng zhèr dào nàr** 从这儿到那儿 [從這兒到那兒]) (tsoong jar daow nar) when you want to indicate the distance from one place to another, you need to use the "distance from" coverb **lí** 离 (離) (lee). The general sentence pattern looks something like this:

Place word + **lí** + place word + description of the distance

For example:

Gōngyuán lí túshūguǎn hěn jìn. 公园离图书馆很近. (公園離圖書館很近.) (Goong-ywan lee too-shoo-gwan hun jeen.) (*The park is very close to the library.*)

Wǒ jiā lí nǐ jiā tǐng yuǎn. 我家离你家挺远. (我家離你家挺遠.) (Waw jyah lee nee jyah teeng ywan.) (*My home is really far from your home.*)

If you want to specify exactly how far one place is from another, you use the number of **lǐ** 里 (lee) (the Chinese equivalent of a kilometer) followed by the word **lí** and then the word **lù** 路 (loo) (Literally: *road*). Whether you say **sì lǐ lù** 四里路 (suh lee loo) (2 *kilometers*), **bā lǐ lù** 八里路 (bah lee loo) (4 *kilometers*), or **èrshísān lǐ lù** 二十三里路 (are-shir-sahn lee loo) (*about 11.5 kilometers*), people know the exact distance when you use this pattern. You also have to use the word **yǒu** 有 (yo) (*to have*) before the number of kilometers. If the answer includes an adjectival verb such as **yuǎn** 远 (遠) (ywan) (*far*) or **jìn** 近 (jin) (*close*) rather than a numerical distance, however, you don't need to specify the number of kilometers or use the word **yǒu**. (Count on Chapter 5 for information on Chinese numbers.)

Check out the following sample questions and answers that use these patterns:

Gōngyuán lí túshūguǎn duō yuǎn? 公园离图书馆多远? (公園離圖書館多遠?) (Goong-ywan lee too-shoo-gwahn dwaw ywan?) (*How far is the park from the library?*)

Gōngyuán lí túshūguǎn yǒu bā lǐ lù. 公园离图书馆有八里路. (公園離圖書館有八里路.) (Goong-ywan lee too-shoo-gwahn yo bah lee loo.) (*The park is four kilometers from the library.*)

Yínháng lí nǐ jiā duō jìn? 银行离你家多近? (銀行離你家多進?) (Een-hahng lee nee jyah dwaw jin?) (*How close is the bank from your home?*)

Hěn jìn. Zhǐ yī lǐ lù. 很近. 只一里路. (Hun jin. Jir ee lee loo.) (*Very close. Just half a kilometer.*)

You may have some other questions when you inquire about locations and distances:

>> **Yào duō cháng shíjiān?** 要多长时间? (要多長時間?) (Yaow dwaw chahng shir-jyan?) (*How long will it take?*)

>> **Zǒu de dào ma?** 走得到吗? (走得到嗎?) (Dzoe duh daow mah?) (*Can I walk there?*)

>> **Zǒu de dào, zǒu bú dào?** 走得到, 走不到? (dzoe duh daow, dzoe boo daow?) (*Can one walk there?*)

GRAMMAR CHAT

To indicate whether something is likely to happen or unlikely to be attained, the pattern you use includes *potential complements*. You use potential complements by putting the word **de** 得 (duh) or **bù** 不 (boo) between the verb and the complement to indicate whether a positive or negative potential is involved, respectively.

Consider the phrase **nǐ kànjiàn** 你看见 (你看見) (nee kahn–jyan) (*you see*). If you say **Nǐ kàn de jiàn ma?** 你看得见吗? (你看得見嗎?) (Nee kahn duh jyan ma?), you mean *Can you see?* If you replace the positive **de** with the negative **bù** to ask **Nǐ kàn bú jiàn ma?** 你看不见吗? (你看不見嗎?) (Nee kahn boo jyan ma?), you mean *You can't see?* Finally, if you use both positive and negative potential forms in the same sentence by asking **Nǐ kàn de jiàn, kàn bú jiàn?** 你看得见, 看不见? (你看得見, 看不見?) (Nee kahn duh jyan, kahn boo jyan?), you mean *Can you see [or not]?*

So in the earlier example **Zǒu de dào, zǒu bú dào?**, what you're really saying is *Can one can walk there [or not]?* Similarly, **Wǒmen lái de jí, lái bù jí?** 我们来得及, 来不及? (我們來得及, 來不及?) (Waw–mun lye duh jee, lye boo jee?) means *Will we make it on time [or not]?*

Here are some other examples of this pattern:

xǐ gānjìng 洗干净 (洗乾淨) (she gahn-jeeng) (*to wash [and make clean]*)

xǐ de gānjìng 洗得干净 (洗得乾淨) (she duh gahn-jeeng) (*can be washed clean*)

xǐ bù gānjìng 洗不干净 (洗不乾淨) (she boo gahn-jeeng) (*can't be washed clean*)

Xǐ de gānjìng, xǐ bù gānjìng? 洗得干净, 洗不干净? (洗得不乾淨, 洗不乾淨?) (She duh gahn-jeeng, she boo gahn-jeeng?) (*Can you wash it clean?/Can it be washed clean?*)

zuò wán 做完 (dzwaw wahn) (*to finish [doing something]*)

zuò de wán 做得完 (dzwaw duh wahn) (*can finish*)

zuò bù wán 做不完 (dzwaw boo wahn) (*can't finish*)

Zuò de wán, zuò bù wán? 做得完, 做不完? (Dzwaw duh wahn, dzwaw boo wahn?) (*Can you finish it?/Can it be finished?*)

Using Ordinal Numbers to Clarify Points of Reference

If someone has ever told you to make a right at the second **jiāotōng dēng** 交通灯 (交通燈) (jyaow-toong dung) (*traffic light*) or that her house is the third one on the left, she's used ordinal numbers. (You can find a list of ordinal numbers in Chapter 5; in this section, I just show you how they're used in giving Chinese directions.)

Simply using a numeral plus a classifier doesn't work in Chinese, such as when you say **sān ge** 三个 (三個) (sahn guh) (*three*) of something. If someone giving you directions says **sān ge jiāotōng dēng** 三个交通灯 (三個交通燈) (sahn guh jyaow-toong dung), you hear *three traffic lights*. To accurately express *the third traffic light*, your helper has to add the word **dì** 第 (dee) before the numeral to create **dì sān ge jiāotōng dēng** 第三个交通灯 (第三個交通燈) (dee sahn guh jyaow-toong dung).

REMEMBER

As I note in Chapter 5, if you use an ordinal number followed by a noun, you must always have a classifier between them. You can't combine **dì sān** 第三 (dee sahn) (*the third*) with **qìchē** 汽车 (汽車) (chee-chuh) (*car*). You have to put the classifier **ge** between the number and the noun to say **dì sān ge qìchē** 第三个汽车 (第三個汽車) (dee sahn guh chee-chuh) (*the third car*).

Following are some examples of ways you may hear ordinal numbers in directions:

dì èr ge fángzi 第二个房子 (第二個房子) (dee are guh fahng-dzuh) (*the second house*)

dì yī tiáo lù 第一条路 (第一條路) (dee ee tyaow loo) (*the first street*)

zuǒ biān dì bā ge fángzi 左边第八个房子 (左邊第八個房子) (dzwaw byan dee bah guh fahng-dzuh) (*the eighth house on the left*)

Specifying Cardinal Points

Your direction-givers can tell you to go right or left until they're blue in the face, but sometimes the best way to give you directions is to point you the right way with the cardinal points: north, south, east, or west.

In Chinese, however, you say them in this order:

>> **dōng** 东 (東) (doong) (*east*)

>> **nán** 南 (nahn) (*south*)

>> **xī** 西 (she) (*west*)

>> **běi** 北 (bay) (*north*)

Not precise enough? Try the following (also in the correct Chinese order):

>> **dōng běi** 东北 (東北) (doong bay) (*northeast*)

>> **xī běi** 西北 (she bay) (*northwest*)

>> **dōng nán** 东南 (東南) (doong nahn) (*southeast*)

>> **xī nán** 西南 (she nahn) (*southwest*)

WARNING

When it comes to indicating north, south, east, and west (as well as left and right), you can use either **-biān** 边 (邊) (byan) or **-miàn** 面 (myan) as a word ending, but not **-tóu** 头 (頭) (toe), which you can use with other position words such as front, back, inside, and outside. (I cover these position words earlier in the chapter.)

GRAMMAR
CHAT

Giving directions often entails multiple instructions. "Make a right, and you're there" or "Go straight, and you'll see it right in front of you" doesn't always cut it. Luckily, a common Chinese pattern makes giving multiple directions easy:

xiān 先 + Verb 1, **zài** 再 + Verb 2. (shyan + Verb 1, dzye + Verb 2.) (*First do Verb 1, and then do Verb 2.*)

Here are some examples:

Xiān wàng dōng zǒu, zài wàng yòu zhuǎn. 先往东走, 再往右转. (先往東走, 再往右轉.) (Shyan wahng doong dzoe, dzye wahng yo jwan.) (*First walk east, and then turn right.*)

Xiān zhí zǒu, zài wàng xī zǒu. 先直走, 再往西走. (Shyan jir dzoe, dzye wahng she dzoe.) (*First go straight, and then turn west.*)

Talkin' the Talk

Julia is walking around Shanghai looking for the Shanghai Museum. She begins to wonder if she's going in the right direction, so she decides to ask a stranger how to get there.

Julia: **Qǐngwèn, Shànghǎi Bówùguǎn lí zhèr hěn yuǎn ma?**
Cheeng-one, Shahng-hi Baw-woo-gwahn lee jar hun ywan mah?
Excuse me, is the Shanghai Museum very far from here?

Stranger:	**Bù yuǎn. Shànghǎi Bówùguǎn jiù zài Rénmín Dàdào.**
	Boo ywan. Shahng-hi Baw-woo-gwahn jyo dzye Run-meen Dah-daow.
	It's not far at all. The Shanghai Museum is on the Avenue of the People.

Julia:	**Rénmín Dàdào lí zhèr duō yuǎn?**
	Run-meen Dah-daow lee jar dwaw ywan?
	How far is the Avenue of the People from here?

Stranger:	**Rénmín Dàdào lí zhèr zhǐ yǒu yì lǐ lù zuǒyòu.**
	Run-meen Dah-daow lee jar jir yo ee lee loo dzwaw-yo.
	The Avenue of the People is only about one kilometer from here.

Julia:	**Cóng zhèr zǒu de dào, zǒu bú dào?**
	Tsoong jar dzoe duh daow, dzoe boo daow?
	Can I walk there from here?

Stranger:	**Kěndìng zǒu de dào. Nǐ xiān wàng nán zǒu, zài dì èr tiáo lù wàng xī zhuǎn. Dì yī ge lóu jiù shì.**
	Kun-deeng dzoe duh daow. Nee shyan wahng nahn dzoe, dzye dee are tyaow loo wahng she jwan. Dee ee guh low jyoe shir.
	It's certainly walkable. First walk north, and then turn west at the second street. It'll be the first building you see.

Julia:	**Fēicháng gǎnxiè nǐ.**
	Fay-chahng gahn-shyeh nee.
	I'm extremely grateful [for your help].

Stranger:	**Méi shì.**
	May shir.
	It's nothing.

. . . .

WORDS TO KNOW

bówùguǎn 博物馆 (博物館)	baw-woo-gwahn	museum
Wǒmen zǒu ba! 我们走吧! (我們走吧!)	Waw-mun dzo bah!	Let's go!
Hǎo bù hǎo? 好不好?	How boo how?	Okay?/How about it?

FUN & GAMES

Use Chinese cardinal directions to indicate whether each building in the illustration faces the north, south, east, or west. Check out Appendix C for the answers.

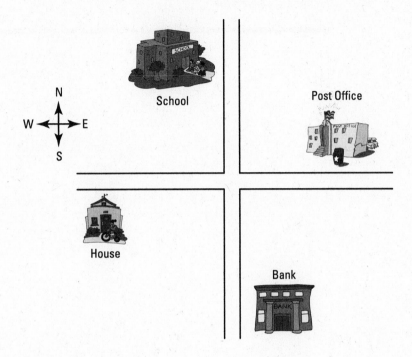

A. School: _____

B. Post office: _____

C. Bank: _____

D. House: _____

Choose somewhere you need to go from one of your new favorite words and write it in the spaces below.

Qǐngwèn, Měiguó dàshǐguǎn zài nǎr?

Cheeng-one, May-gwaw dah-shir-gwahn dzye nar?

Excuse me, where's the American embassy?

Qǐngwèn, _____ zài nǎr?

Cheeng-one, _____ dzye nar?

Excuse me, where's the _____?

Qǐngwèn, _____ zài nǎr?

Cheeng-one, _____ dzye nar?

Excuse me, where's the _____?

Chapter **18**
Finding a Place to Stay

T he right hotel can make or break a vacation. Whether you stay in a capital city or a little backwater town with only one hotel to its name, you still need to know how to check in, check out, and ask for anything you need in between (including the bill). This chapter runs you through the gamut of booking your hotel, checking in at the front desk, checking out at the designated time, and dealing with all sorts of issues that may come up in between.

REMEMBER

First, however, I have an astounding fact for you: You have not one, not two, but as many as five ways to say the word *hotel* in Chinese:

» **bīnguǎn** 宾馆 (宾馆) (been-gwahn) (Literally: *a place for guests*)

» **fàndiàn** 饭店 (飯店) (fahn-dyan) (Literally: *a place for meals*)

» **jiǔdiàn** 酒店 (jyo-dyan) (Literally: *a place for wine*)

» **lǚguǎn** 旅馆 (旅館) (lyew-gwahn) (*hotel*)

» **zhāodàisuǒ** 招待所 (jaow-dye-swaw) (Literally: *a place to receive people*)

Making a Room Reservation

Thinking of **yùdìng** 预定 (預定) (yew–deeng) (*reserving*) a hotel **fángjiān** 房间 (房間) (fahng–jyan) (*room*)? What kind do you want? A single room all for yourself? A double room for you and your special someone? Or perhaps a suite for a special occasion like your 50th wedding anniversary?

You have many kinds of rooms to choose from, depending on your budget and your unique needs:

>> **dānrén fángjiān** 单人房间 (單人房間) (dahn-run fahng-jyan) (*single room*)

>> **shuāngrén fángjiān** 双人房间 (雙人房間) (shwahng-run fahng-jyan) (*double room*)

>> **tàojiān** 套间 (套間) (taow-jyan) (*a suite*)

>> **yíge ānjìng de fángjiān** 一个安静的房间 (一個安靜的房間) (ee-guh ahn-jeeng duh fahng-jyan) (*a quiet room*)

>> **yíge bù xīyān de fángjiān** 一个不吸烟的房间 (一個不吸煙的房間) (ee-guh boo she-yan duh fahng-jyan) (*a non-smoking room*)

>> **yíge cháo yuànzi de fángjiān** 一个朝院子的房间 (一個朝院子的房間) (ee-guh chaow ywan-dzuh duh fahng-jyan) (*a room facing the courtyard*)

>> **yíge dài yángtái de fángjiān** 一个带阳台的房间 (一個帶陽臺的房間) (ee-guh dye yahng-tye duh fahng-jyan) (*a room with a balcony*)

>> **yíge fāngbiàn cánjí rén de fángjiān** 一个方便残疾人的房间 (一個方便殘疾人的房間) (ee-guh fahng-byan tsahn-jee run duh fahng-jyan) (*a room equipped for handicapped people*)

>> **yíge guāngxiàn hǎo de fángjiān** 一个光线好的房间 (一個光線好的房間) (ee-guh gwahng-shyan how duh fahng-jyan) (*a bright room*)

>> **yíge hǎi jǐng de fángjiān** 一个海景的房间 (一個海景的房間) (ee-guh hi jeeng duh fahng-jyan) (*a room with an ocean view*)

>> **yíge yǒu kōngtiáo de fángjiān** 一个有空调的房间 (一個有空調的房間) (ee-guh yo koong-tyaow duh fahng-jyan) (*a room with air conditioning*)

Whatever the occasion and whatever kind of room you want, you need to know how to make a reservation. Just make sure you know your budget in advance (and stick to it). You're sure to find a decent hotel no matter the price range if you spend some time checking out the competition.

Here are some things you may want to ask or specify over the phone as you begin the search for your ideal hotel:

» **Nǐmen de fángjiān yǒu méiyǒu wǎngluò liánjié?** 你们的房间有没有网络连接? (你們的房間有沒有網絡連接?) (Nee-men duh fahng-jyan yo may-yo wahng-lwaw lyan-jyeh?) (*Do your rooms have Internet access?*)

» **Nǐmen hái yǒu fángjiān ma?** 你们还有房间吗? (你們還有房間嗎?) (Nee-mun hi yo fahng-jyan mah?) (*Do you have any rooms available?*)

» **Nǐmen fángjiān de jiàgé shì duōshǎo?** 你们房间的价格是多少? (你們房間的價格是多少?) (Nee-mun fahng-jyan duh jyah-guh shir dwaw-shaow?) (*How much are your rooms?*)

» **Nǐmen shōu bù shōu xìnyòng kǎ?** 你们收不收信用卡? (你們收不收信用卡?) (Nee-men show boo show sheen-yoong kah?) (*Do you accept credit cards?*)

» **Wǒ yào yíge fángjiān zhù liǎng ge wǎnshàng.** 我要一个房间住两个晚上. (我要一個房間住兩個晚上.) (Waw yaow ee-guh fahng-jyan joo lyahng guh wahn-shahng.) (*I'd like a room for two nights.*)

» **Yǒu méiyǒu shāngwù zhōngxīn?** 有没有商务中心? (有沒有商務中心?) (Yo may-yo shahng-woo joong-sheen?) (*Is there a business center?*)

» **Yǒu méiyǒu wúxiàn wǎngluò?** 有没有無線網絡? (有沒有無線網絡?) (Yo may-yo woo-shyan wahng-lwaw?) (*Do you have WiFi?*)

When you do finally pick up your phone to reserve a room, make sure you have your credit card in front of you (refer to Chapter 15 for more money talk).

Talkin' the Talk

Eli calls a well-known hotel chain in Hong Kong to make a three-day reservation for his whole family. The hotel clerk quickly answers his call.

Eli: **Qǐngwèn, nǐmen fángjiān de jiàgé shì duōshǎo?**
Cheeng-one, nee-men fahng-jyan duh jyah-guh shir dwaw-shaow?
May I ask, how much are your rooms?

Hotel clerk: **Wǒmen de fángjiān yìtiān wǎnshàng sānbǎi kuài Měi yuán.**
Waw-men duh fahng-jyan ee-tyan wahn-shahng san-bye kwye May ywan.
Our rooms are USD $300 per night.

Eli:	**Nà shì dānrén fángjiān hái shì shuāngrén fángjiān de jiàgé?**

Eli: **Nà shì dānrén fángjiān hái shì shuāngrén fángjiān de jiàgé?**
Nah shir dahn-run fahng-jyan hi shir shwahng-run fahng-jyan duh jyah-guh?
Is that the price of a single room or a double?

Hotel clerk: **Dānrén fángjiān hé shuāngrén fángjiān de jiàgé dōu yíyàng.**
Dahn-run fahng-jyan huh shwahng-run fahng-jyan duh jyah-guh doe ee-yahng.
The prices of our single and double rooms are the same.

Eli: **Hǎo jíle. Wǒ yào liǎngge dānrén fángjiān yíge shuāngrén fángjiān.**
How jee-luh. Waw yaow lyahng-guh dahn-run fahng-jyan ee-guh shwahng-run fahng-jyan.
Great. I'd like two single rooms and one double.

Hotel clerk: **Méiyǒu wèntí. Nǐmen yào dāi jǐ ge wǎnshàng?**
May-yo one-tee. Nee-men yaow dye jee guh wahn-shahng?
No problem. How many nights will you be staying?

Eli: **Yígòng sān ge wǎnshàng.**
Ee-goong sahn guh wahn-shahng.
Altogether, three nights.

Hotel clerk: **Hǎo. Nà yígòng liǎng qiān qībǎi kuài.**
How. Nah ee-goong lyahng chyan chee-bye kwye.
Very well. That will be $2,700 altogether.

WORDS TO KNOW

qiántái 前台	chyan-tye	reception desk
tuì fáng 退房	tway fahng	check out
rùzhù 入住	roo-joo	check in
yàoshi kǎ 钥匙卡	yaow-shir kah	key card

HOTEL OR APARTMENT?

CULTURAL WISDOM

China's booming economy has become a magnet for foreign businesses, and scores of foreign business people have been taking up residence there for over a decade now. Because living in mainland China can be quite expensive and nice apartments that don't come with long waiting lists are hard to come by, many foreigners opt to stay in a permanent hotel room or a serviced apartment connected to a foreign-run hotel. Rent in Shanghai for a nice-sized apartment is around USD $3,500 per month, comparable to the rent of major U.S. cities like New York or Chicago. And you can expect the hotels to run at least $300 per night, just like in metropolitan U.S. cities.

GRAMMAR CHAT

The coverb **hé** 和 (huh) (*and*), along with the noun that always follows it, precedes the main verb or adjective of a sentence. (What's a *coverb*? Basically, it's a word that's technically a verb but typically acts as a preposition.) Some synonyms of **hé** are **gēn** 跟 (gun), **yǔ** 与 (與) (yew), and **tóng** 同 (toong), although **tóng** translates more closely as *with*.

Checking In Before You Hit the Pool

Before you can take advantage of any conveniences your hotel offers (flip to the following section), you have to officially **bànlǐ rùzhù shǒuxù** 办理入住手续 (辦理入住手續) (bahn-lee roo-joo show-shyew) (*check in*). You don't want to be caught red-handed running in the gym or relaxing in the hot tub unless you're a bona fide guest, right? (Don't answer that.)

When you walk up to the **fàndiàn qiántái** 饭店前台 (飯店前台) (fahn-dyan chyan-tye) (*reception desk*), you invariably find yourself needing to say one of the following sentences:

>> **Nǐmen hái yǒu fángjiān ma?** 你们还有房间吗? (你們還有房間嗎?) (Nee-men hi yo fahng-jyan mah?) (*Do you have any rooms available?*)

>> **Wǒ méiyǒu yùdìng fángjiān.** 我没有预定房间. (我沒有預定房間.) (Waw may-yo yew-deeng fahng-jyan.) (*I don't have a reservation.*)

>> **Wǒ yǐjīng yùdìng le fángjiān.** 我已经预定了房间. (我已經預定了房間.) (Waw ee-jeeng yew-deeng luh fahng-jyan.) (*I already made a reservation.*)

If you're in luck, the hotel has at least one **kōng** 空 (koong) (*empty/vacant*) room. If the hotel has no available space, you'll hear **Duìbùqǐ, wǒmen kèmǎn.** 对不起, 我们客满. (對不起, 我們客滿.) (Dway-boo-chee, waw-men kuh-mahn.) (*Sorry, there are no vacancies./We're full.*).

The **qiántái fúwùyuán** 前台服务员 (前台服務員) (chyan-tye foo-woo-ywan) (*front desk clerk*) asks you to **tián** 填 (tyan) (*fill out*) a couple of **biǎo** 表 (byaow) (*forms*) to book your room, so have a pen and some form of **zhèngjiàn** 证件 (證件) (juhng-jyan) (*ID*) ready — especially your **hùzhào** 护照 (護照) (hoo-jaow) (*passport*). Voilà! You're officially a hotel **kèrén** 客人 (kuh-run) (*guest*).

After you successfully manage to check in, a **xínglǐ yuán** 行李员 (行李員) (sheeng-lee ywan) (*porter/bellboy*) immediately appears to help take your **xínglǐ** 行李 (sheeng-lee) (*luggage*) to your room. After he lets you in, he gives you the **yàoshi** 钥匙 (鑰匙) (yaow-shir) (*key*) if you didn't get it from the **qiántái fúwùyuán** downstairs.

Talkin' the Talk

Adele arrives in Taiwan and wants to check into a hotel in downtown Taipei, but the clerk informs her that the hotel has no vacancy.

Adele: **Nǐ hǎo. Qǐngwèn, nǐmen hái yǒu fángjiān ma?**
           Nee how. Cheeng-one, nee-men hi yo fahng-jyan mah?
           Hello. May I ask, do you have any rooms available?

Clerk: **Duìbùqǐ, wǒmen jīntiān kèmǎn. Méiyǒu kōng fángjiān le.**
           Dway-boo-chee, waw-men jin-tyan kuh-mahn. May-yo koong fahng-jyan luh.
           I'm sorry, but we're full today. There aren't any vacant rooms.

Adele: **Zāogāo! Nǐ néng bù néng tuījiàn biéde lǚguǎn?**
           Dzaow-gaow! Nee nung boo nung tway-jyan byeh-duh lyew-gwahn?
           Rats! Could you perhaps recommend another hotel, then?

Clerk: **Kéyǐ. Gébì de lǚguǎn yǒu kōng fángjiān. Nǐ zuì hǎo zǒu guò qù shì shì kàn.**
           Kuh-yee. Guh-bee duh lyew-gwahn yo koong fahng-jyan. Nee dzway how dzoe gwaw chyew shir shir kahn.
           Yes. The hotel next door has vacancies. You may as well walk over there and have a look.

Adele: **Xièxiè.**
           Shyeh-shyeh.
           Thank you.

xínglǐ 行李	sheeng-lee	luggage
xiǎofèi 小费 (小費)	shyaow-fay	tip
diàntī 电梯 (電梯)	dyan-tee	elevator
kèfáng fúwù 客房服务 (客房服務)	kuh-fahng foo-woo	room service

Taking Advantage of Hotel Service

After you check into your hotel (refer to the preceding section), you may find yourself mysteriously lingering a bit in the **dàtīng** 大厅 (大廳) (dah–teeng) (*lobby*), visually casing the joint long enough to take in all sorts of amenities. The following sections introduce you to both the comfort services and customer services hotels have to offer.

REMEMBER

Depending on your service needs, you interact with many different employees on any given hotel stay:

» **fúwùtái jīnglǐ** 服务台经理 (服務台經理) (foo-woo-tye jeeng-lee) (*concierge*)

» **fúwùyuán** 服务员 (服務員) (foo-woo-ywan) (*attendant*)

» **fúwùyuán lǐngbān** 服务员领班 (服務員領班) (foo-woo-ywan leeng-bahn) (*bell captain*)

» **zhùlǐ jīnglǐ** 助理经理 (助理經理) (joo-lee jeeng-lee) (*assistant manager*)

» **zǒngjīnglǐ** 总经理 (總經理) (dzoong-jeeng-lee) (*general manager*)

Counting on convenience

Most hotels let you put in for a wake-up call so that you don't have to worry about setting an alarm. All you have to say is **Qǐng nǐ jiào wǒ qǐchuáng.** 请你叫我起床. (請你叫我起床.) (Cheeng nee jyaow waw chee–chwahng.) (Literally: *Please call me to get out of bed.*).

After you're awake, the luxuries at your disposal may include the following:

» **ànmō yùgāng** 按摩浴缸 (ahn-maw yew-gahng) (*jacuzzi*)

» **diànshì** 电视 (電視) (dyan-shir) (*television*)

- » **gānxǐ fúwù** 干洗服务 (乾洗服務) (gahn-she foo-woo) (*dry cleaning service*)

- » **lǚguǎn fàndiàn** 旅馆饭店 (旅館飯店) (lyew-gwahn fahn-dyan) (*hotel restaurant*)

- » **shāngwù zhōngxīn** 商务中心 (商務中心) (shahng-woo joong-sheen) (*business center*)

- » **jiànshēn fáng** 健身房 (jyan-shun fahng) (*gym*)

- » **xǐyī fúwù** 洗衣服务 (洗衣服务) (she-ee foo-woo) (*laundry service*)

- » **yóuyǒngchí** 游泳池 (yo-yoong-chir) (*swimming pool*)

Getting problems fixed

Uh oh . . . you're finally ensconced in your big, beautiful hotel room when you discover that the **mén suǒ bú shàng** 门锁不上 (門鎖不上) (mun swaw boo shahng) (*door doesn't lock*) and the **kōngtiáo huài le** 空调坏了 (空調壞了) (koong-tyaow hwye luh) (*air conditioning doesn't work*). To make matters worse, your **chuānghu dǎ bù kāi** 窗户打不开 (窗戶打不開) (chwahng-hoo dah boo kye) (*window won't open*). Heat wave! It may be hard to believe, but in addition to all that, your **mǎtǒng dǔzhùle** 马桶堵住了 (馬桶堵住了) (mah-toong doo-joo-luh) (*toilet is clogged*). Time to call the nearest **kèfáng fúwùyuán** 客房服务员 (客房服務員) (kuh-fahng foo-woo-ywan) (*hotel housekeeper*) for help.

Call quick if the following pieces of equipment are **huàile** 坏了 (壞了) (hwye-luh) (*broken*) and need immediate fixing:

- » **chāzuò** 插座 (chah-dzwaw) (*electric outlet*)

- » **kāiguān** 开关 (開關) (kye-gwahn) (*light switch*)

- » **kōngtiáo** 空调 (空調) (koong-tyaow) (*air conditioner*)

- » **mǎtǒng** 马桶 (馬桶) (mah-toong) (*toilet*)

- » **nuǎnqì** 暖气 (暖氣) (nwan-chee) (*heater*)

- » **yáokòng qì** 遥控器 (遙控器) (yaow-koong chee) (*remote control*)

Even if you aren't having an equipment emergency, you may want housekeeping to send the following items right over:

- » **chuīfēngjī** 吹风机 (吹風機) (chway-fung-jee) (*hair dryer*)

- » **máojīn** 毛巾 (maow-jeen) (*towel*)

>> **máotǎn** 毛毯 (maow-tahn) (*blanket*)

>> **wèishēngzhǐ** 卫生纸 (衛生紙) (way-shung-jir) (*toilet paper*)

>> **zhěntóu** 枕头 (枕頭) (jun-toe) (*pillow*)

Maybe you just need someone to **dǎsǎo fángjiān** 打扫房间 (打掃房間) (dah–saow fahng–jyan) (*clean the room*). Oh well. Even the best hotels need some tweaking every now and then.

Hey! I almost forgot one of the best kinds of service you can take advantage of on occasion: room service! Before you decide to order room service for food, however, just remember that it's often twice as expensive as dining in the hotel restaurant, because the service is more convenient.

GRAMMAR CHAT

To make a comparison by saying that something is a number of times more expensive than something else, you first use the word **guì** 贵 (貴) (gway) (*expensive*), followed by the number of times you think it's more expensive and the word **bèi** 倍 (bay) (roughly translated as *times*). You can compare the relative cost of two products or services by using the word **bǐ** 比 (bee) (*compared to*) in the following pattern:

X **bǐ** Y **guì** (number) **bèi**. X 比 Y 贵 (貴) (number) 倍.

(X bee Y gway (number) bay.)

Here are some examples:

Zhège fángjiān bǐ nèige guì shí bèi. 这个房间比那个贵十倍. (這個房間比那個貴十倍.) (Jay-guh fahng-jyan bee nay-guh gway shir bay.) (*This room is ten times more expensive than that one.*)

Zuò chūzūchē bǐ zuò gōnggòng qìchē guì wǔ bèi. 坐出租车比坐公共汽车贵五倍. (坐出租車比坐公共汽車貴五倍.) (Zwaw choo-dzoo-chuh bee dzwaw goong-goong chee-chuh gway woo bay.) (*Taking a cab is five times more expensive than taking the bus.*)

CULTURAL WISDOM

Never drink directly from the tap in your Chinese hotel; the water isn't safe. Every hotel room in China has a large flask of boiling water that you can use to make tea or for drinking water. You can brush your teeth with tap water because you just spit it out. Local Chinese don't dare drink the tap water either, so you're in good company.

Talkin' the Talk

Irma enters her hotel room after she checks in, only to discover the bathroom faucet is broken. She calls for housekeeping and a few minutes later hears a knock on her door.

Housekeeper: **Kèfáng fúwùyuán!**
Kuh-fahng foo-woo-ywan!
Housekeeping!

Irma: **Qǐng jìn!**
Cheeng jin!
Come on in!

Housekeeper: **Yǒu shénme wèntí?**
Yo shummuh one-tee?
What seems to be the trouble?

Irma: **Zhèige shuǐlóngtóu huàile. Yě méiyǒu rèshuǐ.**
Jay-guh shway-loong-toe hwye-luh. Yeah may-yo ruh-shway.
This faucet is broken. There's also no hot water.

Housekeeper: **Hěn duìbùqǐ. Mǎshàng sòng shuǐnuǎn gōng guòlái kànkàn.**
Hun dway-boo-chee. Mah-shahng soong shway-nwan goong gwaw-lye kahn-kahn.
I'm so sorry. We'll send a plumber right away to have a look.

Irma: **Xièxiè.**
Shyeh-shyeh.
Thank you.

As the housekeeper starts to leave, Irma suddenly remembers some other things that the housekeeper may be able to take care of as long as she's there.

Irma: **Xiǎojiě, nǐmen yǒu méiyǒu xǐyī fúwù?**
Shyaow-jyeh, nee-men yo mayo she-ee foo-woo?
Miss, do you have any laundry service?

Housekeeper:	**Yǒu.**
	Yo.
	Yes, we do.

Irma:	**Hǎo jíle. Jīntiān kěyǐ bǎ zhè xiē yīfú xǐ hǎo ma?**
	How jee-luh. Jin-tyan kuh-yee bah jay shyeh ee-foo she how mah?
	Great. Can I have these clothes cleaned today?

Housekeeper:	**Kěyǐ.**
	Kuh-yee.
	Yes.

Irma:	**Yóuqíshì zhèige wūdiǎn. Néng bùnéng qùdiào?**
	Yo-chee-shir jay-guh woo-dyan. Nung boo-nung chyew-dyaow?
	Especially this stain. Can it be removed?

Housekeeper:	**Méiyǒu wèntí.**
	May-yo one-tee.
	No problem.

Irma:	**Hǎo. Xièxiè.**
	How. Shyeh-shyeh.
	Great. Thanks.

● ●

WORDS TO KNOW

jiào xǐng diànhuà 叫醒电话	jyaow sheeng dyan-hwah	wake-up call
Cèsuǒ yìshuǐle. 厕所溢水了.	Tsuh-swaw ee-shway-luh.	The toilet is overflowing.
Xūyào gèng duō de wèishēngzhǐ. 需要更多的卫生纸.	Shyew-yaow gung dwaw duh way-shung-jir.	We need more toilet paper.
Dēng kāiguān bù qǐ zuòyòng. 灯开关不起作用.	Dung kye-gwan boo chee dzwaw-yoong.	The light switch doesn't work.

As you can see in the previous Talkin' the Talk dialogue, the coverb **bǎ** 把 (bah) often appears right after the subject of the sentence, separating it from the direct object, which is always something concrete rather than an abstract idea. It separates the indirect and direct objects.

You don't have the following sentence pattern:

Subject + Verb + Complement (+ Indirect Object) + Object

Instead, you have this one:

Subject + **bǎ** + Object + Verb + Complement (+ Indirect Object)

Here are some examples:

Qǐng nǐ bǎ nǐde hùzhào ná gěi qiántái fúwùyuán. 请你把你的护照拿给前台服务员. (請你把你的護照拿給前台服務員.) (Cheeng nee bah nee-duh hoo-jaow nah gay chyan-tye foo-woo-ywan.) (*Please give your passport to the front desk clerk.*)

Wǒ bǎ shū jiè gěi nǐ. 我把书接给你. (我把書借給你.) (Waw bah shoo jyeh gay nee.) (*I'll loan you the book.*)

Checking Out Before Heading Out

That oh-so-depressing time has come again. Time to say goodbye. Time to **téngchū** 腾出 (騰出) (tuhng-choo) (*vacate*) your hotel room and **tuìfáng** 退房 (tway-fahng) (*check out*).

You may need to say some of the following as you begin the end of your stay:

>> **Jiézhàng yǐhòu wǒ néng bùnéng bǎ bāoguǒ liú zài qiántái?** 结帐以后我能不能把包裹留在前台? (結帳以後我能不能把包裹留在前台?) (Jyeh-jahng ee-ho waw nung boo-nung bah baow-gwaw lyo dzye chyan-tye?) (*After checking out, may I leave my bags at the front desk?*)

>> **Nǐmen jiēshòu shénme xìnyòng kǎ?** 你们接收什么信用卡? (你們接收甚麼信用卡?) (Nee-men jyeh-show shummuh sheen-yoong kah?) (*Which credit cards do you accept?*)

>> **Wǒ bù yīnggāi fù zhè xiàng.** 我不应该付这项. (我不應該付這項.) (Waw boo eeng-gye foo jay shyahng.) (*I shouldn't be charged for this.*)

>> **Wǒ yào fùzhàng.** 我要付账. (我要付賬.) (Waw yaow foo-jahng.) (*I'd like to pay the bill.*)

» **Yǒu méiyǒu qù fēijīchǎng de bānchē?** 有没有去飞机场的班车? (有沒有去飛機場的班車?) (Yo may-yo chyew fay-jee-chahng duh ban-chuh?) (*Is there a shuttle to the airport?*)

» **Zhè búshì wǒde zhàngdān.** 这不是我的账单。(這不是我的賬單。) (Jay boo-shir waw-duh jahng-dahn.) (*This isn't my bill.*)

Talkin' the Talk

Shirley is ready to check out after her three-day stay at a five-star hotel in Shanghai. She approaches the reception clerk to check out.

Shirley: **Nǐ hǎo. Wǒ jīntiān yào tuìfáng, suǒyǐ yào fù zhàng.**
            Nee how. Waw jin-tyan yaow tway-fahng, swaw-yee yaow foo jahng.
            Hello. I'd like to check out today, so I'd like to pay the bill.

Clerk: **Qǐngwèn, nín de fángjiān hào shì duōshǎo?**
            Cheeng-one, neen duh fahng-jyan how shir dwaw-shaow?
            May I ask, what's your room number?

Shirley: **Wǔlíngliù hào fángjiān.**
            Woo-leeng-lyo how fahng-jyan.
            Room 506.

Clerk: **Hǎo. Zhè shì nínde zhàngdān. Yígòng yìqiān wǔbǎi kuài.**
            How. Jay shir neen-duh jahng-dahn. Ee-goong ee-chyan woo-bye kwye.
            Okay. This is your bill. It's $1,500 altogether.

Shirley pays the bill with her credit card.

Shirley: **Zhè shì wǒmen fángjiān de yàoshi.**
            Jay shir waw-mun fahng-jyan duh yaow-shir.
            This is my room key.

Clerk: **Xièxiè.**
            Shyeh-shyeh.
            Thank you.

Shirley: **Jiézhàng yǐhòu wǒ néng bùnéng bǎ bāoguǒ liú zài qiántái?**

Jyeh-jahng ee-ho waw nung boo-nung bah baow-gwaw lyo dzye chyan-tye?

After checking out, may I leave my bags at the front desk?

Clerk: **Kěyǐ. Méiyǒu wèntí.**

Kuh-yee. May-yo one-tee.

Yes. No problem.

WORDS TO KNOW

yājīn 押金	yah-jeen	deposit
xìnyòngkǎ 信用卡	sheen-yoong-kah	credit card
shìnèi bǎoxiǎnxiāng 室内保险箱 (室内保险箱)	shir-nay baow-shyan-shyahng	in-room safe

FUN & GAMES

Fill in the blanks, using the following words: **tuìfáng** 退房, **zhàngdān** 账单 (賬單), **fángjiān** 房间 (房間), **kèmǎn** 客满 (客滿), and **qǐchuáng** 起床. You can find the answer key in Appendix C.

1. **Nǐmen de _____ yǒu méiyǒu wǎngluò liánjié?** 你们的 _____ 有没有网络连接? (你們的 _____ 有沒有網絡連接?)

   Do your rooms have Internet access?

2. **Duìbùqǐ, wǒmen _____ le.** 对不起, 我们 _____ 了. (對不起, 我們 _____ 了.)

   I'm sorry, we have no vacancies.

3. **Qǐng nǐ jiào wǒ _____.** 请你叫我 _____. (請你叫我 _____.)

   Please give me a wake-up call.

4. **Zhè búshì wǒde _____.** 这不是我的 _____. (這不是我的 _____.)

   This isn't my bill.

5. **Wǒ jīntiān yào _____.** 我今天要 _____.

   I'd like to check out today.

Chapter **19**

Handling Emergencies

You can easily plan the fun and exciting things you want to experience while you travel or go out with friends, but you can't predict needing to call the police to report a theft or rushing to an emergency room with **lánwěi yán** 阑尾炎 (闌尾炎) (lahn-way yeahn) (*appendicitis*) on your trip to the Great Wall. Such things can and do happen, and this chapter gives you the language tools you need to communicate your problems during your times of need.

Calling for Help in Times of Need

When you're faced with an emergency, the last way you want to spend your time is searching for an oversized Chinese–English dictionary to figure out how to quickly call for help. Try memorizing these phrases before a situation arises:

» **Jiào jǐngchá!** 叫警察 (Jyaow jeeng-chah!) (*Call the police!*)

» **Jiào jiùhùchē!** 叫救护车! (叫救護車!) (Jyaow jyo-hoo-chuh!) (*Call an ambulance!*)

» **Jǐngwèi!** 警卫! (警衛!) (Jeeng way!) (*Security!*)

» **Jiù mìng!** 救命! (Jyo meeng!) (*Help!/Save me!*)

» **Zháohuǒ lā!** 着火啦! (Jaow-hwaw lah!) (*Fire!*)

» **Zhuā zéi!** 抓贼! (抓賊!) (Jwah dzay!) (*Stop, thief!*)

TIP

Be careful when you say the words **jiào** 叫 (jyaow) (*to call*) and **jiù** 救 (jyo) (*to save*) in the preceding phrases. You don't want to mistakenly ask someone to save the police when you want him to call the police.

Sometimes you have to ask for someone who speaks English. Here are some phrases you can quickly blurt out during emergencies:

» **Nǐ shuō Yīngwén ma?** 你说英文吗? (你說英文嗎?) (Nee shwaw Eeng-one mah?) (*Do you speak English?*)

» **Wǒ xūyào yíge jiǎng Yīngwén de lǜshī.** 我需要一个讲英文的律师. (我需要一個 講英文的律師.) (Waw shyew-yaow ee-guh jyahng Eeng-one duh lyew-shir.) (*I need a lawyer who speaks English.*)

» **Yǒu méiyǒu jiǎng Yīngwén de dàifu?** 有没有讲英文的大夫? (有沒有講英文的 大夫?) (Yo mayo jyahng Eeng-one duh dye-foo?) (*Are there any English-speaking doctors?*)

When you finally get someone on the line who can help you, you need to know what to say to get immediate help:

» **Wǒ bèi rén qiǎngle.** 我被人抢了. (我被人搶了.) (Waw bay run chyahng-luh.) (*I've been robbed.*)

» **Wǒ yào bào yíge chēhuò.** 我要报一个车祸. (我要報一個車禍.) (Waw yaow baow yee-guh chuh-hwaw.) (*I'd like to report a car accident.*)

» **Yǒu rén shòushāngle.** 有人受伤了. (有人受傷了.) (Yo run show-shahng-luh.) (*People are injured.*)

Receiving Medical Care

It's everyone's greatest nightmare — getting sick and not knowing why or how to make it better. If you suddenly find yourself in the **yīyuàn** 医院 (醫院) (ee-ywan) (*hospital*) or otherwise visiting an **yīshēng** 医生 (醫生) (ee-shung) (*doctor*), you need to explain what ails you — often in a hurry. Doing so may be easier said than done, especially if you have to explain yourself in Chinese (or help a Chinese-speaking victim who's having trouble communicating), but don't worry. In the following sections, I walk you through your doctor's visit step by step.

TIP

When you travel, don't forget to bring your prescription medicines. Carry them in a separate carry-on bag or in your purse. You don't want to pack them in a piece of check-in luggage, never to be seen again if the luggage gets lost.

CULTURAL WISDOM

WARNING

Here are a couple of additional medical-emergency tips for traveling in China:

» Unless you're in a big city like Beijing or Shanghai, if you get seriously ill while staying in mainland China, your best bet is to fly to Hong Kong or back home for medical care. Don't forget to check into evacuation insurance before you go.

» Chinese people don't have O-negative blood, so Chinese hospitals don't store it. If you have a medical emergency in China that requires O-negative blood, you should check directly with your country's nearest embassy or consulate for help. You may need to be airlifted out to get the appropriate care. You may also want to take your own hypodermic needles in case you need an injection because you can't guarantee that the needles you may come across are steril-ized. Better safe than sorry away from home.

Deciding whether to see a doctor

If your luck is good, you'll never need to use any of the phrases I present in this chapter. If you end up running out of luck, however, keep reading. Even if you've never smoked a day in your life, you can still develop a cough or even bronchitis. Time to see an **yīshēng**.

Talkin' the Talk

Dàlín and his wife, Miǎn, are on their first trip back to China in 20 years. Miǎn becomes concerned about a sudden onset of dizziness. The two discuss her symptoms.

Dàlín: **Nǐ zěnme bùshūfu?**
Nee dzummuh boo-shoo-foo?
What's wrong?

Miǎn: **Wǒ gǎnjué bùshūfu kěshì bù zhīdào wǒ déle shénme bìng.**
Waw gahn-jweh boo-shoo-foo kuh-shir boo jir-daow waw duh-luh shummuh beeng.
I don't feel well, but I don't know what I have.

Dàlín: **Nǐ fāshāo ma?**
Nee fah-shaow mah?
Are you running a fever?

Miǎn:	**Méiyǒu, dànshì wǒ tóuyūn. Yěxǔ wǒ xūyào kàn nèikē yīshēng.**
	Mayo, dahn-shir waw toe-yewn. Yeh-shyew waw shyew-yaow kahn nay-kuh ee-shung.
	No, but I feel dizzy. Perhaps I need to see an internist.

Dàlín calls the nearest medical clinic to make an appointment and then returns to Miǎn.

Dàlín:	**Wǒ jīntiān xiàwǔ sān diǎn zhōng yuē le yíge shíjiān. Nǐ zuì hǎo zànshí zuò xiàlái.**
	Waw jin-tyan shyah-woo sahn dyan joong yweh luh ee-guh shir-jyan. Nee dzway how dzahn-shir dzwaw shyah-lye.
	I've made an appointment for 3:00 this afternoon. In the meantime, you'd better sit down for a while.

WORDS TO KNOW

liúgǎn 流感	lyo gahn	the flu
lánwěiyán 阑尾炎 (闌尾炎)	lahn-way-yan	appendicitis
biǎntáotǐ yán 扁桃体炎 (扁桃體炎)	byan-taow-tee yan	tonsillitis
bìngdú 病毒	beeng-doo	virus
gǎnrǎn 感染	gahn-rahn	infection

GRAMMAR CHAT

Although verbs don't express tense in Chinese, you often connect them to things called *aspect markers*, which come directly after the verb and indicate the degree of completion of an action. The aspect markers **xiàlái** 下来 (下來) (shyah-lye) and **xiàqù** 下去 (shyah-chyew) are two such examples. **Xiàlái** refers to an action that slowly turns into a non-action or a calmer state, such as **zuò xiàlái** 坐下来 (坐下來) (dzwaw shyah-lye) (*to sit down and rest*) in the preceding Talkin' the Talk section. **Xiàqù** refers to continuing action.

Describing what ails you

First things first: You can't tell the doctor where it hurts if you don't know the word for what hurts. (Sure, you can point, I guess, but that only goes so far; when was the last time you tried pointing to internal organs?) Table 19-1 spells out the general body parts.

TABLE 19-1

Basic Body Words

Chinese	Pronunciation	English
tóu 头 (頭)	toe	*head*
ěrduō 耳朵	are-dwaw	*ear*
liǎn 脸 (臉)	lyan	*face*
yǎnjīng 眼睛	yan-jeeng	*eye*
bízi 鼻子	bee-dzuh	*nose*
bózi 脖子	baw-dzuh	*neck*
hóulóng 喉咙 (喉嚨)	ho-loong	*throat*
jiānbǎng 肩膀	jyan-bahng	*shoulder*
gēbo 胳膊	guh-baw	*arm*
shǒu 手	show	*hand*
shǒuzhǐ 手指	show-jir	*finger*
xiōng 胸	shyoong	*chest*
fèi 肺	fay	*lungs*
xīn 心	shin	*heart*
dùzi 肚子	doo-dzuh	*stomach*
gān 肝	gahn	*liver*
shèn 肾	shun	*kidney*
bèi 背	bay	*back*
tuǐ 腿	tway	*leg*
jiǎo 脚 (腳)	jyaow	*foot*
jiǎozhǐ 脚趾 (腳趾)	jyaow-jir	*toe*
shēntǐ 身体 (身體)	shun-tee	*body*
gǔtóu 骨头 (骨頭)	goo-toe	*bone*
jīròu 肌肉	jee-roe	*muscles*
shénjīng 神经 (神經)	shun-jeeng	*nerves*

Maybe you're just now checking your old **wēndùjì** 温度计 (溫度計) (one-doo-jee) (*thermometer*) and finding out **Wǒ fāshāo le!** 我发烧了! (我發燒了!) (Waw fah-shaow luh!) (*I have a fever!*). Time to figure out what the problem is. Whether you make a sudden trip to the **jízhěn shì** 急诊室 (急診室) (jee-jun shir) (*emergency room*) or take a normal visit to a private doctor's office, you'll probably field the same basic questions about your symptoms. Table 19-2 lists some symptoms you may have.

TABLE 19-2 ## Common Medical Symptoms

Chinese	Pronunciation	English
yāotòng 腰痛	yaow-toong	*backache*
biànmì 便秘	byan-mee	*constipation*
ěr tòng 耳痛	are toong	*earache*
ěxīn 恶心 (噁心)	uh-sheen	*nauseous*
fāshāo 发烧 (發燒)	fah-shaow	*to have a fever*
hóulóng téng 喉咙痛 (喉嚨痛)	ho-loong tung	*sore throat*
lādùzi 拉肚子	lah-doo-dzuh	*diarrhea*
pàngle 胖了	pahng-luh	*gained weight*
shòule 瘦了	show-luh	*lost weight*
tóuténg 头疼 (頭疼)	toe-tung	*headache*
wèi tòng 胃痛	way toong	*stomach ache*
xiàntǐ zhǒngle 腺体肿了 (腺體腫了)	shyan-tee joong-luh	*swollen glands*
yá tòng 牙痛	yah toong	*toothache*

In an emergency, you may not have the energy to remember both the pronunciation *and* the proper tone for the word you mean to use. You may want to say you're feeling kind of **tóuyūn** 头晕 (頭暈) (toe-yewn) (*dizzy*), but if it comes out sounding like **tuōyùn** 托运 (托運) (twaw-yewn) instead, you alert your caregiver that you're sending your luggage on ahead of you.

Talkin' the Talk

Kristen shows up for her appointment to see Huò Dàifu (Dr. Huo). Because this is Kristen's first visit to Dr. Huo, the **jiēdài yuán** 接待员 (接待員) (jyeh-dye ywan) (*receptionist*) needs her to fill out some forms before she sees the doctor to discuss her symptoms.

Jiēdài yuán:	**Nǐ shì lái kànbìng de ma?** Nee shir lye kahn-beeng duh mah? *Have you come to see a doctor?*
Kristen:	**Shì de.** Shir duh. *Yes.*
Jiēdài yuán:	**Yǒu méiyǒu yīliáo bǎoxiǎn?** Yo may-yo ee-lyaow baow-shyan? *Do you have any medical insurance?*
Kristen:	**Yǒu.** Yo. *Yes, I do.*
Jiēdài yuán:	**Hǎo. Qǐng tián yíxià zhèi zhāng biǎo.** How. Cheeng tyan ee-shyah jay jahng byaow. *All right. Please fill out this form.*

A short while later, the receptionist introduces Kristen to a **hùshì** (hoo-shir) (*nurse*), who plans to take her blood pressure.

Jiēdài yuán:	**Hùshì huì xiān liáng yíxià xuèyā.** Hoo-shir hway shyan lyahng ee-shyah shweh-yah. *The nurse will first take your blood pressure.*
Hùshì:	**Qǐng juǎnqǐ nǐde xiùzi.** Cheeng jwan-chee nee-duh shyo-dzuh. *Please roll up your sleeve.*
Hùshì:	**Hǎo. Huò Dàifu xiànzài gěi nǐ kànbìng.** How. Hwaw Dye-foo shyan-dzye gay nee kahn-beeng. *All right. Dr. Huo will see you now.*

Kristen enters Dr. Huo's office, and after a few basic introductory questions, Dr. Huo asks her what brings her to his office.

Huò Dàifu: **Yǒu shénme zhèngzhuàng?**
Yo shummuh juhng-jwahng?
What sorts of symptoms do you have?

Kristen: **Wǒde hóulóng cóng zuótiān jiù tòngle.**
Waw-duh ho-loong tsoong dzwaw-tyan jyo toong-luh.
I've had this pain in my throat since yesterday.

Huò Dàifu: **Hǎo. Wǒ xiān yòng tīngzhěnqì tīng yíxià nǐde xīnzàng.**
How. Waw shyan yoong teeng-juhn-chee teeng ee-shyah nee-duh shin-dzahng.
All right. I'm first going to use a stethoscope to listen to your heart.

Dr. Huo puts the stethoscope to Kristen's chest.

Huò Dàifu: **Shēn hūxī.**
Shun hoo-she.
Take a deep breath.

Dr. Huo finishes listening with the stethoscope and takes out a tongue depressor.

Huò Dàifu: **Qǐng bǎ zuǐ zhāngkāi, bǎ shétóu shēn chūlái . . . duì le. Nǐde hóulóng hǎoxiàng yǒu yìdiǎn fāyán.**
Cheeng bah dzway jahng-kye, bah shuh-to shun choo-lye . . . dway luh. Nee-duh ho-loong how-shyahng yo ee-dyan fah-yan.
Please open your mouth and stick out your tongue . . . yes. Your throat seems to be inflamed.

Discussing your medical history

When you see a doctor for the first time, he or she will want to find out about your **bìng shǐ** 病史 (beeng shir) (*medical history*). You'll hear the following query: **Nǐ jiā yǒu méiyǒu _____ de bìng shǐ?** 你家有没有 _____ 的病史?) (Nee jyah yo may-yo _____ duh beeng-shir?) (*Does your family have any history of _____?*)

Table 19-3 lists some of the more serious illnesses that hopefully neither you nor your family members have ever had.

TABLE 19-3

Serious Illnesses

Chinese	Pronunciation	English
áizhèng 癌症	eye-juhng	*cancer*
àizībìng 艾滋病	eye-dzuh-beeng	*AIDS*
bing xíng gānyán 丙型肝炎	beeng sheeng gahn-yan	*Hepatitis C*
fèi'ái 肺癌	fay-eye	*lung cancer*
fèi jiéhé 肺结核 (肺結核)	fay jyeh-huh	*tuberculosis*
huòluàn 霍乱 (霍亂)	hwaw-lwan	*cholera*
jiǎxíng gānyán 甲型肝炎	jya-sheeng gahn-yan	*Hepatitis A*
lìjí 痢疾	lee-jee	*dysentery*
qìchuǎn bìng 气喘病 (氣喘病)	chee-chwan beeng	*asthma*
shuǐdòu 水痘	shway-doe	*chicken pox*
tángniàobìng 糖尿病	tahng-nyaow-beeng	*diabetes*
xīnzàng yǒu máobìng 心脏有毛病 (心臟有毛病)	shin-dzahng yo maow-beeng	*heart trouble*
yǐxíng gānyán 已型肝炎	ee-sheeng gahn-yan	*Hepatitis B*

Making a diagnosis

Did your doctor say those magic words: **Méi shénme** 没什么 (沒甚麼) (may shum-muh) (*It's nothing*)? Yeah, neither did mine. Too bad. I bet you've heard stories about how doctors who use traditional medical techniques from ancient cultures can just take one look at a person and immediately know what ails that person. The truth is, aside from simple colds and the flu, most doctors still need to take all kinds of tests to give a proper diagnosis. They may even need to perform the following tasks:

- » **huàyàn** 化验 (化驗) (hwah-yan) (*lab tests*)

- » **xīndiàntú** 心电图 (心電圖) (shin-dyan-too) (*electrocardiogram*)

- » **huàyàn yíxià xiǎobiàn** 化验一下小便 (化驗一下小便) (hwah-yan ee-shyah shyaow-byan) (*have your urine tested*)

When the doctor is ready to give you the verdict, here are some of the conditions you may hear (the minor ones, at least; check out Table 19-3 for more serious diagnoses):

- » **bìngdú** 病毒 (beeng-doo) (*virus*)

- » **gǎnmào** 感冒 (gahn-maow) (*a cold*)

- » **gǎnrǎn** 感染 (gahn-rahn) (*infection*)

- » **guòmǐn** 过敏 (過敏) (gwaw-meen) (*allergies*)

- » **liúgǎn** 流感 (lyo-gahn) (*flu*)

- » **qìguǎnyán** 气管炎 (氣管炎) (chee-gwahn-yan) (*bronchitis*)

Talkin' the Talk

Michael takes his daughter, Irma, to the **yīshēng** (doctor) after he notices her bad cough. The doctor takes her temperature and discusses what she may have with the family.

Yīshēng: **Irma, hǎo xiāoxi! Nǐde tǐwēn zhèngcháng.**
Irma, how shyaow-she! Nee-duh tee-one juhng-chahng.
Irma, good news! Your temperature is normal.

Irma: **Hǎo jí le.**
How jee luh.
Great.

Yīshēng:	**Kěnéng zhǐ shì gǎnmào.**
	Kuh-nung jir shir gahn-maow.
	Perhaps it's just a little cold.

Michael:	**Hái chuánrǎn ma?**
	Hi chwahn-rahn mah?
	Is it still contagious?

Yīshēng:	**Bú huì.**
	Boo hway.
	No.

Irma:	**Yánzhòng ma?**
	Yan-joong mah?
	Is it serious?

Yīshēng:	**Bù yánzhòng. Nǐ zuì hǎo xiūxi jǐ tiān hē hěn duō shuǐ, jiù hǎo le.**
	Boo yan-joong. Nee dzway how shyo-she jee tyan huh hun dwaw shway, jyo how luh.
	No. You should rest for a few days and drink lots of liquids, and it should get better.

Michael:	**Tā děi zài chuángshàng tǎng duōjiǔ?**
	Tah day dzye chwahng-shahng tahng dwaw-jyo?
	How long must she rest in bed?

Yīshēng:	**Zuì hǎo liǎng sān tiān.**
	Dzway how lyahng sahn tyan.
	Ideally for two or three days.

• •

WORDS TO KNOW

Fúyòng liǎng piàn āsīpǐlín. 服用两片阿司匹林. (服用兩片阿司匹林.)	Fu-yoong lyahng pyan ah-suh-pee-leen.	Take two aspirin.
Shǐyòng nǐ de xīrù qì. 使用你的吸入器.	Shir-yoong nee duh shee-roo chee.	Use your inhaler.
Yìtiān chī liǎng cì. 一天吃两次. (一天吃兩次.)	Ee-tyan chir lyahng tsuh.	Take the medicine twice a day.

GRAMMAR CHAT

In Chinese, you generally put a negative prefix, such as **bù** 不 (boo), in front of the verb you're negating. It sounds redundant in English to literally translate a response as *not serious* when someone asks about the seriousness of a situation. It's more colloquial and appropriate to translate it as *no*, as you see in the previous Talkin' the Talk section when Irma asks the doctor if her ailment is serious.

Treating yourself to better health

Not everything can be cured with a bowl of **jītāng** 鸡汤 (雞湯) (jee-tahng) (*chicken soup*), despite what my grandmother told me. If your grandmother cooks as well as mine did, however, the soup couldn't hurt . . .

Your doctor may prescribe some **yào** 药 (藥) (yaow) (*medicine*) to make you feel better. After you **tián** 填 (填) (tyan) (*fill*) your **yīliáo chǔfāng** 医疗处方 (醫療處方) (ee-lyaow choo-fahng) (*prescription*), you may find the following instructions on the bottle:

» **Fàn hòu chī.** 饭后吃. (飯後吃.) (Fahn ho chir.) (*Take after eating.*)

» **Měi sìge xiǎoshí chī yícì.** 每四个小时吃一次. (每四個小時吃一次.) (May suh-guh shyaow-shir chir ee-tsuh.) (*Take one tablet every four hours.*)

» **Měi tiān chī liǎng cì, měi cì sān piàn.** 每天吃两次, 每次三片. (每天吃兩次, 每次三片.) (May tyan chir lyahng tsuh, may tsuh sahn pyan.) (*Take three tablets twice a day.*)

Calling the Police

Ever have your pocketbook **tōu le** 偷了 (toe luh) (*stolen*)? Being a victim is an awful feeling, as I can tell you from experience. You feel angry at such a scary experience, especially if it happens in another country and the **zéi** 贼 (賊) (dzay) (*thief*) **táopǎo** 逃跑 (taow-paow) (*escapes*) quickly.

I hope you're never the victim of a crime like theft (or something worse). Still, you should always be prepared with some key words you can use when the **jǐngchá** 警察 (jeeng-chah) (*police*) finally pull up in the **jǐngchē** 警车 (警車) (jeeng-chuh) (*police car*) and take you back to the **jǐngchá jú** 警察局 (jeeng-chah jyew) (*police station*) to identify a potential **zéi**. Hopefully the culprit will be **zhuā le** 抓了 (jwah luh) (*arrested*).

You may also find yourself in an emergency that doesn't involve you. If you ever witness an accident, here are some phrases you can relay to the police, emergency workers, or victims:

>> **Bié kū. Jǐngchá hé jiùhùchē láile.** 别哭. 警察和救护车来了. (别哭. 警察和救護車來了.) (Byeh koo. Jeeng-chah huh jyo-hoo-chuh lye-luh.) (*Don't cry. The police and the ambulance have arrived.*)

>> **Tā bèi qìchē yàzháo le.** 他被车压着了. (他被車压着了.) (Tah bay chee-chuh yah-jaow luh.) (*He was run over by a car.*)

>> **Tā zài liúxiě.** 他在流血. (Tah dzye lyo-shyeh.) (*He's bleeding.*)

Acquiring Legal Help

As with any other country, once in a while foreigners may need legal representation even if they unintentionally break the law. I hope you're not one of these people, but if you are, you'll probably look high and low for the best **lǜshī** 律师 (律師) (lyew-shir) (*lawyer*). The best place to start looking for one is your country's **dàshǐguǎn** 大使馆 (大使館) (dah-shir-gwahn) (*embassy*) or **lǐngshìguǎn** 领事馆 (領事館) (leeng-shir-gwahn) (*consulate*) for advice.

It can be very annoying and stressful to have to deal with **lǜshī,** no matter what country you're in, but you have to admit — they do know the **fǎlǜ** 法律 (fah-lyew) (*law*). And if you have to go to **fǎyuàn** 法院 (fah-ywan) (*court*) for any serious incident, you want the judge to **pànjué** 判决 (判決) (pahn-jweh) (*make a decision*) in your favor. Moral of the story: Good **lǜshī** are worth their weight in gold, even if you still consider them sharks in the end.

FUN & GAMES

Identify the following body parts in Chinese. Check Appendix C for the answers.

1. Arm: _____

2. Shoulder: _____

3. Finger: _____

4. Leg: _____

5. Neck: _____

6. Chest: _____

7. Eye: _____

8. Ear: _____

9. Nose: _____

Fill in the blanks.

You visit a doctor in Beijing, and she asks you: **Nǐ jiā yǒu méiyǒu _____ de bìngshǐ?** (Nee jyah yo mayo _____ duh beeng-shir?) (*Does your family have any history of _____?*) Use two of the many new words in Table 19-3 to answer in the blanks below. (The first one is an example.)

Wǒ jiā yǒu <u>tángniàobìng</u> de bìngshǐ. (Waw jyah yo tahng-nyaow-beeng duh beeng-shir.) (*My family has a history of diabetes.*)

Wǒ jiā yǒu _____ de bìngshǐ.

Wǒ jiā yǒu _____ de bìngshǐ.

4

The Part of Tens

Discover ten practical tips to keep in mind when learning Chinese.

Know the top ten cultural do's and don'ts when you're in China or with Chinese acquaintances.

Chapter **20**

Ten Ways to Learn Chinese Quickly

This chapter contains ten good activities that can help speed up your Chinese learning curve. Having useful, easy-to-access, and easy-to-follow learning tools makes a big difference in your progress. And besides, you can have fun with them, too.

Listen to Chinese Being Spoken

Just imagine trying to figure out what Chinese tones sound like without actually hearing them spoken out loud; it's kind of like imagining what Beethoven's Fifth sounds like based on a written description. Even if you read this book cover to cover, you'll be hard-pressed to figure out just what the first, second, third, and fourth tones actually sound like unless you listen to the accompanying audio files (www.dummies.com/go/chinese).

Be creative with your discovery of the language (and your language listening) by picking up all the language CDs you can find out there. With YouTube, you can see Chinese films or documentaries of people speaking on just about anything. Keep mimicking what you hear over and over again so that your pronunciation and intonation become better with each go-round. Pretty soon, you'll be able to tell a native Mandarin speaker from a native Cantonese speaker.

Check Out a Peking Opera Performance

Okay, I admit that the first time I attended a performance of Peking Opera, I wished I had brought a pair of ear plugs. The opera is an acquired taste, to be sure. Kind of like caviar. But I recommend spending time cultivating an appreciation for it. Peking Opera originated in the late 1700s, when opera troupes originally staged performances for the royal family. Only later did it become such a public art, and now it's all the rage for any person who claims to appreciate Chinese culture. The makeup, costumes, cacophonous music, and stylized movements are predictable and much treasured by the Chinese people. Listening to Peking Opera not only helps you develop an appreciation for a great Chinese art form but also fine-tunes your recognition of the pronunciation of standard Mandarin. You can even learn a few tunes at the same time. A win-win situation all around.

Cook with a Wok

You may be surprised what cooking with a wok can do for your Chinese. Not only do you start eating healthier, but you also soak in Chinese words by osmosis because you're forced to visit some Asian food markets to gather the ingredients you need to cook with. Ever hear of **dòufu** 豆腐 (doe-foo) (*soybean curd*)? How about bok choi? Okay, so that's Cantonese, but the Mandarin is **bái cài** 白菜 (bye tsye) (*Chinese cabbage*). The best traditional Chinese cooking, all done with a wok, puts you in the proper frame of mind to want to absorb some more Chinese language. Try following some recipes from a Chinese cookbook and repeat the names of the ingredients over and over. And if you're not a great cook, get into the habit of eating at Chinese restaurants and mastering the names of at least ten dishes before the end of the meal.

Shop for Food in Chinatown

Mingle with the Mandarin-speaking masses while you attune your ear to the sounds and tones of Chinese. Buying food is only one of the fun things to do in Chinatown, of course, but it's one worth doing often. Not only do you cultivate a good ear for Chinese, but you also become privy to the gestures that often go along with the sounds.

Search Online

Tons of information on Chinese language and culture is only a mouse click away. Now that you're in the information age, take advantage of it. Everything from writing Chinese characters to discovering Peking Opera is out there. (Head to the earlier section "Check Out a Peking Opera Performance" for more on that particular option.) Whatever motivated you to start speaking Chinese in the first place, the World Wide Web keeps you involved. Just do a quick search for places such as Shanghai, Beijing, or Taipei or for cultural keywords such as *wok* or *pagoda.* You'll be amazed at what you can come up with.

Watch Kung-Fu Flicks

Bruce Lee is only the tip of the iceberg. Go to your local public library and ask to see the list of kung-fu movies. Everything from Hong Kong action films to mainland martial arts flicks — you should find them all there. Pick whatever interests you. Directors like Zhang Yimou and Chen Kaige have become famous around the world. (Okay, so they didn't direct kung-fu movies . . . but they're still worth checking out.)

TIP

The best way to grasp Chinese is to watch the films over and over to see how many words and phrases you can pick up in one sitting. You soon become adept at anticipating which gestures go with which words, and you develop a great ear for all those tones.

Exchange Language Lessons

Finding a language partner has to be one of the best ways to pick up Chinese. You get to learn the language, but you also develop a friendship along the way. Tons of students come to the United States every year from China. Whether you're in school at the moment or just live near one, you should have no problem putting up a sign offering a language exchange. And don't forget to ask your language partner to compare notes about Chinese and American culture. That's when the real fun begins.

Make Chinese Friends

Possibilities for meeting Chinese-speaking people are endless. Check out the cubicle next to you at your office or the desk ahead of you in class. Or how about the mother of the kid who's in your child's karate class? Wherever you go, you have a chance to make a new friend who not only knows Chinese but can also teach you a little about the culture. You may even find a new friend to see that kung-fu movie with or to help you navigate grocery shopping in Chinatown (not to mention how to use a wok after you buy all your food).

Study Chinese Calligraphy

Chinese calligraphy is one of the most beautiful art forms in the world. Why not pick up a brush and create those beautiful strokes yourself on rice paper? The whole ritual of preparing the ink and paper is an exercise in patience and meditation, and you get to appreciate the difficulty Chinese schoolchildren have in learning to write Chinese. You can discover how to write your name in Chinese (have your English name transliterated, because there's no alphabet in Chinese) and then practice writing those characters over and over until you can sign your name to a Chinese New Year's card and mail it to a friend.

Be Curious and Creative

If you look for opportunities to practice Chinese, I guarantee you can find them. Be imaginative. And stop worrying about failing. In fact, make as many mistakes as it takes so that you can make a mental note of what you should do or say differently the next time around. Give yourself a pat on the back every time you discover something new in Chinese or figure out a novel way to find out more about the Chinese language and people. Keep yakking away with the new words and phrases you find in this book and enjoy watching the reactions on people's faces when you open your mouth.

Chapter **21**

Ten Things Never to Do in China

This chapter may save you from certain embarrassment and possibly even outright humiliation one day. It gives you ten important tips on what not to do if you really want to win friends and make a good impression with your Chinese acquaintances. Take my tips to heart.

Never Accept a Compliment Graciously

You may find yourself at a loss for words when you compliment a Chinese host on a wonderful meal and you get in response, "No, no, the food was really horrible." You hear the same thing when you tell a Chinese parent how smart or handsome his son is; he meets the compliment with a rebuff of "No, he's really stupid." or "He's not good looking at all." These people aren't being nasty — just humble and polite. Moral of the story here: Feign humility, even if it kills you! A little less boasting and fewer self-congratulatory remarks go a long way toward scoring cultural sensitivity points with the Chinese.

To deflect a compliment, you can say something like **Nálǐ, nálǐ.** 哪里哪里. (哪裡哪裡.) (Nah-lee nah-lee.) if you're speaking with someone from Taiwan or **Nǎr de huà.** 哪儿的话. (哪兒的話.) (Nar duh hwah.) if you're speaking with someone from mainland China. They both mean *No, no, I don't deserve any praise.* (Chapter 4 shows you some other ways to reject compliments.)

Never Make Someone Lose Face

The worst thing you can possibly do to Chinese acquaintances is publicly humiliate or otherwise embarrass them. Doing so makes them lose face. Don't point out a mistake in front of others or yell at someone.

TIP

The good news is that you can actually help someone gain face by complimenting that person and giving credit where credit is due. Do so whenever the opportunity arises. Your graciousness is much appreciated.

Never Get Angry in Public

Public displays of anger are frowned upon by the Chinese and are most uncomfortable for them to deal with — especially if the people getting angry are foreign tourists, for example. This concept goes right along with the faux pas of making someone (usually the Chinese host) lose face, which I cover in the preceding section. The Chinese place a premium on group harmony, so foreigners should try to swallow hard, be polite, and cope privately.

Never Address People by Their First Names First

Chinese people have first and last names like everyone else. However, in China, the last name always comes first. The family (and the collective in general) always takes precedence over the individual. Joe Smith in Minnesota is known as Smith Joe (or the equivalent) in Shanghai. If a man is introduced to you as Lǐ Míng, you can safely refer to him as Mr. Lǐ (not Mr. Míng).

Unlike people in the West, the Chinese don't feel very comfortable calling each other by their first names. Only family members and a few close friends ever refer to Lǐ Míng, for example, as simply Míng. They may, however, add the prefix **lǎo** 老 (laow) (*old*) or **xiǎo** 小 (shyaow) (*young*) before the family name to show familiarity and closeness. **Lǎo Lǐ** 老李 (Laow Lee) (*Old Lǐ*) may refer to his younger friend as **Xiǎo Chén** 小陈 (小陳) (Shyaow Chun) (*Young Chén*).

Never Take Food with the Wrong End of Your Chopsticks

The next time you gather around a dinner table with a Chinese host, you may discover that serving spoons for the many communal dishes are nonexistent. Rather, everyone serves him- or herself (or others) by turning one's chopsticks upside down to take food from the main dishes before putting the food on the individual plates. Why upside down? Because you don't want to put the part of the chopsticks that goes in your mouth in the communal food bowls everyone eats from.

Never Drink Alcohol Without First Offering a Toast

Chinese banquets include eight to ten courses of food and plenty of alcohol. Sometimes you drink rice wine, and sometimes you drink industrial-strength **Máo Tái** 茅台 (Maow Tye), known to put a foreigner or two under the table in no time. One way to slow the drinking is to observe Chinese etiquette by always offering a toast to the host or someone else at the table before taking a sip yourself (yes, before every sip). Toasting not only prevents you from drinking too much too quickly but also shows your gratitude toward the host and your regard for the other guests.

All you need to do is raise your glass with your right hand, holding the bottom of the glass from underneath with your left hand, say the name of the person whom you want to toast, look directly at that person with a smile, give a nod as a form of respect, and then take a little sip.

TIP

If someone toasts you with a **gān bēi** 干杯 (gahn bay), however, watch out. **Gān bēi** means *bottoms up*, and you may be expected to drink the whole drink rather quickly. Don't worry. You can always say **suí yì** 随意 (sway ee) (*as you wish*) in return and take just a little sip instead.

Never Let Someone Else Pay the Bill Without Fighting for It

Most Westerners are stunned the first time they witness the many noisy, fairly chaotic scenes at the end of Chinese restaurant meals. The time to pay the bill has come, and everyone is simply doing what he or she is expected to do — fight to be the one to pay it. The Chinese feel that vociferously and strenuously attempting to wrest the bill out of the very hands of whoever happens to have it is simply good manners. This struggle may go back and forth for a good few minutes until someone "wins" and pays the bill. The gesture of being eager and willing to pay is always appreciated.

Never Show Up Empty-Handed

Gifts are exchanged frequently between the Chinese, and not just on special occasions. If you have dinner in someone's house to meet a prospective business partner or for any other prearranged meeting, both parties commonly exchange gifts as small tokens of friendship and good will. Westerners are often surprised at the number of gifts the Chinese hosts give. The general rule of thumb is to bring many little (gender nonspecific) gifts when you travel to China. You never know when you'll meet someone who wants to present you with a special memento, so you should arrive with your own as well.

Never Accept Food, Drinks, or Gifts Without First Refusing a Few Times

No self-respecting guests immediately accept whatever food, drink, or gift may be offered to them in someone's home no matter how eager they may be to receive it. Proper Chinese etiquette prevents you from doing anything that makes you appear greedy or eager to receive any offerings, so be sure to politely refuse a couple of times. For example, if someone tries to serve you food, immediately say **Zìjǐ lái.** 自己来. (自己來.) (Dzuh-jee lye.) (*I'll take it myself.*). You should do this several times and then let the person serve you anyway. At least he'll know you didn't want him to go to all the trouble.

Never Take the First "No, Thank You" Literally

Chinese people automatically decline food or drinks several times — even if they really feel hungry or thirsty. They may say something like **bú yòng, bú yòng** 不用, 不用 (boo yoong, boo yoong) (*no need, no need*). Never take the first refusal literally. Even if they say it once or twice, offer it again. A good guest is supposed to refuse at least once, but a good host is also supposed to make the offer at least twice.

5 Appendixes

Look up common words in the mini-dictionary, which provides both Chinese-to-English and English-to-Chinese translations.

Because Chinese has no equivalent of English verb conjugation, use the list of Chinese verbs provided when you need help.

Check the answers to the Fun & Games exercises to see how well you did!

Appendix A

Chinese-English Mini-Dictionary

A

ǎi (eye): short

àirén (eye-run): spouse (used only in the PRC)

āiyá (eye-yah): oh my goodness!

ānjìng (ahn-jeeng): quiet

ānpái (ahn-pye): to arrange

ānquán dài (ahn-chwan dye): seat belt

ānquán fúwùqì (ahn-chwan foo-woo-chee): secure server

ānzhuāng tiáozhì jiětiáoqì (ahn-jwahng tyaow-jir jyeh-tyaow-chee) to install a modem

āsīpīlín (ah-suh-pee-leen): aspirin

B

bàba (bah-bah): father

bái cài (bye tsye): Chinese cabbage

bǎifēnbǐ (bye-fun-bee): percentage

bǎihuò shāngdiàn (bye-hwaw shahng-dyan): department store

bàn (bahn): half

bāngmáng (bahng-mahng): to help

bàngōngshì (bahn-goong-shir): office

bàngōng zhuō (bahn-goong jwaw): desk

bànyè (bahn-yeh): midnight

bǎocún (baow-tswun): save

bǎomǔ (baow-moo): nanny

bào tāi (baow tye): flat tire

bàoqiàn (baow-chyan): I'm sorry

bāshì lǚyóu (bah-shir lyew-yo): bus tour

bèixīn (bay-sheen): tank top

Běijīng (Bay-jeeng): Beijing

Bēnchí (Bun-chir): Mercedes Benz

běndì huà shēngchǎn (bun-dee hwah shung-chahn): local production

biǎntáotǐ yán (byan-taow-tee yan): tonsilitis

bǐjìběn diànnǎo (bee-jee-bun dyan-naow): laptop

bìngdú (beeng-doo): virus

bīnguǎn (been-gwahn): hotel

bō (baw): to dial

bókè (baw-kuh): blog

bówùguǎn (baw-woo-gwahn): museum

bù (boo): not; no

bǔchōng (boo-choong): to add

búcuò (boo-tswaw): not bad; really good

bùduì (boo-dway): incorrect

bú kèqì (boo kuh-chee): you're welcome

bùliáng xìnyòng (boo-lyahng sheen-yoong): bad credit

bùzhǎng (boo-jahng): department head; minister

C

cá (tsah): to sweep

cài (tsye): food

cài shìchǎng (tsye shir-chahng): food market

càidān (tsye-dahn): menu

cānguǎn (tsahn-gwahn): restaurant

cānjīnzhǐ (tsahn-jeen-jir): napkin

cèsuǒ (tsuh-swaw): toilet

chá (chah): tea; to look something up

chá diànhuà hàomǎ (chah dyan-hwah how-mah): look up a phone number

chángcháng (chahng-chahng): often

chàngpiàn diàn (chahng-pyan dyan): record store

chángtú diànhuà (chahng-too dyan-hwah): long-distance phone call

chǎnwù (chahn-woo): product

chāojí shìchǎng (chaow-jee shir-chahng): supermarket

chātóu (chah-toe): adaptor

chāzi (chah-dzuh): fork

chēpiào (chuh-pyaow): bus ticket

chéngshì (chung-shir): city

chī yào (chir yaow): to take medicine

chīfàn (chir-fahn): to eat

chōngdiàn qì (choong-dyan chee): charger

chóngxīn kāijī (choong-sheen kye-jee): reboot

chuān (chwahn): to wear

chuáng (chwahng): bed

chuánzhēn jī (chwan-juhn jee): fax machine

chūbù huìyì (choo-boo hway-ee): preliminary meeting

chūkǒu jiégòu (choo-ko jyeh-go): export structure

chūfā (choo-fah): to leave the house; to set off

chún sùshí (chwun soo-shir): vegetarian food

Chūnjià (Chwun-jyah): Spring break

chūzū (choo-dzoo): to rent

chūzū chē (choo-dzoo chuh): taxi

cóng (tsoong): from

cōngmíng (tsoong-meeng): intelligent

cuò (tswaw): mistake

D

dà (dah): big

dǎ (dah): to do, play, or hit

dǎ diànhuà (dah dyan-hwah): to make a phone call

dǎ májiàng (dah mah-jahng): to play mah jong

dǎ wǎngqiú (dah wahng-chyo): to play tennis

dà jiē (dah jyeh): avenue

dǎkāi (dah-kye): to turn something on

dàlù (dah-loo): mainland (China)

dānchéng piào (dahn-chuhng pyaow): one-way ticket

dàng'àn (dahng-ahn): file (noun)

dāngrán (dahng-rahn): of course

dànshì (dahn-shir): but; however

Dào miào (Daow myaow): Daoist Temple

dàotián (daow-tyan): rice paddies

dǎoyóu (daow-yo): guide (noun)

dǎpái (dah-pye): to play cards

dàshǐ guǎn (dah-shir gwahn): embassy

dàtīng (dah-teeng): lobby

dàxué zhuānyè (dah-shyweh jwan-yeh): college major

dǎyìn (dah een): print

děng (duhng): to wait

dēng jī pái (duhng jee pye): boarding pass

dēng kāiguān (duhng kye-gwahn): light switch

diǎn (dyan): to order (food)

diànhuà (dyan-hwah): telephone

diànhuà hàomǎ (dyan-hwah how-mah): telephone number

diànhuà huìyì (dyan-hwah hway-ee): conference call

diànhuàkǎ (dyan-hwah-kah): telephone card

diǎnjī (dyan-jee): click

diànnǎo (dyan-now): computer

diànnǎo chéngxù (dyan-naow chung-shyew): computer program

diànnǎo ruǎnjiàn (dyan-naow rwan-jyan): computer software

diànnǎo shèbèi (dyan-now shuh-bay): computer equipment

diànshì (dyan-shir): television

diàntī (dyan-tee): elevator

diànyǐng (dyan-yeeng): movie

diànzǐ kōngjiān (dyan-dzuh koong-jyan): cyberspace

diànzǐ gōnggào pái (dyan-dzuh goong-gaow pye): e-commerce

diànzǐ yóujiàn (dyan-dzuh yo-jyan): email

diànzǐ yóuxiāng dìzhǐ (dyan-dzuh yo-shyahng dee-jir): email address

diàoyú (dyaow-yew): fishing

dìfāng (dee-fahng): place

dìng wèi (deeng way): to make a reservation

dìnghuò chéngbàn (deeng-hwaw chung-bahn): ordering and processing cost

ding shū jī (deeng shoo jee): stapler

dìqū (dee-chyew): area; location

dìtiě (dee-tyeh): subway

dìtú (dee-too): map

dìzhǐ (dee-jir): address

dōngxī (doong-she): thing

dōu (doe): both; all

dòufu (doe-foo): soybean curd

duìbùqǐ (dway-boo-chee): excuse me; I'm sorry

duìfāng fùfèi diànhuà (dway-fahng foo-fay dyan-hwah): collect call

duìhuàn lǜ (dway-hwahn lyew): exchange rate

duìhuànchù (dway-hwahn-choo): exchange bureaus

duìmiàn (dway-myan): opposite

dùjià (doo-jyah): on vacation

duō (dwaw): many

duō jiǔ (dwaw-jyoe): how long

duōbiān màoyì (dwaw-byan maow-ee): multilateral trade

duōshǎo (dwaw-shaow): how much

dúpǐn zǒusī fàn (doo-peen dzoe-suh fahn): drug smuggler

E

è (uh): hungry

érzi (are-dzuh): son

F

fā yīgè duǎnxìn (fah ee-guh dwan-sheen): send a text

fǎlǜ (fah-lyew): law

fàn (fahn): food

fàndiàn (fahn-dyan): restaurant

fàndiàn qiántái (fahn-dyan chyan-tye): reception desk

fáng jià (fahng jyah): to take a vacation

fángjiān (fahng-jyan): room

fànguǎn (fahn-gwahn): hotel

fángzi (fahng-dzuh): house

fàntīng (fahn-teeng): dining room

fēi zhèngshì huìyì (fay juhng-shir hway-ee): informal meeting

fēijī (fay-jee): airplane

fēijī chǎng (fay-jee chahng): airport

féizào (fay-dzaow): soap

fēn (fun): minute; one cent

fēngxiǎn tóuzī (fung-shyan toe-dzuh): venture capital

fùjìn (foo-jeen): area; vicinity

Fú miào (Foo myaow): Buddhist temple

fùmǔ (foo-moo): parents

fù qián (foo chyan): to pay

fú qiǎn (foo chyan): snorkeling

fùqīn (foo-cheen): father

fúwùqì (foo-woo-chee): server

fúwùtái jīnglǐ (foo-woo-tye jeeng-lee): concierge

fúwùyuán (foo-woo-ywan): attendant

fùyìnjī (foo-een-jee): copier

fùzhì (foo-jir): copy (verb)

fúzhuāng diàn (foo-jwahng dyan): clothing store

G

gǎibiàn (gye-byan): to change (attitude/behavior)

Gǎngbì (Gahng-bee): Hong Kong dollar

gāngbǐ (gahng-bee): pen

gānjìng (gahn-jeeng): clean

gǎnrǎn (gahn-rahn): infection

gǎnxiè (gahn-shyeh): many thanks

gāofēng qī (gaow-fung chee): rush hour

gāogēnxié (gaow-gun-shyeh): high heels

gàosù (gaow-soo): to tell

gàosù gōnglù (gaow-soo goong-loo): freeway

gāoxìng (gaow-sheeng): happy

gěi (gay): to give

gèng (guhng): more

gēnggǎi (guhng-gye): to change

gèrén diànnǎo (guh-run dyan-now): PC (personal computer)

gēshǒu (guh-sho): singer

gōngchē sījī (goong-chuh suh-jee): bus driver

gōngfū (goong-foo): kung fu

gōnggòng qìchē (goong-goong chee-chuh): public bus

gōnggòng qìchē zhàn (goong-goong chee-chuh jahn): bus stop

gōnglù (goong-loo): highway

gōngsī (goong-suh): company

gōngwén bāo (goong-one baow): briefcase

gōngxǐ (goong-she): congratulations

gōngyòng diànhuà (goong-yoong dyan-hwah): public telephone

gōngzuò (goong-dzwaw): to work; job

Gǒu Nián (Go Nyan): Year of the Dog

guà (gwah): to hang up

guǎn (gwan): to care about

guān niǎo (gwahn-nyaow): birdwatching

gǔdōng (goo-doong): shareholder

guāng guāng tuán (gwahn gwahng twahn): tour group

guāngpán (gwahng-pahn): music CD

guānxì (gwahn-shee): relationships

guàtú (gwah-too): flip chart**

gǔdài (goo-dye): ancient; antique

guì (gway): expensive

Gǔgē (Goo-guh): Google

guójì diànhuà (gwaw-jee dyan-hwah): international phone call

guójì mànyóu fèi (gwaw-jee mahn-yo fay): international roaming charges

guójì wǎngluò (gwaw-jee wahng-lwaw): the Internet

guójiā (gwaw-jyah): country

Guóyǔ (Gwaw-yew): Mandarin (term used in Taiwan)

guǒzhī (gwaw-jir): juice

H

hǎiguān (hi-gwahn): customs

háizi (hi-dzuh): child

hángxíng (hahng-sheeng): sailing

Hánjià (hahn-jyah): winter vacation

Hànyǔ (hahn-yew): Chinese language

hǎo (how): good

hǎokàn (how-kahn): pretty

hàomǎ (how-mah): number

Hǎo zàn (How-dzahn): Instagram

hē (huh): to drink

hébìng (huh-beeng): merger

hétóng (huh-toong): contract

Hóu Nián (Ho Nyan): Year of the Monkey

Hǔ Nián (Hoo Nyan): Year of the Tiger

huài (hwye): broken; bad

huàn (hwahn): to change (trains, money)

huánbǎo de jìhuà (hwahn-baow duh jee-hwah): eco-friendly project

huángdēngjī (hwahn-duhng-jee): slide projector

huángdēng piàn (hwahng-duhng pyan): slides

huānyíng (hwahn-yeeng): welcome

huí (hway): to answer; to return

huì (hway): to know how to do something

huí lái (hway lye): to return (come back)

huíkòu (hway-ko): rebate

huí wén zhēn (hway one jun): paper clip

huìyì (hway-ee): meeting

huìyì shì (hway-ee shir): conference room

huòzhe (hwaw-juh): or

huòbì (hwaw-bee): currency

huǒchē zhàn (hwaw-chuh jahn): train station

hùshī (hoo-shir): nurse

hùtóu (hoo-toe): bank account

hùzhào (hoo-jaow): passport

J

jí (jee): hurry

jǐ (jee): several; how many

jíyóu (jee-yo): stamp collecting

Jī Nián (Jee Nyan): Year of the Rooster

jiā (jyah): family; home

jiàgé (jyah-guh): price

jiàn (jyan): to see; also used as a classifier

jiǎnchá (jyan-chah): to examine

jiǎng (jyahng): to talk

jiànpán (jyan-pahn): keyboard

jiànlì yíge zhànghù (jyan-lee ee-guh jahng-hoo): to set up an account

jiǎn qiè (jyan chyeh): cut (from a document)

jiànshēn yùndòng (jyan-shun yewn-doong): to work out

jiǎnsuǒ (jyan-swaw): to search

jiǎnsuǒ guójì yīntèwǎng (jyan-swaw gwaw-jee een-tuh-wahng): search the Internet

jiǎnsuǒ yǐnqíng (jyan-swaw yeen-cheeng): search engine

jiànyì (jyan-ee): to suggest; suggestion

jiào (jyaow): to be called

jiāo (jyaow): to teach

jiàoliàn (jyaow-lyan): coach (noun)

jiàoshòu (jyaow-show): professor

jiāotōng (jyaow-toong): transportation

jiào xǐng diànhuà (jyaow sheeng dyan-hwah): wake-up call

jiǎoyāzi (jyaow-yah-dzuh): foot

jiàrì (jyah-ir): vacation day

jiè (jyeh): to borrow; to loan

jiē (jyeh): to answer the phone; street

jiéhūn (jyeh-hwun): to marry

jiéhūn jìniàn rì (jyeh-hwun jee-nyan ir): wedding anniversary

jiějué (jyeh-jweh): to resolve; to solve

jiérì (jyeh-ir): holiday

jièshào (jyeh-shaow): to introduce

jiéyú (jyeh-yew): account balance

jiézòu lándiào (jyeh-dzo lahn-dyaow): rhythm and blues

jīguāng bǐ (jee-gwahng bee): laser pointer

jìn (jeen): close

jìn pǐn (jeen peen): contraband

jǐngbào xìtǒng (jeeng-baow shee-toong): alarm system

jǐngchá (jeeng-chah): police

jǐngchá jú (jeeng-chah jyew): police station

jīngjì cāng (jeeng-jee tsahng): economy class

jīngjì rén (jeeng-jee run): broker

Jīngjù (Jeeng-jyew): Peking Opera

jīnglǐ (jeeng-lee): manager

jǐnjí chūkǒu (jin-jee choo-koe): emergency exits

jīntiān (jeen-tyan): today

Jǐngwèi (Jeeng-way): Security!!

jìshù fúwù (jee-shoo foo-woo): technical support

jìsuàn qī (ji-swan chee): calculator

jiǔ (jyoe): wine; alcohol

jiùhù chē (jyoe-hoo chuh): ambulance

jiùshēng yī (jyoe-shung ee): life vests

jízhěn shì (jee-juhn shir): emergency room

jué bù (jyweh boo): never

K

kāfēi jī (kah-fay jee): coffee machine

kāfēi (kah-fay): coffee

kāfēi tīng (kah-fay teeng): café

kāi (kye): to open

kāichē (kye-chuh): to drive

kāihuì (kye-hway): to have a meeting

kāimén (kye-mun): to open the door

kāishǐ (kye-shir): to start

kāiwèi cài (kye-way tsye): appetizer

kāiyèchē (kye-yeh-chuh): to pull an all-nighter

kǎlā'ōukè jī (kah-lah-o-kuh jee): karaoke machine

kàn shū (kahn shoo): to read

kànbìng (kahn-beeng): to see a doctor

kàojìn (cow-jeen): next to

kè (kuh): class (academic)

kě (kuh): thirsty

kè hù (kuh hoo): client

kèfáng fúwù (kuh-fahng foo-woo): room service

kěndìng (kuhn-deeng): definitely

kěnéng (kuh-nung): perhaps

kěpà (kuh-pah): scary

kèrén (kuh-run): guest

kěxí (kuh-she): too bad; unfortunately

kěyǐ (kuh-yee): can; to be able to

kǒnglóng (koong-long): dinosaur

Kǒng miào (Koong myaow): Confucian temple

kōngtiáo (koong-tyaow): air conditioning

kòngwèi (koong-way): vacant

kuài (kwye): fast; dollar

kuàijì (kwye-jee): accounting

kuàizi (kwye-dzuh): chopsticks

kuāndài (kwahn dye): broadband

L

lái (lye): to come

láihuí piào (lye-hway pyaow): round-trip ticket

lǎo (laow): old; overdone

lǎobǎn (laow-bahn): a boss

lǎoshī (laow-shir): teacher

lèi (lay): tired

léishè guāngdié (lay-shuh gwahng-dyeh): CD-ROM

lěng (luhng): cold

lěngjìng (lung-jeeng): calm

lǐ (lee): inside; Chinese equivalent of a kilometer

liánghǎo de xìnyòng (lyahng-haow duh sheen-yoong): good credit

liángxié (lyahng-shyeh): sandals

liáotiān (lyaow-tyan): to chat

lǐbài (lee-bye): to pray; week

lǐfǎ shī (lee-fah shir): hairdresser

líkāi (lee-kye): to leave

lǐngqǔ dān (leeng-chyew dahn): luggage claim tag

língshìguǎn (leeng-shir-gwahn): consulate

lǐpǐn diàn (lee-peen dyan): gift shop

lìshǐ yōujiǔ de dìqū (lee-shir yo-jyo duh dee-chyew): historic district

lǐtáng (lee-tahng): auditorium

liúgǎn (lyo-gahn): the flu

liúhuà (lyo-hwah): to leave a message

liúlǎn (lyo-lahn): to browse

liúxíng (lyo-sheeng): popular

lǐwù (lee-woo): gifts

Lóng Nián (Loong Nyan): Year of the Dragon

lóu shàng (low shahng): upstairs

lóu xià (low shyah): downstairs

lù (loo): road

lǚguǎn (lyew-gwahn): hotel

lùshī (lyew-shir): lawyer

lùxiàngjī (loo-shyahng-jee): video recorder

lǚxíng (lyew-sheeng): to travel

lǚxíng dàilǐrén (lyew-sheeng dye-lee-run): travel agent

lǚxíng zhīpiào (lyew-sheeng jir-pyaow): traveler's checks

lǚxíngshè (lyew-sheeng-shuh): travel agency

lǚyóu (lyew-yoe): tour

lǚyóu shǒucè (lyew-yoe show-tsuh): guidebook

M

Mǎ Nián (Ma Nyan): Year of the Horse

máfan (mah-fahn): annoying

mài (my): to sell

mǎi (my): to buy

májiàng (mah-jyahng): mah-jong

màikèfēng (my-kuh-fung): microphone

māma (mah-mah): mother

màn (mahn): slow

mànchē (mahn-chuh): local train

máng (mahng): busy

máojīn (maow-jeen): towel

máotǎn (maow-tahn): blanket

máoyī (maow-ee): sweater

màoyì zhǎnxiāohuì (maow-ee jahn-shyaow-hway): trade show

měi ge (may guh): each

Měiguó (May-gwaw): America

Měiguó ren (May-gwaw run): American

méimáo (may-maow): eyebrow

méiyǒu (mayo): don't have

Měiyuán (May-ywan): U.S. dollar

mén (mun): door

ménkǒu (mun-ko): entrance

miàn (myan): face

miǎnfèi (myan-fay): free

miǎnshuì (myan-shway): duty free

miàntiáo (myan-tyaow): noodles

mǐfàn (mee-fahn): rice

mílù (mee-loo): to get lost

mìmǎ (mee-mah): personal identification number (PIN); password

Míngjiào (Meeng-jyaow): Tweets

míngnián (meeng-nyan): next year

míngpiàn (meeng-pyan): business card

míngtiān (meeng-tyan): tomorrow

mínjiān yīnyuè (meen-jyan een-yweh): folk music

mìshū (mee-shoo): secretary

MP3 bōfàng qì (MP3 baw-fahng chee): MP3 player

mǔqīn (moo-cheen): mother

N

ná (nah): to pick up

nà (nah): that

nǎ (nah): which

nán péngyǒu (nahn pung-yo): boyfriend

nào zhōng (naow joong): alarm clock

nǎr (nar): where

nàr (nar): there

nǐ (nee): you

niánjì (nyan-jee): age

niánqīng (nyan-cheeng): young

Nígū (Nee-goo): Buddhist nun

nǐmen (nee-mun): you (plural)

nín (neen): you (polite)

Niú Nián (Nyo Nyan): Year of the Ox

nuǎnhuó (nwan-hwaw): warm

nuǎnqì (nwahn-chee): heater

nǚ péngyǒu (nyew puhng-yo): girlfriend

O

Ōu yuán (Oh ywan): Euro

Ōuzhōu (Oh-joe): Europe

P

páshān (pah-shan): mountain climbing

pànjué (pahn-jweh): to make a (legal) decision

pēngtiáo yìshù (puhng-tyaow ee-shoo): culinary arts

péngyǒu (puhng-yo): friend

piányì (pyan-yee): cheap

piānzi (pyan-dzuh): movie

piào (pyaow): ticket

piàoliàng (pyaow-lyahng): pretty

píjiǔ (pee-jyo): beer

píngcháng (peeng-chahng): usually; often

píngguǒ shǒujī (peeng-gwaw sho-jee): iPhone

Píngguǒ (Peeng-gwaw): Apple (company)

pìnqǐng (peen-cheeng): to hire

pǐntuō (peen-twaw): pint

pīnyīn (peen-yeen): pinyin (the Chinese Romanization system)

péngkè yáogǔn yīnyuè (pun-kuh yaow-gun een-yweh): punk rock

Pǔtōnghuà (Poo-toong-hwah): Mandarin (term used in mainland China)

Qīngzhēn ròu (Cheeng-jun roe): Halal meat

qítā (chee-tah): other; anything else

qīzhōng kǎo (chee-joong kaow): midterm exam

qīmò kǎo (chee-maw kaow): final exam

qīzi (chee-dzuh): wife

qù (chyew): to go

qǔ qián (chyew chyan): to withdraw money

quánbù (chwan-boo): entire; the whole thing

qùdiào (chyew-dyaow): erase; remove

qùnián (chyew-nyan): last year

qúnzi (chwun-dzuh): skirt

qǔxiāo (chyew-shyaow): to cancel

Q

qián (chyan): front; money

qiān chū (chyan choo): to log off

qiān rù (chyan roo): to log on

qiánbāo (chyan-baow): wallet

qiānbǐ (chyan-bee): pencil

qiántái (chyan-tye): reception desk

qiántái fúwùyuán (chyan-tye foo-woo-ywan): receptionist

qiānzhèng (chyan-juhng): visa

qiáo (chyaow): bridge

qìchē (chee-chuh): car

qǐfēi (chee-fay): to take off (airplane)

qíguài (chee-gwye): strange

qímǎ (chee-mah): horseback riding

qīng (cheeng): clear

qíng (cheeng): affection

qǐng (cheeng): please

qìng (cheeng): to celebrate

qīngzǎo (cheeng-dzaow): time (midnight to 6:00 a.m.)

R

ràng (rahng): to let; to allow

rè (ruh): hot

rén (run): person

rénmínbì (run-meen-bee): PRC dollar

RénRén wǎng (Run Run wahng): Facebook

rènshi (run-shir): to know someone

Rì yuán (ir ywan): Japanese dollar

Rìběn (Ir-bun): Japan

rìlì (ir-lee): calendar

rìqī (ir-chee): date

róngxìng (roong-sheeng): to be honored

róngyì (roong-ee): easy

ròu (row): meat

ruǎnjiàn (rwahn-jyan): software

ruǎnmù sāi bǎn (rwan-moo sye bahn): cork board

rùzhù (roo-joo): check into a room

S

săomiáo yí (saow-myaow ee): scanner

shăndiàn (shahn-dyan): lightning bolt

shàng (shahng): above

shāngdiàn (shahng-dyan): store

shàngge xīngqī (shahng-guh sheeng-chee): last week

shàngge yuè (shahng-guh yweh): last month

shàngwăng (shahng-wahng): to go online

shāngwù cāng (shahng-woo tsahng): business class

shāngwù zhōngxīn (shahng-woo joong-sheen): business center

shāngyè (shahng-yeh): business

shè lù yītǐ jī (shuh loo ee-tee jee): camcorder

Shé Nián (Shuh Nyan): Year of the Snake

shéi (shay): who; whom

shèjiāo wăngluò (shuh-jyaow wahng-lwaw): social network

shēn (shun): dark; deep

shēn qián (shun chyan): scuba diving

shēnfèn dàoyòng (shun-fun daow-yoong): identity theft

shēngqì (shung-chee): angry

shēngrì (shung-ir): birthday

shēngrì dàngāo (shung-ir dahn-gaow): birthday cake

shēngyì huǒbàn (shuhng-ee hwaw-bahn): business partner

shēngyīn (shung-een): voice

shénme (shummuh): what

shēntǐ (shun-tee): body

shì (shir): yes; is

Shìchuāng (Shir-chwahng): Windows (computer platform)

shīfu (shir-foo): master; cook

shíhòu (shir-ho): time

shíjiān biǎo (shir-jyan byaow): schedule

shìnèi bǎoxiǎnxiāng (shir-nay baow-shyan-shyahng): in-room safe

shìpín yóuxì (shir-peen yo-shee): video games

shìpǐn záhuò (shir-peen dzah-hwaw): groceries

shōudào (show-daow): to receive

shòuhuì (show-hway): bribery

shǒujī (show-jee): cellphone

shǒujī hàomǎ (show-jee how-mah): cellphone number

shōujù (show-jyew): receipt

shòushāng (show-shahng): to be injured

shǒutí xínglǐ (show-tee sheeng-lee): carry-on luggage

shǒutíshì (show-tee-shir): laptop

shū (shoo): to lose; book

Shǔ Nián (Shoo Nyan): Year of the Rat

shuāng (shwahng): a pair

shuāngjī (shwahng jee): double-click

shuāngrén fángjiān (shwahng-run fahng-jyan): double room

shuāxīn (shwah-sheen): refresh

shǔbiāo (shoo-byaow): mouse

shūdiàn (shoo-dyan): bookstore

shūfu (shoo-foo): comfortable

shuǐguǒ (shway-gwaw): fruit

shuǐ fèi qiánshuǐ (shway fay chyan-shway): scuba diving

Shǔjià (Shoo-jyah): summer vacation

shuìjiào (shway-jyaow): sleep

shuō (shwaw): to speak

shuōchàng yīnyuè (shwaw-chahng een-yweh): rap music

shuǐzāi (shway-dzye): flood

sījī (suh-jee): driver

sīlì xuéxiào (suh-lee shyweh-shyaow): private school

sìzhōu (suh-joe): around

sòng (soong): to send

sōng (soong): loose

sùcài (soo-tsye): vegetarian dishes

suì (sway): age

suǒ (swaw): to lock

sùshè (soo-shuh): dormitory

T

tā (tah): he; him

tāde (tah-duh): his

tài (tye): too much

táishì (tye-shir): desktop

táishì diànnǎo (tye-shir dyan-now): desktop computer

tàitài (tye-tye): wife (term used mostly in Taiwan)

Táiwān (Tye-wahn): Taiwan

tàiyáng yǎnjìng (tye-yahng yan-jeeng): sunglasses

tāmen (tah-men): they; them

tāng (tahng): soup

tánpàn (tahn-pahn): negotiate

tǎnzi (tahn-dzuh): blanket

tàojiān (taow-jyan): suite

tǎolùn (taow-lwoon): to discuss

tèsè (tuh-suh): special

tián (tyan): to fill out a form

tiándiǎn (tyan dyan): dessert

tiānqì (tyan-chee): weather

tiānxiàn (tyan-shyan): antenna

tiàowǔ (tyaow-woo): to dance

tīng (teeng): to listen to

tóngshì (toong-shir): colleague

tóngwū (toong-woo): roommate

tóngyì (toong-ee): to agree

tóuděng cāng (toe-dung tsahng): first class

tóuténg (toe-tung): headache

Tù Nián (Too Nyan): Year of the Rabbit

tuīchí (tway-chir): postponed

tuìfáng (tway-fahng): to check out of a room

tuìhuí (tway-hway): to return merchandise

tuìkuǎn (tway-kwahn): refund

tuōyùn (twaw-yewn): to check in luggage

W

wài (wye): outside

wàibì (wye-bee): foreign currency

wàijiāo guān (wye-jyaow gwahn): diplomat

wàizǔfù (wye-dzoo-foo): maternal grandfather (formal)

wàizǔmǔ (wye-dzoo-moo): maternal grandmother (formal)

wǎnfàn (wahn-fahn): dinner

wánjù diàn (wahn-jyew dyan): toy store

wǎng chóng (wahng choong): Internet geek; netter

wǎngjì xiéyì (wahng-jee shyeh-ee): Internet protocol

wǎngluò ānquán (wahng-lwaw ahn-chwan): network security

wǎngluò guǎnlǐ yuán (wahng-lwaw gwan-lee ywan): network administrator

wǎngluò kǒngbù zhǔyì (wahng-lwaw koong-boo joo-ee): cyber terrorism

wǎngluò liánjié (wahng-lwaw lyan-jyeh): Internet access

wǎngluò liúlǎn qì (wahng-lwaw lyo-lahn chee): Internet browser

wǎngluò shèxiàng jī (wahng-lwaw shuh-shyahng jee): webcam

wǎngshàng zhīfù (wahng-shahng jir-foo): online payment

wǎngshàng fúwù tígōng shāng (wahng-shahng foo-woo tee-goong shahng): Internet service provider

wǎngsù (wahng-soo): Internet speed

wǎngyè shèjì shī (wahng-yeh shuh-jee shir): web designer

wǎngzhàn (wahng-jahn): website

wǎnhuì (wahn-hway): party

wǎnshàng (wahn-shahng): evening (6 p.m. to midnight)

Wànwéiwǎng (Wahn-way-wahng): World Wide Web

wéi (way): hello (on phone only)

Wěidà de Zhōngguó Fánghuóqiáng (Way-dah duh Joong-gwaw Fahng-hwaw-chyahng): The Great Chinese Firewall

Wēiruǎn (Way-roowan): Microsoft

wèishēng zhǐ (way-shung jir): toilet paper

wèishénme (way-shummuh): why

wénjiàn (wun-jyan): a file

wènlù (wun-loo): to ask for directions

wēnquán (wun-chwan): spa

wèntí (wun-tee): problem

wǒ (waw): I; me

wǒde (waw-duh): mine

wǒmen (waw-men): we; us

wòshì (waw-shir): bedroom

wǔfàn (woo-fahn): lunch

wǔjīn diàn (woo-jin dyan): hardware store

wúxiàn diànhuà (woo-shyan dyan-hwah): cordless phone

wúxiàn wǎngluò (woo-shyan wahng-lwaw): WiFi

Wǔ yuè (Woo-yweh): May

X

X guāng jī (X gwahng jee): X-ray machine

xǐ (shee): to wash

xià (shyah): below; next; to go down; to get off

xiàge (shyah-guh): next

xiàge xīngqī (shyah-guh sheeng-chee): next week

xiàge yuè (shyah-guh yweh): next month

xiǎng (shyahng): to think

Xiānggǎng (Shyahng-gahng): Hong Kong

Xiānggǎng huòbì (Shyahng-gahng hwaw-bee): Hong Kong dollar

xiānghù xìnrèn (shyahng-hoo sheen-run): mutual trust

xiàngmù (shyahng-moo): item

xiàngpí jīn (shyahng-pee jeen): rubber band

xiàngqí (shyahng-chee): chess

xiāngzi (shyahng-dzuh): suitcase

xiànjīn (shyan-jeen): cash

xiánliáo (shyan-lyaow): small talk

xiǎnshìqì (shyan-shir-chee): monitor

xiántán (shyan-tahn): to chat

xiànzài (shyan-dzye): now

xiǎo (shyaow): small

xiǎo cài (shyaow tsye): side dish

xiǎo géjiān (shyaow guh-jyan): cubicle

xiǎo píngbǎn diànnǎo (shyaow peeng-bahn dyan-naow): small tablet PC

xiǎo xīn (shyaow sheen): be careful

xiǎofèi (shyaow-fay): tip

xiàwǔ (shyah-woo): afternoon (noon to 6 p.m.)

xiàzài (shyah-dzye): to download

xīcān (she-tsahn): Western food

xiédiàn (shyeh-dyan): shoe store

xièxiè (shyeh-shyeh): thanks

xiézi (shyeh-dzuh): shoes

xǐhuān (she-hwahn): to like

xīn (sheen): new

Xīn bì (Sheen bee): Singapore dollar

Xīn táibì (Sheen tye-bee): New Taiwan dollar

xīndiàntú (sheen-dyan-too): EKG

Xīnlàng wēi-bó (sheen-lahng way-baw): Twitter

xínglǐ (sheeng-lee): luggage

Xīngqī'èr (Sheeng-chee-are): Tuesday

Xīngqīliù (Sheeng-chee-lyo): Saturday

Xīngqīsān (Sheeng-chee-sahn): Wednesday

Xīngqīsì (Sheeng-chee-suh): Thursday

Xīngqītiān (Sheeng-chee-tyan): Sunday

Xīngqīwǔ (Sheeng-chee-woo): Friday

Xīngqīyī (Sheeng-chee-ee): Monday

xìnxī (sheen-she): message

xìnxī jìshù rényuán (sheen-shee jee-shoo run-ywan): IT person

xìnyòngkǎ (sheen-yoong kah): credit card

xìnyòng píngfēn (sheen-yoong peeng-fun): credit score

xī rù qì (shee roo chee): inhaler

xǐshǒu jiān (shee-show jyan): bathroom

xiūxi (shyo-shee): to rest

xǐyī fúwù (shee-ee foo-woo): laundry service

xuǎnzé (shwan-dzuh): to choose

xuǎnzé yīgè liúlǎn qì (shwan-dzuh ee-guh lyo-lahn chee): choose a browser

xuéshēng (shweh-shung): student

xuéxí (shweh-shee): to study

xuéxiào (shweh-shyaow): school

xuēzi (shweh-dzuh): boots

Xūnǐ Zhuānyòng Wǎngluò (Shyew-nee Jwan-yoong Wahng-lwaw): Virtual Private Network (VPN)

xūyào (shyew-yaow): to need

Y

Yáng Nián (Yahng Nyan): Year of the Sheep

yājīn (yah-jeen): deposit (money)

yǎnjìng (yan-jeeng): glasses

yǎnjīng (yan-jeeng): eye

yǎnshì (yan-shir): a presentation

yǎnyuán (yan-ywan): actor

yào (yaow): to want; medicine

yàofáng (yaow-fahng): pharmacy

yáokòng qì (yaow-koong chee): remote control

yàoshi (yaow-shir): key

yàowán (yaow-wahn): pill

yáshuā (yah-shwah): toothbrush

yáyī (yah-ee): dentist

Yàzhōu (Yah-joe): Asia

yě (yeah): also

yèyú àihào (yeah-yew eye-how): hobby

yèzǒnghuì (yeh-dzoong-hway): nightclub

yī (ee): one

yìchéng (ee-chung): agenda

yídòng hùliánwǎng tígōng shāng (ee-doong hoo-lyan-wahng tee-goong shahng): mobile Internet providers

yīfu (ee-foo): clothing

yǐhòu (ee-ho): after

yìhuǎr jiàn (ee-hwar jyan): see you later

yìhuǎr (ee-hwar): in a little while

yìjiàn (ee-jyan): opinion

yíng (eeng): to win

yìngbì (eeng-bee): coins

yīnggāi (eeng-guy): should

yínháng (een-hahng): bank

yìngjiàn (eeng-jyan): computer hardware

yīnlì (een-lee): lunar calendar

Yīngwén (Eeng-wun): English language

yìngyòng (eeng-yoong): app

yīliáo bǎoxiǎn (ee-lyaow baow-shyan): medical insurance

Yīngyǔ (Eeng-yew): English (language)

yǐnliào (een-lyaow): drinks

yīnwèi (een-way): because

yīnyuè (een-yweh): music

yīnyuè jiā (een-yweh jyah): musician

yìqǐ (ee-chee): together

yīshēng (ee-shung): doctor

yǐwéi (ee-way): to consider

yìxiē (ee-shyeh): a few

yíyàng (ee-yahng): the same

yīyuàn (ee-ywan): hospital

yǐzi (ee-dzuh): chair

yòng (yoong): to use

yònghù xìngmíng (yoong-hoo sheeng-meeng): user name

yǒngyuǎn (yoong ywan): forever

yòu (yo): right

yǒu (yo): to have

yǒu de shíhòu (yo duh shir-ho): sometimes

yóujú (yo-jyew): post office

yóulǎn (yo-lahn): to sightsee

yōusī (yo-suh): to meditate

Yóutài shíwù (Yo-tye shir-woo): Kosher food

yǔ (yew): rain

yuán (ywan): Chinese dollar

yuǎn (ywan): far

yuǎnchéng gōngzuò (ywan-chung goong-dzaw): work remotely

yuányì (ywan-ee): gardening

yùdìng (yew-deeng): to make a reservation

Yuènán (Yweh-nahn): Vietnam

yùfù fèi (yew-foo fay): pre-paid

yùndòng (yewn-doong): exercise

yùndòng shān (yewn-doong shahn): sweatshirt

yùndòng xié (yewn-doong shyeh): sneakers

yùndòngyuán (yewn-doong ywan): athlete

yùnqì (yewn-chee): luck

yǔsǎn (yew-sahn): umbrella

yùsuàn (yew-swan): budget

yǔyī (yew-ee): raincoat

yǔyīn yóujiàn (yew-een yo-jyan): voicemail

yùyuē (yew-yweh): reservation (noun)

Z

zàijiàn (dzye-jyan): goodbye

zàixiàn huìyì (dzye-shyan hway-ee): online meeting

zánmen (dzah-men): we; us (informal)

zǎofàn (dzaow-fahn): breakfast

zāogāo (dzaow-gaow): Rats!; what a shame

zǎoshàng (dzaow-shahng): morning (6 a.m. to noon)

zázhì (dzah-jir): magazine

zéi (dzay): thief

zěnme (dzummah): how

zhàngdān (jahng-dahn): bill

zhàngfu (jahng-foo): husband

zhàntái (jahn-tye): platform

zhāntiē (jahn-tyeh): paste

zhànxiàn (jahn-shyan): the line is busy

zhǎo (jaow): to look for

zhāohu (jaow-hoo): greeting

zhàopiàn (jaow-pyan): photo

zhàoxiàng (jaow-shyahng): to take pictures

zhàoxiàngjī (jaow-shyahng-jee): camera

zhékòu (juh-ko): discount

zhēn (juhn): really; truly

zhèngdiǎn (juhng-dyan): on time

zhèngjiàn (juhng-jyan): ID

zhí (jir): straight

zhǐ (jir): only

zhīdào (jir-daow): to know (about something)

zhìliàng (jir-lyahng): quality

zhìnéng zhǔbǎn (jir-nung joo-bahn): smart board

zhīpiào (jir-pyaow): check (money)

zhīpiào bù (jir-pyaow boo): checkbook

zhōng (joong): time; size medium

Zhōngguó (Joong-gwaw): China

Zhōngguó Yídòng (Joong-gwaw Ee-doong): China Mobile

Zhōngguó Diànxìn (Joong-gwaw Dyan-sheen): China Unicom

Zhōngguó Liántōng (Joong-gwaw Lyan-toong): China Telecom

Zhōngguó rén (Zoong-gwaw run): Chinese (person)

Zhōngwén (Zoong-one): Chinese language

zhōngwǔ (joong-woo): noon

zhōngyú (joong-yew): finally

zhōumò (joe-maw): weekend

zhù (joo): to reside

zhǔ cài (joo tsye): main dish

Zhū Nián (Joo Nyan): Year of the Pig

zhuǎn (jwan): to transfer; to turn

zhūbǎo (joo-baow): jewelry

zhūbǎo diàn (joo-baow dyan): jewelry store

zhǔguǎn (joo-gwan): CEO

zhuólù (jwaw-loo): landing

zhuōzi (jwaw-dzuh): table

zìdòng lóutī (dzuh-doong loe-tee): escalator

zìdòng tíkuǎn kǎ (dzuh-doong tee-kwan kah): ATM card

zìdòng qǔkuǎn jī (dzuh-doong chyew-kwan jee): ATM machine

zìjǐ (dzuh-jee): self

zǒngcái (dzoong-tsye): president of a company

zǒngshì (dzoong-shir): always

zǒngsuàn (dzoong-swahn): finally

zǒu (dzoe): to walk

zūfèi (dzoo-fay): rent

zǔfù (dzoo-foo): paternal grandfather (formal)

zǔhé yīnxiǎng (dzoo-huh een-shyahng): stereo system

zǔmǔ (dzoo-moo): paternal grandmother (formal)

zuì (dzway): the most

zuǒ (dzwaw): left

zuòjī (dzwaw-jee): land line

zuótiān (dzwaw-tyan): yesterday

English-Chinese Mini-Dictionary

A

above: **shàng** (shahng)

account balance: **jiéyú** (jyeh-yew)

accounting: **kuàijì** (kwye-jee)

actor: **yǎnyuán** (yan-ywan)

adaptor: **chātóu** (chah-toe)

add: **bǔchōng** (boo-choong)

address: **dìzhǐ** (dee-jir)

affection: **qíng** (cheeng)

after: **yǐhòu** (ee-ho)

afternoon (noon to 6 p.m.): **xiàwǔ** (shyah-woo)

age: **niánjì; suì** (nyan-jee; sway)

agenda: **yìchéng** (ee-chung)

agree: **tóngyì** (toong-ee)

air conditioning: **kōngtiáo** (koong-tyaow)

airplane: **fēijī** (fay-jee)

airport: **fēijī chǎng** (fay-jee chahng)

alarm clock: **nàozhōng** (naow-joong)

alarm system: **jǐngbào xìtǒng** (jeeng-baow shee-toong)

alcohol: **jiǔ** (jyoe)

all: **dōu** (doe)

allow: **ràng** (rahng)

also: **yě** (yeh)

always: **zǒngshì** (dzoong-shir)

ambulance: **jiùhù chē** (jyoe-hoo chuh)

America: **Měiguó** (May-gwaw)

American: **Měiguó ren** (May-gwaw run)

ancient: **gǔdài** (goo-dye)

angry: **shēngqì** (shung-chee)

annoying: **máfan** (mah-fahn)

answer (the phone): **jiē** (jyeh)

answer (a question): **huí** (hway)

antenna: **tiānxiàn** (tyan-shyan)

antique: **gǔdài** (goo-dye)

anything else: **qítā** (chee-tah)

app: **yìngyòng** (eeng-yoong)

appendicitis: **lánwěiyán** (lahn-way-yan)

appetizer: **kāiwèi cài** (kye-way tsye)

Apple (company): **Píngguǒ** (Peeng-gwaw)

area (location): **dìqū** (dee-chyew)

area (vicinity): **fùjìn** (foo-jeen)

around: **sìzhōu** (suh-joe)

arrange: **ānpái** (ahn-pye)

Asia: **Yàzhōu** (Yah-joe)

ask for directions: **wènlù** (wun-loo)

athlete: **yùndòng yuán** (yoon-doong ywan)

ATM card: **zìdòng tíkuǎn kǎ** (dzuh-doong tee-kwan kah)

ATM machine: **zìdòng tí kuǎn jī** (dzuh-doong tee kwan jee)

attendant: **fúwùyuán** (foo-woo-ywan)

auditorium: **lǐtáng** (lee-tahng)

B

bad: **huài** (hwye)

bad credit: **bùliáng xìnyòng** (boo-lyahng sheen-yoong)

bank: **yínháng** (een-hahng)

bank account: **hùtóu** (hoo-toe)

bathroom: **xǐshǒu jiān** (she-show jyan)

be able to: **kěyǐ** (kuh-yee)

be called: **jiào** (jyaow)

be careful: **xiǎo xīn** (shyaow sheen)

be honored: **róngxìng** (roong-sheeng)

be injured: **shòushāng** (show-shahng)

be sick: **bìng** (beeng)

because: **yīnwèi** (een-way)

bed: **chuáng** (chwahng)

bedroom: **wòshì** (waw-shir)

beer: **píjiǔ** (pee-jyo)

Beijing: **Běijīng** (Bay-jeeng)

below: **xià** (shyah)

big: **dà** (dah)

bill: **zhàngdān** (jahng-dahn)

birdwatching: **guān niǎo** (gwahn nyaow)

birthday: **shēngrì** (shung-ir)

birthday cake: **shēngrì dàngāo** (shung-ir dahn-gaow)

blanket: **máotǎn; tǎnzi** (maow-tahn; tahn-dzuh)

blog: **bókè** (baw-kuh)

boarding pass: **dēngjī pái** (dung-jee pye)

body: **shēntǐ** (shun-tee)

book: **shū** (shoo)

bookstore: **shūdiàn** (shoo-dyan)

boots: **xuēzi** (shweh-dzuh)

borrow: **jiè** (jyeh)

boss: **lǎobǎn** (laow-bahn)

both: **dōu** (doe)

boyfriend: **nán péngyǒu** (nahn pung-yo)

breakfast: **zǎofàn** (dzaow-fahn)

bribery: **shòuhuì** (sho-hway)

bridge: **qiáo** (chyaow)

briefcase: **gōngwén bāo** (goong-wun baow)

broadband: **kuāndài** (kwahn-dye)

broken: **huài** (hwye)

broker: **jīngjì rén** (jeeng-jee run)

browse: **liúlǎn** (lyo-lahn)

Buddhist nun: **Nígū** (Nee-goo)

Buddhist temple: **Fú miào** (Foo myaow)

budget: **yùsuàn** (yew-swan)

bus driver: **gōngchē sījī** (goong-chuh suh-jee)

bus stop: **gōnggòng qìchē zhàn** (goong-goong chee-chuh jahn)

bus ticket: **chēpiào** (chuh-piaow)

bus tour: **bāshì lǚyóu** (bah-shir lyew-yo)

business: **shēngyì** (shung-yee)

business card: **míngpiàn** (meeng-pyan)

business center: **shāngwù zhōngxīn** (shahng-woo joong-sheen)

business class: **shāngwù cāng** (shahng-woo tsahng)

business partner: **shēngyì huǒbàn** (shung-ee hwaw-bahn)

busy: **máng** (mahng)

but: **dànshì** (dahn-shir)

buy: **mǎi** (mye)

C

café: **kāfēi tīng** (kah-fay teeng)

calendar: **rìlì** (ir-lee)

calculator: **jìsuàn qī** (ji-swan chee)

calm: **lěngjìng** (lung-jeeng)

camcorder: **shè lù yītǐ jī** (shuh loo ee-tee jee)

camera: **zhàoxiàngjī** (jaow-shyahng-jee)

can: **kěyǐ** (kuh-yee)

cancel: **qǔxiāo** (chyew-shyaow)

car: **qìchē** (chee-chuh)

care about: **guǎn** (gwan)

carry-on luggage: **shǒutí xínglǐ** (show-tee sheeng-lee)

cash: **xiànjīn** (shyan-jeen)

CD (music): **guāngpán** (gwahng-pahn)

CD-ROM: **léishè guāngdié** (lay-shuh gwahng-dyeh)

celebrate: **qìng** (cheeng)

cellphone: **shǒujī** (show-jee)

cellphone number: **shǒujī hàomǎ** (show-jee how-mah)

CEO: **zhǔguǎn** (joo-gwan)

chair: **yǐzi** (ee-dzuh)

change (attitude/behavior): **gǎibiàn** (guy-byan)

change (trains, money): **huàn** (hwahn)

charger: **chōngdiàn qì** (choong-dyan chee)

chat: **liáotiān; xiántán** (lyaow-tyan; shyan-tahn)

cheap: **piányì** (pyan-yee)

check (money): **zhīpiào** (jir-pyaow)

check-in luggage: **tuōyùn** (twaw-yewn)

check into a room: **rùzhù** (roo-joo)

check out of a room: **tuìfáng** (tway-fahng)

checkbook: **zhīpiào bù** (jir-pyaow boo)

chess: **xiàngqí** (shyahng-chee): chess

child: **háizi** (hi-dzuh)

China: **Zhōngguó** (Joong-gwaw)

China Mobile: **Zhōngguó Yídòng** (Joong-gwaw Ee-doong)

China Telecom: **Zhōngguó Liántōng** (Joong-gwaw Lyan-toong)

China Unicom: **Zhōngguó Diànxìn** (Joong-gwaw Dyan-sheen)

Chinese (language): **Hànyǔ; Zhōngwén** (Hahn-yew; Joong-one)

Chinese cabbage: **báicài** (bye-tsye)

Chinese dollar: **yuán** (ywan)

Chinese (person): **Zhōngguó rén** (Joong-gwaw run)

Chinese Romanization system: **pīnyīn** (peen-yeen)

choose: **xuǎnzé** (shywan-dzuh)

choose a browser: **xuǎnzé yīgè liúlǎn qì** (shwan-dzuh ee-guh lyo-lahn chee)

chopsticks: **kuàizi** (kwye-dzuh)

city: **chéngshì** (chung-shir)

class (academic): **kè** (kuh)

click: **diǎnjī** (dyan-jee)

clean: **gānjìng** (gahn-jeeng)

clear: **qīng** (cheeng)

client: **kè hù** (kuh hoo)

close: **jìn** (jeen)

clothing: **yīfu** (ee-foo)

clothing store: **fúzhuāng diàn** (foo-jwahng dyan)

coach: **jiàoliàn** (jyaow-lyan)

coffee: **kāfēi** (kah-fay)

coffee machine: **kāfēi jī** (kah-fay jee)

coins: **yìngbì** (eeng-bee)

cold: **lěng** (luhng)

colleague: **tóngshì** (toong-shir)

collect call: **duìfāng fùfèi diànhuà** (dway-fahng foo-fay dyan-hwah)

college major: **dàxué zhuānyè** (dah-shyweh jwan-yeh)

come: **lái** (lye)

comfortable: **shūfu** (shoo-foo)

company: **gōngsī** (goong-suh)

computer: **diànnǎo** (dyan-now)

computer equipment: **diànnǎo shèbèi** (dyan-now shuh-bay)

computer hardware: **yìngjiàn** (eeng-jyan)

computer program: **diànnǎo chéngxù** (dyan-naow chung-shyew)

computer software: **diànnǎo ruǎnjiàn** (dyan-naow rwan-jyan)

concierge: **fúwùtái jīnglǐ** (foo-woo-tye jeeng-lee)

conference call: **diànhuà huìyì** (dyan-hwah hway-ee)

conference room: **huìyì shì** (hway-ee shir)

congratulations: **gōngxǐ** (goong-she)

consider: **yǐwéi** (ee-way)

consulate: **lǐngshìguǎn** (leeng-shir-gwahn)

contraband: **jìn pǐn** (jeen peen)

contract: **hétóng** (huh-toong)

cook (noun): **shīfu** (shir-foo)

cooking (verb): **pēngtiáo** (pung-tyaow)

copier: **fùyìnjī** (foo-een-jee)

copy: **fùzhì** (foo-jir)

cordless phone: **wúxiàn diànhuà** (woo-shyan dyan-hwah)

cork board: **ruǎnmù sāi bǎn** (rwan-moo sye bahn)

country: **guójiā** (gwaw-jyah)

credit card: **xìnyòngkǎ** (sheen-yoong-kah)

credit score: **xìnyòng píngfēn** (sheen-yoong peeng-fun)

cubicle: **xiǎo géjiān** (shyaow guh-jyan)

culinary arts: **pēngtiáo yìshù** (puhng-tyaow ee-shoo)

currency: **huòbì** (hwaw-bee)

customs: **hǎiguān** (hye-gwahn)

cut (from a document): **jiǎn qiè** (jyan chyeh)

cyberspace: **diànzǐ kōngjiān** (dyan-dzuh koong-jyan)

cyber terrorism: **wǎngluò kǒngbù zhǔyì** (wahng-lwaw koong-boo joo-ee)

D

dance: **tiàowǔ** (tyaow-woo)

Daoist Temple: **Dào miào** (Daow myaow)

dark: **shēn** (shun)

date: **rìqī** (ir-chee)

deep: **shēn** (shun)

definitely: **kěndìng** (kuhn-deeng)

dentist: **yáyī** (yah-ee)

department head: **bùzhǎng** (boo-jahng)

department store: **bǎihuò shāngdiàn** (bye-hwaw shahng-dyan)

deposit (money): **yājīn** (yah-jeen)

desk: **bàngōng zhuō** (bahn-goong jwaw)

desktop: **táishì** (tye-shir)

desktop computer: **táishì diànnǎo** (tye-shir dyan-now)

dessert: **tiándiǎn** (tyan-dyan)

dial: **bō** (baw)

dining room: **fàntīng** (fahn-teeng)

dinner: **wǎnfàn** (wahn-fahn)

dinosaur: **kǒnglóng** (koong long)

diplomat: **wàijiāo guān** (wye-jyaow gwahn)

discount: **zhékòu** (juh-ko)

discuss: **tǎolùn** (taow-lwun)

do: **dǎ** (dah)

doctor: **yīshēng** (ee-shung)

dollar: **kuài** (kwye)

don't have: **méiyǒu** (may-yo)

door: **mén** (mun)

dormitory: **sùshè** (soo-shuh)

double room: **shuāngrén fángjiān** (shwahng-run fahng-jyan)

double-click: **shuāngjī** (shwahng-jee)

download: **xiàzài** (shyah-dzye)

downstairs: **lóuxià** (low-shyah)

drink: **hē** (huh)

drinks: **yǐnliào** (een-lyaow)

drive: **kāichē** (kye-chuh)

driver: **sījī** (suh-jee)

drug smuggler: **dúpǐn zǒusī fàn** (doo-peen dzoe-suh fahn)

duty free: **miǎnshuì** (myan-shway)

E

each: **měige** (may-guh)

easy: **róngyì** (roong-ee)

eat: **chīfàn** (chir-fahn)

eco-friendly project: **huánbǎo de jìhuà** (hwahn-baow duh jee-hwah)

e-commerce: **diànzǐ gōnggào pái** (dyan-dzuh goong-gaow pye)

economy class: **jīngjì cāng** (jeeng-jee tsahng)

EKG: **xīndiàntú** (sheen-dyan-too)

elevator: **diàntī** (dyan-tee)

email: **diànzǐ yóujiàn** (dyan-dzuh yo-jyan)

email address: **diànzǐ yóuxiāng dìzhǐ** (dyan-dzuh yo-shyahng dee-jir)

embassy: **dàshǐ guǎn** (dah-shir gwahn)

emergency exits: **jǐnjí chūkǒu** (jeen-jee choo-ko)

emergency room: **jízhěn shì** (jee-jun shir)

English (language): **Yīngwén; Yīngyǔ** (Eeng-one; Eeng-yew)

entire: **quánbù** (chwan-boo)

entrance: **ménkǒu** (mun-ko)

erase: **qùdiào** (chyew-dyaow)

escalator: **zìdòng lóutī** (dzuh-doong loe-tee)

Euro: **Ōuyuán** (Oh-ywan)

Europe: **Ōuzhōu** (Oh-joe)

evening (6 p.m. to midnight): **wǎnshàng** (wahn-shahng)

examine: **jiǎnchá** (jyan-chah)

exchange bureaus: **duìhuàn chù** (dway-hwahn choo)

exchange rate: **duìhuàn lǜ** (dway-hwahn lyew)

excuse me: **duìbùqǐ** (dway-boo-chee)

exercise: **yùndòng** (yewn-doong)

expensive: **guì** (gway)

export structure: **chūkǒu jiégòu** (choo-ko jyeh-go)

eye: **yǎnjīng** (yan-jeeng)

eyebrow: **méimáo** (may-maow)

F

face: **miàn** (myan)

family: **jiā** (jyah)

Facebook: **Rén Rén Wǎng** (Run Run Wahng)

far: **yuǎn** (ywan)

fast: **kuài** (kwye)

father: **bàba; fùqīn** (bah-bah; foo-cheen)

fax machine: **chuánzhēn jī** (chwahn-juhn jee)

few: **yìxiē** (ee-shyeh)

file: **wénjiàn; dàng'àn (noun)** (wun-jyan; dahng ahn)

fill out (a form): **tián** (tyan)

finally: **zhōngyú** (joong-yew)

first class: **tóuděng cāng** (toe-dung tsahng)

fishing: **diàoyú** (dyaow-yew)

flat tire: **bào tāi** (baow tye)

flip chart: **guàtú** (gwah-too)

flood: **shuǐzāi** (shway-dzye)

flu: **liúgǎn** (lyo-gahn)

folk music: **mínjiān yīnyuè** (meen-jyan een-yweh)

food: **cài; fàn** (tsye; fahn)

food market: **cài shìchǎng** (tsye shir-chahng)

foot: **jiǎoyāzi** (jyaow-yah-dzuh)

foreign currency: **wàibì** (wye-bee)

fork: **chāzi** (chah-dzuh)

free: **miǎnfèi** (myan-fay)

freeway: **gāosù gōnglù** (gaow-soo goong-loo)

Friday: **Xīngqīwǔ** (Sheeng-chee-woo)

friend: **péngyǒu** (puhng-yo)

from: **cóng** (tsoong)

front: **qián** (chyan)

fruit: **shuǐguǒ** (shway-gwaw)

G

gardening: **yuányì** (ywan-ee)

get lost: **mílù** (mee-loo)

get off: **xià** (shyah)

get on: **shàng** (shahng)

gifts: **lǐwù** (lee-woo)

gift shop: **lǐpǐn diàn** (lee-peen dyan)

girlfriend: **nǔ péngyǒu** (nyew puhng-yoe)

give: **gěi** (gay)

glasses: **yǎnjìng** (yan-jeeng)

go: **qù** (chyew)

go down: **xià** (shyah)

go online: **shàngwǎng** (shahng-wahng)

go up: **shàng** (shahng)

good: **hǎo** (how)

good credit: **liánghǎo de xìnyòng** (lyahng-haow duh sheen-yoong)

goodbye: **zàijiàn** (dzye-jyan)

Google: **Gǔgē** (Goo-guh)

Great Chinese Firewall: **Wěidà de Zhōngguó Fánghuǒqiáng** (Way-dah duh Joong-gwaw Fahng-hwaw-chyahng)

greeting: **zhāohu** (jaow-hoo)

groceries: **shípǐn záhuò** (shir-peen dzah-hwaw)

guest: **kèrén** (kuh-run)

guide (noun): **dǎoyóu** (daow-yo)

guidebook: **lǚyóu shǒucè** (lyew-yo show-tsuh)

H

Halal meat: **Qīngzhēn ròu** (Cheeng-jun roe)

half: **bàn** (bahn)

hairdresser: **lǐfà shī** (lee-fah shir)

hang up: **guà** (guah)

happy: **gāoxìng** (gaow-sheeng)

hardware store: **wǔjīn diàn** (woo-jin dyan)

have: **yǒu** (yo)

have a meeting: **kāihuì** (kye-hway)

he: **tā** (tah)

headache: **tóuténg** (toe-tuhng)

heater: **nuǎnqì** (nwahn-chee)

hello (on phone only): **wéi** (way)

help: **bāngmáng** (bahng-mahng)

high heels: **gāogēnxié** (gaow-gun-shyeh)

highway: **gōnglù** (goong-loo)

him: **tā** (tah)

his: **tā de** (tah duh)

historic district: **lìshǐ yōujiǔ de dìqū** (lee-shir yo-jyo duh dee-chyew)

hire: **pìnqǐng** (peen-cheeng)

hit: **dǎ** (dah)

hobby: **yèyú àihào** (yeh-yew eye-how)

holiday: **jiérì** (jyeh-ir)

home: **jiā** (jyah)

Hong Kong: **Xiānggǎng** (Shyahng-gahng)

Hong Kong dollar: **Xiānggǎng huòbì** (shyahng-gahng hwaw-bee)

horseback riding: **qímǎ** (chee-mah)

hospital: **yīyuàn** (ee-ywan)

hot: **rè** (ruh)

hotel: **bīnguǎn; fànguǎn; lǚguǎn** (been-gwahn; fahn-gwahn; lyew-gwahn)

house: **fángzi** (fahng-dzuh)

how: **zěnme** (dzummuh)

however: **dànshì** (dahn-shir)

how long: **duō jiǔ** (dwaw jyoe)

how many: **jǐ** (jee)

how much: **duōshǎo** (dwaw-shaow)

hungry: **è** (uh)

hurry: **jí** (jee)

husband: **zhàngfu** (jahng-foo)

I

I: **wǒ** (waw)

ID: **zhèngjiàn** (juhng-jyan)

identity theft: **shēnfèn dàoyòng** (shun-fun daow-yoong)

I'm sorry: **bàoqiàn; duìbùqǐ** (baow-chyan; dway-boo-chee)

in a little while: **yīhuǐr** (ee-hwar)

in-room safe: **shìnèi bǎoxiǎn xiāng** (shir-nay baow-shyan shyahng)

incorrect: **bùduì** (boo-dway)

infection: **gǎnrǎn** (gahn-rahn)

informal meeting: **fēi zhèngshì huìyì** (fay juhng-shir hway-ee)

inhaler: **xī rù qì** (shee roo chee)

inside: **lǐ** (lee)

install a modem: **ānzhuāng tiáozhì jiětiáoqì** (ahn-jwahng tyaow-jir jyeh-tyaow-chee)

Instagram: **Hǎo zàn** (How dzahn)

instant messaging: **jíshí tōngxùn** (jee-shir toong-shwun)

intelligent: **cōngmíng** (tsoong-meeng)

international phone call: **guójì diànhuà** (gwaw-jee dyan-hwah)

international roaming charges: **guójì mànyóu fèi** (gwaw-jee mahn-yo fay)

Internet: **guójì wǎngluò** (gwaw-jee wahng-lwaw)

Internet access: **wǎngluò liánjié** (wahng-lwaw lyan-jyeh)

Internet browser: **wǎngluò liúlǎn qì** (wahng-lwaw lyo-lahn chee)

Internet geek: **wǎng chóng** (wahng choong)

Internet protocol: **wǎngjì xiéyì** (wahng-jee shyeh-ee)

Internet service provider: **wǎngshàng fúwù tígōng shāng** (wahng-shahng foo-woo tee-goong shahng)

Internet speed: **wǎngsù** (wahng-soo)

introduce: **jièshào** (jyeh-shaow)

iPhone: **Píngguǒ shǒujī** (Peeng-gwaw show-jee)

is: **shì** (shir)

IT person: **xìnxī jìshù rényuán** (sheen-shee jee-shoo run-ywan)

item: **xiàngmù** (shyahng-moo)

J

Japan: **Rìběn** (Ir-bun)

Japanese dollar: **Rì yuán** (Ir ywan)

jeans: **niúzǎikù** (nyo-dzye-koo)

jewelry: **zhūbǎo** (joo-baow)

jewelry store: **zhūbǎo diàn** (joo-baow dyan)

job: **gōngzuò** (goong-dzwaw)

juice: **guǒzhī** (gwaw-jir)

K

karaoke machine: **kǎlā'ōukè jī** (kah-lah-o-kuh jee)

key: **yàoshi** (yaow-shir)

keyboard: **jiànpán** (jyan-pahn)

kilometer (Chinese equivalent): **lǐ** (lee)

know (how to do something): **huì** (hway)

know (information): **zhīdào** (jir-daow)

know (someone): **rènshi** (run-shir)

Kosher food: **Yóutài shíwù** (Yo-tye shir-woo)

kung fu: gōngfū (goong-foo)

L

landing: **zhuólù** (jwaw-loo)

landline: **zuòjī** (dzwaw jee)

laptop: **bǐjìběn diànnǎo** (bee-jee-bun dyan-naow)

laptop: **shǒutíshì** (show-tee-shir)

laser pointer: **jīguāng bǐ** (jee-gwahng bee)

last month: **shàngge yuè** (shahng-guh yweh)

last week: **shàngge xīngqī** (shahng-guh sheeng-chee)

last year: **qùnián** (chyew-nyan)

laundry service: **xǐyī fúwù** (she-ee foo-woo)

law: **fǎlǜ** (fah-lyew)

lawyer: **lǜshī** (lyew-shir)

leave: **líkāi** (lee-kye)

leave a message: **liúhuà** (lyo-hwah)

leave the house: **chūfā** (choo-fah)

left: **zuǒ** (dzwaw)

let: **ràng** (rahng)

life vests: **jiùshēng yī** (jyoe-shung ee)

lightning bolt: **shǎndiàn** (shahn dyan)

like: **xǐhuān** (she-hwahn)

line is busy: **zhànxiàn** (jahn shyan)

listen to: **tīng** (teeng)

loan: **jiè** (jyeh)

lobby: **dàtīng** (dah-teeng)

local train: **mànchē** (mahn-chuh)

local production: **běndì huà shēngchǎn** (bun-dee hwah shung-chahn)

location: **dìqū** (dee-chyew)

lock: **suǒ** (swaw)

log off: **qiān chū** (chyan choo)

log on: **qiān rù** (chyan roo)

London: **Lúndūn** (Lwun-duhn)

long-distance phone call: **chángtú diànhuà** (chahng-too dyan-hwah)

look for: **zhǎo** (jaow)

look something up: **chá** (chah)

look up a phone number: **chá diànhuà hàomǎ** (chah dyan-hwah how-mah)

loose: **sōng** (soong)

lose: **shū** (shoo)

luck: **yùnqì** (yewn-chee)

luggage: **xínglǐ** (sheeng-lee)

luggage claim tag: **lǐngqǔ dān** (leeng-chyew dahn)

lunar calendar: **yīnlì** (een-lee)

lunch: **wǔfàn** (woo-fahn)

M

Mac (computer): **Píngguǒ** (Peeng-gwaw)

magazine: **zázhì** (dzah-jir)

main dish: **zhǔ cài** (joo tsye)

mainland (China): **dàlù** (dah-loo)

make a legal decision: **pànjué** (pahn-jweh)

make a phone call: **dǎ diànhuà** (dah dyan-hwah)

make a reservation (seats): **dìng wèi** (deeng-way)

make a reservation: **yùdìng** (yew-deeng)

manager: **jīnglǐ** (jeeng-lee)

Mandarin: **Guóyǔ; Pǔtōnghuà; Hànyǔ** (Gwaw-yew [term used in Taiwan]; Poo-toong-hwah [term used in mainland China]; Hahn-yew [politically neutral term used in both Taiwan and mainland China])

many: **duō** (dwaw)

many thanks: **gǎnxiè** (gahn-shyeh)

map: **dìtú** (dee-too)

marry: **jiéhūn** (jyeh-hwun)

master: **shīfu** (shir-foo)

maternal grandfather (formal): **wàizǔfù** (wye-dzoo-foo)

maternal grandmother (formal): **wàizǔmǔ** (wye-dzoo-moo)

May: **Wǔ yuè** (Woo yweh)

me: **wǒ** (waw)

meat: **ròu** (row)

medical insurance: **yīliáo bǎoxiǎn** (ee-lyaow baow-shyan)

medicine: **yào** (yaow)

meditate: **yōusī** (yo-suh)

meeting: **huìyì** (hway-ee)

menu: **càidān** (tsye-dahn)

Mercedes Benz: **Bēnchí** (Bun-chir)

merger: **hébìng** (huh-beeng)

message: **xìnxī** (sheen-she)

microphone: **màikèfēng** (my-kuh-fung)

Microsoft: **Wēiruǎn** (Way-roowan)

midnight: **bànyè** (bahn-yeh)

midterm exam: **qīzhōng kǎo** (chee-joong kaow)

mine: **wǒ de** (waw duh)

minister (official): **bùzhǎng** (boo-jahng)

minute: **fēn** (fun)

mistake: **cuò** (tswaw)

mobile Internet providers: **yídòng hùliánwǎng tígōng shāng** (ee-doong hoo-lyan-wahng tee-goong shahng)

Monday: **Xīngqīyī** (Sheeng-chee-ee)

monitor (computer): **xiǎnshìqì** (shyan-shir-chee)

money: **qián** (chyan)

more: **gèng** (guhng)

morning (6 a.m. to noon): **zǎoshàng** (dzaow-shahng)

most: **zuì** (dzway)

mother: **māma; mǔqīn** (mah-mah; moo-cheen)

mountain climbing: **páshān** (pah-shan)

mouse: **shǔbiāo** (shoo-byaow)

movie: **diànyǐng; piānzi** (dyan-yeeng; pyan-dzuh)

MP3 player: **MP3 bōfàngqì** (MP3 baw-fahng-chee)

multilateral trade: **duōbiān màoyì** (dwaw-byan maow-ee)

museum: **bówùguǎn** (baw-woo-gwahn)

music: **yīnyuè** (een-yweh)

musician: **yīnyuè jiā** (een-yweh jyah)

mutual trust: **xiānghù xìnrèn** (shyahng-hoo sheen-run)

my: **wǒ de** (waw-duh)

nanny: **bǎomǔ** (baow-moo)

napkin: **cānjīnzhǐ** (tsahn-jeen-jir)

need: **xūyào** (shyew-yaow)

negotiate: **tánpàn** (tahn-pahn)

neighborhood: **fùjìn** (foo-jeen)

network administrator: **wǎngluò guǎnlǐ yuán** (wahng-lwaw gwan-lee ywan)

network security: **wǎngluò ānquán xìng** (wahng-lwaw ahn-chwan sheeng)

never: **jué bù** (jyweh boo)

new: **xīn** (sheen)

New Taiwan dollar: **Xīn táibì** (Sheen tye-bee)

New York: **Niǔyuē** (Nyo-yweh)

newspaper: **bàozhǐ** (baow-jir)

next: **xiàge** (shyah-guh)

next month: **xiàge yuè** (shyah-guh yweh)

next to: **kàojìn** (cow-jeen)

next week: **xiàge xīngqī** (shyah-guh sheeng-chee)

next year: **míngnián** (meeng-nyan)

nightclub: **yèzǒnghuì** (yeh-dzoong-hway)

no: **bù** (boo)

noodles: **miàntiáo** (myan-tyaow)

noon: **zhōngwǔ** (joong-woo)

not bad: **búcuò** (boo-tswaw)

not: **bù** (boo)

notebook: **bǐjìběn** (bee-jee-bun)

now: **xiànzài** (shyan-dzye)

number: **hàomǎ** (how-mah)

nurse: **hùshì** (hoo-shir)

of course: **dāngrán** (dahng-rahn)

office: **bàngōngshì** (bahn-goong-shir)

often: **chángcháng; píngcháng** (chahng-chahng; peeng-chahng)

Oh my goodness!: **āiyà** (eye-yah)

old: **lǎo** (laow)

on time: **zhèngdiǎn** (juhng-dyan)

on top: **shàng** (shahng)

on vacation: **dùjià** (doo-jyah)

one: **yī** (ee)

one cent: **fēn** (fun)

one-way ticket: **dānchéng piào** (dahn-chuhng pyaow)

online meeting: **zàixiàn huìyì** (dzye-shyan hway-ee)

online gaming: **zàixiàn yóuxì** (dzye-shyan yo-shee)

online payment: **wǎngshàng zhīfù** (wahng-shahng jir-foo)

online shopping: **wǎngshàng gòuwù** (wahn-shahng go-woo)

only: **zhǐ** (jir)

open: **kāi** (kye)

open the door: **kāimén** (kye-mun)

opinion: **yìjiàn** (ee-jyan)

opposite: **duìmiàn** (dway-myan)

or: **huòzhe** (hwaw-juh)

order (food): **diǎn** (dyan)

ordering and processing cost: **dìnghuò chéngbàn** (deeng-hwaw chung-bahn)

other: **biéde** (byeh-duh)

other: **qítā** (chee-tah)

overdone: **lǎo** (laow)

outside: **wài** (wye)

P

pair: **shuāng** (shwahng)

paper clip: **huí wén zhēn** (hway wun jun)

parents: **fùmǔ** (foo-moo)

party: **wǎnhuì** (wahn-hway)

passport: **hùzhào** (hoo-jaow)

password: **mìmǎ** (mee-mah)

paste: **zhāntiē** (jahn tyeh)

paternal grandfather (formal): **zǔfù** (dzoo-foo)

paternal grandmother (formal): **zǔmǔ** (dzoo-moo)

pay: **fù qián** (foo chyan)

PC (personal computer): **gèrén diànnǎo** (guh-run dyan-now)

Peking Opera: **Jīngjù** (Jeeng-jyew)

pen: **gāngbǐ** (gahng-bee)

pencil: **qiānbǐ** (chyan-bee)

percentage: **bǎifēn bǐ** (bye-fun bee)

perhaps: **kěnéng** (kuh-nuhng)

person: **rén** (run)

pharmacy: **yàofáng** (yaow-fahng)

photo: **zhàopiàn** (jaow-pyan)

pick up: **ná** (nah)

pill: **yàowán** (yaow-wahn)

PIN: **mìmǎ** (mee-mah)

pint: **pǐntuō** (peen-twaw)

place: **dìfāng** (dee-fahng)

platform: **zhàntái** (jahn-tye)

play: **dǎ** (dah [used with a follow-up word referring to a particular sport])

play: **wán** (wahn [general usage])

play cards: **dǎpái** (dah-pye)

play mah-jong: **dǎ májiàng** (dah mah-jahng)

play tennis: **dǎ wǎngqiú** (dah wahng-chyo)

please: **qǐng** (cheeng)

police: **jǐngchá** (jeeng-chah)

police station: **jǐngchá jú** (jeeng-chah jyew)

popular: **liúxíng** (lyo-sheeng)

post office: **yóujú** (yo-jyew)

postponed: **tuīchí** (tway-chir)

pray: **lǐbài** (lee-bye)

PRC dollar: **rénmínbì** (run-meen-bee)

pre-paid: **yùfù fèi** (yew-foo fay)

preliminary meeting: **chūbù huìyì** (choo-boo hway-ee)

presentation: **yǎnshì** (yan-shir)

president (of company): **zǒngcái** (dzoong-tsye)

pretty: **hǎokàn** (how-kahn)

pretty: **piàoliàng** (pyaow-lyahng)

price: **jiàgé** (jyah-guh)

print: **dǎyìn** (dah-een)

private school: **sīlì xuéxiào** (suh-lee shweh-shyaow)

problem: **wèntǐ** (wun-tee)

product: **chǎnwù** (chahn-woo)

professor: **jiàoshòu** (jyaow-show)

public bus: **gōnggòng qìchē** (goong-goong chee-chuh)

public telephone: **gōngyòng diànhuà** (goong-yoong dyan-hwah)

pull an all-nighter: **kāi yèchē** (kye yeh-chuh)

punk rock: **péngkè yáogǔn yīnyuè** (pung-kuh yaow-gwun een-yweh)

Q

quality: **zhìliàng** (jir-lyahng)

quiet: **ānjìng** (ahn-jeeng)

R

rain: **yǔ** (yew)

raincoat: **yǔyī** (yew-ee)

rap music: **shuōchàng yīnyuè** (shwaw-chahng een-yweh)

Rats!: **zāogāo** (dzaow-gaow)

read: **kàn shū** (kahn shoo)

really: **zhēn** (juhn)

really good: **búcuò** (boo-tswaw)

rebate: **huíkòu** (hway-ko)

reboot: **chóngxīn kāijī** (choong-sheen kye-jee)

receipt: **shōujù** (show-jyew)

receive: **shōudào** (show-daow)

reception desk: **qiántái** (chyan-tye)

receptionist: **qiántái fúwùyuán** (chyan-tye foo-woo-ywan)

record store: **chàngpiàn diàn** (chahng-pyan dyan)

refresh: **shuāxīn** (shwah-sheen)

refund: **tuìkuǎn** (tway-kwahn)

relationships: **guānxì** (gwahn-shee)

remote control: **yáokòng qì** (yaow-koong chee)

remove: **qùdiào** (chyew-dyaow)

rent (noun): **zūfèi** (dzoo-fay)

rent (verb): **chūzū** (choo-dzoo)

reservation (noun): **yùyuē** (yew-yweh)

reservation (verb: to make): **yùdìng** (yew-deeng)

reside: **zhù** (joo)

resolve: **jiějué** (jyeh-jweh)

rest: **xiūxi** (shyo-she)

restaurant: **cānguǎn; fàndiàn** (tsahn-gwahn; fahn-dyan)

return: **huí** (hway)

return (come back): **huílái** (hway-lye)

return (merchandise): **tuìhuí** (tway-hway)

rhythm and blues: **jiézòu lándiào** (jyeh-dzo lahn-dyaow)

rice: **mǐfàn** (mee-fahn)

rice paddies: **dàotián** (daow-tyan)

right: **yòu** (yo)

road: **lù** (loo)

room: **fángjiān** (fahng-jyan)

room service: **kèfáng fúwù** (kuh-fahng foo-woo)

roommate: **tóngwū** (toong-woo)

round-trip ticket: **láihuí piào** (lye-hway pyaow)

rubberband: **xiàngpíjīn** (shyahng-pee-jeen)

rush hour: **gāofēngqī** (gaow-fuhng-chee)

S

sailing: **hángxíng** (hahng-sheeng)

same: **yíyàng** (ee-yahng)

sandals: **liángxié** (lyahng-shyeh)

Saturday: **Xīngqīliù** (Sheeng-chee-lyo)

save: **bǎocún** (baow-tswun)

scanner: **sǎomiáo yí** (saow-myaow ee)

scary: **kěpà** (kuh-pah)

schedule: **shíjiānbiǎo** (shir-jyan-byaow)

school: **xuéxiào** (shweh-shyaow)

scuba diving: **shēn qián** (shun-chyan)

search: **jiǎnsuǒ** (jyan-swaw)

search engine: **jiǎnsuǒ yǐnqíng** (jyan-swaw een-cheeng)

search the Internet: **jiǎnsuǒ guójì yīntèwǎng** (jyan-swaw gwaw-jee een-tuh-wahng)

seat belt: **ānquán dài** (ahn-chwan dye)

secretary: **mìshū** (mee-shoo)

secure server: **ānquán fúwùqì** (ahn-chwan foo-woo-chee)

Security!: **Jǐngwèi!** (Jeeng-way!)

see: **kàn** (kahn)

see a doctor: **kànbìng** (kahn-beeng)

see you later: **yīhuǐr jiàn** (ee-hwar jyan)

see: **jiàn** (jyan [also used as a classifier])

self: **zìjǐ** (dzuh-jee)

sell: **mài** (my)

send: **sòng** (soong)

send a text: **fā yīgè duǎnxìn** (fah ee-guh dwan-sheen)

server: **fúwùqì** (foo-woo-chee)

set off (leave): **chūfā** (choo-fah)

set up an account: **jiànlì yíge zhànghù** (jyan-lee ee-guh jahng-hoo)

several; how many: **jǐ** (jee)

shareholder: **gǔdōng** (goo-doong)

shoe store: **xié diàn** (shyeh dyan)

shoes: **xiézi** (shyeh-dzuh)

short: **ǎi** (eye)

should: **yīnggāi** (eeng-guy)

side dish: **xiǎo cài** (shyaow tsye)

sightsee: **yóulǎn** (yo-lahn)

Singapore dollar: **Xīn bì; Xīnjiāpō yuán** (Sheen bee; Sheen-jya-paw ywan)

singer: **gēshǒu** (guh-show)

skirt: **qúnzi** (chwun-dzuh)

sleep: **shuìjiào** (shway-jyaow)

slide projector: **huàndēngjī** (hwahn-duhng-jee)

slide projector: **huángdēng piàn** (hwahn-duhng- pyan)

slow: **màn** (mahn)

small: **xiǎo** (shyaow)

small tablet PC: **xiǎo píngbǎn diànnǎo** (shyaow peeng-bahn dyan-naow)

small talk: **xiánliáo** (shyan-lyaow)

smart board: **zhìnéng zhǔbǎn** (jir-nung joo-bahn)

sorkeling: **fú qiǎn** (foo chyan)

soap: **féizào** (fay-dzaow)

social network: **shèjiāo wǎngluò** (shuh-jyaow wahng-lwaw)

software: **ruǎnjiàn** (rwahn-jyan)

solve: **jiějué** (jyeh-jweh)

sometimes: **yǒu de shíhòu** (yo duh shir-ho)

son: **érzi** (are-dzuh)

soup: **tāng** (tahng)

soybean curd: **dòufu** (doe-foo)

spa: **wēnquán** (wun-chwan)

speak: **shuō** (shwaw)

special: **tèsè** (tuh-suh)

spouse: **àirén** (eye-run [used only in the PRC])

Spring break: **Chūnjià** (Chwun-jyah)

stamp collecting: **jí yóu** (jee yo)

stapler: **dìng shū jī** (deeng shoo jee)

start: **kāishǐ** (kye-shir)

stereo system: **zǔhé yīnxiǎng** (dzoo-huh een-shyahng)

store: **shāngdiàn** (shahng-dyan)

straight: **zhí** (jir)

strange: **qíguài** (chee-gwye)

street: **jiē** (jyeh)

student: **xuéshēng** (shweh-shung)

study: **xuéxí** (shweh-she)

subway: **dìtiě** (dee-tyeh)

suggest: **jiànyì** (jyan-ee)

suggestion: **jiànyì** (jyan-ee)

suitcase: **xiāngzi** (shyahng-dzuh)

suite: **tàojiān** (taow-jyan)

summer vacation: **Shǔjià** (Shoo-jyah)

Sunday: **Xīngqītiān** (Sheeng-chee-tyan)

sunglasses: **tàiyáng yǎnjìng** (tye-yahng yan-jeeng)

supermarket: **chāojí shìchǎng** (chaow-jee shir-chahng)

sweater: **máoyī** (maow-ee)

sweatshirt: **yùndòng shān** (yewn-doong shahn)

sweep: **cá** (tsah)

T

table: **zhuōzi** (jwaw-dzuh)

Taiwan: **Táiwān** (Tye-wahn)

take a vacation: **fàng jià** (fahng jyah)

take medicine: **chī yào** (chir yaow)

take off (airplane): **qǐfēi** (chee-fay)

take pictures: **zhàoxiàng** (jaow-shyahng)

talk: **jiǎng** (jyahng)

tank top: **bèixīn** (bay-sheen)

taxi: **chūzū chē** (choo-dzoo chuh)

tea: **chá** (chah)

teach: **jiāo** (jyaow)

teacher: **lǎoshī** (laow-shir)

technical support: **jìshù fúwù** (jee-shoo foo-woo)

telephone: **diànhuà** (dyan-hwah)

telephone card: **diànhuàkǎ** (dyan-hwah-kah)

telephone number: **diànhuà hàomǎ** (dyan-hwah how-mah)

tell: **gàosù** (gaow-soo)

thanks: **xièxiè** (shyeh-shyeh)

that: **nà** (nah)

That's awful!: **Zāogāo!** (Dzaow-gaow!)

them: **tāmen** (tah-men)

there: **nàr** (nahr)

they: **tāmen** (tah-men)

thief: **zéi** (dzay)

thing: **dōngxi** (doong-she)

think: **xiǎng** (shyahng)

thirsty: **kě** (kuh)

Thursday: **Xīngqīsì** (Sheeng-chee-suh)

ticket: **piào** (pyaow)

ticket office: **piàofáng (pyaow-fahng)**

time: **shíhòu** (shir-ho)

time (midnight to 6 a.m.): **qīngzǎo** (cheeng-dzaow)

time: **zhōng** (joong)

tip: **xiǎofèi** (shyaow-fay)

tired: **lèi** (lay)

today: **jīntiān** (jeen-tyan)

together: **yìqǐ** (ee-chee)

toilet: **cèsuǒ** (tsuh-swaw)

toilet paper: **wèishēng zhǐ** (way-shung jir)

tomorrow: **míngtiān** (meeng-tyan)

too bad: **kěxī** (kuh-she)

too much: **tài** (tye)

toothbrush: **yáshuā** (yah-shwah)

tour: **lǚyóu** (lyew-yo)

tour group: **guāng guāng tuán** (gwahng gwahng twahn)

towel: **máojīn** (maow-jeen)

toy store: **wánjù diàn** (wahn-jyew dyan)

trade show: **màoyì zhǎnxiāohuì** (maow-ee jahn-shyaow-hway)

train station: **huǒchē zhàn** (hwaw-chuh jahn)

transfer: **zhuǎn** (jwan)

transparency: **tóuyǐngpiàn** (toe-eeng-pyan)

transparent tape: **jiāo dài** (jyaow dye)

transportation: **jiāotōng** (jyaow-toong)

travel: **lǚxíng** (lyew-sheeng)

travel agency: **lǚxíngshè** (lyew-sheeng-shuh)

travel agent: **lǚxíng dàilǐ rén** (lyew-sheeng dye-lee run) traveler's checks: **lǔxíng zhīpiào** (lyew-sheeng jir-pyaow)

truly: **zhēn** (juhn)

Tuesday: **Xīngqī'èr** (Sheeng-chee-are)

turn: **zhuǎn** (jwan)

turn something on: **dǎkāi** (dah-kye)

turn something off: **guāndiào** (gwan-dyaow)

TV: **diànshì** (dyan-shir)

Tweets: **Míngjiào** (Meeng-jyaow)

U

U.S. dollar: **Měiyuán** (May-ywan)

umbrella: **yǔsǎn** (yew-sahn)

unfortunately: **kěxī** (kuh-she)

upstairs: **lóushàng** (low-shahng)

us: **wǒmen** (waw-men)

us (informal): **zánmen** (dzah-men)

use: **yòng** (yoong)

user name: **yònghù xìngmíng** (yoong-hoo sheeng-meeng)

usually: **píngcháng** (peeng-chahng)

V

vacant: **kòngwèi** (koong-way)

vacation day: **jiàrì** (jyah-ir)

vegetarian dishes: **sùcài** (soo-tsye)

vegetarian food: **chún sùshí** (chwun soo-shir)

venture capital: **fēngxiǎn tóuzī** (fung-shyan toe-dzuh)

vicinity: **fùjìn** (foo-jeen)

video games: **shìpín yóuxì** (shir-peen yo-shee)

video recorder: **lùxiàngjī** (loo-shyahng-jee)

Vietnam: **Yuènán** (Yweh-nahn)

villa: **biéshu** (byeh-shoo)

virus: **bìngdú** (beeng-doo)

visa: **qiānzhèng** (chyan-juhng)

voice: **shēngyīn** (shung-een)

voice mail: **yǔyīn yóujiàn** (yew-een yo-jyan)

VPN (Virtual Private Network): **xūnǐ zhuānyòng wǎngluò** (shyew-nee jwan-yoong wahng-lwaw)

W

wait: **děng** (duhng)

wake-up call: **jiào xǐng diànhuà** (jyaow sheeng dyan-hwah)

walk: **zǒu** (dzoe)

wallet: **qiánbāo** (chyan-baow)

want: **yào** (yaow)

warm: **nuǎnhuó** (nwan-hwaw)

wash: **xǐ** (shee)

we: **wǒmen** (waw-men)

we (informal): **zánmen** (dzah-men)

wear: **chuān** (chwahn)

weather: **tiānqì** (tyan-chee)

webcam: **wǎngluò shèxiàng jī** (wahng-lwaw shuh-shyahng jee)

web designer: **wǎngyè shèjì shī** (wahng-yeh shuh-jee shir)

website: **wǎngzhàn** (wahng-jahn)

WeChat: **Wēixìn** (Way-sheen)

wedding anniversary: **jiéhūn jìniàn rì** (jyeh-hwun jee-nyan ir)

Wednesday: **Xīngqīsān** (Sheeng-chee-sahn)

week: **lǐbài** (lee-bye)

weekend: **zhōumò** (joe-maw)

welcome: **huānyíng** (hwahn-eeng)

Western food: **Xīcān** (Shee-tsahn)

what: **shénme** (shummuh)

what a shame: **zāogāo** (dzaow-gaow)

where: **nǎr** (nar)

which: **nǎ** (nah)

who: **shéi** (shay)

whom: **shéi** (shay)

whole thing: **quánbù** (chwan-boo)

why: **wèishénme** (way-shummuh)

wife: **qīzi** (chee-dzuh)

wife: **tàitài** (tye-tye [used mostly in Taiwan])

WiFi: **wúxiàn wǎngluò** (woo-shyan wahng-lwaw)

Windows: **Shìchuāng** (Shir-chwahng)

win: **yíng** (eeng)

wine: **jiǔ** (jyoe)

winter vacation: **Hánjià** (hahn-jyah)

withdraw money: **qǔ qián** (chyew chyan)

work: **gōngzuò** (goong-dzwaw)

work out: **jiànshēn yùndòng** (jyan-shun yewn-doong)

work remotely: **yuǎnchéng gōngzuò** (ywan-chung goong-dzwaw)

World Wide Web: **wànwéiwǎng** (wahn-way-wahng)

X

X-ray machine: **X guāng jī** (X gwahng jee)

Y

Year of the Dog: **Gǒu Nián** (Go Nyan)

Year of the Dragon: **Lóng Nián** (Loong Nyan)

Year of the Horse: **Mǎ Nián** (Ma Nyan)

Year of the Monkey: **Hóu Nián** (Ho Nyan)

Year of the Ox: **Niú Nián** (Nyo Nyan)

Year of the Pig: **Zhū Nián** (Joo Nyan)

Year of the Rabbit: **Tù Nián** (Too Nyan)

Year of the Rat: **Shǔ Nián** (Shoo Nyan)

Year of the Rooster: **Jī Nián** (Jee Nyan)

Year of the Sheep: **Yáng Nián** (Yahng Nyan)

Year of the Snake: **Shé Nián** (Shuh Nyan)

Year of the Tiger: **Hǔ Nián** (Hoo Nyan)

yes: **shì** (shir)

yesterday: **zuótiān** (dzwaw-tyan)

you: **nǐ** (nee)

you (plural): **nǐmen** (nee-mun)

you (polite): **nín** (neen)

you're welcome: **búkèqì** (boo-kuh-chee)

young: **niánqīng** (nyan-cheeng)

Appendix B

Chinese Verbs

Here's a handy list of useful Chinese verbs. For a general description of how verbs work in Chinese, see Chapter 3.

àn (ahn): to press

ānpái (ahn-pye): to arrange; to schedule

ānzhuāng (ahn-jwahng): to install

bāngmáng (bahng-mahng): to help

bō (baw): to dial

cānjiā (tsahn-jyah): to participate

chàng (chahng): to sing

chī (chir): to eat

chídào (chir-daow): to be late

chóngxīn kāijī (choong-sheen kye-jee): to reboot

chuān (chwan): to wear

chuī (chway): to blow

cún qián (tswun chyan): to deposit money

dǎ (dah): to hit; to strike; to play

dài (dye): to bring; to carry; to wear (accessories)

děng (duhng): to wait

dēnglù (duhng-loo): to log on

diǎn (dyan): to order (food)

dǒng (doong): to understand

è (uh): to be hungry

fēi (fay): to fly

fù zhàng (foo-jahng): to pay a bill

gǎibiàn (gye-byan): to change

gǎnjué (gahn-jweh): to feel

gǎnxiè (gahn-shyeh): to thank

gàosù (gaow-soo): to tell

gāoxìng (gaow-sheeng): to be happy

gěi (gay): to give

gōngzuò (goong-dzwaw): to work

guà (gwah): to hang up

guān (gwan): to close

gūjì (goo-jee): to estimate

guò (gwaw): to pass

hē (huh): to drink

hézuò (huh-dzwaw): to cooperate

huà (hwah): to paint

huàn (hwahn): to exchange

huānyíng (hwahn-eeng): to welcome

huí (hway): to return

huì (hway): to know how to do something

hūxī (hoo-she): to breathe

jiàn (jyan): to see

jiǎng (jyahng): to speak

jiànlì (jyan-lee): to set up

jiànyì (jyan-ee): to suggest

jiào (jyaow): to call

jiē (jyeh): to answer (a phone call)

jiè (jyeh): to loan; to borrow

jiěfàng (jyeh-fahng): to liberate

jiéhūn (jyeh-hwun): to marry

jiějué (jyeh-jweh): to solve

jièshào (jyeh-shaow): to introduce

jiēshòu (jyeh-show): to accept (money, tickets, and so on) jiézhàng (jyeh-jahng): to pay the bill

jiù (jyoe): to save (a life)

juédìng (jyweh-deeng): to decide

kāi (kye): to open

kāi chē (kye chuh): to drive

kāihuì (kye-hway): to have or be in a
   meeting

kàn (kahn): to read; to look; to see

kě (kuh): to be thirsty

lái (lye): to come

liànxí (lyan-she): to practice

líkāi (lee-kye): to leave

liú (lyoe): to leave (an object; a
   message)

mà (mah): to scold

mǎi (my): to buy

mài (my): to sell

máng (mahng): to be busy

mílù (mee-loo): to get lost

ná (nah): to pick up; to take

néng (nuhng): to be able to

pànjué (pahn-jweh): to make a legal
   decision

qǐng (cheeng): to invite

qù (chyew): to go

qǔ qián (chyew chyan): to withdraw
   money

qǔxiāo (chyew-shyaow): to cancel

ràng (rahng): to permit

rènshi (run-shir): to know (a person);
   to recognize

shàng (shahng): to get on

shàngwǎng (shahng-wahng): to go
   online

shì (shir): to be

shōu (show): to receive

shū (shoo): to lose

shuō (shwaw): to speak

sòng (soong): to send

tánpàn (tahn-pahn): to negotiate

tǎolùn (taow-lwun): to discuss

tián (tyan): to fill out (a form)

tīng (teeng): to hear; to listen to

tóngyì (toong-ee): to agree

tuìchū (tway-choo): to log off

tuìfáng (tway-fahng): to check out
   (of a hotel room)

tuìhuí (tway-hway): to return
   (merchandise)

tuōyùn (twaw-yewn): to check in
   luggage

wán (wahn): to play

wàng (wahng): to forget

wèn (one): to ask

xǐ (she): to wash

xià (shyah): to get off

xiǎng (shyahng): to think; to miss

xiàzǎi (shyah-dzye): to download

xǐhuān (she-hwan): to like; to enjoy

xīn (sheen): to believe

xuǎnzé (shwan-dzuh): to choose

xuéxí (shweh-she): to study

yǎnshì (yan-shir): to give a
   presentation

yào (yaow): to want

yíng (eeng): to win

yòng (yoong): to use

yǒu (yo): to have; there are

yóulǎn (yo-lahn): to sightsee

yóuyǒng (yo-yoong): to swim

yuànyì (ywan-yee): to be willing to

yùsuàn (yew-swan): to budget

zhǎo (jaow): to look for

zhàoxiàng (jaow-shyahng): to take pictures

zhīdào (jir-daow): to know (a fact)

zhù (joo): to reside; to extend wishes

zhuā (jwah): to catch

zhuǎn (jwan): to transfer; to turn

zhuāngrù (jwahng-roo): to pack

zhuǎnzū (jwan-dzoo): to sublet

zhǔchí (joo-chir): to lead; to be in charge

zǒu lù (dzoe loo): to walk

zū (dzoo): to rent

zuò (dzwaw): to do; to make; to sit

zuò fàn (dzwaw-fahn): to cook

Appendix C

Fun & Games Answer Key

The following are all of the answers to the Fun & Games exercises. For chapters that feature fill-in-the-blank questions that could have more than one answer, no answers appear in this appendix.

Chapter 2

c, a, d, c, c

Chapter 3

b, e, a, d, c

Chapter 4

Activity 1: **hǎo, míngzi, Déguórén, bàofēngxuě, jiàn**

Activity 2:

1. **(C) Hǎo jiǔ méi jiàn.**
2. **(D) Wǎn ān.**
3. **(E) Zǎo.**
4. **(F) Nǎr de huà.**
5. **(A) Hěn gāoxìng jiàndào nǐ.**
6. **(B) Yílù píng'ān.**

Chapter 5

wǔ, qī, shí, sānshí, liùshí, jiǔshí

Chapter 6

yùshì: *bathroom*

wòshì: *bedroom*

fàntīng: *dining room*

tǎnzi: *blanket*

yángtái: *balcony*

zhěntóu: *pillow*

bèizi: *quilt*

shūzhuō: *desk*

shāfā: *sofa*

Chapter 7

yīshēng: *doctor*

lǎoshī: *teacher*

fēixīngyuán: *pilot*

kuàijì: *accountant*

Chapter 8

A. **píngguǒ** (*apple*)

B. **júzi** (*orange*)

C. **shēngcài** (*lettuce*)

D. **fānqié** (*tomato*)

E. **hú luóbō** (*carrot*)

F. **yángcōng** (*onion*)

G. **xīlánhuā** (*broccoli*)

Chapter 9

A. **zhūbǎo diàn** (*jewelry store*)

B. **cài shìchǎng:** (*food market*)

C. **huādiàn:** (*flower shop*)

D. **yàofáng:** (*drugstore*)

E. **wánjù diàn:** (*toy store*)

Chapter 10

1. f

2. e

3. d

4. c

5. a

6. b

Chapter 11

Just a moment.: **Shǎoděng.**

Is she at home?: **Tā zài ma?**

Hello?: **Wéi?**

Sorry, you dialed the wrong number.: **Duìbùqǐ, nǐ bōcuòle hàomǎ.**

Please leave a message.: **Qǐng nǐ liú yíge huà.**

Chapter 12

1. b

2. a

3. d

4. c

5. e

Chapter 13

A. dǎ pīngpāng qiú

B. tán gāngqín

C. dǎ gōngfu

D. chuī chángdí

E. pá shān

Chapter 14

1. a
2. c
3. b
4. a
5. b

Chapter 15

1. yuán (formal) or kuài (informal)
2. jiǎo (formal) or tmáo (informal)
3. fēn (formal or informal)

A. zìdòng tīkuǎnjī (*ATM*)

B. chūnà yuán (*bank teller*)

C. yínháng (*bank*)

D. hùzhào (*passport*)

E. xìnyòngkǎ (*credit card*)

F. qiánbāo (*wallet*)

Chapter 16

A. fēijī

B. huǒchē

C. dìtiě

D. gōnggòng qìchē

E. chūzū chē

Chapter 17

A. **Xuéxiào zài běibiān/běimiàn.** (*The school is to the north.*)

B. **Yóujú zài dōngbiān/dōngmiàn.** (*The post office is to the east.*)

C. **Yínháng zài nánbiān/nánmiàn.** (*The bank is to the south.*)

D. **Fángzi zài xībiān/xīmiàn.** (*The house is to the west.*)

Chapter 18

1. **fángjiān**
2. **kèmǎn**
3. **qǐchuáng**
4. **zhàngdān**
5. **tuìfáng**

Chapter 19

1. **gēbō:** *arm*
2. **jiānbǎng:** *shoulder*
3. **shǒuzhǐ:** *finger*
4. **tuǐ:** *leg*
5. **bózi:** *neck*
6. **xiōngqiāng:** *chest*
7. **yǎnjīng:** *eye*
8. **ěrduō:** *ear*
9. **bízi:** *nose*

Index

bathroom, 90, 92, 128–129
be, 40
Běijīng, 62
bean curd, 121
bedrooms, 90–92
beef balls, 128
beer, 120, 124
behavior, culturally acceptable, 57
best, 145
binoculars, 36
biology, 189
bird-watching, 36
birthday cake, 80
birthday gift, 80
black, 150
blue, 150
bodily functions, culturally acceptable
    behavior and, 57
body, 301
bone, 301
books, 35
bookstore, 138, 268
boots, 145
boss, 53
bowl, 114
boyfriend, 53
breakfast, 112
bribery, 198
British Consulate, 270
broccoli, 121
Buddhist nun, 108
Buddhists, 211
buns, steamed, 112, 128
bus driver, 261
bus ticket, 261
bus tour, 227
buses, getting onto, 260–261
business class, 252
business school, 188
businesses, calling, 174–175
busy, 195
buy, 40

C

cabbage, 121
calligraphy, 25, 152, 316
calm, 108
Canada, 224
cancel, 250
cancer, 305
Canton. *See* Guangdong
Cantonese, 11
cardinal points, specifying, 276–278
carpentry workshop, 94
cartoon, 165
castle, 85
cellphones, 171–172
centimeter, 82
Cháng'é, 81
chair, 192
change, small, 235
characters, 28–29
    direction of, 26–28
    overview, 21–22
    radicals, using, 24
    Six Scripts, classifying using, 22–23
    stroke order for, 25
    traditional versus simplified, 2, 28–29
chat, 99
cheap, 241
cheaper, 241
Cheat Sheet, 4
check, paying, 129, 319–320
check in, 284
check out, 284
check-in counter, getting passed, 250–252
chemistry, 189
Chen Kaige, 315
chest, 301
chicken, fried, 124
chicken pox, 305
Children's Palace, 189
China, moving to
    apartments, searching for, 86–88
    homes, decorating, 89

drinks, 119, 199

drug smuggler, 256

drugstore, 138

dry red wine, 124

dryer, 94

dumplings, 112

duty free, 256

dysentery, 305

E

ear, 301

earache, 302

earth, 91

east, 276

eat, 40

economy, 285

economy/coach, 252

egg drop soup, 122

egg tarts, 128

eggplant, 121

eight, 66

eight o'clock, 72

eighteen, 67

EKG, 305

elementary school, 188

elevator, 287

eleven, 67

eleven o'clock, 72

email, 180–182, 185

emergencies

  help, calling out for, 297–298

  legal help, acquiring, 309

  medical care, receiving

    ailments, describing, 300–305

    diagnosis, making, 306–308

    doctor, deciding to go to, 299–300

    overview, 298–299

    prescription instructions, 308

  overview, 297

  police, calling, 308–309

emergency room, 305

energy, 89

engineering, 202

English, 190

entertainment, 202

Eritrea, freedom of press and, 184

Euro, 234

evil spirits, 95

exams, phrases for, 190–191

exchange rate, 238

exist, 38

expensive, 289

export structure, 201

expressions, basic

  conversing

    compliments, rejecting, 63

    goodbye, saying, 63

    hometowns, finding out, 61–62

    new friends and strangers, addressing, 55–56

    overview, 55

    times of day, 56–59

    weather, 59–61

  introductions

    acquaintances, making, 52

    friends and family, introducing, 52–53

    names, asking for, 53–55

    overview, 52

  overview, 51

eye, 301

F

Facebook, 204

family, introducing, 52–53

father, 16

fēngshuǐ

  attic, 95

  basement, 94–95

  bathroom, 92

  bedrooms, 91–92

  kitchens, 92–93

  living room, 93–94

  overview, 89–91

February, 78

fifteen, 67

finals, 14–15

finger, 301

I

icons used in this book, 4
ID, 285
ideographs, 23
idiomatic expressions, 17–18
inch, 82
indefinite articles, 36–38
infection, 300
informal meeting, 176
initials, 13–14
initial greetings, 196–198
in-room safe, 294
inside, 271
Instagram, 204
instant messaging, 182, 204
insurance, 202
international relations, 189
Internet, 205
    connection speed, 185
    Internet protocol, 185
    online, going, 182–183
    online courses, 188
    online material, 32, 51, 85, 315
    online meeting, 176
    online payment, 183
    online shopping, 183
interrogative expressions, 113
interrogative pronouns, 48–49
introductions, 52–53
introductory questions, 102
Ireland, 224
Israel, 224
Italian, 190

J

jade, 26
Jade Emperor, 93
January, 78
Japan, 224
Japanese dollar, 234
jeans, 140
jewelry store, 138
Jiāngsū province, 115

Jiéfàng Lù. *See* middle mountain
joined meaning, 23
journalism, 202
July, 78
June, 78

K

Kadoorie, Elly, 212
key, 88
key card, 284
KFC, 123
kidney, 301
kilogram, 82
kilometer, 82
kindergarten, 188
kitchen, 90, 92–93
Kitchen God, 93
knife, 114
Korea, freedom of press and, 184
kosher food, 134
kung-fu, 165, 315

L

Lǎozǐ, 28
Labor Day, 223
lake, 36
lamb chops, 124
language lessons, exchanging, 315
Lantern Festival, 81
last month, 78
law school, 188
lawyer, 55
leg, 301
lemonade, 124
liter, 82
literature, 190
Liúlì cháng, 151
liver, 301
living room, 90, 93–94
local production, 201
London, 62
lost weight, 302
lower berth, 262

outdoor markets
  comparisons, making, 131–132
  cost, asking, 132–134
  overview, 131
outside, 271
ox, 80

P

Paris, 62
particles, 33
passive voices, 39
passports, 227–228
paste, 194
paternal grandfather, 55
paternal grandmother, 55
Peking Opera
  attending, 314
  history of, 161
  music and, 159
People's Republic of China
  characters used in, 9, 28
  pīnyīn, adoption of, 11
peppers, stuffed, 128
performances, attending, 157–160
pharmaceuticals, 202
philosophy, 190
phone calls
  to clients, 175–176
  to friends, 173–174
  to hotels and businesses, 174–175
  overview, 172–173
phonetic compounds, 23
phonetic loan characters, 23
physical contact, culturally acceptable behavior and, 57
physics, 190
pīnyīn
  defined, 2
  reading, 11–12
pictographs, 23
picture, 207
pig, 81
pink, 150
pint, 82
pizza, 124

plants, 89
plate, 114
plural nouns, 35–36
points of reference, using ordinal numbers to clarify, 276
political science, 190
pool table, 94
pork
  fried pork dumplings, 128
  pork chops, 124
  steamed pork buns, 128
possessive article, 27
possessive particle, 47
potato, 121
potential complements, 275
poultry dishes, 119
pound, 82
preliminary meeting, 176
pre-paid phone card, 174
prescriptions, 308
presentations, making, 198–199
prices
  markets, asking at, 132–134
  night markets, negotiating at, 153–155
print, 194
private school, 59
product, 201
pronouns, 33
property, 86
Pǔdòng, growth of, 88
Pǔtónghuà. See Mandarin
public relations, 202
public school, 59
publishing, 202
purchases, paying for, 154
purple, 150

Q

Qín Shǐhuáng, 163
Qū Yuán, 81
quality, comparing, 145–146
quart, 82
question particle, 47
questions, asking, 47–49, 70, 102

verbs
  aspect markers, 41–43
  overview, 39–40
  shì, 40
  yào, 44–45
  yǒu, 43–44
Vietnam, 62, 224
Virtual Private Network (VPN) services, 204
virus, 300
visas, 227–228
vocational school, 188

W

waitstaff, talking with, 125–127
wake-up call, 291
walk, 40, 273
Wángfǔjǐng, 141
want, 40, 44–45
warm, 57
washing machine, 94
water, 91
Wēibó, 1
weather, conversing about, 59–61
web designer, 183
website, 185
WeChat, 204
wedding anniversary, 80
Wednesday, 76
weights, 81–82
west, 277
white, 150
wife, 53
Windows, 205
wind/water style
  attic, 95
  basement, 94–95
  bathroom, 92
  bedrooms, 91–92
  kitchens, 92–93
  living room, 93–94
  overview, 89–91

wine, 120
winter, 78
winter vacation, 231
woks, cooking with, 314
wood, 91
work, 105–108
writing
  calligraphy, 25, 152, 316
  in general, 21
writing brush, 25

X

Xī'ān, 163
Xiǎomǐ, 171
X-ray machine, 305
Xǔ Shèn, 22

Y

Yáo Míng, 44
Yangzi River, 10
Yáo Míng, 207
yard, 82
Year of Dog, 222
yellow, 150
Yellow Mountain, 207
yes/no questions, 47–48
YouTube, 204
yuándàn. *See* New Year's Day

Z

Zaire, 224
zero, 66
Zhang Yimou, 315
Zhèjiāng province, 115
Zhōnghuá rénmín gònghé guó. *See* People's Republic of China
Zhōngwén. *See* Mandarin
Zhōu Ēnlái, 12
zìmǔ, 21

About the Author

Dr. Wendy Abraham has lived, studied, and worked in both the People's Republic of China and Taiwan, directed Chinese language programs for American students, researched oracle bones and bronze inscriptions (the origins of the Chinese writing system), and gathered oral histories of the oldest generation of Chinese Jewish descendants in Kaifeng — the subject of her doctoral dissertation. She has interpreted for high-level arts delegations and has taught Chinese language, literature, history, and culture at universities throughout the United States. An inveterate world traveler, Dr. Abraham has written widely and continues to lecture frequently on the subject of the Chinese Jews. Her interest in all things Chinese since the age of 3 continues unabated.

Dedication

This book is dedicated to my wonderful and fun-loving family:

My mother, Marilyn, whose marathon Tuesday mahjong games have become the stuff of legend on the Upper West Side; my father, George, connoisseur of Shakespeare and meanest chess player in all of Vegas; sister, Susan, sculptor of Italian marble and mother of poodle Irma; brother-in-law, Michael Fogarty, sculptor of hair and father of poodle Irma; niece, Irma (the poodle); cousin, Michael Ian, painter, photographer, and everyone's favorite brunch buddy; and dear family friend (and fellow mahjong fiend), Helayne Kamenoff, whose love and support have been unwavering throughout it all.

Acknowledgments

This third edition of *Chinese For Dummies* can only hope to replicate the energy, enthusiasm, and sense of humor of the entire Advanced Chinese class of Appo High, budding linguists and scholars all: William Haskell, Elijah Hadley, Malachi Duff, Andrew Pao, and Charles Bibus. They made the teaching of Chinese a delight, and single-handedly restored my faith in humanity (and in teenagers).

This book was written with the support and help of many people, in more ways than one. Deep gratitude goes first to Rev. James Harvey III and Melody Harvey, and to childhood friend Cynthia (Sargent) Reidlinger, all of whose lives and faith have been a great inspiration these past few years.

Special thanks go to Lindsey Lefevere, Executive Editor at John Wiley & Sons, Inc., for the opportunity to write this third edition, and for her clear leadership as it got underway. To Chrissy Guthrie, Editorial Project Manager and Development Editor for Wiley, a great debt of thanks for taking the publication process through all sorts of twists and turns with encouragement, patience, humor, and plain old thinking outside the box. (It worked.) Thanks also to Christy Pingleton, Copy Editor, for her painstaking attention to detail as she slogged through the uncharted territory of Chinese characters, pinyin, and four different tone marks.

Lastly, a great debt of thanks goes to Chinese language editor for the first, second, and now third editions of *Chinese For Dummies*, State Department linguist and longtime friend, Wen Yang. Poring over every inch of a Chinese character is a skill he's honed fine since our days at Georgetown when he got roped into hand writing dozens of Chinese characters for the index to my master's thesis. (No easy feat in the days before cellphones, email, the personal computer, and something called Google that could just "will" a Chinese character into perfect, printed existence.)

To all of these people (and the latest technology), I say thank you for helping to create a book within a brand that never fails to put a smile on the face.

Publisher's Acknowledgments

Executive Editor: Lindsay Sandman Lefevere

Editorial Project Manager and Development Editor: Christina Guthrie

Copy Editor: Christine Pingleton

Technical Editor: Wen Yang

Production Editor: G. Vasanth Koilraj

Cover Image: © Gwoeii/Shutterstock

Take dummies with you everywhere you go!

Whether you are excited about e-books, want more from the web, must have your mobile apps, or are swept up in social media, dummies makes everything easier.

Find us online!

dummies.com

Leverage the power

Dummies is the global leader in the reference category and one of the most trusted and highly regarded brands in the world. No longer just focused on books, customers now have access to the dummies content they need in the format they want. Together we'll craft a solution that engages your customers, stands out from the competition, and helps you meet your goals.

Advertising & Sponsorships

Connect with an engaged audience on a powerful multimedia site, and position your message alongside expert how-to content. Dummies.com is a one-stop shop for free, online information and know-how curated by a team of experts.

- Targeted ads
- Video
- Email Marketing
- Microsites
- Sweepstakes sponsorship

20 MILLION PAGE VIEWS **EVERY SINGLE MONTH**

15 MILLION UNIQUE VISITORS PER MONTH

43% OF ALL VISITORS ACCESS THE SITE **VIA THEIR MOBILE DEVICES**

700,000 NEWSLETTER SUBSCRIPTIONS TO THE INBOXES OF *300,000* UNIQUE **INDIVIDUALS EVERY WEEK**

# of dummies

Custom Publishing

Reach a global audience in any language by creating a solution that will differentiate you from competitors, amplify your message, and encourage customers to make a buying decision.

- Apps
- Books
- eBooks
- Video
- Audio
- Webinars

Brand Licensing & Content

Leverage the strength of the world's most popular reference brand to reach new audiences and channels of distribution.

For more information, visit **dummies.com/biz**

PERSONAL ENRICHMENT

Staying Sharp
9781119187790
USA $26.00
CAN $31.99
UK £19.99

Facebook
Carolyn Abram
9781119179030
USA $21.99
CAN $25.99
UK £16.99

Guitar
Mark Phillips
Jon Chappell
9781119293354
USA $24.99
CAN $29.99
UK £17.99

Investing
Eric Tyson, MBA
9781119293347
USA $22.99
CAN $27.99
UK £16.99

Beekeeping
Howland Blackiston
9781119310068
USA $22.99
CAN $27.99
UK £16.99

Digital Photography
Julie Adair King
9781119235606
USA $24.99
CAN $29.99
UK £17.99

Meditation
Stephan Bodian
9781119251163
USA $24.99
CAN $29.99
UK £17.99

Pregnancy ALL-IN-ONE
9781119235491
USA $26.99
CAN $31.99
UK £19.99

Samsung Galaxy S7
Bill Hughes
9781119279952
USA $24.99
CAN $29.99
UK £17.99

iPhone
Edward C. Baig
Bob "Dr. Mac" LeVitus
9781119283133
USA $24.99
CAN $29.99
UK £17.99

Crocheting
Karen Manthey
Susan Brittain
9781119287117
USA $24.99
CAN $29.99
UK £16.99

Nutrition
Carol Ann Rinzler
9781119130246
USA $22.99
CAN $27.99
UK £16.99

PROFESSIONAL DEVELOPMENT

Windows 10
Andy Rathbone
9781119311041
USA $24.99
CAN $29.99
UK £17.99

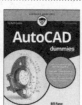
AutoCAD
Bill Fane
9781119255796
USA $39.99
CAN $47.99
UK £27.99

Excel 2016
Greg Harvey, PhD
9781119293439
USA $26.99
CAN $31.99
UK £19.99

QuickBooks 2017
Stephen L. Nelson, MBA, CPA, All-in-Function
9781119281467
USA $26.99
CAN $31.99
UK £19.99

macOS Sierra
Bob "Dr. Mac" LeVitus
9781119280651
USA $29.99
CAN $35.99
UK £21.99

LinkedIn
Joel Elad, MBAs
9781119251132
USA $24.99
CAN $29.99
UK £17.99

Windows 10 ALL-IN-ONE
Woody Leonhard
9781119310563
USA $34.00
CAN $41.99
UK £24.99

SharePoint 2016
Rosemarie Withee
Ken Withee
9781119181705
USA $29.99
CAN $35.99
UK £21.99

Fundamental Analysis
Matt Krantz
9781119263593
USA $26.99
CAN $31.99
UK £19.99

Networking
Doug Lowe
9781119257769
USA $29.99
CAN $35.99
UK £21.99

Office 2016
Wallace Wang
9781119293477
USA $26.99
CAN $31.99
UK £19.99

Office 365
Rosemarie Withee
Ken Withee
Jennifer Reed
9781119265313
USA $24.99
CAN $29.99
UK £17.99

Salesforce.com
Liz Kao
Jon Paz
9781119239314
USA $29.99
CAN $35.99
UK £21.99

Coding
Nikhil Abraham
9781119293323
USA $29.99
CAN $35.99
UK £21.99

dummies.com

dummies®
A Wiley Brand

Learning Made Easy

ACADEMIC

9781119293576
USA $19.99
CAN $23.99
UK £15.99

9781119293637
USA $19.99
CAN $23.99
UK £15.99

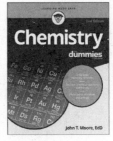

9781119293491
USA $19.99
CAN $23.99
UK £15.99

9781119293460
USA $19.99
CAN $23.99
UK £15.99

9781119293590
USA $19.99
CAN $23.99
UK £15.99

9781119215844
USA $26.99
CAN $31.99
UK £19.99

9781119293378
USA $22.99
CAN $27.99
UK £16.99

9781119293521
USA $19.99
CAN $23.99
UK £15.99

9781119239178
USA $18.99
CAN $22.99
UK £14.99

9781119263883
USA $26.99
CAN $31.99
UK £19.99

Available Everywhere Books Are Sold

dummies.com

Small books for big imaginations

GETTING STARTED WITH Coding
Get Creative with Code!
Camille McCue, PhD

9781119177173
USA $9.99
CAN $9.99
UK £8.99

MODDING Minecraft
Build Your Own Minecraft Mods!
Sarah Guthals, PhD
Stephen Foster, PhD
Lindsay Handley, PhD

9781119177272
USA $9.99
CAN $9.99
UK £8.99

MAKING YouTube VIDEOS
Star in Your Own Video!
Nick Willoughby

9781119177241
USA $9.99
CAN $9.99
UK £8.99

DESIGNING Digital Games
Create Games with Scratch!
Derek Breen

9781119177210
USA $9.99
CAN $9.99
UK £8.99

GETTING STARTED WITH Raspberry Pi
Program Your Raspberry Pi!
Richard Wentk

9781119262657
USA $9.99
CAN $9.99
UK £6.99

EXPERIMENTING WITH Science
Think, Test, and Learn!

9781119291336
USA $9.99
CAN $9.99
UK £6.99

CREATING Digital Animations
Animate Stories with Scratch!
Derek Breen

9781119233527
USA $9.99
CAN $9.99
UK £6.99

GETTING STARTED WITH Engineering
Think Like an Engineer!
Camille McCue, PhD

9781119291220
USA $9.99
CAN $9.99
UK £6.99

WRITING Computer Code
Learn the Language of Computers!
Chris Minnick and Eva Holland

9781119177302
USA $9.99
CAN $9.99
UK £8.99

Unleash Their Creativity

dummies.com

dummies
A Wiley Brand